MEMOIRS

OF

PRINCE METTERNICH

SECOND VOLUME

LONDON : PRINTED BY
SPOTTISWOODE AND CO., NEW-STREET SQUARE
AND PARLIAMENT STREET

MEMOIRS

OF

PRINCE METTERNICH

1773–1815

EDITED BY

PRINCE RICHARD METTERNICH

THE PAPERS CLASSIFIED AND ARRANGED BY M. A. de KLINKOWSTRÖM

TRANSLATED BY MRS ALEXANDER NAPIER

VOL. II.

LONDON
RICHARD BENTLEY & SON, NEW BURLINGTON STREET
Publishers in Ordinary to Her Majesty the Queen
1880

CONTENTS

OF

THE SECOND VOLUME.

———◦◦◦———

THIRD BOOK (*continued*).

METTERNICH'S ENTRANCE INTO THE IMPERIAL SERVICE.

HIS FIRST STATE-PAPER (NOTE 10, VOLUME I.).

1801.

Instructions to Count von Metternich-Winneburg as Austrian Ambassador at the Electoral Court of Saxony (Vienna, November 2, 1801). Drawn up by Metternich himself.

54. IT being our pleasure to appoint Count von Eltz, who has for several years been our authorised Minister at the Court of Saxony, to be our Ambassador Extraordinary at the Court of Spain, we think it in the interest of our service at this important moment immediately to fill the vacant post at the Saxon court. Our choice has fallen on Count von Metternich, confiding as we do in his experience, zeal for the state, and fidelity. We provide him, therefore, with the necessary credentials, which he will deliver to the Elector, with the assurance of our highest regard and esteem.

With respect to the ceremonials, about which doubts have so often prevailed at the Saxon court, we refer him solely to the instructions which he will receive thereupon from the Imperial Chancery.

As it is necessary, however, for the welfare and better execution of our service, that he should have a thorough knowledge of the circumstances under which he enters upon this post of Ambassador, we have

thought it advisable to place in his hands the following
statement. . . . .

A. *The present State of European Politics with special
regard to Austria.*

The events of the last eleven years have been of a
character to change entirely the whole political situation
of Europe.

The French Revolution and the change of one of the
most important Monarchies into a Republic; the thorough
overthrow of the independence of Holland; the union
of the Netherlands, the left bank of the Rhine, Savoy
and part of Switzerland, and Holland with France; the
change in that constitution which had rendered Switzerland happy for centuries; the formation of a new
democratic republic in North Italy; the altered conditions of Venice; the taking possession of the Grand-
Duchy of Tuscany; the partition of Poland; the extraordinary acquisitions of Prussia; the temporary monopoly of England, as a consequence of the destruction of
the mercantile navies of her enemies, and the taking of
almost all the French colonies, many Spanish, and all
the Dutch colonies; the vast conquests of Great Britain
in the East Indies, and the complete overthrow of
Tippoo Sahib, who had long been her formidable enemy;
the actual occupation of Egypt by the French; the
Cape of Good Hope and Malta, these two most important
points for the commerce of the world, in the possession
of that Power which already had the monopoly of
trade; and lastly, the impending changes in consequence
of the Peace of Luneville—this state of things, as the
result of the French Revolution and of the general war
arising from it, far exceeds the changes caused by

the three great wars of the past century : namely, the
Spanish Succession war, which decided the superiority of
France; the Northern war, which opened to Russia the
political gates of Europe; and the Prussian war with us
in 1740, the consequence of which was the Seven Years'
war.

The attempt to create from the present chaos of
elements a settled European state-system for the immediate future would be impossible. The consequences
of such vast changes, together with the still pending
struggle of political principles, relegate the hope of a
general peace to a very distant period. Every year
since 1790 has produced changes in the political condition of Europe which would have been thought impossible in the year which preceded them, and could hardly
be believed in the year which followed them. Compare only the state of the French Republic in November, 1799, with that in April, 1801 ; the close alliance
of Russia in 1799 with the Russian Embassy to Paris
in March of the present year. And what differences
in English policy in the last eleven years ! Obstinately
neutral in 1792, England was latterly the most active
member of the Coalition, and is now herself the object
of an entirely different Coalition headed by France and
Russia, which the hitherto neutral Northern Powers
have been persuaded to join. These few points, selected
from so many changes and modifications, are more than
sufficient to prove how hazardous must be a prediction
of probable events, even in the next ten years.

The relations, external and internal, of our monarchy
have experienced changes which even the most powerful
state cannot escape. All our former and even our
recent alliances with other Powers have ceased to exist ;
in many cases even the very motives are forgotten

which produced them ; a brief survey of these alliances will make this clear.

It was the object of the alliance with France in 1756 to secure our more remote Dutch and Italian provinces, to check the ever-increasing malignant influence of the French in the Empire, and to enable the forces of the Archducal house of Austria, secure from the hostile designs of France, to be directed to every point which promised advantage.

For France, the chief advantage of this alliance consisted in the entire security of her frontier, enabling her to save a great part of the subsidies which she had to pay every year to less powerful states, and to apply these to the improvement and reinforcement of her navy.

An intimate friendship and alliance had been formed between the courts of Russia and Austria at a time when Russia could hardly be ranked with the European Powers as a civilised state. Until the accession of Peter III. both Powers considered themselves natural allies, and for this feeling there were many reasons. They were not immediate neighbours, did not therefore envy each other's increase of territory, but even promoted it ; whilst they had a common enemy in the Porte ; and latterly they both found in Prussia a dangerous neighbour, who became more and more so to both of them, as her encroachments on Poland seemed to have some probability of success.

But hardly had Peter III. mounted the throne than he threw himself blindly into the arms of Prussia. The alliance with Austria, renewed under the Empress Katherine, was founded principally on the personal liking of the Empress for Austria, the above-mentioned reasons for an alliance gradually disappearing.

Prussia, an ever-increasing state owing to her geographical situation, and always our rival, has since the reign of Frederick II. shown the ambition of a Power of the first rank, although her small financial resources and her population have made her only a secondary Power. Her whole policy was directed to the enlargement of her territory and the extension of her influence, and that with a total disregard of all acknowledged international and moral principles. The alliance of the year 1791 hardly deserves mention. Its immediate abolition shows the degree of confidence placed in it.

The often-renewed alliances with England had a natural ground in the political and geographical relations of the two countries; between a merely commercial and an exclusively continental power there was no natural ground for rivalry. Our Netherlands, besides, afforded the nearest and most convenient points of contact with the Continent, and in our political strength there lay a powerful counter-balance to the jealousy of the French. The advantages of the alliance were, however, and especially latterly, on the side of England, for during the alliance with France we had no need of the English, and since the war with France the support given to our finances was not at all in proportion to the extraordinary efforts and sacrifices from which Great Britain derived the greatest advantage.

We joined the Triple Alliance of 1798, between England, Russia, and the Porte, only to have a direct interest in the war.

It is evident from all this how different were the circumstances, which led us to join these alliances, from our present political point of view.

Our more remote Dutch and Italian provinces— the former of which gave us an immediate frontier with France, brought us into connection with Holland, and separated that country from France—were, by the last Peace, ceded partly to France itself, and partly went to form new republics subject to France.

In consequence of the occupation of the Netherlands by the French and the opening up of the Scheldt, the greater part of the commerce which had been transferred to Amsterdam, Rotterdam, and other places, has returned to its old convenient centre; and if this state of things continue, the probable fate of Holland will be to become a French province.

Being no longer in immediate contact with France, the loss of the Netherlands, the remotest, and as regarded defence the most expensive, of all our states, gives us indirectly many advantages. The rivalry of France with our House in the internal affairs of Italy, after having lasted for centuries, will now find other material. The erection of a considerable republic after the French model, which, with the other republics and the smaller Italian states, is to be reckoned among the actual possessions of France; the laying out of strong military lines against our frontier; and, lastly, the destruction of all means of defence which could in the remotest degree be turned against France : all this gives to the French Republic a preponderance in Italian affairs such as we never possessed. The possession of the important Venetian provinces, on the other hand, gives us advantages which France never had even at the height of her protectorate.

The fickle character of the Russian Emperor, easily estranged by trifles, and often not to be won by the greatest sacrifices, makes a durable alliance with that empire extremely difficult for us, as well as for others. By internal resources not possessed by any other civilised state, able to terminate every alliance and every war at her own pleasure, merely by the retreat of her army, unassailable within her frontiers, Russia is, by virtue of her geographical and political situation, always dangerous, but especially so under a government which, without principles, acts from the convenience of the moment. Our present relations with Russia in regard. to the extensive frontiers common to both Empires give rise to the following considerations :—

The existence of Poland was equally important for us, for the interests of the adjacent states, and for the general peace of Europe. Situated between three great states, Poland prevented the frequent collisions which always occur if there is immediate contact, and for that reason alone it had a decided value for each of the three Powers; this value was, however, doubled for Prussia and for ourselves. Only the blind desire of aggrandisement in the Berlin cabinet, and the revolutionary period, which the Empress Katherine made use of for the execution of her long-cherished intentions, could have brought about the partition of Poland, contrary to all principles of sound policy. Our part was and could only be conservative. The pressure of circumstances, the impossibility of preventing the aggrandisement of the two Powers, and the necessity of diminishing the inevitable evil by obtaining some compensation, alone induced us to give our long-delayed assent. The advantage to Prussia of an increased population and extended frontier is counter-balanced by the disadvantage of having these frontiers in common with Russia and with us. We are in a similar position; no country but Russia could, in spite of her enormous extension towards the East, still nourish the desire of approaching the centre of European politics; but it remains to be seen whether the partition of Poland has promoted this object.

Prussia, which was before, during, and after her alliance with us always true to the same principles and views, has during the last ten years much increased in importance. The part which she has maintained at the expense of political morality; events the most adverse which she has turned to her own advantage, without regard to engagements and promises; her acquisitions, made and intended, have placed her for several years among Powers of the first rank. The influence of Prussia in the affairs of the Empire attained, by the unconstitutional adhesion of its most powerful estates, a height which was denied to the Imperial dignity itself.

The present sketch sufficiently shows how remote we still are from the restoration of the European balance of power, and with it from general peace. The extraordinary acquisitions of France must undergo modifications. England, still at war with France, and apparently with all the naval Powers of Europe, has made so many conquests that peace can only be secured with this state by a great retrocession on her part.

With our possessions well defined we thus enter into quite new relations. It is incumbent upon our present policy to choose new and appropriate alliances, the main object of which must be the invigorating of our political forces, the preservation of internal peace, and the attainment of a position which, as far as unforeseen circumstances allow, will enable us to act a part corresponding to the extent and power of a state of the first rank.

B. *Austria's Relations with Saxony.*

The geographical position of the Electorate of Saxony deprives it of any claim to independence, as far as that word can be applied to a third-rate Power. Closed in between two powerful monarchies, its destiny seems to be that it should be governed only by influences from without.

A war between ourselves and Prussia would no doubt be the very worst thing which could happen to Saxony. Every attitude she assumed in such a case would be sure to turn out to her disadvantage. None would probably prove to her advantage. If she were to remain neutral, she would succumb to the fate of smaller states, which can support their neutrality only by protestations, and which are exposed sometimes to the devastations of the conqueror, sometimes to those of the conquered. In this latter respect she has experienced the misery of the most ruinous requisitions on the side of Prussia. If she declared for either side, she ran into dangers which she had no power either to avert or to diminish. United with Prussia, her people would merely serve to recruit the allied armies, and her stores of corn to feed them. Saxony's only rational policy lay and lies in her using all means to maintain friendly relations between her two powerful neighbours, or at least, in taking every possible care, so far as depends on her, to avoid the outbreak of any war; so that she may use the time of peace for the promotion of internal prosperity, the extension of her commercial relations, and the healing of the wounds made by the Seven Years' war and the oppressive reigns of the two Kings of Poland.

The choice of the part she has to take in future can,

unfortunately, no longer be doubtful for Saxony. The preponderance Prussia has gained, and the acquisitions of this Power around or in the neighbourhood of the Saxon frontier in the last ten years, press hard upon Saxony. By the possession of Ausbach and Bayreuth, Saxony is bounded north and south by Prussia ; and by Prussia's occupation of her former Polish provinces she is threatened on the east. The most important part of the trade and commerce of Saxony fell, in consequence of this, under the power of Prussia ; any assertions of neutrality or declarations for us are for the future not unfeasible.

The conviction that Saxony would be able to maintain its own independence by its important position in the German Empire, and by the guarantee of its being a constituent member of the Empire, should never have influenced the Dresden cabinet more powerfully than at that time when the designs of Prussia manifested themselves so nakedly that even the existence of states of the Empire, and especially of those in immediate proximity to Prussia, was placed in a state of jeopardy. The cabinet of Dresden should never have deviated from the constitutional path and followed the lead of the peculiarly Prussian policy ; but the blindness which seems to have fallen upon the Northern courts determined, alas ! the Saxon court to play in this later period a part running so counter to its true interests.

The influence of the Elector, as one of the most powerful estates of the Empire, had formerly been very considerable. As head of the *corpus evangelicorum*, he stood at the head of a party increasing in strength, especially in recent times. But the daily increasing influence of Prussia in the external affairs of the Empire, the despotic supremacy with which she maintained the neutrality of Northern Germany by uniting the most powerful Protestant states under her protection, together with the majority she was always able to secure by means of the sixteen votes of the Houses of Brandenburg and Brunswick in the Imperial Diet, rendered the part of the Saxon Ministry almost illusory.

The adhesion of the Elector to the Prussian neutrality was a mistake which can only be considered as the consequence of an earlier one. The League of Princes (*Fürstenbund*) directed against the constitution itself, under the pretext of the purest constitutional principles, and founded by Prussia (1785) for the convenient execution of her long-cherished plans of subjugation, contained the germ of all the mischief which was diffused over the whole Empire.

This League was ostensibly founded for the preservation of the Imperial constitution, and the principles upon which it rested were concealed by the Prussian cabinet in a manner to flatter the private interests of each member of it, so that only a practised eye was able to discover the assaults on the constitution, and to see through the hideous designs of Prussia— designs which had no other purpose than to subjugate the affairs of the Empire to her own arbitrary guidance, and to make the greater part of Germany subservient to Prussian plans of aggrandisement.

The conduct of this Power in Franconia in 1792 and afterwards, and, indeed, during the whole war waged with the Empire, caused the mask to fall. Every article of the Peace of Basel, and especially the separate article which came to the knowledge of the whole world, effaced even the most remote appearance of constitutional intentions. If Saxony had been less deluded and more open

to the candid examination of consequences, every
hope of disinterested protection from Prussia would
have disappeared ; but the astute policy of Prussia
constantly contrived to involve the members of the
League in her designs, and knew so well the weak side
of the great Protestant Estates that she could venture
in 1796, at the head of the most considerable section of
the German Empire, to revolt against her most important duties as a member of the Empire, and to proclaim
the necessity of an actual division of the Imperial body.

We touch upon the League of Princes (*Fürstenbund*)
because, although in opposition, it still maintains a considerable influence on the policy of the courts.

Since the final partition of Poland, Saxon policy has
confined itself to the internal relations of the Empire. Its geographical position and the relations of the
Electorate arising therefrom weighed on the political
attitude of the court and caused it to be constantly fearful of giving any occasion of complaint to the cabinets
of neighbouring states, and everything betrayed the
greatest want of independence. Since its unreserved
adoption of Prussian neutrality the influence of the
Berlin cabinet has been unbounded.

The hope of seeing the peace of Northern Germany
secured has now disappeared by the adhesion of Prussia
to the coalition of the Northern Powers. Should Prussia
also succeed in keeping free from active participation
in the war from the consideration of the advantages
which the monopoly of the trade of the North under a
neutral flag must give it, the prospects of internal peace
in the countries in that part of the Empire must be
extremely small, now that Prussia has revealed her
designs upon Hanover and other parts of Lower Saxony,
and are replaced by the painful consciousness that we

have co-operated in the ambitious designs of so dangerous a neighbour.

C. *Conduct of our Plenipotentiary at the Electoral Court.*

The Peace of Luneville, signed in our name and in the name of the Empire deserves pre-eminent attention among the real points of negotiation between us and the Electoral court.

The epistle despatched to the Electoral and more important princes contained the most authentic statement of the pressure of those circumstances under which the Peace was so hastily signed in the name of the Empire without its previous approval. Our patriotic conduct and the reservation by the Estates of the constitutional right of interference in the concerns of the Empire were at the time most thankfully acknowledged by the Estates and afterwards by the Imperial Diet.

The exhibition of our principles in the matter of this Peace furnishes a new and undeniable proof how much we lay to heart, under the most unfavourable circumstances, the preservation so far as possible of the constitution of the Empire and the protection of each member of it.

The severe conditions, provisionally conceded by us as head of the Empire, in the name of the Empire— after the example of the Rastadt Peace of 1714—did not go beyond the concessions made in 1798 and 1799 at the Congress of Rastadt by the deputies sent to conclude peace: nay, we endeavoured, so far as circumstances permitted, to soften these.

A comparison with the Prussian Peace concluded in 1795 at Basel, and an observation of the contrast between the private peace concluded in a most unconstitutional manner after the Prussian fashion with each of the Estates of the Empire, will convince every impartial person of the remarkable difference in our conduct, which aimed at avoiding the least appearance of unconstitutional action.

An impartial judgment, however, can by no means be expected from the evil disposed, whose interests might be threatened if our principles were seen to be true. The Prussian court, whose unconstitutional procedure in the course of the last six years exceeds all measure, will leave no stone unturned to carry out the designs which are clearly revealed in the separate articles of the Basel Treaty, and will strain every nerve to extend its character of protector of North Germany, asserted since that date to the whole of Germany. All the artifices of Prussian policy will be brought into play to bring the more powerful Estates of the Empire to oppose our well-intentioned designs, and to use language which enables the King of Prussia to appear in the position of a mediator.

.   .   .   .   .   .

The principal point of view under which all negotiations with the cabinet of Dresden are to be considered is to remove, or at least to modify, as much as possible the influence of the Prussian court. Where the existence of the Empire is at stake no opportunity is to be neglected of directing the attention of the Elector and his ministry to the great truth, that the political existence of Saxony is not to be severed from that of the Empire, and that the latter is to be saved only by the utter disregard of all private designs, and by the strictest alliance between the members of the Empire and the head of the Empire.

The situation of Dresden and the numerous *corps diplomatiques* usually found there make this post even in normal times most appropriate for the observation of foreign courts and especially of the Russian court ; at the present moment this is especially the case.

The Berlin cabinet, which endeavours most carefully to conceal its political course in Berlin itself from every foreign ambassador, but especially from ours, attains this object with more difficulty at a court where its predominance is especially visible. The fact that our ambassador in Dresden was often able to learn the designs of Prussia, especially in the concerns of the Empire, earlier even than the ambassador in Berlin, should be sufficient to show that he ought to apply his whole attention to the policy of that court, and trace its most secret ways.

The critical character of our relations with the Russian court has prevented all direct communication with St. Petersburg. Dresden is now the nearest point where any of our ambassadors meet with Russian officials. The number of individuals of this nation living there, mostly of the first families, facilitates the possibility of collecting important news from a country almost closed to us. With regard, however, to the news gathered, this must be carefully sifted, since it comes mostly from men who, though well informed, yet being much out of humour, either see what is false or wish to see it.

The observation of the French representative at any of the important meetings of the Aulic Council will present much interesting matter, and will afford glimpses of the designs of the French Government in the affairs of the Empire. Another important object relative to

our monarchy may also be observed—namely, the care-
lessness of the Saxon Government with regard to the
propagation of the new political infatuation which
makes such rapid strides in the Protestant states of
Germany.   The propinquity of Electoral Saxony to
our states and the presence of a French agent there
during these later years has facilitated a system of
espionnage in all our military institutions and attempts
also to enlist friends and adherents in the very heart of
the monarchy.   The French representative found abun-
dant means for the easier execution of his purpose in the
ready compliance of the multitude of Poles there, who,
impelled by the promise of the French Government to
restore Poland—in which, of course, the most important
parts were to be distributed among them—allowed themselves to be used as active spies for all purposes.   The
Elector, from religious principles and unbounded devotion to the Polish nation, permitted even the most
obnoxious individuals of this nation to reside in his
states.

The revolutionary influence of the French agent
did not confine itself, however, only to these movements.
Many of the secret clubs scattered over Germany since
the departure of Alquier also aided the action of the
Dresden agent.

It would be superfluous to direct attention to
the most exact observance of all that relates to an
object so nearly affecting the repose of our states.

The neighbourhood of Electoral Saxony will frequently necessitate negotiations which concern the
welfare of our lands and the affairs of our subjects ; and
precise instructions will be given for every such occasion.

In conclusion, weekly, and if occasion demands it
more frequent, accounts must be sent, and at the end of
every year a full account drawn up which shall contain
a complete survey of the home affairs, statistics, policy,
finances, and military constitution of Saxony.

AT THE CLOSE OF THE EMBASSY AT DRESDEN.

1803.

(Note 10, Vol. I.)

Count Metternich to Count Cobenzl, Dresden, Nov. 20,
1803.

55. At the very moment of my departure from this place, I desire to have the honour of submitting to your Excellency the result of the orders which you were pleased to give me on going to Dresden.

I am more and more convinced that the ways of the Ministry here will always be the same ; the most solemn protestation of principles, abandoned the moment that their application seems in the least to compromise the court of Saxony with Prussia, and the express desire of playing merely a secondary part in all serious discussions, is the key to all their determinations. I have spoken here of the surprise of the Imperial court at seeing the court of Saxony abandon the cause of justice and sound policy in the important discussion just opened at Ratisbonne. I have heard nothing everywhere but protestations of attachment to the principles formerly brought forward by the Imperial court for the maintenance of the Germanic Constitution, and the instructions given to the Minister at the Diet are animated by the sole desire of seeing the majority of votes he desires accorded to the Elector. Count de Loss even ended by telling me that the Imperial court could assuredly have nothing to complain of this court, in the course of the deliberations on the introduction of new votes; that it held to the principle that no new vote could be exercised without the Imperial ratification, and that the Minister had precise instructions to take a perfectly passive part. I could not help seizing the occasion to make him see that this part did not suit a court of such weight in Germany; that the Constitution of the Empire would necessarily fall if the chief courts adopted a purely passive system in such important discussions. He did not reply, but took up the conversation a moment afterwards, protesting the purity of the principles of his court. Baron de Vrintz, who arrived here yesterday evening from Berlin, where he has finished the commission with which he was charged, confided to me this morning that one of the principal reasons for his remaining here some days was to arouse the attention of the Ministry to the projects which he believes are adopted in Berlin for the establishing of a line of communication from Erfurt, through Schönburg and Reuss, to Hof. Your Excellency will deign to recall those discussions which were raised between the court here and the court at Berlin, for the free passage of Prussian posts as far as Erfurt, and which I had the honour to make the subject of several despatches during my mission at Dresden. M. de Vrintz, instructed in all the details of this negotiation, asserts that he found here so much submission and cowardice on the part of the court, that he has no doubt of the success of this new enterprise of the Prussians, which, in buying up the most important and lucrative lines of the Saxon posts, de-

prives this country of all means of communication with
foreigners, except by the Prussian lines, the frontier of
Bohemia alone excepted.

I have the honour to assure your Excellency that
all the reports which have reached Vienna of the unfavourable reception which M. le Baron de Schall may
meet with from this court are entirely without foundation. It renders the most complete justice to all his
personal qualities, and, I am convinced, will see him
arrive with great pleasure, whenever his Imperial
Majesty thinks fit to send him.

AT THE TIME OF THE EMBASSY IN BERLIN,

1804—1806.

1804.

56. Metternich to Colloredo, Berlin, September 24, 1804.
57. Metternich to Colloredo, Berlin, December 4, 1804.
58. Metternich to Colloredo, Berlin, December 5, 1804.
59. Metternich to Colloredo, Berlin, December 27, 1804.
60. Hardenberg to Metternich, Berlin, December 26, 1804.
61. Metternich to Hardenberg, Berlin, January 15, 1805.

Metternich's first steps towards preparing the way for the Admission of Prussia into the Austro-Russian Coalition.

56. Never, assuredly, could two monarchies, formerly rivals, find their interests more intimately bound together than are those of Austria and Prussia at this moment. Situated between two states which seem destined to change the face of the Continent of Europe, which can only be rivals with any success at the expense of the countries which separate them; both strengthened, if they require it, by the chances which seem exclusively reserved to the early years of individuals and states, the dangers of Austria and Prussia being the same, their views should be in common. The germs of destruction in the Prussian monarchy have been prepared by its own government, and have originated in those very acquisitions which seemed to ensure its strength and splendour. All comparison between the loss which the Austrian monarchy has sustained in the course of a disastrous war—principally rendered so by the false calculations of the Prussian Minister—and the advantages which at the first glance seemed to have been gained by the court of Berlin, will ultimately be in our favour. The geographical situation of the new Prussian acquisitions presents all the disadvantages which we have got rid of in the division of our country; and if the Low Countries compensate in part, by their intrinsic value, for the enormous expenses and the embarrassing political discussions which their possession entailed, assuredly the Westphalian provinces, and the line of petty scattered provinces which bound the Prussian monarchy, offer nothing of the kind. The genius of M. d'Haugwitz—whose ministry is, without doubt, only a most extraordinary series of abandonment of all principle, of perfidy, and false measures—has never reached the height of rejecting a bait which by multiplying the political embarrassments of a state surrounded by powerful neighbours, and lacking interior resources, must necessarily end by endangering its very existence. Frederick II. would never have ruined Europe by the Peace of Basel, or would have come out from the unequal struggle which was its result the most powerful monarch of the Continent. It would not be difficult to prove that the Prussian monarchy, whose extent is nearly tripled since the death of that king, has lost its real strength. Frederick William III., will assuredly never from the centre of his vast states, use a language to France, Russia, and Austria, like that which Frederick II. used to send forth from his capital, which was always the headquarters of an intrenched camp.

Among all the bad services rendered to his king by

M. d'Haugwitz, one cannot forget his having sapped the foundations of the military spirit, sole foundation as it is of the Prussian power and the result of the assiduous care of three great princes. There is no longer a Minister of War. The great genius of Frederick II. was able to include the management of his whole army. It is certain that the military standard is so fallen from its ancient grandeur, and has lost so much of its importance, that the first war in which Prussia may find herself engaged, perhaps in spite of herself, will prove that she has receded as much as her neighbours have gained in strength and experience.

The man who will succeed M. d'Haugwitz (whether he will continue in power or fall, no one can calculate), and the one who at present is the most immediate and active agent of the political system (if it may be called one) of that minister, is M. Lombard, secretary to the King's cabinet. His office gives him extensive influence in all political affairs. His colleague Beyme directs, with power equally large, all branches of the Interior administration. The interests of both are united.

M. de Hardenberg, whose political principles have not had time to develop, but who, in many ways, seems to wish to follow a different line from that of his predecessor, notwithstanding the positive assurances of M. d'Haugwitz, that their principles are always the same, owes his present influence to the absence of three months which the latter had the imprudence to allow himself during the summer. He has but two chances —either to join with Lombard, or to dismiss him for good. The first would certainly deprive him of his independence ; the second would give him the opportunity of placing near the King some individual of his own creation. No one can doubt his choice in this

alternative, but time alone will show us its success.
The Secretary of the Cabinet has been occupying himself for some time in preparing the way for one of his
brothers employed in the department of Foreign Affairs.
The youngest of these is very young ; the eldest, who
is older than the secretary himself, has not so much
talent and astuteness, and the reign of the Lombard
seems likely to end with him who is now at the head of
affairs.   It is this man, one of the principal sources of
the evils which afflict Europe—a man doubtless devoted
to the interests of France, paid by her, and not to be
bought by anyone else, because she pays for any services
rendered to her as much as and more than anyone else
is able to do—who makes the most direct opposition to
our union with Prussia.   We shall in vain act,
in a sense most agreeable to the personal sentiments
of the King, if ever we aim at any result which shall
have for its object to counterbalance the disastrous
influence of France.   Every overture will be received
with eagerness and conviction on the part of the King,
and all happy results will be carefully stifled in the bud
by Lombard.

The King yields only to one predominant feeling,
which those about him have carefully nourished for
years — it is assuredly the only one that is shared
by them, for the reasons I have shown above—that of
fear.   We cannot conceal from ourselves that they fear
us no longer ; and t will be only the Power that inspires
some terror here which can direct the movements of the
Prussian cabinet, with some chance of success.

France and Russia exercise this power, and the time
for making Prussia enter into our views, which ought
to be essentially her own, could not be more favourable
than when there is an open quarrel between those two

Powers ; but it is not we who will be able to manage this. It appears certain that it is only at St. Petersburg, that the court of Prussia can be conquered ; and the most perfect agreement of our views, the most intimate combination of our means with those of Russia, seem to offer every probability of success in attaining this end. The alliance should in that case be demanded by Russia, who would risk nothing by involving herself with France, and our part should be confined to the most positive assurances that we have for some time pledged ourselves to the inauguration of a new system, based on the common interests of the two monarchies : assurances given so often, and which up to the present time have only served as a pretext for urging the boundless attachment of the King for all the French governments to which the Revolution has given birth, although diametrically opposed to the personal sentiments of that sovereign. The Prussian cabinet will not reject overtures which are made by Russia, because it will be afraid of offending that Power ; it would enter into them willingly, if it did not believe that it ought not to be foremost in trying to prevent Europe from affording new means of aggrandisement to France, and it is the court of Russia alone that can ever determine it to an alliance bringing with it some chance of war.

The most essential service which the court of St. Petersburg can render to us, and at the same time to the whole of Europe, would be to employ itself in getting Lombard removed from his post, where he is placed as a scout of Bonaparte's to hinder everything, or what is equivalent to that, to acquaint him with every measure which is not his own. The present moment would seem favourable to secure to Russia the success of a negotiation which may be a delicate one,

but would really destroy one of the greatest obstacles
to an understanding between the three Powers : her
quarrel with France, the change of the Prussian ministry, in which probably personal interest would second
her views; and, above all, the momentary embarrassment in which the King would find himself by the
chances of a war with Sweden on behalf of the French
in the north of Germany. The conduct of Lombard,
his well-known principles, his league with France, the
impossibility of our confiding in that man—all will
serve as a pretext, if it were difficult to find one, for
his removal from a place where he must necessarily
give umbrage to every Power not exclusively devoted
to France. The difficulty of replacing Lombard by a
man more worthy to serve his master is great ; never,
perhaps, was the scarcity of fit men to be employed in
the diplomatic career felt more strongly than now ; but
certainly a more dangerous man than Lombard could
not be found. It would be a very happy thing if this
agreement could be established, supported by the
authority of Russia, and cemented by our sincere desire
to unite our dearest interests with those of a state
which for some time has had no right to treat us as
a rival ; the Ministers of Austria and Russia at the
court of Berlin receiving orders to be open to all overtures, and to agree in their expressions regarding all
objects of common interest. This unity of will and
expression would prove to the cabinet here that there
exists between us and Russia an agreement to dominate
Prussia, and at the same time open to her certain
methods of extrication from a dilemma in which she
has been for more than a year, by uniting its interests
to those of these two Powers.

Metternich to Colloredo, Berlin, December 4, 1804.

57. In obedience to the wishes of your Excellency, I repaired, the day after the receipt of the despatches of the 15th November, to the house of M. d'Alopéus, to communicate to him the orders I had received relative to the last overtures he made to me. I thought I could not give him a better proof of the confidence of his Imperial Majesty's Ministry than by reading to him the despatch itself. He showed the greatest satisfaction with its contents, and we are agreed on a uniform line of conduct in a delicate negotiation, which cannot be conducted with too much prudence, so as not to excite the attention of our two colleagues, the Ministers of France and England, who are equally interested in spreading it about, though for entirely opposite reasons; and above all taking care that it is not abused by the disaffected, who are employed here even in the offices. It was decided that I should go to M. de Hardenberg to make him aware of the wishes of my august master for a real union between our courts, the sole end of which would be to maintain the equilibrium of Europe, and to ensure the independence, tranquillity, and safety, individual and general, of Powers equally menaced by the proceedings of the French Government. M. d'Alopéus satisfied me of the good disposition of the Minister, and informed me of two subjects of disquietude touched upon by M. de Hardenberg, which he advised me to remove: first, that an agreement between Prussia and Austria might bring about an offensive alliance directed by the British cabinet; and that there should enter into our plans no ideas of aggrandisement. My instructions being perfectly precise in these two respects, and the

intentions of my court free from suspicion, I promised
him to mention these two matters in the conversation
which I should have with M. de Hardenberg. M.
d'Alopéus insisted, with all the ardour for the good
cause which animates him, that I should press my overtures and offer to the King the direct guarantee of the
Emperor as to the purity and sincerity of our intentions. We agreed on our individual conduct, and
(being obliged to give some reason for the arrival of my
courier) that I should make no mystery of the assent of
his Imperial Majesty to the measures employed by the
court here to procure the deliverance of Chevalier
Rumbold.[1]

M. de Hardenberg being that day at Potsdam, I
could not ask him for an interview till the following day,
November 22. I explained the conduct which his
Imperial Majesty had believed up to this time must
convince the French Government of his desire—shared
by the King—to maintain the peace of the Continent,
and to abstain from all participation, direct or indirect,
in the maritime war. The results have not at present
shown the same sentiments on the part of the French
Government, which rests apparently on constant encroachments and a system of extension incompatible
with the repose and equilibrium of Europe. His Imperial
Majesty desires that those princes who may be considered the mutual protectors of this equilibrium should
dismiss all subjects of disunion, and unite in their principles of conduct. I dwelt on all the reasons given in
your Excellency's despatch to prove that such an agreement could in no wise disturb harmony with France, if
its views did not exceed bounds ; and that, supposing

---

[1] Rumbold, the English Resident in the Circle of Lower Saxony, taken
prisoner by Napoleon, and subsequently released.

the contrary, this agreement would become necessary
to save the Powers most exposed from inevitable ruin.
I was firm on the point that assuredly his Imperial
Majesty was very far from wishing for more than Providence had placed under his sceptre, and that he
regarded it as superfluous even to mention the first
principle of all agreement—namely, the putting away
of all thoughts of acquisition or encroachment.

M. de Hardenberg listened to these overtures with
attention and with an air of great satisfaction. He
assured me that his own views had been for some time
exactly the same, and that his greatest desire was to be
able to justify the flattering confidence I had placed in
him by contributing with all his power towards the
success of these salutary measures, which alone can
save Europe from the ruin which seems to threaten it.
He told me of the great difficulty he should have to get
the King to agree to any measure which would in the
least resemble a coalition, the result of the last having
given him an aversion to any similar idea; 'but,' added
he, 'be convinced that your principles are ours, and
provided that you wish neither for an offensive league
with England, nor to enter into any scheme of aggrandisement for any one Power, I will do all I possibly can
to forward the measures, convinced that nothing would
be more distasteful to the King than either of these two
things. You understand,' said he to me, 'that one of
the first precautions necessary is the observation of the
most profound secrecy: and that can only be secured by
confiding the matter to the smallest number of persons
possible. On this account I would desire that your
Minister make not the least allusion to this affair to Count
de Finkenstein,[1] and that you alone should have charge

---

[1] Count Carl Finkenstein, Prussian Ambassador at Vienna.

of all the communications concerning it.   I shall not
myself make use of the confidence of your court, except to the King.   You understand that if France heard
one word, that would suffice to render all union impossible; she rules by the division of states, flattering us
alternately, at the expense of one another.'   I promised
to tell your Excellency of his remark concerning Count
de Finkenstein.

I took the opportunity of showing that the agreement of our views in relation to France was a pledge
of their sincerity, and I assured him that every precaution he thought fit to propose to us would be accepted
with pleasure.   M. de Hardenberg told me that he did
not intend to go to Potsdam, having been there so
recently, but that he preferred to await the return of
the King, fixed for Wednesday, November 28, so as not
to arouse the suspicion of the people about his Majesty
as to the subject on which he wished to speak alone
with him.   As this delay might make some difference in
such an important negotiation, he asked me if I could
not remit to him in writing the essential points of what
I had just said, his desire being to use the very words
I had employed.   Having foreseen this demand, I had
made an extract of the despatch, without headings or
signature, which I sent to him.

He gave me his word of honour that the only use
he would make of it would be to master its contents, so
that he might render them faithfully to his master.

By chance M. d'Alopéus being announced at this
moment, M. de Hardenberg asked me if he would be
in the way, and I agreed with pleasure that he should
take part in our conversation.   Having told him the
object of my visit to M. de Hardenberg, M. d'Alopéus
hastened to fulfill the promises which he had made in

private, and expressed himself fully authorised to trust the sincerity and loyalty of the terms of agreement between the courts of Vienna and Berlin, and even undertook that every guarantee to the King should be made from the Emperor direct, his Imperial Majesty being perfectly cognisant of our views, and sharing the conviction of the sincerity and agreement of the three Powers. The conversation I had just had with M. de Hardenberg was repeated word for word, and we apprised the Minister of the mutual engagement we had made, to confide the secret to one of our *employés* only ; M. de Hardenberg begged M. d'Alopéus that he would not acquaint M. de Goltz with any communication relating to the object of a negotiation which he wished to be restricted to himself, M. d'Alopéus, and myself.

The King returned to town on November 28, and M. de Hardenberg having had an interview with him, begged me to call at his house. He told me that, having only seen his Majesty for a few moments, he was unable to do more than transmit the overtures to him without discussing them ; that his Majesty had declared without hesitation that his intentions and views were exactly the same as those of his Imperial Majesty, but that the mode of execution appeared to him to offer so many subjects for meditation that he wished to reflect on it for some days. 'If Bonaparte hears of it,' added the King, 'he will fall on one or other of us, to prevent the union ; I should like to see you one of these days to discuss the thing quietly. I await,' continued he, 'the return of a courier whom we have sent from Potsdam, and who ought to be in Paris in three or four days, the object of his journey being to carry our offers of mediation between France and Russia, and the proposition of the evacuation of the country of Hanover by the French.

His return must necessarily bring modifications even to the measures necessary for the alliance.' I replied that I did not think I could defer sending a courier with the report of our first conversation, and begged him to tell me what information I might give concerning the one which had just taken place.

M. de Hardenberg replied : 'I am strongly of your opinion that you should inform your court of our conversations, and of my own words of this day. I even authorise you to guarantee the most absolute agreement of the King's principles and his way of looking at things; it is only in the method of carrying them out that I have difficulties to overcome.' He repeated what he had said to me in our first conversation as to the King's ideas about coalition, and of his difficulty in disabusing him of them in regard to what we now propose. 'Do you wish,' added he, 'that I should seek an interview with the King ? But I assure you that I would not have waited so long if I did not know him, and if I had not the conviction that it is better not to press him personally on decisions of this kind.' I replied that I believed I could not leave the management of our affairs in better hands, based as it was on the most intimate knowledge of his master, and that I was far from wishing to press him. I finished this conversation, during which he could not hide his embarrassment at the indefiniteness of his communica- tion, by telling him that I could add nothing to what I had confided to him at the time of our first interview, and that I contented myself with referring him to the contents of the paper which I had sent him ; which, while containing the principles of his Imperial Majesty, must furnish him with the most powerful weapons for reassuring the fears of the King, if haply any existed ;

that, not being informed of the intentions of my court relative to the mode of agreement, I was hardly in a condition to insist upon any one form as preferable to another, but that I would undertake with pleasure to make known to his Imperial Majesty all ideas suggested by M. de Hardenberg which would tend to ensure the accomplishment of a junction, of the necessity of which neither of us entertained any doubts. M. d'Alopéus, for whose support I could not be thankful enough, had warned me of the difficulties which M. de Hardenberg experienced, about which he had expressed himself still more freely to him. The personal character of the King is repugnant to any measure which obliges him to act with decision; on the other hand, he is not ignorant of the dangers with which Europe is menaced; but, unhappily, the man on whom he depends shrinks at the least appearance of war. M. de Hardenberg appears to me to have entered into the views of the courts of Vienna and St. Petersburg without any reserve, and we may hope from him and his efforts all that can ever be expected from the court of Berlin.

Metternich to Colloredo, Berlin, December 5, 1804.

58. Convinced of the necessity of the court of Russia being exactly informed of the progress of our negotiation, I expressed the preceding despatch so that it might be read by M. d'Alopéus. The account of my conversations is such as I have had the honour to describe there, and I do not think I have omitted a single word of importance.

M. de Hardenberg has expressed himself to me with the greatest freedom, and it is impossible to doubt the sincerity of his intentions with respect to us. He knows all the dangers of his position, and has little confidence in the cabinet of the King, and above all in Lombard, whom he appreciates at his just value, thwarting him in all his plans, although the success of the negotiation relative to Chevalier Rumbold allows him to display a more decided character than he would have dared to show before that event. He seems determined to use every means to reduce Lombard's party, and was not afraid to admit to M. d'Alopéus the necessity under which he believed himself to be in this respect. The measures he has proposed to me to ensure secrecy, the zeal with which he received my first overtures, the state of suffering in which I found him yesterday (which he could not conceal from me) at seeing the inaction and the weakness of his master, the strong conviction he entertains as to the gigantic extent of the Emperor Napoleon's views—all speak in favour of the sincerity of his promises to support our salutary views; and if the result is not perfectly successful, the fault cannot be attributed to him.

M. d'Alopéus has an abrupt and excitable manner, but yet shows great coolness and circumspection in the negotiation. I am convinced that the renewal of the war does not enter into his plans, and that he has not neglected the calculation of all the chances which in that case would be found on the side of France. He appears to me to observe scrupulously the orders of his court, and I am more and more strengthened in the conviction that it is by the court of St. Petersburg alone that we can conquer Prussia. All depends on the course which the Russian cabinet follows at Berlin, above all on the perseverance in which it enters on the negotiations, and on the support which it continues to give to ours. The King has himself shown that he has great confidence in the straightforwardness and right principle of the Emperor Alexander ; but if his reason cannot refuse to acknowledge the necessity of joining in the views of the two courts, the fear of becoming involved with France troubles him, and it is Russia alone which will ever be able to conquer this feeling or to force him to act in spite of himself. I have rested all my reasonings with M. de Hardenberg on the perfect agreement of our position under all possible circumstances, not forgetting at the same time that we cannot do anything more than offer ourselves. Prussia has certainly as much need of us as we can possibly have of her : a truth which sad experience will not fail to bring to light, if the indecision of the King and his aide-de-camp, General Köckritz, does not bring this monarch to an agreement equally useful to both parties.

M. d'Alopéus has just come to see me. I communicated to him my despatch under letter A (No. 55), and he says that he does not think he could do better than found his despatch to his court on its contents.

Metternich to Colloredo, Berlin, December 27, 1804.

59. M. de Hardenberg has had many conferences with the King, who at last has made up his mind with respect to the overtures which I was charged to make to the Minister here. You will find in the verbal declaration enclosed (No. 60) which was given to me by M. de Hardenberg, at a conference which I had with him yesterday, and which I have the honour to transmit to you in the original, M. le Comte, an expression of the sentiments of the King which, I dare to flatter myself, surpasses what might have been expected.

M. d'Alopéus, who during the kind of stagnation in

which we have been has taken care to keep me well
informed of the views which M. de Hardenberg communicated to him, tells me that that Minister had certain
difficulties in proposing to his master, first, the form of
a Convention to ensure the principles common to the
three Sovereigns, because of the danger which might
ensue personally to the King of Prussia from the existence of such an agreement if it were discovered and
misrepresented by the cabinet of the Tuileries; then,
secondly, the manner of bringing in the interests of
Italy, from which the Prussian states are far removed,
by the support which he proposes to give to our overtures.   M. d'Alopéus warned me that the last point was
the most difficult of all to introduce.   Indeed, M. de
Hardenberg, after having given me the verbal note yesterday, told me he felt obliged to make known to me,
in their full extent, the sentiments and views of his
master; his Majesty believes he could not meddle in the
affairs of Italy, whose geographical position, and that
of his states, makes it impossible to render any effectual
help at such a distance. In support of this argument, he
alluded to the possibility of a war in Denmark, which,
with the best will to help on our part, we should find
equally beyond our reach.   I thought it right to observe
that Italy, and everything relating to it might be considered from two different points of view.   That we, as
neighbours, and a Power bordering on that country,
had a more direct and individual interest in it than the
more remote Powers could have; but that it could not
be concealed that the encroachments of France on that
side must affect the whole of Europe as her extensions
had other parts of the Continent; that assuredly
Prussia, Russia, and Austria would not see with indifference the Emperor Napoleon at some future time

unite the throne of Spain to the crown of France, and
that they could not but be equally interested that the
crown of Naples, Lombardy, and perhaps that of the
whole of Italy, should not come to him or his family,
supposing such a project enters his head. That my
august master, far from wishing to encroach on the
rights of any of his neighbours, only founded his views
on general principles; that I was convinced that if ever
there was a question of personal interest in the
agreement of the Powers, it could only be on grounds
applicable to the principles of general utility, and that
Italy seemed to me to be as little able to separate herself from this point of view as any other European
state. M. de Hardenberg assured me that what he
had just said had much the same meaning, but that he
thought he ought to explain the King's views as frankly
as possible.

. . . M. d'Alopéus having started the idea of an
engagement between the three Sovereigns which should
be contained in autograph letters, M. de Hardenberg
assured him, privately, of the King's assent to this
method, at the same time begging him not to mention it.

. . . The present state of our negotiation appears
to me as advantageous as possible. Prussia is included in
the general cause; she is directly and explicitly one with
us and Russia. It would have been a real gain merely to
have induced her not to obstruct the views of the two
courts; but she has engaged to support them. M. de
Hardenberg has declared twenty times in the course of
our conversation that it is the King's wish to hold the
same language as ourselves and Russia, and to agree in
all our measures. From that, added he, we may expect
the most immediate influence on the fate of Europe;

the King is convinced of it, and his resolutions once taken are immovable.

. . . I think I could reduce all the elements contained in the verbal note, and touched on in my conversation with the Minister, to the following :—Prussia desires to come to an understanding with the two Imperial courts on all the principles necessary to guarantee and consolidate the peace of Europe, and applicable to any pretensions the French Government may develop (Italy not excepted) tending to disturb peace, to disunite the Powers among themselves, and to necessitate a language and agreement of measures proper to maintain and re-establish the political equilibrium of Europe. She is also desirous of arranging with us the interior affairs of the German Empire, in which she believes us more immediately interested at the present moment. It will not have escaped the penetration of your Excellency that the affairs of Germany are expressly mentioned in the verbal note.

M. de Hardenberg professed in our conversation yesterday that his master has a great desire to come to an understanding as soon as possible with us on all the points of discussion which may still exist concerning the final arrangements of Germany. He said to me that it would suffice that his Majesty the Emperor should make clear : first, what are the objects which it would be better to put aside, or of which he wished to adjourn the discussion ; secondly, what are those which he wishes submitted to discussion at once ; so as to be sure of the King's assent, which he will pronounce in the most unequivocal manner at the Diet. He added, 'Nothing is more necessary for the removal of all foreign influence from Germany than that we should be of one mind ; and it will not escape your court how

essential it is to destroy all those elements which are
suited to keep up the hope the French have of disuniting
us.' I assured M. de Hardenberg of the satisfaction his
overtures had given at Vienna, and of the eagerness with
which his Imperial Majesty responded to the confidence
of the King, the proofs of which I had transmitted to
him, and which he fully appreciated. I am convinced
on this occasion, as in all the preceding ones, of the
sincere desire of the Minister to do his best to bring our
two courts together. He has spoken much to me of his
conviction that France will continue to amuse us, at the
expense of each other : and of his wish to get rid of all
the false notions which are consequently suggested to
each of us, as the simplest and surest method of de-
feating these manœuvres.

Hardenberg to Metternich, Berlin, December 4, 1804.

60. The King, in adhering most rigidly to the
system of neutrality which he prescribed to himself
during the present war, is constantly animated with the
desire of seeing peace and tranquillity maintained on
the Continent, and the benefits which would accrue
therefrom to the whole of Europe, settled as soon as
possible on solid and equitable bases.

His Majesty evinces the most lively satisfaction at
finding the sentiments of his Imperial Majesty in this
respect agreeing so entirely with his own ; and it is
with sincere thankfulness that he has received the overtures made by M. le Comte de Metternich for an agreement of principles and conduct, and, if it be necessary,
of measures between their Majesties and his Imperial
Majesty of All the Russias. From the happy connection
which exists between the two sovereigns of Russia and
Prussia, and the confidence which the King justly places

in the character of his Majesty the Emperor of the Romans and Austria, his Majesty most willingly gives his hand to such an agreement, and will be ready to concert with their Majesties on all that the critical circumstances of the moment demand, or that can in any way help towards the desired end. His Majesty consents with pleasure to put on one side all subjects of disunion between the two courts. It would be the fulfilment of his wishes to see them dismissed for ever, and to be able to come to an understanding with his Imperial Majesty on the affairs of Germany.

Further communications on the part of the Imperial court on any subject which may supervene will be received with equal satisfaction and confidence.

Metternich to Hardenberg, Berlin, January 15, 1805.

61. The salutary dispositions contained in the verbal note of M. le Baron de Hardenberg, with the overtures which the Minister of State has added to them, correspond exactly with those of the Emperor.

All that is passing in Europe, and especially in Germany, is assuredly calculated to arouse the attention of the Great Powers in alliance with that great national body; and the court of Vienna, as little hides from itself as that of Berlin the frightful consequences which seem to be the inevitable result of the protection which France accords to all intrigues, at the head of which she is not to be found openly. The ways and means employed by her to gain a decisive influence over the courts of Portugal and Spain, and to subdue still more effectually Holland, Switzerland, and nearly the whole of Italy, present unequivocal prognostications of the fate which Germany may expect when her turn comes: that is to say, after the fulfilment of the fate which

Napoleon destines for the Republics with which he is surrounded, and at whose independence we may every instant expect to see him give the last blows.

The following reasoning appears at least conclusive: If the present sovereign of France, not content with the degree of power to which he has brought his empire, really entertains the views that are supposed, and which all his actions authorise one to suppose, of arrogating to himself either the domination or a dictatorial power over all his neighbours, doubtless he entertains similar views towards Germany. Those who foresaw the absolute sovereign of France in the proceedings of the First Consul are equally authorised to extend their conjectures as to the further designs of the Restorer of the Empire of Charlemagne, in calling about him the Sovereign Pontiff, the legislative authorities of the Italian Republics, and as many of the princes of Germany as he has found disposed to assist as vassals at his coronation; lastly, seeking, or rather expecting, still more certain guarantees of the success of his plans, in the adoption of the same military government and the same political principles which brought the Roman Empire to a universal monarchy.

The fate of Europe depends on the determination of the sovereigns of Austria, Russia, and Prussia; on the sincerity and energy they throw into their union, and on the elevation of the point of view from which they act in concert. Peace even could not be maintained without the union of the Great Powers. The ease with which one predominating Power is already allowed to oppress her weak neighbours, and to attack the South if she is on good terms with the North, or the North if she spares the South, can hardly be considered as a state of peace; it is, on the contrary, a state of war so much the more dangerous, inasmuch as the attacking party only is in arms, making conquests without striking a blow, and swaggering on without fear of resistance, till the time will come when even an alliance of the enfeebled Powers will not suffice to stem the torrent.

The Emperor of Germany and Austria loves peace as much as his Prussian Majesty, and has perhaps more need of it than any other sovereign.

The Emperor of Russia is as pacific, and as little animated with the thirst of ambition and conquest; but it depends neither on their desires nor their isolated measures to maintain the peace of the Continent, and in consequence the tranquillity, and, above all, the importance and the glory of their monarchies. They can only reckon on a true and lasting peace when all three Powers shall be sincerely united to make peace by the only proper means, to preserve it from all check, or at least to establish it for the future on a solid foundation. Such a union should rest, above all, on the most entire confidence in the purity, moderation, and energy of the sentiments of each.

Francis II. will omit nothing to prove that he is worthy of such trust on the part of Alexander I. and Frederick William. The confidence which his Majesty the Emperor of Russia inspires in the sovereign of Prussia induces his Imperial Majesty to leave to that monarch the glorious privilege of bringing about by his intervention the formation of a triple agreement, by which Germany and the greater part of Europe may expect peace, safety, and independence. His Imperial and Royal Majesty begs to assure his Prussian Majesty, in the most positive manner, that, far from its ever entering into his thoughts to expose the interests of Prussia, on the contrary, he will regard the dangers of

Prussia as his own, subordinating every individual view to the public interest, making no difference between objects more or less remote, whenever they seem to cause any anxiety. Lastly, nothing will prevent Austria from forming the triple alliance, not even the temptation of the greatest advantages for herself alone. His Imperial and Royal Majesty hopes, on his side, that the determination of his Prussian Majesty will be absolutely the same in this respect.

WINTZINGERODE'S MISSION IN BERLIN.

(Note 11, Vol. I.)

1805.

62. Metternich to Colloredo, Berlin, February 18, 1805.
63. Metternich to Wintzingerode, Berlin, March 3, 1805.
64. Metternich to Colloredo, Berlin, May 16, 1805.

62. I hasten to have the honour of informing your Excellency of the arrival of M. le Baron de Wintzingerode and the first conversations I have had with him.[1] . . .

M. de Wintzingerode came to see me. I told him I had been informed of his arrival, and had received orders to consult with him as to all the steps to be taken.

' Pray believe me,' said he to me, ' that the sole aim of the Emperor Alexander is to draw as close as possible the ties which unite our two states. We have decided no longer to suffer the neutrality of Prussia; in case of a war, the chances of which increase daily, it would be far better to have an open enemy than a so-called friend favouring all the enterprises of the common enemy. . . . I suppose the first courier who arrives will bring you the statement of our views on the points

---

[1] Baron de Wintzingerode, Major-General and Adjutant of the Russian Emperor was, together with Herr von Alopäus, entrusted with the negotiations respecting the admission of Prussia into the Coalition against France.

essential to the agreement; which may all be reduced
to bringing the King to a decision, and not to commit
yourself. If the King really wishes for the agreement,
he will not refuse to take the first step, to write to
your Emperor and to beg mine to forward his advances. The Emperor of Russia has direct proofs that
Prussia formerly involved him with France, as you have
been many times; it is for him to furnish us now with
the first pledges of his desire to join with us. I believe
then that it would be better that we should not seem
to have arranged these things together; it seems to
me natural that if the Minister here thinks that Austria
and Russia are entirely agreed, and that they will only
permit him to accede to measures already taken, he will
be more afraid of committing himself, than if he supposes the contrary.'

I observed to the General that I need make no
change in the conduct I had observed up to this time,
to enter exactly into his views.

The General assured me that he knew the whole
progress of our negotiation; he did not hesitate to
tell me that the contents of my despatches had always
met with his master's approbation, and that one of the
causes of his dissatisfaction with M. d'Alopéus was that
up to this time he has been so slow to second me; that
all my despatches had been strong in principle, and that
the manner in which I declared myself demanded that
the vigour and strength of the Minister of Russia should
be doubled.

'M. d'Alopéus,' said he, 'supposed the Emperor to
be the same as he was at the Conferences at Memel,
and he deceives himself. The Emperor is personally
attached to the King, but he would be very sorry if
anyone thought that feeling would influence in the least

his way of looking at things, and he will convince the King of this himself.'

We agreed on our line of conduct : that I should wait for M. d'Alopéus to come to me to make the first confidences relative to the despatches brought by M. de Wintzingerode ; that in public we should avoid all appearance of treating directly of affairs, and that I should beg him to come always to me, to avoid the surveillance to which we should be exposed in the house where he lives, which is one of those most watched by the police, of which fact I shall take care to warn him.

The present position of affairs, all the chances of war which have shown themselves lately, the presence of the former minister, who, encouraged and sustained by certainly the most numerous party, thinks of nothing but the moment when he can resume his former influence, all contribute to the embarrassment of the present minister. He does not know how to refuse the proposition of Russia to make the King take the first direct step in the agreement, and in the way indicated by himself, without endangering the purity of his master's intentions, or without confessing how little power he can exercise on the King's final determinations.

The part taken by M. de Haugwitz in the embarrassment of his rival cannot escape any observer on the spot. He has the air of ignoring all that is going on at present, and seems very intimate with Lombard. Some words which the *employés* of the French mission let fall, and the continuance of his connection with Chevalier de Bray, prove that the avowed partisans of France have not lost all hope of seeing him at the helm again.

I confine my own conduct strictly to the orders of

your Excellency. It is infinitely less difficult than I
could have supposed, considering the apparently amicable
footing on which General Wintzingerode is with the
Russian ambassador. The former, in a conversation
which I had with him this morning, in which he told
me of his interview with the King, confirmed his
opinion, already declared in the present despatch, that
M. d'Alopéus does not unite the energy necessary for
a Russian ambassador with the other qualities which he
undeniably possesses.

Metternich to Wintzingerode, Berlin, March 3, 1805.

63. The Prussian minister having promised to
send to the Austrian minister, in a short time, a summary of the King's intentions relative to the agreement,
all conjecture must remain in suspense until that time.
The replies of the Berlin cabinet to the different overtures which the court of Vienna and recently that
of St. Petersburg have made to it can only offer two
points of view : they will either consent explicitly to
enter into an agreement of ways and means to oppose the encroachments of France, or they will be
evasive and dilatory. This last supposition is equivalent
to a negative reply, with this difference only, that the
way to a negotiation will still remain open.

In considering the present position of Prussia relative to Swedish Pomerania, there is no doubt that the
declared wish of the King and the hope with which
the Ministry flatters itself is, that no question relating
to it may be discussed.

The King will undoubtedly be exposed through his
own fault to see his system of inaction threatened from
three sides ; and this system, the only one compatible
with his personal inclinations, has been dressed up by

his counsellors and perfidious courtiers in a mask of neutrality, all the advantages of which are constantly in favour of France.

Russia has peremptorily declared against the project for the occupation of Pomerania.

Sweden confines herself to an expression of principles, without explaining her future intentions.

They hope here that France will make no enquiries about the discussions which are being raised between the cabinets of St. Petersburg and Berlin, and that she will trust to the engagements contracted with her by Prussia.

The first news from Paris will doubtless supply us with the views of Napoleon, and the interest he may have in augmenting or diminishing the embarrassment of this court. His conduct will also show what intentions he could have had in provoking, through his Minister at Berlin, the measures which have brought about the present discussion. If he thought it well to depend now on the above-mentioned engagements with Prussia, what reason could he have to excuse himself in the eyes of the King for not having done so at a time when it only depended on him to appear to ignore the direct part which Russia will be forced to take in the cause of Sweden?

Can anyone suppose, even on the very simplest calculation, that the King flatters himself that he can remain much longer in his state of inaction? Does there seem to him to be the possibility of a chance that Prussia could in a general movement withdraw from all participation?

Lastly, What will bring about the concurrence of Prussia?

The solution of these three questions will require a

profound discussion, which will embrace the whole policy of this court, and a full knowledge of the engagements contracted with France.

Two considerations inseparable from his personal character will necessarily present themselves to the King, if he finds himself forced to choose between the two Imperial courts and France, namely :—

1st. Which side offers the most chance of safety and exemption from present exertion ?

2nd. Which of the two seems to promise the larger indemnity for the expenses a war would occasion ?

One might, and assuredly with reason, be astonished that the question of the choice of an ally could be the subject of any discussion whatever, looking at it from the sole point of view of the principles and inclinations of the King himself. It seems probable that the wish of the Powers, and the impossibility of his escaping a decision, will make him decide at last.

He would endure anything if he thought he could avoid taking an active part ; and if he sees the passive *rôle* can no longer be sustained, there is no doubt he will declare for the side which offers the most chances of safety with the least exertion, and he cannot hide from himself that these are only to be found in his alliance with Austria and Russia.

Metternich to Colloredo, Berlin, May 16, 1805.

64. Baron de Wintzingerode having announced his intention of returning to St. Petersburg, the King invited him to Potsdam to be present at a review of the garrison, after which his Majesty gave him an audience to take leave. The General was received by the King with a great many protestations of friendship for the Emperor Alexander ; they had more than an hour's conversation, chiefly on ordinary topics, and the King seemed infinitely more at his ease than on any former occasion. . . .

The political system of Prussia cannot but be shaken by an intimate alliance of Russia and Austria. She ought not to think of escaping, or doubt the impossibility of inaction, when these two Powers declare that her decision will be for the good of the whole of Europe. It is not enough to leave her at the present time no means of escape, it will be necessary to keep her in that state. Anything which in the least resembles incoherence on the part of the Powers will always serve as a pretext for slipping her neck out of the collar. Anything, which in the least gives the idea of a retrograde step, will be explicitly declared to be one, and the King's cabinet will extract from it something favourable to its former principles.

One cannot deny that the mission of Baron de Wintzingerode, and the energetic language which the Emperor Alexander has caused to be used here by that ambassador, have recently only had the effect of intimidating the King, and of making the Minister assume positively that the Prussian court will not refuse to cooperate with the allied Powers when the moment for action has arrived. . . .

Three consequences equally annoying appear to me to have resulted from the course the cabinet of St. Petersburg has thought fit to follow in an affair of which I am far from being able to judge the motives exactly :—

1. That Prussia is authorised to hope that, being an intermediary, she will continue to be the arbiter of the rival Powers in Europe.

2. That in not deciding too quickly on a question

advanced by Russia, there is at any rate a chance of seeing it presently offered with essential modifications.

3. That they like to persuade themselves here that the league between the two Imperial courts is not as strong as they supposed it to be a short time ago.

We learn here that the decision of M. Novosiltzoff's mission [1] is the only result of the negotiation with England, and Baron de Hardenberg expressly told me that he believed this would be as much news for Vienna as it had been here.

Prussia ignores the stipulations which bind the two Imperial courts ; but she ought to believe in them without knowing the terms, and it is from that persuasion alone that we can expect happy results. The conviction of the impossibility of detaching Russia from the interests of Austria will always be most powerful with the two Powers, and the idea submitted by M. d'Alopéus to Baron de Wintzingerode, a short time before the arrival of the news of the mission of M. Novosiltzoff, of establishing at Berlin points for negotiation between France, Russia, and England, would be certainly the most unhappy of all determinations. The idea of combating any conception of that kind on the spot, however unlikely it might be either on the side of Russia or France, is one of the motives which has made him hasten his departure.

---

[1] M. Novosiltzoff, a young Russian diplomatist, who was sent on a confidential mission to London, for the purpose of negotiating with Pitt a coalition between England and Russia.

THE APPROACHING ENTRANCE OF RUSSIAN TROOPS ON PRUSSIAN TERRITORY.

(Note 12, Vol. I.)

65. Metternich to Colloredo, Berlin, September 26, 1805.
66. Metternich to Colloredo, Berlin, September 27, 1805.

65. I hasten to have the honour of submitting to your Excellency the following details of a conference which I had with Baron de Hardenberg this morning.

This minister having begged me to go to see him, I went to call upon him about noon. He told me that he desired an interview in consequence of the resolutions which his Majesty had taken after receiving the last autograph letter of the Emperor Alexander. 'You doubtless know through M. d'Alopéus,' said the minister to me, 'that he has been charged with a mission for the King; perhaps you are even informed of its contents.' I replied that I was certainly aware of the fact, but that M. d'Alopéus had assured me he was ignorant of the contents himself. 'The Emperor,' continued the minister, 'begs the King in the most polite terms to grant his troops a free passage through his dominions; he also proposes an interview with him, which the King has decided to accept. I have just seen M. d'Alopéus, and I have begged him to inform his august master of it as soon as possible, and his Majesty also will send an officer this evening to inform the Emperor on his part. The King having decided

to send Count de Haugwitz to Vienna, I beg you
to send passports for that minister; he intends to set
out to-morrow morning, and you would perhaps like to
see him again before his departure ; he is in the next
room, and I will ask him to come in. His Majesty has
commanded all his army to be immediately put on a
war footing. We hope by that energetic measure,
after the explanations which will take place between
the two sovereigns, to put ourselves in a position to be
of real assistance to the common cause.'

I detained Baron de Hardenberg, who had risen to
fetch M. de Haugwitz. I wished first to speak to him
confidentially, which was not easy, as M. de Haugwitz
was in an adjoining room, and the minister is exceedingly deaf. I said to Baron de Hardenberg that I
should have the honour of sending him the passport he
asked for, but that I could not but express my conviction that the journey of Count de Haugwitz would
bring about no other results than those which Count
de Merveldt and myself had been charged to present
to the Prussian cabinet. 'Your Excellency ought
to be convinced,' said I to him, 'that the principles
of the Imperial court are no longer open to modification. I forewarned you of the reply which would be
made to the last propositions of France, transmitted
by the court here, and I was not deceived ; I now tell
you for a certainty that this journey of M. de Haugwitz will have no other effect but to convince him
of the unalterable determination of his Majesty the
Emperor to follow the course which the two Imperial courts have marked out. The most exact means
of deciding have been given to France. We have explained the purity of our intentions ; and assuredly no
Power could have declared its sentiments with more

dignity and sincerity than ours. You have a much
more direct means of taking an active part in our
pacific negotiations : join our common armaments. M.
de Haugwitz will convince himself that it is only in that
way that Prussia can succeed.   Announce to France the
object for which you have given the order to put your
army on a war footing, which you assure me is for
the purpose of coming to our support ; by that fact
alone you will render the most signal service to the
good cause, from which I defy you ever to separate
your interests without preparing certain ruin for yourself ; let this step precede all others, and I shall see some
chance of a good result from the journey of M. de
Haugwitz.'

Baron de Hardenberg interrupted me to say that
his Majesty had thought he must reply to the mission
of M. de Merveldt,[1] by sending one of his ministers, a
man whose rank and public character corresponded
perfectly to the respect which the King entertained for
his Imperial Majesty ; that he would be charged to
explain at Vienna the motives of the King's journey
and the Prussian armaments. Perhaps, continued he,
all hope of avoiding the breaking out of war is not impossible ; perhaps one might be able to take up the
thread of the negotiations, even if hostilities have
begun, which is very possible ; you have not communicated to us all your negotiations—I am ready, therefore, to be informed on those points.   I replied to
Baron de Hardenberg that this supposition astonished
me more than anyone else, having myself been charged
with all the communications relative to our negotiations

---

[1] General Count Merveldt was sent as Austrian Plenipotentiary Extraordinary to Berlin, to negotiate, with Metternich, the admission of Prussia
into the coalition.

with France. ' You perhaps are not informed yourself,'
said the Baron ; ' but what I tell you is quite true, and
I can prove it.   I must persist in declaring that I cannot
admit your statement.'

Count de Haugwitz entering at this moment, he
came towards me and reiterated with his habitual
phrases assurances of his satisfaction at having been
chosen by his Majesty for the most agreeable mission
that could have been entrusted to him.   I had no hesitation in repeating to him all that I had said to his colleague ; I dwelt principally on my conviction of the
uselessness of this step, and took it for granted that all
these armaments were assembled with the same views
as those of the Imperial courts. Messieurs de Haugwitz
and de Hardenberg exclaimed anew about the views and
intentions of the King being in exact conformity with
our own.   ' There would be one way only,' added
Baron de Hardenberg, ' by which our military measures
could be made to turn against the wishes of the King.
You know, doubtless, as well as I do, ·the rumours
which are publicly circulated of the entrance of the
Russian troops into our territory.   It is with the view
of enlightenment on all these measures, that the King
undertakes a long journey ; the entrance of the Russians in spite of him would be undoubtedly the signal
for war.' The two ministers were profuse in assurances of the signal service which these same armaments
rendered to the cause.   They maintained that France
would abate her pretensions on seeing such serious
preparations, especially as she could not see any opening by which to rally these forces to her side.   I interrupted these gentlemen by submitting to them the
remark that if his Majesty and his minister were as
convinced as they seemed to be that these energetic

demonstrations could not fail to produce an effect on the
French Government, they could not but trust to the plan
which I had been the first to advance in the name of
my court. ' Do not content yourselves,' said I, ' with
allowing France to guess your intentions ; declare them
in concert with the Imperial courts, and you will
ensure every chance of success. Count de Haugwitz
joined me, and paraphrased my argument, adding at
the same time that it was to come to a complete understanding with us that he went to Vienna.

This conversation, which lasted more than an
hour, turned always more or less on commonplaces :
many words and phrases and little sense. I do not
think I need give in detail all the phrases repeated
over and over again. I flatter myself that his Imperial
Majesty will deign to approve the modification which
circumstances have forced upon me as to refusing the
mission of M. de Haugwitz. The refusal at a moment
when his mission coincides with the journey which the
King is going to undertake would certainly have made
no change in the dispositions which are the result of it, so
the two ministers declared to me at the conference held
yesterday. I should, besides, have been letting M. de
Haugwitz himself know that his presence was not
acceptable, which would only have served to exasperate
him at a moment when his councils are needed by the
King. His personal character is too well known at
Vienna to need description, and your Excellency in your
wisdom will be able to judge to what point you would
wish me to go in controlling his reports. His journey in
any case is destined to produce no result ; I wish I
could say as much of that of the King. I confess that
my intimate connection with Baron de Wintzingerode, who knows his master thoroughly, has only served

to make me dread the results of any interview of that nature.

Your Excellency is as able to judge as we who are on the spot of the present dispositions of the court of Prussia. They spread yesterday the most alarming reports of the part which the King will take in consequence of the views of his assembled council ; to-day it is all reduced to mere military demonstrations. The journey of the King has evidently but one object, to try to wheedle the Emperor, and to gain at least time, if the first of these objects does not succeed : the mission of M. de Haugwitz was nothing more than a manœuvre of the same kind. Everything seems to depend now on the firmness which the Emperor Alexander assumes in his interview with the King, and the effect which the entrance of the Russian troops produces, a step which is the consequence of engagements too serious and measures too well concerted to allow of delay.

Metternich to Colloredo, Berlin, September 27, 1805.

66. Baron de Hardenberg, having returned from Tempelberg yesterday, sent this morning at seven o'clock to beg M. d'Alopéus to go and see him. A delay in the message prevented the Russian Minister from going to Baron de Hardenberg before half-past eight o'clock, and he found him just entering his carriage to go to the King. He was only able to tell him the news which had just arrived from Poland confirming the immediate entrance of the Russian troops ; he begged M. d'Alopéus to try once more to prevent this step, and to avoid the most horrible catastrophe to the good cause. The latter confined himself to saying that the commands to the army were out of his jurisdiction, and that he had made known to the court

here some time ago the determination of his Imperial
Majesty, so that he could give the necessary orders for
the free passage of their troops. This conversation
having lasted only a few minutes, the Russian Minister
returned home, where he found Count Ozarovski, one
of the *attachés* to the mission, who had just arrived
from St. Petersburg.

His despatches, dated the 18th, enclose the order
to M. d'Alopéus to declare to the Ministry 'that his
Imperial Majesty, in the hope of the King's agreement
to the interview which he proposed to him in his last
letter, has suspended the entrance of his troops till
that date, convinced, however, that the King will not
hesitate to make common cause with him.'

These orders were to be regarded as not having been
given if the King had acceded to the passage of the
troops before their arrival, and a result from the reply
of the King to the first letter from the Emperor.

M. d'Alopéus repaired immediately to the Cabinet
Minister; they made some difficulty about announcing
him, Messieurs de Laforest and Duroc being expected
every moment. He persisted, and they ushered him
into a room where Baron de Hardenberg was not accustomed to receive. He acquitted himself of his orders,
and added (as was expressly commanded him in his
despatches) that his Majesty being immovable in all his
resolutions, he had no doubt the King would at last
take the only step conducive to his interests and his
glory. Baron de Hardenberg showed the greatest
pleasure at this news, and told him that it had come
just in time; that he would see his Majesty before
dinner at Charlottenburg, and that would put him at
ease with the French Ambassadors, whom he expected
every moment. M. d'Alopéus asked him if it were

true that the French had proposed again to the King to occupy Hanover, and they would guarantee him the possession of it. ' Ah, it is a question of much more than that,' replied the Baron ; ' they propose an alliance, and a good deal besides. I hope,' added he, ' that we shall make the most of this interview, and who knows whether the King may not be persuaded ! '

Baron de Hardenberg, in the course of this conversation, showed some impatience at not seeing the English embark for Hanover. ' No one,' said he, ' can prevent them from taking possession of their own country again.'

All these details, which I had from M. d'Alopéus, who came on to me, and in whose presence I noted down the sentence above quoted, which he tells me is the substance of his orders, appear to me to be of a nature to be brought as soon as possible to the knowledge of your Excellency. . . .

The military preparations go on here with great vigour : a camp is now being made between Kalisch and Sieradz, in Poland, evidently directed against the march of the Russian troops, and it is said that some regiments destined to form another in Pomerania will assemble on October 2. A great quantity of siege artillery is being embarked on the Spree, which can only be intended to go towards the mouth of the Oder.

The avowal that renewed propositions of an alliance with France are being listened to, formally contradicts the statement lately made by Baron de Hardenberg of the real advantage the good cause would gain from the present state of the army and affairs in Prussia.

INROAD OF THE FRENCH AT ANSBACH.

(Note 12, Vol. I.)

67. Metternich to Colloredo, Berlin, Oct. 7, 1805.
68. Alopéus to Czartoryski, Berlin, Oct. 6, 1805.
69. Metternich to Colloredo, Berlin, Oct. 10, 1805.
70. Metternich to Colloredo, Berlin, Oct. 15, 1805.
71. Metternich to Colloredo, Berlin, Oct. 16, 1805.
72. Metternich to Colloredo, Berlin, Oct. 18, 1805.
73. Hardenberg to Duroc, and Laforest, Berlin, Oct. 19, 1805.

Metternich to Colloredo, Berlin, October 7, 1805.

67. I hasten to have the honour of announcing to your Excellency the first results of an event which has doubtless already been made known directly to his Imperial Majesty. A body of 4,000 Frenchmen surrounded a Prussian lieutenant with 24 Hussars at Sickardsreuth, on the road between Wurzburg and Ansbach. This officer, in spite of his protestations that he could not allow the passage of troops, was obliged to yield to force. The French, 20,000 strong—so it is said—are now traversing the whole of the region about Ansbach, on their way to Neuburg, on the Danube. They live by requisitions, without indemnifying the people for their supplies, as if they were in an enemy's country.

Prince Dolgorouki having had his audience at Potsdam yesterday, Baron de Hardenberg remained afterwards with the King. Just as the minister was getting into his carriage, a despatch was brought to him which contained the above-mentioned news. Your Excellency will be able to judge by the annexed report (No. 68) which M. d'Alopéus forwarded the same night

to Pularia, of the effect which this unexpected event
has had on the King. I am obliged to refer entirely to
my colleague's account, not having yet spoken myself to
Baron de Hardenberg, with whom I have begged an
hour's interview this evening, as I missed him at his
house this morning.

Bonaparte has on this occasion done more good to
the cause than any negotiation. He throws the King
into the arms of the allies, by wounding him in his most
sensitive part. He has shown the value of his promises,
and has not hesitated to insult him in the face of Europe.
It seems as if he had wished to take away from him
every reason against joining the coalition or even detaching himself from it. The King, overcome by the
course of the negotiation alone, always inclines towards
the latter course; forced to abandon all hope of remaining aloof from the great political crisis, and treated
personally like all the other monarchs of Europe, he
finds himself as intimately bound to the general cause
as it is possible for him to be.

Another remark not less important is, that the annoyance caused to the King by the supposition that
Russia intended to force his hand has excited him to
exert himself in a manner the coalition could hardly
have expected. If the Russian troops have been stopped
on the remote frontiers of the Prussian kingdom, an
army of two hundred thousand men is now organised,
equipped, and ready to march on the flank of the
enemy; the fifty thousand men, who were to come, find
themselves replaced by four times the number to carry
on the operations.

The sudden resolution to quarrel with Prussia, and
to overthrow with a stroke of the pen the alliance most
useful to France, has given rise to the following conjec-

tures, partly supported by secondary circumstances. The order given to the French army not to respect the neutrality of the Prussian territory coincides, as to its date, with the arrival of the despatches of M. de Laforest and of General Duroc, which contained the first rumours spread here of the determination of the Emperor of Russia that his troops should pass the Prussian frontiers on September 28, either amicably or by force. Supposing that these two ambassadors had pretended to know this fact from a source which could not be disputed, and that they had depended on the assurance which doubtless M. de Hardenberg, and still more their secret agents, would have given them, that the king would regard this measure as a declaration of war, might not the Emperor Napoleon have despatched this order (which would doubtless, infinitely facilitate his immediate operations) in the hope that the news of its execution would arrive at Berlin at a time when the King would be either closely allied or in open war with Russia, conscious that in either case it would do no harm ? . . . .

P.S. News has arrived to-day of the landing of the Russians in Pomerania : I am still ignorant of their numbers.

Alopéus to Czartoryski, Berlin, October 6, 1805.

(Addition to No. 67.)

68. While Baron de Hardenberg was with the King, a courier arrived from Ansbach with the unexpected news that on September 23 (October 3) the French had forced their way through the Prussian territory by Franconia. . . .*

---

* ' M. d'Alopéus describes the event in the same terms as Metternich in the preceding despatch.'

The King, on hearing of this invasion of his territory, in the first moment of anger, ordered Baron de Hardenberg to send back M. Duroc and M. Laforest immediately. An instant afterwards he begged him to suspend their recall, return without delay to Berlin, and assemble a council, composed of the Duke of Brunswick, Marshal de Möllendorf, Count de Schulenburg, and Baron de Hardenberg himself, and to send the result of their deliberations to his Majesty. M. de Hardenberg has been to the above-mentioned generals, who are all to assemble this evening, with the exception of Count de Schulenburg, who is kept in bed by an illness which came on suddenly some days ago. All have heard with joy the news, which relieves them of much anxiety.

The Cabinet Minister began by observing to the King that now his Majesty was released from all promises or engagements contracted with France, and that nothing should prevent him from declaring openly for his august ally. This will no doubt be the result of the deliberations of the generals and ministers above mentioned. This result will be sent to the King to-morrow at Paretz; and the day after to-morrow we shall learn the final determination of his Majesty. According to all appearances Prince Dolgorouki will be the bearer of the decisions. All being ready for the departure of the King, it is probable that his Majesty will not defer it longer than is absolutely necessary to give the orders made necessary by the incident which I have the honour to report to you.

Metternich to Colloredo, Berlin, October 10, 1805.

69. The Prussian minister, Baron de Hardenberg, has told me in confidence that the King has come over to our side entirely. Prince Dolgorouki brings the permission for the entry of the Russians, which the King wished to be effected through Silesia and Bohemia, as the shortest route. Early this morning, an urgent request has been sent from the King to the Russian general in Pomerania, to advance immediately with the twenty thousand Russians and Swedes who are there. A courier has been despatched to Dresden, requesting the Elector immediately to mobilise his army, which is assembled behind that of the Prussians. In a council of war to be held to-day, the chief point to be arranged will be a diversion to be promptly taken to favour our Imperial army. The regiments in Ansbach have received orders to march to Bayreuth. Baron de Hardenberg requests me to have a courier ready this evening or early to-morrow morning, by which time he will have given me the official notice. A certain secrecy is observed for the moment, in order to secure the troops and treasure at Ansbach.

Metternich to Colloredo, October 15, 1805.

70. M. le Baron de Hardenberg has just enabled me to communicate to your Excellency the measures which are to be taken in consequence of the violation of Prussian territory by the French, and which are now going on with great promptitude. Four armies are being formed at the following points : namely, one of from forty to fifty thousand men, in the neighbourhood of Bayreuth, under the command of the Prince of Hohenlohe ; a second, in Hanover, under the Duke of Brunswick ; a third, in Westphalia ; and a fourth in reserve.

The Elector of Saxony has been asked to assemble his troops and join the Prussian army in Franconia. The different corps will be prepared to join the common cause as soon as they are assembled, and in a state to undertake the operations, which it is now extremely urgent should be agreed upon. Baron de Hardenberg desires * that we should make as much haste as possible in commencing negotiations to this end, and it is greatly to be wished that an able man, instructed in the details of our military operations, should be sent to help us.

The court here believes it ought to follow a line of conduct which will not expose it to seeing its views (worthy as they are of the principles of the King and his minister) shackled, or perhaps annihilated, by some French operation before all the means of striking the blow are ready and on the spot. It will take four or five weeks for the army to assemble in the neighbour-hood of Bayreuth ; and by that time the Russian column which is marching through Silesia will have reached the frontier of Bohemia, and the united armies will then be able to take the offensive † as agreed upon.

The King is quite decided to support the good cause by all the means in his power ; he will show that the violation of his territory by our common enemy has been as vigorously resented by him as the measures which he thought it his duty to carry out have been prompt and decided.

Baron de Hardenberg begged me this morning to regard his confidential communications, which are con-fined to the above-mentioned data, as official communi-cations proper to enlighten our august master on the real intentions and projects of the King, and to submit them immediately to your Excellency, and I hasten to

---

* 'It is much to be desired'—addition by Baron de Hardenberg. See explanation in the following despatch, No. 71.

† ' " Offensive " in the sense of resulting from an agreement to be made on which all the general measures depend.' (Correction by Baron de Hardenberg.)

send off a courier this very day with the present despatch.

Conclusion, added by Baron de Hardenberg.

The King has made known to the French Minister and to General Duroc, in a very decided manner, that the unexpected violation of his neutrality puts him under the necessity of making his army take up positions to ensure the safety of his kingdom, and that he regards the engagements (known to us) which have subsisted between France and himself entirely annulled. Baron de Hardenberg has promised me in a short time the communication of the declaration itself.

Metternich to Colloredo, Berlin, October 16, 1805.

71. The corrections on the margin of my first report were dictated to me by Baron de Hardenberg himself, with whom I have passed more than two hours. . . . Baron de Hardenberg commenced the conversation, by saying : 'That his Majesty acceded to the armed mediation which the two Imperial courts had proposed to him, and that in consequence he had put the whole army in motion.' He added, 'that he believed the most urgent necessity existed for our agreeing on the measures, both political and military, which would tend to this object, and that M. de Kalkreuth had been charged to declare this determination to his Majesty the Emperor of All the Russias ; that he would enter here into a negotiation with M. d'Alopéus, and that it was much to be desired that I should be invested with full powers to that end, the welfare of the cause depending on the most perfect unity of our principles and measures.'

I replied to Baron de Hardenberg that the resuming of the armed negotiation appeared to me not suitable to the circumstances, and that what would have saved all Europe a short time ago was no longer applicable to the circumstances of the moment. ' But you have never asked anything else of us,' replied he. I observed to him that in truth the same step had preceded the rupture with France, who had refused to lend herself to it; but that I believed the court of Prussia should separate entirely the two questions; namely, the demand of the two Imperial courts, and the injury which the King had sustained at the hand of France, and wished to wipe out. I proposed to him that he should read over my despatch, in which I begged him to make the meaning clear, that the Emperor might not be deceived as to the real intentions of the King, besides that by analysing it we should both better understand the views of his Majesty.

He proposed the first amendment * to me, not having been charged to make such a demand, although he had adopted it in its full extent.

The second † was the consequence of a long discussion. I had expressly used the word ' offensive ' in my paper ; he had used it to my face twenty times, and it alone described exactly the meaning of the present armament. He could not erase it, but subordinated it as the result of a previous agreement. I observed to him that such an amendment seemed inexplicable to me, when it was a question of avenging a personal insult, and that it could only be expressed in that way, after having plainly declared, face to face with the friendly Powers, that any injury to territory even on

* See the note to the last despatch, No. 70.
† See note to No. 70, p. 67.

their side would be regarded as a declaration of war.
'I conceived,' said I to him, 'that it was necessary to
be open and explicit to the Allies regarding the mode of
action decided on, but the question itself is certainly
settled by the simple fact of the insult.'

Baron de Hardenberg, not being able to retreat from
this position, had recourse to the most detestable of all
statements—namely, to deny that the King had ever said
that he would regard an injury to his territory as a
declaration of war. I objected that in this case
assuredly the two Imperial courts were under a great
mistake; that the Emperor of Russia would only regret
that he had not made his armies advance farther; and
that Count de Haugwitz must himself be deceived in
expressing himself in the same manner on this question.
'How can you wish that we should have said such a
thing to the Emperor of Russia?' interrupted he; 'he
has never said to us that he would force a passage.'
'Ah,' replied I, 'you confess then what you have always
denied, that the rumour of the entrance of the Russian
troops was only a vague report without foundation;
what, then, did your military measures signify?' 'They
were ready for anything that might happen,' said he,
'and are now ready for the French. We are going at
once to Hanover, and it is a question now what measures
we shall adopt there towards the French. They will
probably be ordered to withdraw their troops immediately.' 'But if they will not?' said I. 'Then means
will be found of surrounding them, and shutting them
up in one place. But all I am saying to you is of no
value, for even this question will not be decided till to-
morrow.'

Our conversation was interrupted by a messenger
from General Köckritz, to tell Baron de Hardenberg that

his Majesty would return to town the day after to-morrow, at eleven o'clock in the morning, and had fixed upon that hour to give him an audience. The Baron begged me to retain my courier till that time, because he would then be able to add his official declarations to what he had just said to me. I told him I did not think I could delay sending my despatches, but that I would send a second courier with the fresh communications, being most anxious to make known at my court as soon as possible the principles of the King, and the measures which will result from them.

I begged him to reply exactly to one single question : ' If an unexpected success, brought about no doubt by the principles of the King's neutrality, respected by our allies, and violated by our enemy, should expose the states and the centre of the Austrian kingdom, would you act then without delay ? ' ' The case is not to be thought of,' said the minister to me, ' for we shall be at war long before that, and our negotiations, which I beg you to hurry on, will have long ago decided both the question and its means of execution.'

The rest of our conversation turned only on the misfortune of knowing the King to be surrounded as he is. Hardenberg assured me that the malevolence of the cabinet secretaries, of which I gave him full details, only exercised an indirect influence on the King.*

---

* In a despatch to Count Colloredo of the same date, Metternich speaks of the influence of these men on the King in the following terms :—' It is certain that the Duke of Brunswick, Marshal de Möllendorf, and the Ministers de Hardenberg and de Schulenberg have all tried to induce the King to retire to Paretz, whence at this critical moment the manœuvres of the secretaries of the cabinet can exercise a still greater influence than they could either at Berlin or Potsdam. They have all thrown off the mask; Lombard had the impudence to pass the evening of the day on which we heard here of the entrance of the French into the country of Ansbach with M. de Laforest and M. Duroc ; and Beyme said at a dinner he was at

He could not but confess that a mere delay in the most vigorous determinations is often of more consequence than the loss of a battle.

We discussed the point whether France would declare war with the King. Notwithstanding all that he said to me, I am sure that he does not conceal from himself that the chances are rather against than for it; it is, then, ourselves and Russia, and the latter principally, who can decide this question, and I hope the first instructions to M. d'Alopéus will be with this object.

I beg to have the honour of submitting to your Excellency, in my first despatches, everything that may serve to elucidate the line taken by this court, although I am convinced that till the negotiators have opened their protocols, we shall never arrive at fixing the points of view in such a way as not to revoke one day all that has been settled the day before. We have rather more than four weeks for negotiations; the armies will be assembled by that time, and anything that is not determined by then can only retard the operations. M. de Hardenberg has not concealed from me that Count de Merveldt will be the General most likely to succeed with the King; I am convinced of this

about a fortnight ago, that the Austrian Monarchy might be considered as put up to auction; that the neighbouring Powers did well to arm themselves, in order to be ready to snatch the morsel which suited them best. To the objection some one made that the colossal power of Bonaparte would still increase under such auspices, he said he did not know that there would be any harm if he established one of his brothers at Vienna. All this is known, the whole town is full of it; even M. de Haugwitz in his conversation with the Emperor and your Excellency was not afraid to lay it at their door, and nothing reaches the King that these two men do not stifle in the bud. M. de Hardenberg has taken upon him lately to make a complaint of Lombard to the King, by telling him the fact above mentioned, and adding that there is a general conviction that he has sold himself to France; the King got angry, and said with a frown, " I ought to know better than you what he is ! " '

myself, and do not wish to lose this opportunity of doing him this well-deserved justice. The Baron de Hardenberg is entirely taken up with the idea of making a general arrive *incognito* ; the time for half-measures appears to me to have passed away as well as that of pretences of all kinds.

Metternich to Colloredo, Berlin, October 18, 1805.

72. Baron de Hardenberg yesterday morning begged me to call upon him in the course of the evening. When I went to him, he told me he had been charged by his Majesty to give to me a copy of the enclosed note (No. 73), which he had ordered to be addressed (dated the 14th) to the French Ambassadors ; and he gave it to me to read. Having read it, I begged Baron de Hardenberg to allow me to analyse an essential part of it, and returned to the words, 'Consecrate to the great work his active mediation,' &c.

'I am far,' said I to him, ' from allowing myself to question whether it is dignified of a great monarch to speak again of any mediation whatever after an insult as grave as that which the King has sustained at the hands of Bonaparte, but I beg you to explain to me the precise point of view from which the mediation proceeds. You told me yesterday that the King acceded to the mediation proposed recently by us and accepted by his Majesty the Emperor Alexander, who in his turn supported it by military demonstrations well worthy of the energy of a great prince. I do not conceal from you that your adhesion to a thing which no longer exists seems to me to need explanation ; I see now that it is again a question of your mediation. But for whom do you take the part of a mediator ? Is it for the two Imperial courts ? In that case it seems to me that you

ought to see that none of the belligerent parties wish
for such a step. The King seems then to wish to be a
mediator in his own cause. With regard to the whole
matter of your declaration to France, I cannot help
telling you that it will cause great astonishment at
Vienna. May not the principles which we profess, and
the declarations which you have formerly made at
Vienna and St. Petersburg about the revenge you would
take at any violation of the King's neutrality, have led
them to expect a declaration of war? What meaning
would you have the Emperor, my master, attach to a
pacific declaration after what has passed at Ansbach?
It is the French alone who violate your territory with
impunity; and you believe you have avenged the perhaps incalculable evil, which may result from the un-
limited confidence we had in the positive assurances of
the King, by declaring to Bonaparte that you regard all
your engagements to him annulled, which he has taken
care to prove to you himself in the most arrogant
manner, assuring him, notwithstanding all this, that
peace with him is your only wish, and mediation your
first duty.'

Baron de Hardenberg begged me to assure my court
that the King and his minister had only thought such
a measure necessary to insure the success of those which
were preparing on all sides. . . . 'I may tell my court,
then,' said I to him, 'that we may count on you?'

'Most assuredly,' replied the Cabinet Minister.' 'Do
you suppose that at this moment Bonaparte will listen
to any propositions of peace whatever? I am expressly
commanded to beg you to transmit to his Imperial
Majesty expressions of the most profound gratitude
from the King for the reception he has deigned to give
to Count de Haugwitz, and above all for the reply of

which he was the bearer ; the personal friendship of the
King needed no fresh proofs of that of the Emperor ;
but believe me, the mission of M. de Haugwitz will
have contributed much to it.'

There is such a change in the language of the Minister since the day before yesterday that I could not
help remarking upon it. He confessed to me that he
had never found the King better disposed than in the
conference of that morning. Baron de Hardenberg and
the Duke of Brunswick confirmed this observation to
M. d'Alopéus, and the Duke even added that he was
astounded at hearing Beyme speaking in a tone of
entire agreement with the measures which the success
of the good cause demands. To judge by the hearty
and really touching way in which M. de Hardenberg
dwelt on the happy effect which the reports of M. de
Haugwitz had produced on the King personally, there
can no longer be any doubt that the comparison of the
proceedings of our august master with those of the
usurper who menaces the whole of Europe has turned
entirely to our advantage.

All these measures indeed show dispositions which
must be improved and secured by a definite negotiation.
The Baron de Hardenberg received yesterday the order
to declare to M. de Laforest that there could no longer
be any question of negotiations relative to the conduct
of the King's troops in Hanover. I suppose that the
opinion of the Duke of Brunswick has contributed to
this determination ; his opinion was, even before the
council of yesterday, pronounced most decidedly on the
business of treating with the French in that country,
declaring that in that case he would not continue to
take the command. . . .

I hasten to send off this courier, whose despatches

will prove to his Imperial Majesty the extreme vacilla-
tion of the court here. We have reached the point
which from the first months of our negotiations has
seemed to me the only one which could bring us to any
result whatever. I have never hesitated to declare my
conviction that all negotiations would be useless ; that
the King would never lend himself to any energetic
measure, unless he was forced to it by the absolute impossibility of giving way any longer to his system of
forbearance ; that, in fact, he would not act till all the
Powers being arranged on one side, and France on the
other, he would be under the necessity of sacrificing his
so-called neutrality to the interests of his people ; and
this confession is really contained in his own declaration of the 14th. The great secret of the perfidious
counsellors who surround this prince and are sold to
France is thus disclosed in the face of Europe. The
King himself proclaims that nothing has been less neutral
than his neutrality. The discovery will not be new
either to us or the French ; but it belongs to us to use
every effort to take advantage of the moment when it is
made known in Prussia.

Hardenberg to Duroc and Laforest, Berlin, October 14,
1805.

73. The King charges me to make known the
following to his Excellency M. le Maréchal Duroc and
to M. de Laforest, Envoy Extraordinary, &c. :—

His Majesty hardly knows whether to be more
astonished at the outrages which the French troops
have committed in his provinces, or at the inconceivable
arguments by which they are attempted to be justified.
Prussia had proclaimed her neutrality ; but faithful to
her anterior engagements, the advantages of which

were entirely for France, she has made sacrifices to
them which may endanger her dearest interests. This
unfailing probity, this connection which, costing France
nothing, gave her an important security on all essential
points, how has it all been repaid? Justly jealous of a
consideration which is due to his power as well as to
his character, the King has read with a sentiment
it would be useless to deny the despatch communicated
by the French Legation to his cabinet. An appeal is
made to the example of the late wars and the analogy
of circumstances, as if the exceptions admitted then
had not been founded on positive transactions, long
since annulled by the Peace—as if the Emperor had remembered these transactions when he took possession of
Hanover, a country which had been placed for so many
years under the protection of Prussia! Ignorance of
our intentions is alleged, as if the intention were not
here in the nature of the thing, inasmuch as the contrary
is not stipulated! as if the solemn protestations of the
authorities of the province and of his Majesty's minister
with his Highness the Elector of Bavaria had not sufficiently proclaimed that there was no need of it, and
that I myself, map in hand, in my conferences with his
Excellency M. le Maréchal Duroc and M. de Laforest,
had not long ago declared the inadmissibility of any
passage of troops through the Margraviates, indicating
the route of communication stipulated by Bavaria, as the
only one where the troops would meet with no obstacles.
It is observed that in such serious matters it is necessary
to speak peremptorily, as if the duty of an explanation
belonged to him who rests quietly on the faith of a
principle, and not to him who proposes to reverse it.
Lastly, a pretence is made of things that never existed,
except in lying reports, and by attributing faults to the

Austrians which they have not committed, the King is forced to reflect on the contrast of their conduct towards him, and that of the French troops.

The King has drawn from this contrast very grave conclusions concerning the Emperor's intentions. He is bound to think that his Imperial Majesty had some reason for regarding the positive engagements which existed between him and Prussia as having no longer any value under present circumstances, and consequently he, on the eve perhaps of sacrificing everything in regard for his promises, considers himself now free from all obligation after the present moment.

Reduced to that state of things in which our first duties are those of our own safety and common justice, the King will not the less show that the same principles always animate him.

To see Europe enjoy the peace which he aspires to preserve to his people will be his only desire; to contribute with all his power to place it on a stable footing, and to consecrate to that great work his active mediation and most assiduous care will be his first duty.

But impeded on all sides in his generous intentions, the King can do no more than declare his anxiety to watch over the safety of his people. Without obligations from this time, but also without guarantees, he is constrained to make his army take up the positions indispensable for the defence of his state.

Begging his Excellency, &c., &c., to transmit these explanations to his Imperial Majesty, I have the honour, &c.

METTERNICH'S FIRST MEETING WITH THE EMPEROR ALEXANDER IN BERLIN.

74. Metternich to Colloredo, Berlin, October 29, 1805.
75. Metternich to Colloredo, Potsdam, October 31, 1805.

74. . . . . I wrote to Prince Czartoryski that, finding myself charged to deliver a letter from my august master to the Emperor Alexander, I begged him to find out from his Imperial Majesty in what way he would deign to receive it.

The prince gave me notice of the intention of his master to grant me an audience the following day.

His Imperial Majesty came to meet me, and deigned to say, with the gracious manner which characterises him, that he was very happy to make my personal acquaintance, as he already knew me well in diplomatic relations. 'You are not ignorant either of my way of thinking,' added the Emperor; 'therefore let us talk like old acquaintances.' I replied to him that his Majesty the Emperor, my master, could not possibly have given me a commission more calculated to crown all my hopes than that which he had desired me to deliver in person. I gave him the letter, and added that new assurances of the friendship and intense admiration of my august master for his person would only be repeating what he must be quite convinced of; that as for the exceedingly flattering reception his Imperial Majesty had deigned to give me personally, I could only attribute it to his extreme indulgence. 'You are, sire,'

said I to him, 'about to take one of the most generous
and at the same time one of the happiest resolutions,
in place of our long and dry negotiations; which
is rightly reserved for the deliverer of Europe, and
you will put the finishing touch to a work worthy of
the august negotiator who is entrusted with it.'

'That depends,' said the Emperor; 'first of all, I
am resolved not to move till we are in clear water,
and I confess that up to the present time I am better
pleased than I had expected. You have guided the
ship perfectly well; it now only needs the last blow to
set it afloat. I have found very many well-disposed persons: Möllendorf thinks wonderfully; even Haugwitz has
expressed himself very frankly to me. I have found
the Queen, too, more courageous than I had expected;
there is only that miserable Köckritz! * But we shall
get through it all in time. They hold to their idea of
mediation; we shall see. This mediation can only end
in an ultimatum, which Bonaparte certainly will not
accept, and in this case we shall receive an insolent
reply before the three weeks which are still necessary
for all the armies to be in readiness.'

I took the liberty of observing to his Majesty that
he had judged the individuals wonderfully well, and
that all the ministers and generals here were well
affected; that the persons immediately about the King
were alone to be feared; 'as for the Queen,' said I to
him, 'your Imperial Majesty has more direct influence
over her than anyone. Haugwitz always goes with
the stream, and Köckritz will no doubt be obliged to
hold his peace if ever she admits him into her presence.
You deign to speak to me so graciously and with such

---

* Köckritz, general adjutant to the King, was a partisan of Lombard
and Beyme in all political questions.

flattering confidence, sire, that I should be neglecting one of my first duties, if I did not lay before you most fully my way of looking at things.   It is impossible that your Majesty has not seen breaking through all the assurances which have been given him, either directly or through his ministers, the constant desire of this court to put off, what it does not see its way to refuse. I believe that the promptest declaration would be most desirable for the cause, without exposing any of our valuable resources.   Our army has unhappily sustained reverses, doubtless exaggerated by the French accounts, the only ones we have had since the 14th, but it is not to be supposed that Bonaparte, active as he is, will not immediately direct all his operations towards the centre of the Austrian Empire.   A Russian army and a very strong Austrian army are, no doubt, defending the approaches.   We are ignorant how many of our troops may be harassing the rear of the enemy's army; but what would Prussia risk by saying at last and in the face of Europe that she had at length taken the only part worthy of a King?   Supposing that Bonaparte is going towards the North, he will divide his forces, and will go to meet the armies which are advancing towards the Elbe and Voigtland, consequently he will divide his strength, and will be forced at length to do himself what up to the present time has been the one aim of his policy towards others.

The Emperor concurred entirely in my opinion. ' Also,' added he, ' I would take care, that if they do not give up the ultimatum, it should be a thorough declaration of war.   Your reverses are no doubt unfortunate, and I believe that Mack is to blame; it would be difficult after his affairs of Naples and Germany to have a very high opinion of him; but after all, it is only one more misfortune to repair, and twenty thousand men do not form the Austrian Power.'

I replied to his Majesty that I thought I ought to suspend my judgment on the unfortunate events in Swabia until the arrival of official news. I had expressly provided myself with several extracts of letters from Swabia and the Empire which prove that our army fought vigorously (this the Bavarians tried to misrepresent!), and that the most treacherous exaggeration prevails in all the reports which are circulated here. The Emperor allowed me to read them to him, and lost no opportunity of doing justice to our army. 'If I am forced,' said I at length, 'to suspend my opinion on the last military events, this can only be with regard to the results; the causes unhappily are too apparent: they are owing in a great measure to the inconceivable defection of one of the most powerful princes of the Empire, and to a proceeding of Bonaparte's, which it is to be hoped will be repaid to him with interest.'

The Emperor replied with vivacity: 'Ah, as to the Elector of Bavaria, my dear friend, we will punish him, I hope, severely; there is not another such case in all the annals of war.' . . .

This conversation, of which the present report only contains a brief statement, lasted more than half an hour. There was no subject we did not discuss, and I found his Majesty as familiar with the ground here as if he had lived here for years. Having asked me who I thought was the worst, Lombard or Beyme, I could only tell him that one being a French Jacobin, and the other a German Jacobin, the only thing to do was to distrust them both. . . .

My pen refuses to retrace, in detail, the personal reception which the Emperor deigned to give me. I have never seen such frank kindness and confidence, except in our august master, whose servant has been received with an attention, confidence, and kindness sufficient to flatter a man grown old and tried in his service. . . .

All the court went in the evening to the theatre; the opera was *Armida*, with a ballet. The Emperor's arrival was made known by trumpets and cries of ' Long live the Emperor!' and ' Long live the King!' which needed no command to be taken up generally. The presence of the Emperor has altogether produced here upon the public a sensation difficult to describe, and the ambassadors of France and Bavaria, who yesterday occupied the same box, would hardly be able to extract from it matter for any flattering reports.

Metternich to Colloredo, Potsdam, October 31, 1805.

75. For two days I was expecting at Berlin the results of the conferences of Prince Czartoryski with the Prussian Ministers; it is only on my arrival here to-day that I am convinced the questions may be reduced summarily thus :—

1st. Yielding to the King's one idea, to make propositions of peace to Bonaparte.

2nd. To declare to him that if he does not accept them, Prussia will be obliged to act in concert with the Powers.

3rd. To accelerate as much as possible the march of the troops towards the places mentioned below.*

---

* The army forming in Voigtland shall march into the Margraviate, and the Lower Saxon army to a part of Westphalia near the Maine.

4th. To agree with the Russians on an operation towards Holland. . . .

I had the honour of another interview with the Emperor Alexander, whom I found disposed as at the first ;
he regards our reverse as a misfortune which demands
prompt reparation.   The views, principles, and general
conduct of this prince, are above all praise. . . .

To-morrow I shall have a conference with the Russian
and Prussian Ministers together.   I beg your Excellency
to be convinced that my one aim will be, on this occasion
as on all others, to justify, so far as I am able, the
flattering confidence which our august master has placed
in me, at a time when the welfare of the Monarchy
and the whole of Europe is centred in the determinations which will crown our labour.   I could not have
a greater support than I have in Prince Czartoryski ;
who in the short conference I had with him to-day
entered entirely into my views, and above all has
rendered the fullest justice to the great character
shown by our own august master under circumstances
so disastrous that military annals can hardly offer a
parallel.

THE POTSDAM TREATY OF ALLIANCE.

76. Metternich to Colloredo, Potsdam, November 4, 1805.
77. Additional Article to Metternich's Proposition, and the remarks thereupon.
78. Metternich's remarks on the first secret article of the Treaty.
79. Metternich to Colloredo, Berlin, November 6, 1805.
80. Cobenzl to Metternich, Brünn, November 10, 1805.

76. I have the honour to submit for the ratification of his Imperial Majesty the enclosed * triple agreement concluded and signed yesterday at eight o'clock in the evening between the Plenipotentiaries of his Imperial Majesty of all the Russias, his Majesty the King of Prussia, and to-day between the Russian Plenipotentiaries and myself; the Prussian copies not being yet ready, the exchange with the Prussian Plenipotentiaries will not take place till the day after to-morrow at Berlin, and Monsignor the Archduke † will undertake to bear this copy of the Treaty to his Imperial Majesty. I choose this mode of assent, to avoid the embarrassment in the matter of precedence. We worked three consecutive days and nights at the definite completion of a work, which I beg his Imperial Majesty to regard as the best it was possible to attain.

. . . . .

On arriving here I found that the Russian and Prus-

---

* We here omit the well-known Treaty of Alliance which has been many times published. See, amongst others, Marten's ' Recueil des Traités,' ii. 481, and Hardenberg's ' Memoirs,' by Ranke, ii. 324.

† Archduke Anton, brother of the Emperor Francis, who was on a diplomatic mission in Berlin.

sian negotiators had been occupied for several days in completing a work which was disputed step by step by the latter. The Emperor began the negotiation by sending through his ministers a project of assent to the coalition pure and simple. The King replied by a counterproject full of words, and showing anything but the active co-operation of Prussia. They had long ago abandoned all idea of revenging the personal injury of Napoleon, except by seizing the opportunity furnished by himself of breaking off every inconvenient engagement with him. Prussia is only accustomed to work when it is clearly for her own benefit; that is all she looks to, and Europe would disappear before her eyes if it depended on her efforts to save it. Without the Emperor Alexander, without his final resolution to take a fatiguing journey, the results of which might have involved his personal dignity, without the generous devotion whereby he regards himself as a simple negotiator, never allowing himself to be repulsed by delays and annoyances of every kind—Prussia would have been immovable. The singular inertness of the King, the frightful malevolence of those who surround him, did not suffice for Napoleon's star; that we have suffered unheard-of reverses, that the Emperor had not one single piece of good news to offer to the King, that all the complications of a scarcity more or less general, of a season destroying in its germ the hope of the next year's harvests: all these things came to his assistance. I believe that, considering all these things, his Imperial Majesty will find more to hope from the efforts of Prussia, in the agreement signed by us and ratified by the two Sovereigns present, than he had allowed himself to expect.

The Russian negotiators will do me the justice to

admit that I yielded nothing, till I saw that my refusal would bring about the rupture of all negotiation ; and if the additional article, which I thought I ought to propose relative to the unhappy possibility that the enemy might pursue his success on the road to Vienna, has been rejected, it is assuredly not for the want of care on my part (No. 77). I urged and sustained the demand, conjointly with the Russians, up to the moment when Count de Haugwitz declared that he considered the negotiation as broken off.

The armies are marching with all haste. Your Excellency will see that the King has fixed upon points of junction so dangerous to Bonaparte that he will risk much in advancing inconsiderately beyond the Inn. I hope I have not committed any errors of mere diplomatic form. I have neither materials nor assistance within reach, and if your Excellency should discover any such faults, I beg · you to believe that they have crept into the work in spite of myself.

Baron de Hardenberg having been unfortunately almost entirely confined to bed, M. de Haugwitz constantly presented us, at the sitting on the following day, with the corrections and additions agreed upon the evening before, but drawn up in a sense contrary to ours, and some quite omitted. We frequently recognised the hand of Lombard, whose influence assuredly has not been slight in the whole course of the negotiation. We therefore agreed yesterday—Prince Czartoryski and myself—that we would not separate any more till we had signed the minutes, which at last took place at three o'clock this morning. The two Sovereigns signed the treaty at his Majesty the Emperor's, and the exchange of treaties was made in their presence, half an hour after the signature of the Plenipotentiaries : circumstances which assuredly add to the extraordinary manner, in which the whole negotiation has been conducted.

I cannot insist too much upon the undoubted truth, that we had to choose between nothing and what we have obtained. This fact is obvious when we consider the extreme pains the Emperor Alexander has taken to support our negotiations with the King personally. This monarch has followed our work step by step; he has done me the honour, among others, to speak to me almost every hour of his efforts to get my supplementary article accepted; he himself undertook, on my proposition, as a last resource, to persuade the King to put at least the sense of my request in the letter which he gave into the charge of Monsignor the Archduke. Nothing discouraged him, neither the news, more and more afflicting in their details, of our reverse in Germany, nor the annoyances which he personally endured.

Your Excellency will find in the enclosed some short reflections on the first secret article (No. 78).

Supplementary Article proposed by Metternich.

77. 'In the unforeseen case of an actual defeat of the Imperial army on the Inn, and of a movement of Bonaparte's which would menace the capital of the Austrian Empire, the Prussian negotiator, according to the wish of his Majesty the King to help to protect so important a point by all the means in his power, will demand a definite response from Bonaparte in the shortest time (which in any case should not exceed forty-eight hours), declaring that he will leave his head-quarters if he does not obtain it, and that he will regard any uncertainty in his reply as a refusal to accede to the ultimatum agreed upon.'

I have supposed the case of the Prussian negotiator

arriving at Napoleon's head-quarters at a moment when the safety of the capital was threatened in a manner still more imminent than at the time of the first defeat of our army. Bonaparte, anxious to finish his work, to press on to other places, putting us consequently out of the game one after the other, would only have to carry with him the Prussian Ambassador, pretending meanwhile to listen to his proposals: in a word, continuing his actions and at the same time deceiving the negotiator, in spite of the hostile attitude which the Prussian armies would assume in the meantime, and in the hope that the part taken by Prussia would soften in proportion as the danger was seen to be more immediate. I believed, at least in the case of the most decided danger, that it would be well to put in our balance the weight of a prompt declaration of Prussia that she would regard the refusal to explain, in a certain fixed time, as a definite refusal to accede to the ultimatum agreed upon. M. de Haugwitz began by refusing even to submit this wish to the King, 'injurious' as he pretends 'to his dignity,' 'as the thing is taken for granted.' Having pressed him for a change in this objection, on the ground that it contained a contradiction, as an injury to the King could never be taken for granted, and that which would be taken for granted (and consequently could not be injurious) 'could not possibly offer any difficulties to be explained,' he then adopted a new form. 'We could not fight the enemy,' said he to me, 'before we had reached him.' I proved to him that it was not a question of fighting when the two armies were separated; but I insisted on the real difference between a declaration of war and a battle; that the first could and must precede the last, therefore there could be no reason for not securing both kinds of help, and that I desired the King would assure us of his wish to employ the one means, while waiting the possibility of employing the other.

M. de Haugwitz ultimately became so excited that, seeing I could obtain nothing from him, I said: 'You will not refuse, M. le Comte, to submit to his Majesty a desire which I beg you to regard as very decided on my part. The Emperor, my mast͏ ͏ ͏ ͏ as always been ready to make sacrifices ; we have d͏ ͏ ͏ ͏d your cause as much as our own, and if the approach of the enemy to our capital—in case of a reverse always possible in the chances of war—does not alarm us when it is a consequence of defending the independence of Europe, it seems to me that we have a right to demand that it is not left to the good pleasure of the negotiator to hasten the matter, and cut short all negotiation before the expiration of a month ; especially in the case of the French army being removed farther and farther from your outposts, so that it would not be possible to reach them until the time fixed in our agreement.'

M. de Haugwitz, seeing that I was not to be trifled with, told me that he would submit my article to the King, and begged me to send him a copy of it the following morning, which I did not fail to do.

Metternich's Remarks on the First Secret Article of the Treaty.

78. The text of this Article* will prove to your Exlency that the views of Prussia with respect to Hanover

---

* The first secret article to the Potsdam Treaty runs thus:—'As Prussia could only with difficulty obtain a safe frontier on the French side by an arrangement which would put her in possession of Hanover, his Imperial Majesty of All the Russias, who, in virtue of his intimacy and alliance with his Britannic Majesty, could not make any engagements on this subject, has nevertheless promised—from regard to the urgency of the present circum-

have for some time been understood by our court. It will show, on the other hand, that that Power dreads every day more and more the contact with France. She offers to the King of England her Westphalian provinces beyond the Weser; the ports of Emden and the North Sea, and the direct influence which they will bring to bear on Holland, will perhaps serve as a bait to the English minister and induce him to second our efforts to overcome the predilection—natural enough—which the King has for the patrimony of his family.

The execution of this clause certainly offers very great difficulties. We had agreed that in any case the negotiations for the subsidies and for the cession of Hanover should not go together; it was only on the day of the signature of the minutes that the Prussian Plenipotentiaries declared to Prince Czartoryski, in a private interview, that the King absolutely demanded that the second negotiation should be begun as soon as possible. The Prince came to me to communicate his grievances, and I thought it as well to propose to him that if we did not absolutely resist the Prussian Minister in his pretension, we should be the better able to insist that the two Imperial courts were exclusively

stances, and a desire to gratify as much as possible his Prussian Majesty, and to dispose him to the co-operation to follow—that he will employ his good offices to effect this arrangement, either by making an exchange, or in any other way which would indemnify the Electoral House of Brunswick, and best conciliate all interests. If the latter agrees to this arrangement, and if England consents to the payment of subsidies for all the troops, which his Majesty the King of Prussia will place in the country during the war, his Majesty engages to make neither peace nor armistice, nor to lay down his arms, except by a common agreement with his august ally and his Britannic Majesty. If the above conditions are not complied with in a manner which will leave no doubt in the mind of his Prussian Majesty, he will have but one duty, resulting from the present convention, to forewarn his ally six months in advance that his safety and the want of pecuniary resources have decided him to make common cause with the enemy.'

charged with the proposition to and the negotiation with the King of England, Prussia remaining perfectly passive. They could hardly refuse, on the consideration that we at least would negotiate with a view to the thing succeeding, whereas the Prussian negotiators, with the malevolence which we have reason always to expect from them, would find some means of paralysing the whole concern. We have proposed this amendment, and the Cabinet Ministers have given their word of honour that the court here will undertake to furnish us with an estimate, which is to include the political views most in favour of England.

Metternich to Colloredo, Berlin, November 6, 1805.

79. I have waited to submit to your Excellency my observations on the present relations of Baron de Hardenberg with M. de Haugwitz, in order not to mislead by inexact information. Unfortunately, it cannot be concealed that the former has lost much of his influence. His bad health, the confidence he places in the personal feelings of M. de Haugwitz, who aims only at his destruction ; his principles, which are known and feared by many people ; above all, the difficulties which up to the present time have hampered him—all paralyse his powers, and perhaps may permanently stultify them. He will yet have an opportunity, which he ought to turn to profit—the time of his colleague's absence. I shall not fail to press this upon his notice ; if he loses this chance, it cannot be supposed that his ministry will be of much longer continuance, unless, indeed, some event very favourable to him should occur. It is not only that we theoretically owe to him what has been made possible by circumstances independent of him —he alone has guided them aright. If the mildness and weakness of his character have deprived us of many advantages which he would no doubt have gained by unhesitatingly saving the cause, or at once taking us to the point where the middle course adopted by him must lead us, it is yet a fact that the retirement of this minister will be a real calamity both from the choice of a successor and his own loss. We know that M. de Haugwitz entered the department *ad latus*, but no official announcement has yet been made of it, and M. de Hardenberg, since his colleague's stay at Vienna, has assured me of his ardent desire for his return, and seemed to attach to it no cause for anxiety.

Cobenzl to Metternich, Brünn, November 10, 1805.

80. The declarations signed and exchanged between the Plenipotentiaries of his Prussian Majesty and his Imperial Majesty of All the Russias, to which you have acceded in the name of our august master, have been brought here by the courier Beck, to whose care you confided them.

The Emperor, having examined these documents with the attention their importance deserves, is quite satisfied, and has ordered us to prepare the acts of ratification, which will be sent to you as quickly as possible. His Majesty charges you to show to the King through his ministers, how delighted he is at last to see the work concluded which consolidates the union so long and so ardently desired by our august master, and which corresponds so well with his sentiments of cordial friendship for his Majesty the King of Prussia.

You will have observed, sir, that the two letters addressed by our august master to the Emperor of the French had partly the same objects as the plan just agreed on between the three courts—namely, to give place to a negotiation between all the interested parties, and to begin by a short armistice in order to have time to save Vienna.

We have as yet no news as to the result of the mission of General de Giulay; but from what we hear we can hardly expect success, and Vienna will probably be in a few days in the enemy's hands. However sad may be this event — easy to foresee when so small a number of troops could be brought to oppose Bonaparte's passage of the Inn—his Majesty will none the less persist in the arrangements made between the three courts, and will fulfil all the engagements you contracted in his name, particularly that of receiving nothing from Bonaparte or treating with him, except in the most perfect agreement with the allied courts. Of this you will not fail to assure Baron de Hardenberg. At the same time, nothing shall be omitted on our part to employ every possible effort against the enemy. By the 20th of this month our forces, united with those of the Imperial court of Russia, will amount to nearly a hundred thousand men, and if at the same time the strong Prussian diversion is accelerated as the urgency of the case requires, the Emperor Napoleon may come to repent having provoked the Powers.

Your conduct, sir, in the important negotiation confided to you deserves the full approbation of our august master, as a proof of which we have the pleasure of announcing to you that his Majesty has nominated you for the Grand Cross of the Order of St. Stephen; the insignia and necessary documents will be sent to you by the first courier. We are certain that this proof of his Majesty's goodness, which you have shown yourself so worthy to receive, will only redouble your zeal in his august service.

ON THE FRENCH ARMY-BULLETINS, AND SUGGESTIONS FOR THE ISSUING OF A NEWSPAPER.

(Notes 14 and 20, Vol. I.)

81. The French Government has for some time resorted to the most atrocious and systematic calumny against the princes and people with whom it desires to break, or with whom it may be at war. This device ought not to produce any great effect, resting as it generally does on the grossest falsehoods; we cannot, however, help seeing that public opinion ends by taking more or less the shape that our enemies wish to give it. The dignity of silence observed by the right side does not impress the people; they blame us for keeping silence, and it is only necessary to be in a foreign country, especially at a place where Bonaparte has chosen to spread all that the odious pamphleteers emit daily against us, to be convinced of the truth of what I say. The daily Bulletins which are published for the French army, and which inundate Germany and the whole of Europe, are a new invention which deserve the most serious attention. Designed less to report military facts than to mislead the public as to the spirit and principles of our government and our people, Bonaparte's cabinet thus brings itself into daily contact with all classes of society. It has given up the official style, and adopted that of familiar conversation; each Bulletin brings on to the scene personages whose respectability inspires confidence, and men of the people, who confirm what they wish to be taken for public feeling in the Austrian monarchy, and which is at last accepted as such by millions of readers.

Nobody, either in Berlin or the rest of Germany, doubts but that Hungary will be declared neutral, and that even by the very organ of the Palatine. Newspaper articles have thus so misled the public mind that all that is said to put matters in a right light is opposed by documents held to be official. The so-called translation of a speech of Count Palffy's seemed to me to necessitate a refutation, because of the great importance which is attached to it. I have sent an article to the newspaper editors in Berlin, and to M. de Höfer at Hamburg. I do not know whether it has been accepted by the editors, for M. Bourienne still exercises an authority so severe over these journals that they are always submitted to him before they appear, that he may erase or alter the articles which do not please him.

As the Hamburg Gazettes are circulated all over Europe, this surveillance was not likely to escape the care of the French Government, and it is much to be desired that some decided steps—easily taken at the moment of contracting the closest engagements among so many great Powers—may at last put an end to the odious pretension of France to corrupt the mind of Germany by means of its own public journals.

These different points have been mentioned in my previous despatches; but I have thought it right again to direct the attention of the court to this object, which is of the greatest importance since it concerns the most wide-spread interests. It is absolutely indispensable that public opinion should be as quickly as possible instructed with respect to the step taken by Count Palffy, Commandant of Presburg, and the unworthy interpretation which has been put upon it by Marshal Davoust. The honour of his Imperial Highness the Archduke Palatin has been endangered, as well as that of a brave and loyal nation, which has always given proof of the most constant devotion to the august House of Austria. I shall wait the orders of your Excellency concerning the measures to be taken, and execute them with all the promptitude and zeal which the case demands. The manner in which it has been thought fit to make known to the public the proposed armistice has made no less sensation here, and it will be equally necessary to re-establish these facts, which furnish ample matter for the malevolence which will become more active and more infuriated in proportion as Bonaparte's difficulties increase.

Ideas on the Establishment of a Newspaper under the Protection of, and Published by, the Allied Powers. Berlin, December 5, 1805.

82. This journal shall be an organ of the good cause, a depository of official news regarding the Allied armies, and a critic of the enemy's proceedings. It will consist of:—

    1. A Political section.
    2. A Literary section.
    3. A kind of Fly-sheet.

No. 1.—The Political section will include: *a)* Official news of the Allied armies, which shall be as well as all the *Inserenda* communicated to the editor by the ministers of the Allied Powers. *b)* The news officially published by the enemy, with remarks by the editors explaining and criticising these documents. *c)* Political memoirs, suitable to guide public opinion.

No. 2.—The Literary section shall relate chiefly to the verification and criticism of the political works published by France and her adherents; references to works which will refute error, and to good political works in general.

No. 3.—The Fly-sheet shall be devoted to articles of less importance, anecdotes, &c.

This journal shall either be printed with two columns, one German, the other French; or contain particular articles in the two languages, at the choice of the *collaborateurs*.

THE BATTLE OF AUSTERLITZ.

(Note 14, Vol. I.)

83. Metternich to Cobenzl, Berlin, December 13, 1805.
84. Metternich and Alopäus to Hardenberg.
85. Metternich to Cobenzl, Berlin, December 16, 1805.

83. I resume my pen in order to have the honour to inform your Excellency of the frightful position in which I have been for some days. A despatch from Count Finkenstein, dated Olmütz, December 3, informs us of the loss of the battle of Austerlitz and the transference of the department of Foreign Affairs to Teschen. All the subsequent accounts, founded on vague and contradictory data, lead us to expect the official news with the greatest impatience.

Marshal de Möllendorf was to leave Berlin tomorrow ; the courier—intended to take the order, already signed by the King—was in Baron de Hardenberg's anteroom, when a courier from Count Haugwitz, sent from Vienna on the 6th, came to bring a despatch informing the Court, in a few words :

'Of the battle of the 2nd ; of an interview between the Emperors Francis and Napoleon, who promised each other to make peace ; of a suspension of arms, and of the sudden departure of the Counts de Stadion and Giulay from Vienna to Nicolsburg, where they are to sign a separate peace.' He adds that Count Stadion had promised him to inform him of his departure, which he had foreseen the evening before, but that he had not done so.

To this report was joined the false and exaggerated Bulletins published by Bonaparte about the day of Austerlitz, and a letter from Bacher* to M. de Laforest, which the envoys of France, Holland, and Bavaria had taken care to spread through the city in a few hours.

M. d'Alopéus, who was present at the arrival of this despatch, which, considering the gravity of the occasion, was as insulting from its brevity as from the malice of its style, came at once to find me, and we agreed to approach Baron de Hardenberg simultaneously, to beg him to influence the King not to suspend any of the military measures, and to cause the armies to advance towards the place indicated on the frontiers of Bohemia, where he would always be able to stop them if between this and then the news was confirmed. The Baron de Hardenberg brought us in the morning the King's assurance that the military measures dictated by his own security should not be suspended, but that his Majesty would send orders to Count de Haugwitz to await the fresh instructions which could not be sent until a clearer view of the state of things was obtained. The departure of Marshal de Möllendorf was postponed till further orders.

Four weeks having elapsed since the departure of Count de Haugwitz, M. d'Alopéus and I, undeterred by vague and indirect news, yesterday addressed, *mutatis mutandis*, the enclosed Note (No. 84) to Baron de Hardenberg—a measure agreed upon beforehand with him. His reply, also delayed, must be the declaration of war against France. We thought it necessary to enforce our arguments by citing the treaty relative to the division of Poland—a country of which the present con-

* Bacher Theobold was at that time a French agent at Regensburg. His letters contained exaggerated news from the seat of war.

stitution is directly menaced by all the measures of
Bonaparte, whether public or private.

The united efforts of M. d'Alopéus and myself could
accomplish no more than to secure that the military
measures should not be relaxed or impeded. We did
accomplish this object, but the state of things was one
of extreme tension, so that we cannot answer for them
beyond a certain point. Another point of view, which
seemed to me suitable to the loyal principles of our
court, made me offer my personal guarantee that his
Imperial Majesty would never draw back from anything
which had been dictated by friendship for his Prussian
Majesty.

The style of Count de Haugwitz's despatch; the
circumstance that M. de Laforest had up to this time
received no official information from M. de Talleyrand;
the little confidence felt in the Prussian negotiators;
lastly, the notorious facts of the unworthy means lately
employed by the French to deceive the Prince of Auers-
perg, all contribute to leave the King, the ministry,
and the public in suspense, and prevent the armistice
from being looked upon as anything but a purely military measure. His Majesty has, nevertheless, charged
his minister to request M. d'Alopéus to convey to his
august master that he was not offended but excessively
grieved at his silence.

In one way or other, we certainly ought to be
immediately relieved from a state of uncertainty which
is worse than death. I believe I cannot better serve the
interests of our august master than by continuing without alteration the course pointed out to me in the last
despatches of your Excellency, until fresh orders are
transmitted to me. I shall, however, be careful to let
my conduct be coloured by the first news which M.

d'Alopéus will probably receive within the next twenty-four hours. If recent times have brought me many a thorn, assuredly the present epoch is the most painful of all, my position being greatly aggravated by the fresh impulse given to all the French party. It cannot be doubted that the day of the dissolution of the coalition will be that of the fall of the present Ministry, and that M. de Haugwitz will only return here to resume the portfolio.

Minute of a Note sent by Metternich and Alopéus to Hardenberg.

84. The sincere and inviolable friendship which unites their Majesties the Emperors of Germany and Austria, the Emperor of All the Russias, and the King of Prussia ; the close agreement cemented between them by the Treaty of Potsdam ; the conformity of their views and principles, and that of the interests of Russia and Prussia in the present crisis, leave the undersigned no doubt that in here pointing out what the Emperor, his august master, now expects from the King—his friend and ally—M. de Hardenberg will hasten to report it to his Prussian Majesty, and to enable the undersigned to give his court the positive and consoling assurance that the orders which he begged to be sent have already been despatched to those concerned.

The sentiments entertained for the Emperor by the King of Prussia make it quite superfluous to remind him of the dangers which have recently accompanied the courageous efforts which their Majesties have made to sustain a cause which they perhaps would consider as desperate if it were not for the certainty that in four weeks after the departure of Count de Haugwitz—the armistice not being concluded between the belligerent

Powers—the Prussian forces will unite with those of the Allies to combat the common enemy, whose rapid progress and exaggerated pretensions leave to Europe no hope of safety but in an obstinate and energetic resistance. The views and principles of the three Sovereigns cannot differ in this respect : all three know their duties ; they can no longer be doubtful ; the moment for conquering or perishing has arrived, and if their wisdom has long foreseen this sad alternative, new enterprises on the part of the head of the French Government, again identify the interests of their States, and compel a redoubled activity to arrest new disorders and avert new dangers.

The head of the French Government loudly proclaims his desire to support or rather to excite against their sovereigns the peoples whom Austria and Prussia, in concert with Russia, have brought into submission, in order to preserve them from the misfortunes and the crimes which the French Revolution brought forth, and which a vigorous and wise policy knows how to remove ; but Bonaparte does not confine himself to this in his plans for disorganisation. The German Empire, having fallen under his power, feels the effects of his influence, and propriety is sacrificed to the desire to recompense those who have been constrained, enticed, or misled to make common cause with the oppressors of their country. The Electors of Bavaria, Würtemburg, and Baden have violated every right in defiance of those of the head of the Empire and of their fellow states, by seizing the possessions of the House of Austria, of the *Noblesse immédiate*, the Teutonic orders and those of Malta, included in their territories or adjacent to them. This forgetfulness of all that the laws of the German Empire prescribe to its members is a frightful presage of what may be expected from Bonaparte's views with regard to this part of Europe; and who can calculate the effects of the success of his plans respecting what was once Poland?

These misfortunes can only be avoided by the immediate carrying out of the measures agreed to on November 3, and therefore the undersigned reminds his Excellency Baron de Hardenberg that it is four weeks to-day since the departure of Count Haugwitz, who was entrusted with the negotiation of the armistice to Berlin, and that at present no happy success has crowned these new efforts to restore peace to Europe. He consequently urges the sending of necessary orders, so that the Prussian armies may immediately advance to the positions which they had occupied, towards points where they can meet the enemy and fight them, according to the tenor of the engagements made between Austria, Prussia, and Russia, in case the armistice should not be concluded within the four weeks after the departure of the Russian Plenipotentiary.

The undersigned, in thus acquitting himself of a duty required by the most imperative circumstances, awaits a reply thoroughly conformable to the expectations of his august master, with a certainty founded on the principles of the King, the enlightened judgment of his minister, and the importance of the object itself; and Baron de Hardenberg will surely recognise the justice of not leaving for a moment in uncertainty his Imperial Majesty, who, at the head of his armies, will announce to them as the reward of their courage what a powerful ally is marching against their enemies.

1805.

Metternich to Cobenzl, Berlin, December 16, 1805.

85. Baron de Stutterheim,* who arrived here yes-terday morning, has informed me of the present posi-tion of affairs. The certainty that the evil is frightful has brought me out of a still worse condition, which your Excellency will have found described in the last despatch which I sent by the courier Beyer on the 13th of this month. I feel my head and hands free. I start again on sure foundations from known data. I know the worst, and may hope once more to serve the Emperor in the most horrible crisis which has ever overtaken his august House. . . . All our troubles arise from one single cause. Our utter want of agreement will end by doubling the power of the enemy ; a hundred thousand men will have conquered or paralysed five hundred thousand—the real force at the disposal of the coalition. But this same fault leaves us on one line alone more than two hundred thousand fighting soldiers intact, thoroughly equipped, and who, led by a man of spirit, will yet rescue the prey from our common enemy. It is this point of view which has sus-tained me in our frightful position, and this I submitted yesterday to General Stutterheim. I have pointed out to him the existence of these resources, of which a mass of more than a hundred thousand men would have entered Bohemia from the 21st to the 23rd of this month, if the unhappy day—the 2nd—and its immediate consequences had not prevented this operation, which would have been easily combined with our other mili-

* Baron Stutterheim, an Austrian general, was sent to Berlin with a letter from the Emperor Francis to King William III.

tary operations, if the least agreement, if even a quicker communication had existed between our different headquarters.

While proving to the General the real existence of these large resources, which he assured me he had hitherto doubted, I did not conceal my fears as to the impossibility of making the best use of them at the present moment, but insisted on the absolute necessity of immediately concerting with him the best plans for preventing the King from giving up, to the great detriment of the cause, the part dictated by honour and his own safety. Being convinced that the most perfect candour towards the King would not fail to have an effect, we concerted our measures and our language, and agreed on the following points :—

1. That the General, in the audience which the King would certainly give him during the day, should admit the full extent of the misfortune.

2. That we should go at once to Baron de Hardenberg with the same object.

3. That we should reduce all the arguments to be put before the King and his ministers to the following facts :—

That if Austria falls, she will drag with her the independence of the whole of Europe.

That Prussia has gone too far to be able henceforth to reckon on the friendship of France, and that she will not help herself by holding back from the Allies ; that, if she was not afraid of uniting her cause to that of the Powers by the treaty of November 3, she ought not to be afraid of actively assisting the three contracting Powers whose fate is bound up in the most intimate manner with her own.

That the present negotiation between Austria and

France cannot be regarded as an infraction of the Treaty of Potsdam, but as a measure dictated by irresistible strength.

That if Austria was in a position to diminish her stipulations by the above-named treaty, she was directly authorised by Prussia to do so, in virtue of Article II.

That we ask a decided answer from the King as quickly as possible, informing us of his intentions, desires, and means of assistance, to prevent our being compelled to make a peace which would sap the foundations of the Austrian Power; or else a decided refusal, which, by setting us free from every tie and every consideration for Prussia, will leave us simply to the calculations of our own convenience.

That we are justified in suspecting the sincerity of the feelings which have guided him in all his stipulations.

These points, which I have drawn from my knowledge of the country and the persons concerned, being entirely approved by M. de Stutterheim, will guide all our arrangements.

One of the chief motives which ought now to influence Prussia is the question of Hanover. No doubt Napoleon, intoxicated with success, will not give up the provinces upon which the court of Berlin has explained its views to us. The force of the arguments to be drawn from this happy circumstance has not escaped us, and Baron de Hardenberg quite enters into our feeling.

Baron de Hardenberg having privately shown that he was sensible of the thorough want of confidence which we have had in the King's proceedings, I did not conceal from him that two causes have greatly contributed to this: the choice of Count Haugwitz as negotiator,

and the delay which had taken place in sending an
officer to our general quarters. Baron Hardenberg
endeavoured to escape from the first of these points,
and I therefore inquired if he himself was satisfied with
the conduct of Count de Haugwitz since his departure
from this place, and he confessed that he was not.
' Well, then,' said I to him, ' how can you expect that
we shall be so? This minister leaves the King in perfect ignorance of all that is passing round him, and his
Majesty himself begins to suspect him of ill-feeling.'

Such are the matters which we thought it right to
discuss. I desire that his Imperial Majesty should deign
to approve the steps we have taken. I only regard
myself as an auxiliary to the commission with which
Baron de Sutterheim is charged. He has found the
questions stated very differently at Berlin from what he
had expected ; it is only from him that I have learned
the real state of affairs with us. It seems to me that
the means of arriving at a peace less humiliating than
the one to which we must subscribe if we are deserted
by our allies is now all that we can hope for ; it is the
only point of view we can present to the court of
Berlin, and apparently the only one for which we can
expect any support. The present position of affairs is
so new here that it has been impossible to extract
anything more from the King or the Ministry to send
by the present courier. Prince Dolgorouki and the
Grand-Duke come to-day. From one moment to another
news is expected from Count de Haugwitz, and the
despatches which the next courier carries to your Excellency will contain a definite reply from Prussia, and
state the means she thinks she can make use of to serve
us, or rather to serve herself, by preventing us from
becoming the prey of our common enemy. The most

decided feeling, and the one which is least concealed from us, is that of fear lest we should sign a separate peace before our communications can reach Hollitsch.

I beg your Excellency to reply to us as quickly as possible, and to inform us most fully of the views and intentions of our august master. The fulfilment of this request seems to me all-important for the attainment of our object. It would also be well that we should be informed of the maximum of the sacrifices that his Imperial Majesty feels that he could make, in case of the active co-operation of Prussia. This knowledge will enable us to reply more decidedly to the different questions which may be proposed to us.

THE HAUGWITZ MISSION
1806.

(Note 15, Vol. I.)

86. Metternich to Stadion, Berlin, January 10, 1806.
87. Metternich to Stadion, Paris, April 7, 1807.

86. Your Excellency is doubtless convinced by the official letters I have addressed to Count de Cobenzl, since the conclusion of the armistice, of the uneasiness manifested on every occasion to see us abandon a cause we are at last believed to understand.

There is no doubt that war was decided on independently of the Second* of December and its immediate consequences ; the mission of M. de Phull † had cut short all further evasion. The march of the troops was no longer problematical, and the outposts are spread over all Franconia. In fact, they have entered Bohemia, and it is no longer left to the King to palliate, in the eyes of Bonaparte, a determination which by consolidating the Ministry will raise Prussia, at any rate for the moment, to his system.

Nothing is more unlike this state of things than the conduct of M. de Haugwitz at Vienna. He seized the moment when the arrival of the Austrian negotiators

---

* The day of the battle of Austerlitz.

† Phull, a Prussian colonel, who, with the English military plenipotentiary, Colonel Anstruther, and the Austrian general, Grenneville, arranged (at Berlin) the plans for the campaign.

was announced, to carry out a plan conceived just at
the time of the signing of the Treaty of Potsdam. . . .

Never has public opinion been more decided than
at the moment of the frightful epoch which saw abo-
lished, in a few hours, the results which should have
crowned a long series of cares and labours. Everyone
looks on M. de Haugwitz as ruined. He is included in
the proscription of the many other instruments whom
Bonaparte employed with so much success to neutralise the Prussian power. The news of the negotiation of an armistice, announced here by the Ministry
with the greatest anxiety, and accompanied with the
most positive assurances, not only that we are about to
conclude peace with France, but that we considered an
alliance offensive and defensive as certain, has suspended
all opinions, paralysed all resources, and was, especially
for Baron de Hardenberg, a clap of thunder, which
foretold what must necessarily be expected.

I have repeated here what your Excellency will
have found in my different despatches, my sole aim
being to implore you, M. le Comte, to convince yourself
of the incontestable truth that views and affairs at
Berlin have gone on an entirely different line from the
views and the negotiation of M. de Haugwitz. He
would have succeeded entirely but for a blunder of
Napoleon's, the matter of the army Bulletin, which
showed plainly to the least penetrating eyes who were the
friends of France, and produced an effect here entirely
contrary to that which its author expected. The only
respectable man whose name was included in the list,
Marshal de Möllendorf, did not hesitate to say that he
would rather have been hanged than have found his
name printed in that Bulletin.

The progress of our negotiation, and the silence which

we observed, were eagerly seized upon by the Count de Haugwitz to bring forward a plan concerted with Bonaparte, in the long and frequent conferences he had with him at Brünn and Schönbrunn. His return to Berlin was as quick as his journey to Vienna had been long. He approached the questions directly with the King, in the hope, no doubt, of gaining his assent by main force, and it was Baron de Hardenberg who insisted that M. de Haugwitz should be enjoined to put down in writing the objects of the negotiations and propositions with which he was charged. His report has up to the present time furnished material for many councils of state, and an impenetrable secrecy envelops the objects of deliberation and the resolutions they may have given rise to. The French Minister alone is in full negotiation with M. de Haugwitz and M. Lombard ; he passes daily several hours with the latter, who up to this time has carefully avoided the appearance of having any connection whatever with the *Corps Diplomatique.*

On the day of the arrival of my last courier, I went to Baron de Hardenberg to tell him the confidential communications I had received. He complained much of the obstinate silence we had hitherto preserved, on the ground that we had thus allowed the French agents to see how little confidence we placed in the determinations of the King. It was not difficult for me to reply to these reproaches by the proofs with which I was furnished of the conduct which M. de Haugwitz had observed at Vienna. . . .

It is impossible for me to submit to your Excellency any other reports of the present position of affairs than those I have drawn, like all the public, from appearances and vague probabilities. None of my colleagues can learn anything positive with respect to that which M. de Haugwitz—whom one can only consider on this occasion as a direct organ of Bonaparte about the King —has included in a report submitted some days ago to his Majesty. The Russian minister, Prince Dolgorouki, even the Grand-Duke, is not more advanced in the affair than I am, notwithstanding the weight which is undoubtedly given to them by the resolution of the Emperor to place at the command of the King the troops who are now in Lower Saxony and Silesia, and who are in a position to contribute perhaps immediately to views entirely opposed to those of their sovereign. M. d'Alopéus and Prince Dolgorouki sent some days ago a courier to St. Petersburg to inform his Imperial Majesty that all their efforts to learn the least detail of the objects of negotiation between Prussia and France were vain. It is supposed that the Emperor will withdraw his troops immediately, and that the explanations between him and the King will be of a very decided character.

I cannot doubt that M. de Haugwitz has been the bearer of many plans of aggrandisement and of indemnity for the expenses of the Prussian armament. Knowing the character of this minister, and observing the documents published by France herself, we cannot but suspect that it is Napoleon's desire to satisfy and disgrace the King by the single fact of an amicable arrangement for a grave and direct insult; to establish the theory that what France attempts is right for her alone, and that we shall see an advantageous arrangement for Prussia result from a universal struggle which M. de Haugwitz will make use of to the detriment of the Allies and the general cause. It is no less true that no territorial acquisition, no exchange of domains,

can ever compensate for the losses which that monarchy sustains by the extreme aggrandisement of
France, and above all by the absolute influence which
that colossal power will exercise in Germany. The
lines of the Weser, so ardently desired by the court of
Berlin, will no longer offer any defence against an
enemy which is established behind them. The Bavarian
army, which may be regarded henceforth as in the pay
of France, will avoid in every war with Napoleon the
trouble of attacking the points of defence, which are to
be from Minden to the North Sea. The time has gone
by when the malevolence of a minister could make the
most of the losses of a neighbour. Prussia suffers
directly with us, and the Memoir of M. de Stutterheim
contains some very correct views on the urgent necessity
of the two Powers uniting in their interests and their
measures.

Baron de Hardenberg, seeing the difficulty of his
principles being brought forward, has begged his
Majesty to accept his resignation. He has given as a
cause for his request the state of his health, which is
certainly very much shattered, and among other considerations the impossibility of serving the interests of
the King in France after the calumnious accusation
which Napoleon made against him in his official reports.
The King told him in the most flattering terms ' that
he could not part with him, and that it was owing to
him that the last report had given him so much satisfaction.' The Queen herself has written a most touching
letter to him, begging him not to abandon the King
at such a critical moment. This minister has therefore decided to keep the portfolio; but it is said that
he has declared emphatically that he would not be
charged with the present negotiation with France, and

it is certain that M. de Laforest sees only M. de Haugwitz.

The Baron de Hardenberg informed me yesterday confidentially of the steps he means to take, using the words that without the blackest ingratitude it would have been impossible for him not to yield to the wishes of the King. I replied to him that I thought he could hardly separate his personal interests from those of the good cause. I congratulated him on his determination, but as a personal friend and a public man connected with our common interests I implored him never to forget that he could ruin the cause in two ways—either by abandoning it, or lending his name and his reputation to the malevolent people who surround him. He reassured me on this last fear, and reiterated what he assuredly thinks. Time alone will show us to what extent he will be able to realise his good intentions. It is impossible not to see that the men who alone can be taxed with his removal are at this moment the most interested in keeping him at his post, and the French diatribe above mentioned has injured them in the opinion of the public more than could have been expected.

Our relations lately established with Prussia may now be regarded as extinct; they could only be reestablished on a new basis, on the choice of which will, no doubt, greatly depend the future welfare of the two monarchies.

Metternich to Stadion, Paris, April 7, 1807.

87. It is with political crimes as with all others: time, which lays all things bare, reveals them sooner or

---

* The close connection of the subject of this despatch with that of the preceding one has induced us to place it here, although it belongs to the time of the Paris Embassy of the year 1807.

later, and never do they remain unpunished. I could
not resist recording in my despatches, and consequently
in the archives of the Department of Foreign Affairs,
the following fact, which, although entirely foreign to
the epoch and to my present sphere, seems to me too
characteristic not to mention. My despatches of the
end of the year 1805 contain, as far as I remember,
the reproach which met me at Berlin, either from
Baron de Hardenberg (making allusion at that time to
the policy of Count de Haugwitz), or from M. de Haugwitz himself, of having betrayed the secret of the triple
convention signed at Potsdam, November 3, 1805. I
even think that your Excellency was directly accused
by Count de Haugwitz of having divulged to the Emperor Napoleon, at the time of his conferences at Brünn,
the engagements which the court of Prussia had contracted with Russia and ourselves. I know only too well
that the thing was said over and over again to the
King, and it caused a great deal of ill will against us.

M. de Laforest, who since his departure from Berlin
has been here, and has no longer any reason for being
on good terms with Count de Haugwitz, told me a
few days ago that that minister, immediately after the
signing of the Treaty of Potsdam, went to him and read
the whole document to him; that he, Laforest, having
reproached him for affixing his signature to such a
paper, and not having employed all his influence to
prevent the King making the engagements it contained:
'We could not do otherwise,' replied Count de Haugwitz: 'and you see that I have taken care to stipu-
late everything so vaguely, and left ourselves so much
latitude, that we are bound to nothing. Assure the
Emperor that it is only a joke, and that we are and will
remain his best friends.'

Any remark on such a thing is superfluous. The author of so many troubles which have since fallen on his country could not more worthily crown his work than by making use of a treaty which he had just signed to violate the intentions of his master, thus endeavouring to embroil the contracting Powers among themselves, and throwing himself into the arms of the only Power whom Prussia had to fear.

THE INFLUENCE OF THE PEACE OF PRESBURG.

(Note 14, Vol. I.)

88. Metternich to Stadion, Berlin, January 10, 1806.
89. Metternich's Treatise on a Political Plan, January, 1806.

88. . . . . To express to you, sir, what I suffered on reading the treaty of December 27 is impossible. I pray you to judge from the intimate knowledge you have of my principles, of my attachment for the person of our august master, and his House, what I feel on reading through a document of which every article only offers subjects of regret. The consequences of the Treaty of Presburg seem to me incalculable. What is the side which Russia believes she must take? What will be the fate of the Ottoman Empire placed in immediate contact with France on her weakest side? What will be the final issue of the Prussian negotiations? The peace, nay the very existence, of the Austrian monarchy, appears to me to depend on these three questions, selected from a crowd of others which present themselves to my mind, but which are beyond my sphere to touch upon.

My preceding despatches will unhappily prove that all matters here are more or less disordered by the same causes which have brought about the present state of things. Time and unforeseen circumstances will, perhaps, do more for us than I can at present allow myself to hope; this moment, when all the elements are in combustion, when nothing is in its place, when one man alone in Europe holds the helm with an all-powerful hand, rendered so doubtless by successes far exceeding what even he himself had dared to hope, is so little suited for any conjectures whatever that I suspend all mine.

Your Excellency will be convinced by my former accounts that the attempts of Bonaparte to crush us with odious calumnies, even at a time when we are no longer his enemies, are as active as ever. Whilst placing us by the public articles in the most complete dependence, his agents owe everything to the secret articles of the Treaty of Presburg. He wishes to deprive us of the interest even which is accorded to misfortune, and follows his usual principle by throwing brands of discord among the Powers, the agreement of whose views should result from their common interests. The twelfth article of the Treaty, which leaves Germany entirely in suspense as to the fate reserved for his Royal Highness the Archduke Ferdinand, has produced here, chiefly on that account, an effect contrary to our wishes. I will not detain you longer than to give the explanations made necessary by one of the paragraphs of the principal despatch of your Excellency.

My different reports will have proved to you, sir, that the certainty that we were really in negotiation for a separate peace has stopped all the King's measures towards bringing us direct help, of which M. de Stutterheim's despatches, and my own of December 16 (No. 85), contained the hope. A prince of reasonable energy, whose best policy would have been to force us to get free, would doubtless not have waited till we called him to our aid, at a time when we are visibly falling beneath the weight which crushes us ; but your Excellency knows the King, and the arrival of

M. de Haugwitz paralysed all that we might have expected from the feeble will of that prince. I was sure of his active and decided co-operation if an appeal for help had been addressed to him by us at the time of his signature of the armistice ; but that which, according to my firm conviction, was indubitable then could not be attained eight days afterwards.

METTERNICH'S SKETCH OF A POLITICAL SCHEME, JANUARY, 1806.

89. The Peace of Presburg, and the part which Russia and Prussia played there, have sapped the foundations of the independence of the Great Powers. The only means possible for the preservation of the old alliances appears to me the following:—

1st. To draw a line from the mouth of the Weser, and following the course of this river, to join the Harz; from there, along the course of the Saale as far as the beginning of the Erzgebirg; the woody and mountainous frontiers of Bohemia, the Inn, the cleared frontiers of the country of Salzburg and Tyrol, the Tagliamento, as far as its mouth in the Adriatic. North Germany being less covered by the Weser than the other parts behind the said line, Prussia should keep the Principality of Minden, and another point suitable for an advanced corps on the left bank of the Weser.

2nd. As one line of fortresses will not bring about the equilibrium between the means of attack and defence, a second chain of fortresses should be established on the Elbe, in the interior of Bohemia, on the Ems, and in Carniola. Places on the Oder, in Prussian and Austrian Silesia, the Riesengebirge, Pless and Theresienstadt, on the Danube, the Save, and the Bukowine, would serve for the third line.

3rd. The three principal Powers—Austria, Russia,

and Prussia—should enter into an alliance, purely defensive, of which the conditions should be :—

a) A total abandonment beyond this line of the interests of Western Europe, over which France at this moment exercises an influence impossible to destroy.

b) The express stipulation of the integrity of the Ottoman Empire.

c) An offer on the part of the united Powers of mediation between France and England, supported by a declaration to the latter that the Eastern Confederation would break off all commercial relations in case of her refusing to treat with them.

d) The cession of Dalmatia, which, united to the ex-Venetian isles, would form an independent state under the guarantee of Austria, France, Russia, and Prussia. The reunion of Venetian Istria and the Isles of Quarnero with the Austrian Provinces and Croatia.

e) Austria would offer in compensation the abdication of the Imperial Roman crown, on condition of its perpetual extinction.

f) The reunion of Hanover with Prussia, in return for the cession of the Westphalian Provinces and the country of Ansbach.

g) Russia would make peace with France on these conditions, and would recognise the Imperial and Royal title of Napoleon and the new kings.

h) A federal system in the west of Europe, with France at the head, should not be opposed.

i) The Eastern Confederation should take the offensive the very moment that France entertained any project of extension beyond the line marked out, and she would regard herself as forming but one whole.

k) The military system of the three Powers should be established on a scale and a plan agreed upon, in which the Prussian and Saxon armies would form the right wing, Russia the army in reserve. The latter would, with this purpose in view, keep a body of a hundred and fifty thousand men in her possessions in Poland, and would place the rest of her army in *échelons*, to be ready on the shortest notice to go to any place where their presence was required.

l) The Eastern Confederation would declare by a . manifesto the object of its formation, and the grounds on which it would rest.

CHANGE OF PRUSSIAN POLITICS AFTER AUSTERLITZ.

(Note 16, Vol. I.)

90. Metternich to Stadion, Berlin, February 28, 1806.
91. Metternich to Stadion, Berlin, February 28, 1806.

90. The chaos has cleared, and Napoleon has gained without a blow a complete victory over Prussia. Your Excellency would learn soon after the reception of the present courier the occupation of the country of Ansbach by the French. All that we know positively about the conditions of arrangement, to which the King thought himself obliged to consent, is limited to the cession to France of the Margraviate of Ansbach, and the Prussian provinces contiguous to the Rhine to be disposed of in favour of a German prince, and the final incorporation of the Electorate of Hanover with the Prussian monarchy. There seems to be no doubt that such were the principal stipulations which M. de Haugwitz signed on December 15, and which the King desired to modify. Napoleon has only followed his usual method in not giving up the least of his demands ; and to understand the conduct of the King's cabinet, we must observe the complicity of a minister who, reckoning on the inconceivable weakness of his master, has dared to dispose of integral parts of his kingdom, not only without instructions and unknown to him, but even in direct contradiction to the orders with which he was furnished.

We know now that the order to place the army on
a peace footing at the time of the return of the courier
sent to Munich, which did not contain a word of ratification on the part of Bonaparte, was signed by the
King unknown to Baron de Hardenberg.   Count de
Haugwitz and his accomplices would of course try
to disarm the King, and give Napoleon time to bring
the greater part of his army to situations where he
could effectually support his threats in case of a refusal
from the King to renounce the modifications proposed
by Baron de Hardenberg.   M. de Haugwitz, without
loss of time, sent one of his most intimate friends here
to support Bonaparte's views, fearing no doubt the
influence of the Cabinet Minister, and the strength of
the weapons furnished by the turn that affairs had
taken, so shameful for Prussia.   The Marquis de Lucchesini,* doubtless never was entrusted with a mission
more in accordance with his principles than that of
which he has just acquitted himself with so much success.   He will return to Paris in a short time to share
with his worthy chief the marks of the high satisfaction
of the Emperor, whom on this occasion they have marvellously gratified at their master's expense.

The stipulations above mentioned will continue to
be enveloped in secresy until the time when they are
brought to the knowledge of the public by the fact
itself.   I am quite ignorant what are the motives which
can guide the King's advisers on this occasion, and that
contrary to the advice of Baron de Hardenberg.

It would be difficult to foresee what side England
and Russia will take in the actual position of affairs.
There seems to be no doubt that Bonaparte will show

* Lucchesini, the Prussian Envoy to Paris, entrusted with the negotiations concerning Hanover.

boundless resentment against the first of these Powers for having deprived him of Hanover ; the King having consented to all that Bonaparte demanded from him, the complete demobilisation of the army would probably soon follow, the King fearing to meet with a refusal if he should insist on the closing of the ports of the North Sea and Baltic. Will this calculation lead the English Minister to forestall the blow by measures against Prussian commerce ? The solution of this question would seem to be equally fatal to both countries ; Prussia, at any rate, will be ruined the very day her trade fails.

Baron de Hardenberg has again sent in his resignation. The King obstinately refuses to accept it, and becomes furious when it is mentioned to him. Seeing that he cannot obtain his release, he has refused to sign any documents relative to the present arrangements, even those to which the King has consented; this Prince, therefore, finds himself in the peculiar situation of having two Ministers of Foreign Affairs, of whom one negotiates and disposes of his provinces unknown to him, and the other refuses to add his name to his own. Count de Schulenberg is expected here to concert with him the measures for the incorporation of Hanover.

It would be difficult to form an idea of the indignation which reigns in the Prussian army ; the military spirit was in the height of its energy at the moment the army was set in motion, and it vigorously resists the attempts which are made to stifle it for ever.

Metternich to Stadion, Berlin, February 28, 1806.

91. Baron de Hardenberg, with whom I had a long conversation this morning, in which he confirmed the data contained in my first despatch of this day,

which I had collected shortly after the signature of the
Articles, from a trustworthy source, and begged me
to transmit them to my court as a confidential communication on his part. He told me that later on he
would make it to me officially. Having informed him
that his Imperial Majesty had left it to me to choose
the time I thought suitable for my journey,* I begged
him to tell me if he still thought he could explain his
views to me on the future relations between our two
courts—relations which became daily more urgent—and
that if he thought them impossible in consequence of the
victory which the opposite party had obtained, I would
no longer delay my departure. He said to me ' that
his only hope lay in the closest agreement of our two
cabinets ; that I must know too well how invariable
his principles had been to doubt them on this occasion,
but that other people had taken great pains constantly to
interfere with his views, and do away with their effects.'
' I will remain in the Ministry,' continued he, ' as long
as the King wishes me to hold the portfolio of Foreign
Affairs ; I will retire for good whenever he orders me
to return it to him. I have always acted from the same
point of view, to remove Haugwitz, and work for the
union of our courts. Remain here until the return of
the courier from Paris ; we shall not know till then
whether Napoleon regards our affair as terminated. I
will then tell you everything ; I will speak to you of
my fears and hopes for the future, and will regard you
as the safest medium by which to transmit them to your
master.'

I promised to fulfil his wishes, which I had, as your
Excellency would see by my last despatches, already

* This refers to Metternich's journey to St. Petersburg, to which place
he went as Ambassador.

taken into my calculations, and he seemed perfectly satisfied.

Our conversation turned on the progress of his colleague's negotiation, about which he spoke in no measured terms; on the necessity of the two courts agreeing about the future arrangements of the Empire, of which among other things he promised me the details; and lastly, he spoke of his anxieties, which at this moment chiefly concern the evacuation of Germany by the French. This last question is too closely connected with others politically independent of Prussia, such as the course which the King of Sweden will take, who will not give up the country of Lauenburg, and above all the important consideration of the advantage which Bonaparte derives from the panic caused by a great army, for me to be able to promise direct results from our efforts.

In reiterating to Baron de Hardenberg assurances of the falsity of the imputations which the French party have never ceased to spread here of a projected offensive alliance between the courts of Vienna and Paris, he said he had never believed it himself, but could tell me something confidentially which would prove what means have been used to act on the King. Count de Haugwitz has declared here that he had read letters from Count de Stadion to Talleyrand in which he begged that minister to engage Napoleon to consent to an alliance, of which the end should be, if not the actual division of Prussia, at least the diminishing of her power. I asked him how that minister could hope to find dupes to believe an allegation so improbable. . . .

I found Baron de Hardenberg heart-broken at the cession of Ansbach, and above all at the form of the cession, without any stipulations whatever in favour of its inhabitants ; first, abandoning them to the vexatious conduct of the French, and then giving them over bound hand and foot to the administrative principles of Bavaria. He also appeared to me to have decided as to the part he would take, and to desire to draw from the present situation of affairs everything possible in favour of the common cause of all the Governments. It is not difficult to foresee that the exercise of his influence will not be tolerated much longer by France, who sees him to be a zealous adversary and an inconvenient observer of the manœuvres of her friends.

THE PRUSSIAN-FRENCH ALLIANCE.

(Note 17, Vol. I.)

92. Metternich to Stadion, Berlin, March 7, 1806.
93. Metternich's report of a conversation with Hardenberg, April 12, 1806.
94. Metternich's Questions and Hardenberg's Answers.

92. . . . . Every day brings forth new motives, which explain the reticence of the Minister (Baron de Hardenberg) in his communications to the members of the *Corps Diplomatique* in whom he most confides, and the secrecy which the King's cabinet has so well preserved about the progress and the bases of Count de Haugwitz's negotiation.

The rumour of an alliance being concluded between Prussia and France having in the last two days acquired a sort of certainty which it is easy for any man cognisant with Berlin to appreciate at its true value, I went this morning to Baron de Hardenberg, determined to put my question in such a manner that he would either confess or formally disavow it.

I said to him that I thought I ought to tell him at once without any disguise the object of my visit— namely, to ask him a question, an answer to which was clearly due to me, as I had explained everything to Prussia and reassured the King as to all the false rumours which had been spread concerning our relations with France. 'Persons well versed in affairs assert,' said I to him, 'that M. de Haugwitz has not confined

himself to a simple reconciliation, but that he has signed
an alliance with France; the French party themselves
support this rumour. You must, then, be interested in
disavowing it if it is false, or informing me of a truth
which you can no longer conceal from the knowledge
of the Powers.'

Baron de Hardenberg replied 'that the direct question addressed to him deserved an equally frank reply,
and that he would not hesitate to tell me what he had
intended to make known with the detailed communications he had promised; that the Count de Haugwitz
had really pushed the neglect of his instructions to the
point of signing at Vienna an alliance offensive and defensive with Napoleon; that the King having refused to
sanction that article, the Emperor had in his ultimatum
brought here by the Marquis Lucchesini consented to the
omission of the words " offensive " and " defensive," and
had contented himself with declaring the *casum fœderis*
to be the reciprocal guarantee of the possessions.' ' It is,'
added he, ' the only amendment which the King has obtained of all the modifications which he desired to make
to the treaty of December 16.'

Having observed to him that this treaty must essentially change the state and nature of the relations of the
Powers with Prussia, who, seeming to ally her cause with
France, could no longer be counted among those who
only desired repose and stability in Europe, Baron de
Hardenberg interrupted me hastily, and assuring me
' that no views offensive to any Power entered into the
King's plans; an alliance other than that which depended only on words, and implied other obligations
than that of preserving our own possessions, would not
agree,' said he, ' with the principles of the King, and our
relations with Russia especially. Believe me, and do all

K 2

you can personally not to allow any other meaning to
be put upon words to which it would be horrible to
sacrifice the remains of the hope we may still indulge
of stemming the torrent, by understanding one another and together making the most of our ways and
means.'

I could not but observe to him that the facility with
which Napoleon had consented to the omission of terms
consented to by M. de Haugwitz, proved more than
anything one could say what a wide meaning was in
Paris attached to the alliance.

The Minister begged me not to make use of his confidential communication, and zealously protested that
he would not cease to maintain and strengthen the
most intimate connection with us. I thought myself
bound to take *ad referendum* what I had just heard,
and renewed my assurances of the great care I would
take to contribute as much as possible to the closest
agreement between the two courts.

The silence which Baron de Hardenberg has observed to all my colleagues in this interesting matter,
and the care which the French party have taken not to
let the secret ooze out till quite lately, are sufficiently
explained by the desire not to let it reach the ear of
the cabinet of St. Petersburg until the last courier sent
to the Duke of Brunswick.

Baron de Hardenberg, in his conversation, particularly insisted on the fact that by the unhappy stipulations of December 16 the King's relations would not
be altered with any other Power, except England, who
would certainly look upon the incorporation of Hanover
as a hostile measure. The supposition that the closing
of the ports might really be stipulated by the treaty
seemed to me to come out too clearly from the avowal

that M. de Hardenberg had made to me, for me not to interrogate him on that point. He assured me that there was no question of it, and said the same to the Russian Minister. It is, however, impossible not to see what side the King would take if Bonaparte insisted on putting this new curb on English trade, and the omission of an article relative to it in the Treaty would certainly not be a proof against the possibility of an engagement, either contracted, or concerted, with the Count de Haugwitz, whose simplest promises assuredly deserve every credit on the part of the French cabinet.

The French have spread about lately that the time of Bonaparte's entry into Ansbach was concerted with Prussia; this was also reported by the agents of the Prussian government, and I therefore demanded explanations from Baron de Hardenberg: he told me that not only was there nothing, but that M. de Lucchesini had been as much astonished as himself at learning this new act of violence. ' On the other hand,' said he, ' what would you wish the King to do? He has been betrayed and sold, and it only remains for him to put a good face on a bad game.'

It is certain that the King was deeply affected on learning the details of the open violation of a territory which, according to all received principles, could not be regarded as ceded till after his ratification.

Baron de Hardenberg, on his side, is inconsolable at the loss of a province whose prosperity he regarded as his work, and which is now crushed under the weight of forty thousand men, of which she has to bear the burden alone.

The manner in which the secret has been kept throughout the course of Count de Haugwitz's negotiation is worthy of remark; your Excellency knows the ground at Berlin too well not to see that this one proof shows how much all branches of the departments are gained over to the interests of France. No such secret could have been kept concerning any other Power treating of affairs with the Prussian cabinet.

The Marquis de Lucchesini went away to-day, well satisfied, no doubt, with his work, and the bearer of a star for M. de Talleyrand of the Order of the Black Eagle set in diamonds, which cost the King six thousand crowns. The price of this gift is as new in Prussian annals as the kind of decoration, the statutes of the Order having up to this time forbidden the luxury of having the stars set in jewels.

MEMOIR BY METTERNICH, APRIL 12, 1806.

93. To undertake to sketch the political situation of Prussia at this present moment is an attempt the more difficult as the men who have reduced the King to this melancholy state have taken great care to conceal their plots from the public. Up to this moment we had merely a summary of the terms of the Treaty signed at Vienna on December 16, between Count de Haugwitz, M. de Talleyrand, and M. Duroc; and now we know them only from their effect; and it is by the little trouble the French took to conceal or to mask the loss of Prussian independence that we have acquired the full knowledge of the demands of Napoleon, and the concessions of Count de Haugwitz. The intentions of this minister should not in any case be confounded with those of the King. To separate them as to the result of the negotiations is unfortunately no longer possible, and will be still less so when Count de Haugwitz returns to the Department of Foreign Affairs.

Having been commanded by his Imperial Majesty to submit to him on my arrival here a general idea of the political situation of Prussia, and what might in the end be expected from that Power—a question which certainly must have an immense influence on our political system in general, and not less directly on our course with regard to Prussia in particular—I have thought it right to prolong my stay at Berlin, until the time which appeared to me the most decisive for the progress of affairs: namely, that of the final conclusion of arrangements with France, and the resumption of the portfolio by Count de Haugwitz—a portfolio which, since the month of December last, has been nothing more than a phantom of power in the hands of a minister of probity, attached to the principles of a sound and loyal policy, and too honest a man to suspect that those whom he believed his friends were occupied in preparing his fall, which in any case the force of general circumstances would have brought about.

Feeling sure that the falling minister would only give evasive replies to any questions I might put to him ; and that, on the other hand, all he could say to me about the future would only be conjectures drawn from the character of his successor, whom unhappily the whole of Europe had judged rightly long before his colleague had done so, I did not the less think that I ought to note the annexed Questions (No. 94), and begged him on this important occasion to explain them with all the frankness demanded by his desire to promote the union of our two courts. The replies, written for the most part at his dictation, or faithfully drawn from his own words, prove but too surely that I was not deceived in my expectation.

It appears to me that the political situation of Prussia offers three essential points of view, which, although bound together in their effects, should first be treated separately. I take then the following questions :—

1st. What will be the consequences of the Treaty of Alliance with France, as far as Prussia is concerned?

2nd. What may the general cause expect from the future co-operation of that Power?

3rd. What can we in particular expect?

It is certain that Prussia has gained nothing for herself by sacrificing all her relations through the conduct of her minister, and isolating her political course from Powers jealous of their independence, but who yet will find in their close union alone the physical and moral means of securing it.

The negotiations of Potsdam have revealed to us without disguise the views of Prussia respecting an amelioration of her frontier on the French side. The banks of the Weser undoubtedly present the only points suitable for a chain of fortifications; and the country of Hanover, exchanged for the Prussian provinces, offers ample compensation for the concessions projected in Westphalia. The changes effected in the Germanic Constitution, or rather her final destruction, and the extraordinary reinforcement of the Bavarian power, have deprived of their former value the lines formed by one of the most active allies of France; the loss of the Margraviate of Ansbach and Cleves, with other losses which Prussia undoubtedly has still to suffer, lessens in a great measure the value of a country seized by a friendly Power under the mask of the most disinterested service.

What may the general cause expect from the future co-operation of Prussia?

This question appears to me to be resolved by the fact that the minister who has brought things to the state in which they are has to justify conduct condemned by everybody without exception. He must therefore try to redeem by utility what he has made his master lose in honour. It is assuredly not by such a calculation or line of conduct that the general cause can hope to derive any benefit. The obstacles which in future will be most directly opposed to the agreement of our views with those of the King will be the intermediaries who constantly come between him and us, if ever we attempt to approach him personally. To develop a plan, to ⸢allow a glimpse of the first hints of a regenerative system, would be to confide them to the most trusted adherents of France. All promises to the contrary would be vain, and the attempt more dangerous than any good the side could possibly gain by it.

It seems clear to me then, that it is necessary to regard Prussia as directly included in the devastating progress of Bonaparte's policy, and that she must be treated as such.

It is from time alone, circumstances unforeseen but necessary, infallible, and above all from the manner in which we are able to seize them and turn them to profit, that we may hope and expect that which all care, all negotiation, cannot procure for us. Everyone who surrounds the King, and his minister for the time being (who, without having his confidence, has all the power), are either weak or sold to Bonaparte; but how much has Bonaparte strengthened our cause by his excessive demands, by the harshness with which he flaunts them in the face of a Power which has done too much to inspire him henceforth with confidence, and too little to save itself and Europe ; lastly, in the public opinion which he has entirely turned against him in a state which he already treats as one of his prefectures! Amicable relations not committing us dangerously are the only proper ones for us in future. It seems superfluous to add that the humble labours I have had the honour to lay before his Imperial Majesty have far from exhausted the matter, even so far as the questions themselves are concerned.

How many different points of view are necessary to be touched upon—what a crowd of ideas offer themselves to be discussed, in order to fathom the newly-founded system of a Power of the first rank! But all these points of view are exhausted, all these replies are given by the single fact of the most perfect submission of Prussia to the French system, of her excessive tolerance for any future demands of Bonaparte, all which may be clearly seen in the few lines Baron de Hardenberg has enabled me to send you.

METTERNICH'S QUESTIONS AND HARDENBERG'S ANSWERS.

(Enclosure in 93.)

94. *Question.* What meaning does Prussia attach to her new treaty of alliance with France; does she limit it merely to a reciprocal guarantee of territory; is a certain *status quo* established as its basis, or does it include also the guarantee of the French Empire, with all possible extensions of territory?

Answer. Baron de Hardenberg declares officially that Prussia attributes no other than a merely defensive sense to her alliance. The guarantee of the possession itself is only to be taken in a general sense; the *status quo* is not specially stated. Count Haugwitz, however, understood this to be the same as the treaties with other Powers, as the Presburg Peace with Austria, &c., &c. Baron de Hardenberg believes that these guarantees will not extend to new acquisitions.

Question. Would it be agreeable to Prussia, in respect of her new relations, to solidify, by the closest alliance with Austria, a system through which both kingdoms may be saved from the foreign pressure which threatens both equally?

Answer. Baron de Hardenberg appeals to the sentiments I know him to entertain—namely, that such a union is the only means of safety; but he referred me to the feeling of the future ministry.

Question. Since Prussia believes she can enter into

an alliance with France and Russia, would she consider an alliance with Austria, which would in any case be founded on the mutual guarantee of possessions, as incompatible?

Answer. Idem.

Question. Would not Prussia agree to a convention by which the influence of the two Powers in the German Empire can alone be equally maintained?

Answer. Idem.

Question. Since, nevertheless, there exists in the Empire only one influence, the French, and one law, which consists of the Imperial authority, which last can only be maintained as far as possible by a special union, will Prussia instruct her Comitial ambassadors in their future deliberations of the Empire, to agree with the Imperial voice, either following up the negotiation in this way, or, for special cases, imparting to the Comitial ambassadors the general directions therefor?

Answer. Baron de Hardenberg considers these principles excellent, and wishes that the future ministry may find them so. As for what concerns the Comitial ambassadors, Baron de Hardenberg believes that the King is personally much inclined to such an alliance, and that Count Haugwitz, too, had been of that opinion before his departure for Paris.

Question. What is the Prussian cabinet's point of view with respect to the future formation of *circles* in Germany?

Answer. At the most this desire can only be considered as a possibility.

Question. What is the future arrangement already agreed on, or contemplated, between Prussia and France as to the Westphalian circles?

Answer. Nothing with regard to this has been stipulated ; no cession has been made besides Cleves, and even on the French side there has been no question of any.

Question. Prussia's protectorate of North Germany has ceased. In the future will she draw back entirely into herself, or use the remains of her influence to maintain the old or establish a new order of things ?

Answer. The King's wish would certainly be to retain the old as much as possible, but he will also not neglect the establishment of the new. Count Haugwitz has busied himself, as we know, with this object.

Question. What does the Prussian court think of the possibility of a system of Imperial defence ? It cannot be concealed that a line from the North Sea to the Croatian frontier, and formed of the united forces of Austria, Prussia, and Saxony, must be a great advantage for that part of the kingdom, and prevent it from being so easily threatened by France ?

Answer. He quite agreed with me, and protested that his own efforts had been directed on similar principles. He feared, however, that Count Haugwitz had been so in love with his work that all Prussia's guarantees had been disposed of.

Question. Will Prussia in no case allow the French army to march through her states to the obstruction of trade ?

Answer. This question can only be answered according to the measure of our weakness at the time. Most certainly up to this time no such question has been mooted.

AT THE TIME OF THE EMBASSY TO PARIS,
1807—1809.

1807.

THE PEACE OF TILSIT AND THE SITUATION OF PRUSSIA.

(Note 19, Vol. I.)

Metternich to Stadion, Paris, July 26, 1807.

95. I have the honour to send to your Excellency the Treaty concluded on the 7th and the 9th of this month, between France, Russia, and Prussia, which was communicated yesterday to the Senate.* . . .

People here are not much occupied with the results which the peace may bring to the political relations of Europe. The Parisians, accustomed to see so many thrones fall, and so many new states rise from their dust, are not astonished at the position to which the Prussian monarchy is reduced. Their imagination carried them much further in the time which elapsed between the news of the signature of the two treaties, and their communication to the Senate.

They remodelled the whole of Europe. Two empires, one in the west and the other in the east, would draw round them the small confederate States to serve

---

* This has been already published. See Marten's *De Clercq*.

as reciprocal intermediaries. Seventeen new kingdoms, among which figured Austria, Hungary, Bohemia, &c., given to as many princes of our house, a displacement more or less general of the reigning sovereigns, nothing scared these politicians of the *cafés* and the *salons*, until at length all their uncertainties were determined by the text of the Treaty itself.

I only repeat these rhapsodies to prove that the whole of Europe might fall without exciting a single sentiment, either of pain, astonishment, or satisfaction, in a people degraded below all others, beneath all imagination, and who, fatigued and demoralised, with all trace of national spirit destroyed by eighteen years of revolution and crime, now look on with the greatest calmness at all which passes beyond their frontiers. Wise men say that the treaties, being as much for the advantage of Russia as France, necessarily contain a germ which in development can only prove fatal to the latter. The remark is commonly made that the Emperor sacrifices to his resentment a Power which he should have protected to serve him as a counterpoise against Russia ; and they repeat the very just reasoning which Napoleon used one day to General de Vincent * in a conference at Warsaw on the true interest of France, which is the very reverse of that excited by his fury and his desire to destroy and to reconstruct. . . . .

Prussia has descended from the first rank to be ranged among Powers of the third order. We shall no longer have a powerful enemy on our right flank ; but neither shall we find any support there, and even her neutrality will be a drawback in case of a war with France. This latter exercises the most direct influence

---

* Nicolas Carl Baron Vincent, an Austrian general and landed proprietor in Galicia, afterwards Austrian Ambassador at the Court of Louis XVIII.

as far as the centre of what was formerly Poland. The Confederation of the Rhine embraces us on both sides. Any war with France would begin at the same time on the borders of the Inn and the Wieliczka. Our position is infinitely worse by the Treaties of Tilsit; but the monarchy is intact and it is defined. The present state of things in Europe carries the seed of destruction in itself, and the wisdom of our Government should bring about a day when three hundred thousand men united, ruled by one will and directed towards one end, will play the first part in Europe at a time of universal anarchy—one of those epochs which always follow great usurpations and almost efface the traces of the conqueror; an epoch of which no one can foretell the date, but which nothing can retard, save the life of one man, and which all the genius of that same man can the less delay as he has never yet made the least attempt to prevent its certain effects.

It is in truth curious that Napoleon, continually troubling and changing the relations of the whole of Europe, has never taken one single step tending to insure the existence of his successors.

THE TREATY OF FONTAINEBLEAU BETWEEN AUSTRIA AND FRANCE.

(Note 22, Vol. I.)

Metternich to Stadion (Private).

96. At last you receive the result of more than a month's labour, anxiety, and especially disgust, impossible to describe. You will judge me, my dear Count, with the same impartiality as I would you; you will read the Convention of October 11, and be terrified at it. I have acted according to my sole and entire conviction; I have acted as a man who is not afraid of committing himself when he desires to avoid greater losses to the Monarchy; I have at length cut the Gordian knot, and if you do not give to my work the respect which I am far from claiming for it, you will at least render justice to my position and intentions. I have never found more bad faith, more impudence, in any of the tortuous negotiations with which I have been charged. Judge me with kindness! I do not think I should be obliged to ask this if things could be understood at a distance as well as they are close at hand.

Metternich to Stadion, Paris, October 12, 1807.

97. I have the honour to submit herewith to your Excellency the Convention which I believed it necessary to sign on the 10th of this month, at Fontainebleau, after eight days of debate.*

I submit for the sanction of our august master a work certainly far below what we had a right to expect in the most just of causes; but his Imperial Majesty may believe that nothing could be obtained beyond what he will find in the present Convention. I broke off the negotiation three times, only retaining a single thread, so as to have the power of renewal; I have yielded at last, not only to the firmest conviction, but to irresistible proofs that each delay would only bring the chance of new sacrifices, without hope of anything better. Your Excellency will see by the project of the Convention that the few days that intervened between my last conversation with M. de Champagny and the date of the minister's letter which caused my journey to Fontainebleau were sufficient to bring forth new demands and pretensions altogether unjust on the part of a cabinet which, in the painful negotiation from which I have just come, has never ceased to pretend it was making sacrifices to us, while we alone have had to bear them. It was necessary, no doubt, to trust very much to the confidence of my master to dare to sign articles which so entirely lack all appearance of reciprocity, and which bring such real losses on the kingdom; but his Majesty will deign to consider all my position: that we were negotiating no longer, and that all litigious questions only ended in more exaggerated demands; that the last word of the French cabinet has always been to declare without any disguise that it expected to be deprived of what it holds, and to be prevented from seizing what it most desires. M. de

---

* The Treaty of Fontainebleau concerning the boundary between Austria and Italy has already been published. See Neumann, II., 236 and 239.

Champagny said to me when I declared that I had neither the will nor the power to sign without receiving new orders from my court : ' You may demand them, but events march, and we march with them.' It is impossible to oppose anything to an argument of this nature when it comes from a Sovereign who, far from following events, has acquired such power that he prepares and develops them at his will.

The court having returned to Fontainebleau on September 21, I thought it better to wait quietly, after having settled all questions of an external character with the minister, till he should make known to me the time when his Majesty would grant me the private audience I had requested from him.   Three days passed uselessly ; at last I received, on September 3, a letter from M. de Champagny, to which was annexed a project of the Convention, very different from all we had agreed upon in our last conference.   I had declared I could not sign the cession of the territory beyond the Canale : they demanded it as far as the Saga.   The questions of the military route, of the passage of Russian garrisons through our states—an odious article which I find upon inquiry would cost an enormous sum— in short, all these demands, totally foreign to the former points of discussion, were offered for my consent without any explanation or excuse.

I went the same night to Fontainebleau, and yesterday had the first conference with M. de Champagny. The refusal of the Emperor to see me, the part which M. de Champagny has taken in sending me his project of the Convention, rather than inviting me to his house to see it, altogether prevented me from hoping for the smallest success.   Decided not to sign it unless I ob-

tained real modifications, I explained myself to the
minister with the greatest frankness; I did not spare
him a single truth on the proceedings of his master
towards a Power which lately he had deceived by promises and protestations entirely different from what he
now proposed. I told him that I should quit Fontainebleau the following morning, very undecided if I should
even take *ad referendum* the articles of his project of
the Convention. We separated without having advanced a single step. I dined with him the same day,
and he begged me to come again the following morning.

Three hours of discussion led to another meeting on
the following day, when we drew up an agreement
which I thought I should be able to sign. M. de
Champagny undertook to submit it to the Emperor.
We worked anew for more than two hours; I had three
other conferences in the following days, and longer discussions than he thought necessary for debating a treaty
of peace brought us at length to the signature of the
informal work which your Excellency receives by the
present courier. . . . . .

. . . . Some extremely remarkable circumstances in my last conference, at ten o'clock this morning, are, however, of a kind which necessitates my re-
porting them here.

Resolved to allow things to come to the last extremity before renouncing all hope of saving the Valley
of Robij and the sources of the Natizone, the importance of which is very great in all military aspects, I
commenced by declaring the impossibility of acceding
to this demand, which had only been made to me the
evening before. I resisted to the point of rising to leave
the minister's room, saying :—' The Emperor my master
can alone dispose of his kingdom : we have reached the

limits of my powers, and I can only beg you to send me this afternoon an exact copy of this article as well as of those we have both agreed upon; I will submit them to the decision of his Imperial Majesty by a courier, whom I will send to-morrow.' As I left the room, M. de Champagny said to me, ' But do you know the consequences of your step?'

'I have calculated everything,' I replied, 'and no secondary consideration shall ever make me deviate from the line I think it right to follow.' ' Ah well,' said M. de Champagny, ' our negotiations must then be regarded as broken off; all the points on which we have yielded must be taken up again—we cannot renew the negotiation here: but I must tell you that we shall immediately send the order to General Andréossy * to demand from your court the cession of the whole course of the Isonzo; in fact, the signature of the Convention such as I communicated to you in the first project, and to insist upon it peremptorily.'

Thus there only remained to me the alternative of breaking off the discussion, and consequently leaving it to an undetermined period, and to all the malevolence of General Andréossy, who, away from his master, would certainly be much less accommodating about external affairs than the minister himself; or to proceed at once *sub spe rati* to the signature of the articles already drawn up. The first of these alternatives could meet neither the intentions nor the interests of his Imperial Majesty. The second only concerns myself; for even admitting that the Convention was not ratified, the different questions must remain at least in suspense until the return of the courier.

* French Ambassador at Vienna.

I did not hesitate, and fell back on one modification : I proposed to him the first article as enclosed. But nothing would move him. The line traced by the Emperor's own hand on a map which served us as a basis was the barrier against which all my efforts were broken. After arguing for three hours, we agreed to meet again in the evening to allow his officials time to make the copies.

A singular indiscretion of M. de Marescalchi* has contributed not a little to this decision. This minister has been kept entirely away from the present negotiation. I was convinced of this by the question he put to me some days after I had commenced it with M. de Champagny—namely, why I had not raised the question. He even promised to mention it again to the Emperor, who never wished to listen when he spoke of the subject to him. Having dined with him at Fontainebleau, three days ago, he said to me with an air of satisfaction, 'Well, your affair will be arranged now. I have succeeded in making the Emperor listen to me ; he told me that he had ordered M. de Champagny to come to an understanding with you on many points, and he wishes everything settled immediately.' 'I know that,' replied I, 'but it is not easy to settle with you, although you have such a simple way with you : you demand everything and give nothing !' 'Ah !' said M. de Marescalchi, with a knowing air, 'you know the Emperor, and there are many people about him who suggest ideas to him which he has often never had himself ; have they, then, already demanded Trieste from you ?' 'No,' said I, 'and the Emperor cannot be ignorant that, all compliance having a limit, there are some questions to which there can

---

* Marescalchi, the Italian Ambassador in Paris from 1802 to 1814.

only be one way of replying!' M. de Marescalchi, seeing he had gone too far, said with an embarrassed air, ' Well I can assure you that many people torment him to demand this cession, and do you try to arrange matters as soon as possible, if they have not already demanded it from you.'

It cannot be denied that this is rather a favourable omen than otherwise, but it contains nothing new. It is not only Trieste which the Emperor covets, and the rapacity of all those who think it their duty to make their court to him by submitting projects of this kind to him : all extension of every kind suits his views, and those who procure him the means of commerce and navigation undoubtedly minister to his favourite ideas. There has, however, been no question of cessions beyond that contained in the project of Convention by M. de Champagny, of September 30.

I am unhappily but too well convinced in every moment of our negotiation, not only that there is no limit to Napoleon's ambition, but that he has now completely thrown off the mask. M. de Champagny does not use a single expression to me which is not either dictated immediately by the Emperor, or founded on his words. I believed myself authorised to say in the frankest manner, from the time we had agreed to sign, all that I thought of the actual position of affairs and the proceedings of the Emperor. M. de Champagny cannot object to the justice of my reasonings ; he therefore constantly falls back on the *beati possidentes*, assuredly the most injurious and the most unworthy of foundations in its present application.

The fact remains, that all my cares to procure any indemnity whatever for Austria have been vain. The Isles of the Quarnero were declared indispensable and necessary for the Italian navigation. The same with Muggia, which, according to other reports, could not be separated from Venetian Istria. I passed at least six hours in refuting all M. de Champagny's sophistical reasons; who in the course of the discussion, declared himself alternately a scribe, a minister, and an impartial judge. Seeing that no territory was to be obtained, I fell back on the numerous estates which are in the districts to be given up. I claimed the right of the Imperial Treasury to the profits from the sale of them in a certain number of years. This proposition, which M. de Champagny took *ad referendum*, was refused, as not terminating the discussion. Braunau and the friendship between the two Empires, so easy to cement when no subject of discussion existed any longer between them, were thrown into one scale, and our cessions into the other. It is worthy of remark that I had never been able to arrive at making M. de Champagny understand that, instead of exchange, there had been nothing but cession on our part; he was constantly objecting the extraordinary advantages that we should derive from the objects of compensation above mentioned. Nothing assuredly could have less resemblance to a negotiation than all the discussions we have had together; but I thought it all the more necessary to terminate them. Three weeks of delay did not seem to me to offer us the least chance of success. From the analogy of the unhappy experiences in all the negotiations with the French Revolutionary Governments—and which of them was ever more revolutionary than this one?—I am convinced that these same conditions, however painful it is to me to submit them for the ratification of his Imperial Majesty, can no longer be obtained on the morrow. I have no doubt that the more your Excellency compares the different data I have sent to-day, the more you will be convinced yourself of this sad truth.*

Metternich to Stadion, Paris, November 12, 1807.

98. I have the honour to lay at the feet of his Imperial Majesty the definite result of the negotiation with which he has deigned to trust me. . . .

The exchange of ratifications has taken place with the usual formalities, and it was on that occasion that M. de Champagny said he was commanded by the Emperor to tell me 'that he saw with pleasure the dawn of a new era in our relations with him, that his Majesty had expressly added that he fully recognised the conciliatory spirit I had personally shown in the delicate negotiation I had undertaken; and was satisfied that a success very promising for the general tranquillity had crowned my efforts.'

It would be superfluous to add any reflections to the present despatch. The facts speak for themselves.†

One single and important remark I think ought not to be omitted, because it must necessarily serve as the basis of our present and future political conduct with regard to this cabinet. We find ourselves for the first time in a situation clearly defined and understood by France; no question is left open; it is established that Napoleon has nothing more to demand from us; that our intercourse with him can in future only be

---

* Here follow the 'Remarks on the Articles of Convention' signed at Fontainebleau, October 10, 1807, which we put aside as they are lengthy and in substance contained in the above.

† The despatch also mentions the subsequent recognition of the Kings of Holland, Westphalia, and Naples by Austria, and the instruction which our Ambassador Count Starhemberg received on the occasion, which led Napoleon to remark 'that he considered all difficulties with Austria as wholly terminated.'

friendly and peaceable. They have expressed a wish for an alliance : it is for our dignity to wait for them to apply to us, if they wish for it, and that we should recall with firmness the Emperor's own words, on the first occasion he seeks a quarrel with us.

This occasion will present itself; it may present itself soon ; it is even necessary for the progress of French politics that it should come.

NAPOLEON'S WAR WITH PORTUGAL, AND THE CONTINENTAL STRUGGLE.

(Note 31, Vol. I.)

99. Metternich to Stadion, Paris, October 16, 1807.

99. I went to Fontainebleau the day before yesterday to be present at the *fêtes* of the next day. The first news I heard there privately was the declaration of war with Portugal. I have received the following information from a perfectly safe source. Since then it has been partly confirmed to me by the Ambassador of Portugal himself.

My report dated September 23 mentions a violent attack made by the Emperor on M. de Lima at a diplomatic audience.* He had just at that time addressed to Portugal the demand that she would close her ports to England, immediately sequestrate all estates belonging to Englishmen, and retain as prisoners of war all the individuals of that nation of whatever age or sex.

The Prince Regent commanded his ambassador to reply to the cabinet of the Tuileries that he was ready to close his ports to the English; he would even allow the Emperor to choose the means of opposing their commerce; but that as his principles were against any oppressive measure on innocent individuals living in his country and trusting to the common rights of men, he would never yield to this last demand.

* See page 291, vol. i.

The Emperor, for all reply, declared war with Portugal; and sent an order to General Junot, who has been for some time commander-in-chief to the army assembled at Bayonne, destined to act against that country, to put it in motion immediately. He sent at the same time a courier to Madrid to demand the co-operation of Spain, of which he had taken care to assure himself beforehand. M. de Lima begged the Emperor to suspend these hostile measures, to grant him a passport to enable him to go to the Prince Regent, and only to regard as an *ultimatum* the determination which his Royal Highness should have taken after his arrival at Lisbon. The passport was granted; the Emperor even promised not to publish his declaration till the end of the delay requested by the Ambassador; but he would not consent to revoke the order given to the army to march forward.

M. de Champagny communicated to the Ambassador his master's reply in a private interview, in which the Minister of Foreign Affairs kept back nothing. He said, after long explanations of the part the Emperor had taken of having nothing more to do with England, that, that Power being the sovereign of the sea, the moment had come in which Napoleon wished to be the ruler of the Continent; that all who opposed his views, or made the least resistance, should be crushed; that, in alliance with Russia, he no longer feared anyone; that in fact the die was cast.

M. de Lima returned to Paris, to send a courier to announce his near arrival at Lisbon. He committed the great blunder of returning the same night to Fontainebleau, to be present at the diplomatic audience yesterday.

The Emperor began his circuit with me. He spoke

to me, in a polite manner, of things altogether indifferent. He only said one word to my neighbour, the
Spanish Ambassador; and approaching the Portuguese
Ambassador, who by chance found himself beside the
Danish Minister, he addressed to both of them one of
the most violent tirades that have ever been made to a
diplomatic circle. He used almost the same words as
M. de Champagny, suppressing, however, that of his
pretension to universal domination. He added, 'if Portugal does not do what I wish, the House of Braganza
will not be reigning in Europe in two months.

'I will no longer tolerate an English Ambassador in
Europe; I will declare war against any Power who
receives one at his court after two months from this
time. I have three hundred thousand Russians at
my disposal, and with that powerful ally I can do
everything. The English declare that they will no
longer respect neutrals on the sea: I will no longer recognise them on the land.' And, addressing the Danish
Minister, he continued: 'The events at Copenhagen
are horrible, but the declaration of the King is an
infamy.'

Continuing his circuit, he apostrophised the Ambassador of Etruria: 'Your Queen is in secret correspondence with England,' said he to him, 'but I have set that
to rights.'

Stopping before the Senator Groening, he asked him
if he were the Deputy of Brême? On his responding
in the affirmative, he asked him: 'How are things going
on with you?' 'Badly, Sire,' replied M. de Groening.
'Ah well, you will do worse yet. Brême and Hamburg
are English towns, consequently I shall know how to
treat them.' He retraced his steps, and concluded the
audience after speaking to me about the present place

of his Imperial Majesty's residence, and some details of his journey.

Your Excellency can easily picture to yourself the effect these violent outbreaks produced on everybody, which I have only weakened by trying to describe. They immediately gave rise to the most extraordinary conjectures, which we too cannot but entertain.

An hour after this audience I repaired to the Minister of Foreign Affairs.

I had hardly taken a seat, when M. de Champagny told me that he had an entirely confidential communication to make to me. ' You see,' began he, ' what the intentions of England are now.   She has lately taken as a basis, and even the King himself has proclaimed, principles incompatible with social order in Europe.   The Emperor is determined to oppose with all his might the success of such scenes as are now taking place in Denmark ; he cannot content himself with half-measures. England has refused the mediation of Russia.   I cannot enter into details enough to prove to you that the propositions I was charged to make last year to Lord Lauderdale, containing abnegation on the Emperor's part, were little consistent with the dignity of his position. England refused peace when he offered it to her ; it is therefore necessary to force her to make it.

' There remain only three Powers in Europe— France, Russia, and Austria.   It is worthy of you to contribute directly to the salutary work which the Emperor proposes.   You have seen for some time that your flag is no more respected than others ; but the King has just declared openly that he will no longer recognise neutrality ; he asserts that he only seized the Danish fleet to prevent it protecting and covering the commerce of neutrals ; he makes use of the specious pretext of taking it from France, while the Emperor has never dreamt of making use of it. Russia makes common cause with us. The whole of Italy obeys the impulsion of France; it only remains that you close all access to the Continent. I believed it right to propose to his Majesty the confidential manner that I use with you to-day. You will thus have the chance of taking the initiative in measures of common interest. This communication is between ourselves. M. d'Andréossy even has not been told.'

M. de Champagny, having at length broken off this sort of discourse, at least ten times longer than I have thought it necessary to report, I took the opportunity of assuring him that I recognised with pleasure as a particular attention the way which he had chosen to make this communication. 'But what is the end at which you wish to arrive? You cannot deny that our relations with England are certainly not of a nature to alarm you; our ports even are closed to her, while they are open to the Russians.'

'Very well,' replied M. de Champagny, 'that is one good step; but as to commerce?'

'As to commerce,' said I to the Minister, interrupting him, 'you will do a real service to our custom-house if you denounce the importation of English merchandise; I can speak for that in this case.'

'I know,' continued he, 'that your laws are altogether prohibitive; but it is for that reason that you are less inclined to submit to vigorous measures when they are taken. You are more than any other Power, a Continental monarchy. You are, also more than any other interested in seeing the re-establishment of peace and tranquillity; it is impossible without maritime peace. The Emperor will be obliged until its conclusion to allow his troops to occupy almost all the places they do at present; he desires nothing more than to recall them; you too must wait with eagerness for the moment when you may also reduce your military system; it is therefore necessary to help to bring it about. The Emperor desires that you should declare that, if England does not restore the Danish fleet, and does not revoke the principles announced in her last declaration, you will recall your Minister from London, and that at that date, December 1, you will send the English Minister from Vienna.'

'I can do no more,' said I to him, 'than take the Emperor Napoleon's desire *ad referendum*; but without even allowing myself to state the question thoroughly, have you well calculated the loss you will sustain by the total suppression of our navigation? We alone make the coast trade; our flag carries provisions to your coasts and those of the kingdom of Italy. What, then, will you gain by our adding to measures which are already far from bearing the impress of amicable relations?' 'We shall lose more than you,' replied M. de Champagny; 'no one will suffer more from the present state of things and that which would immediately take place; but we intend to force England to peace, and we shall do it.'

'Will Russia second you in these measures?' I asked M. de Champagny.

'We feel sure she will; the Emperor Alexander will adopt any measure of Napoleon's to arrive at the object we both equally desire. Send a courier to Vienna with the communication I have just made to you. We shall have an answer at the same time as you will receive news relative to the Convention. I ought at the same time to tell you that if the reply were negative,

the Emperor would oblige you to make the same declaration in an official manner.' Here you see all the
principal features of a conversation which never lost
the most confidential and most amicable tone. I thought
I would seize the occasion to touch the chord of the
alliance for the first time since the return of the ostensible despatch.

I said to M. de Champagny that the confidential
manner he had adopted on this occasion authorised me
to be explicit with him. 'How is it that you ask us to
depart from a state of tacit war (for the closing of the
ports cannot be looked upon in any other way), to
declare against England in the most decided manner,
while when we propose to you to trust to our relations
of friendship and 'good-will on a basis much more
decided, you give us no answer? For some time I
have not spoken to you of our more intimate alliance,
because it was, doubtless, your part to reply to the last
communication which I was authorised to make to you,
in the sense and under the same forms that you desire ;
but this circumstance gives me a right to ask the
question.'

M. de Champagny involved himself in a sentence
which contained no reply to the direct question I
had addressed to him; he finished by saying : ' But
really, by binding your interest to ours, in bringing our
interests together, in fact, an intimate connection must
follow.'

' But I am astonished,' said I, ' that with one of
these propositions the idea of the other has not come to
you.'

The same ambiguous response, of which I could
only gather the question : ' What, then, do you really
desire ? '

'We desire,' said I, 'to see the end of all these unfortunate prejudices on the one side, and on the other the restoration of a state of security, which can only rest on suitable and certain foundations.'

'But a guarantee of your possessions would be given to you,' said M. de Champagny; 'you know that the Emperor has no other views for you—be well convinced of that.'

Nothing is more striking, and at the same time more painful for the negotiator charged to treat with M. de Champagny, than the extreme difference there is between his studied part and his improvised response. He rattles off the former with a veritable flow of words; in the latter one can only extract from him detached phrases which have no connection. It is therefore always perfectly easy to see where the lesson for the day stops.

All reflection on the communication which the present report contains seems to me to be rendered superfluous by the positive fact that Napoleon, passing all bounds, beyond even all calculations, has made it understood that he accompanies the official demand, which he addresses now to us in a confidential form, by a declaration of war in case of refusal. I can guarantee this assertion.

He has publicly boasted of having three hundred thousand Russians at his command. I am not convinced of the truth of this, as M. de Champagny would doubtless have been commanded to confirm it to me if the certainty really existed. My question seemed to have taken him unawares; he returned several times to this article, and only used such phrases as 'I believe—I have every reason to believe—we have no doubt,' &c.

But be that as it may, it does not alter the question

of the moment. There has been a total change in Napoleon's manner lately; he seems to think he has reached a point where moderation only exposes him to useless annoyance. The Peace of Tilsit and the extreme weakness of the Emperor Alexander have brought this about. Sure of having paralysed the cabinet of St. Petersburg for a certain space of time, which the Emperor of the French can calculate better than anyone else, it is only necessary to keep his former and future enemies in a passive attitude. He has never lost time, he will lose very little in the interval, and Alexander will recover from his illusions when Napoleon in the course of time leaves him to share his regrets with the rest of Europe, preparatory to his being crushed in an immense crucible.

We are of all the Continental Powers that which is the most directly and the most immediately menaced. The ancient and venerable union of so many happy peoples under the tutelary sceptre of the august House of Austria, will not sustain the first shock—a shock directed by the fury of a man who knows our vulnerable sides better than we do, who has meditated on the most direct means for our destruction in a way almost incredible, who the day when he entered the lists with us could have no other object than that of annihilating his last and unhappily too feeble counterweight.

But the fate, the duration, of an empire, can they depend on the frail existence of a single individual? It is no more than right to put this question when the means of avoiding an unhappy conflict are so problematical.

What is the case at present? Does it not offer to us any precious opportunities of replacing our existence entire and intact on a firm foundation? Would it be possible to elude a demand which, by its extreme use-lessness in every political point of view, seems to be put forward only to furnish pretexts for embarrassment and confusion, if the counter-blow, which will not fail to act in the most injurious manner on French commerce, does not give it the character of an act of pure and blind rage? These are some of the questions which I do not allow myself to approach. Their solution is reserved for the wisdom of his Imperial Majesty; but it is my most imperative duty to submit to him my firm con-viction that on this occasion more than any other the fury of Napoleon will know no bounds, and that his thirst for universal dominion could not be better seconded than by an inadequate measure on our part.

ARRIVAL OF THE RUSSIAN AMBASSADOR TOLS-
TOY IN PARIS, AND THE FRENCH REFERENCE
TO RUSSIA.
(Note 23, Vol. I.)

100. Metternich to Stadion, Paris, November 12, 1807.

100. Count de Tolstoy arrived at Paris November
1, accompanied by M. de Nesselrode, counsellor to the
embassy, half-a-dozen attachés, and an aide-de-camp.

. . . . It would be difficult to describe to your
Excellency the simplicity and perfect freedom with
which he explained everything to me. He repeated
what had been said to me by Count Nesselrode, that
his instructions were to hold by me entirely. He added
that he was able to tell me quite confidentially that the
Emperor his master remembered with pleasure having
known me personally at a time when great hopes had
bound the two Empires together; that the position of
Russia and Austria had grown worse since then, but that
we were happily still standing, and that he reckoned on
the kindness I would show to his ambassador here.

I said to Count de Tolstoy: ' We all have and
can have but one aim, that of preserving our integrity
in the midst of the general convulsion. Europe, or
rather some parts of ancient Europe, place themselves
on one side—the Emperor Napoleon on the other. He
will caress you to-day to fall on you to-morrow: he will
do the same to us ; we both shall have to struggle constantly against his projects of subversion and invasion ;
the struggle has been open for some time, and un-

happily has been but too badly managed; our mutual
position now demands that it should be confined to the
defence of principles which are the foundation of
your existence and our own. We have both the same
dangerous rocks to avoid—that of open quarrel or that
of false caresses: we shall swim between the two, if we
are wise and friendly.'

'I am quite of your opinion,' said Count de
Tolstoy to me; 'believe me that my court has absolutely the same views, notwithstanding false appearances. I do not know what these men wish to make
of me; but they are fools if they think I shall be
their dupe.' 'Have the air of being so and be not,'
interrupted I; 'let us be friends and communicate our
ideas to each other, which taken singly often lead only
to mistakes, but which taken as a whole will conduct
us to those truths which they naturally wish to conceal.'

He informed me that the Emperor had told him, the
evening before, that all his differences with Austria
were smoothed over, that he had signed a Convention
which had cut short everything, and that he would
immediately evacuate Braunau. He added, said Count
Tolstoy: 'The Emperor of Austria has yielded with
perfect grace to the equitable measures which I proposed to him concerning England, and I am now about
to give the necessary passes to a courier whom Count
Metternich is going to send to London.'

'Well, what will you do with regard to England?'
I asked him. 'It would be better,' replied he, 'that
we should let that pass; and you have done well to
follow the path you have chosen.'

He asked me for details of our new frontier in
Italy, and the terms of the evacuation of Braunau. I
told him I saw no difficulty in letting him know of the

Convention of the 10th, inasmuch as it contained an article regarding the passage of the Russian troops in Cattaro. 'It is, according to all appearance,' added I, ' a treat they wished to give you here. They would be eager to grant you this demand at Vienna, if it arrived there by your ambassador. I declare to you that this conviction alone has made me put it into our Convention here, where it otherwise would not have been.' ' You are right,' replied the ambassador ; ' the Emperor has been most eager in telling me this, exactly in the sense you suppose. I am going to ask you a singular question,' added he, ' but it is necessary that we speak frankly. Have you any secret articles in your Convention ? '   ' I am sure that they wish to make you think so,' interrupted I ; ' and I will easily prove the contrary by showing you the very copy of the Convention I am going to exchange, the only one I have here.' ' No,' replied he, ' they have not said so explicitly, but they have done all they could to make me suspect it.' ' Ah, well,' said I, ' you see the fruits of your embassy to Paris, and you will see many more like it.'

Wishing to sound him on the degree of confidence which he would show me in respect to Turkey, I said that I had heard here on good authority that the fate of that country was to be brought in question. ' You are then going to make your peace here with the Porte ? ' I asked him. ' Yes,' replied he ; ' but it is of all the negotiations the most simple, because we want nothing. I wish you could have seen the astonishment of these gentlemen when I said to them, in the plainest and simplest way, that we should demand no cession from the Porte. I know that it is generally believed among you that we wish to acquire Moldavia and Wallachia ; I swear to you there is no truth in it : and what should we do with it?' I remarked to him that the present time appeared to me to induce a preference for Conservative measures, and that a third party could not be injured without a new aggrandisement of France; he was entirely of my opinion, and begged me to assure my court most positively that Russia aspired to no aggrandisement at the expense of Turkey, and begged me to get rid of the false ideas which had taken root among us.

I do not pretend to judge from these appearances the depth of Russian policy; but I have been for some time settled in my own mind that there was extreme exaggeration about the friendly relations between the cabinets of St. Petersburg and the Tuileries, which it is part of the French policy to encourage. My statements support this truth; and I have no doubt now that every day will bring fresh evidence.

Our part seems to me to be determined, and the wisdom of his Imperial Majesty has prepared every means of following a line of conduct marked out by general circumstances and our individual position. We had cause to dread, more than any other conjuncture, the complete union of our two neighbouring Powers. This danger is averted; we may, most probably, find ourselves at some time exposed to great preparations on the part of Russia, and to the embarrassment which would necessarily result to us, but we shall have gained one, perhaps two years; our existence, our integrity will be preserved; and if it is impossible to live otherwise than from day to day, we have not less but more chances than any other European Power of arriving intact at the great day which will put an end to a state necessarily precarious, because it is contrary to nature and civilisation.

REPORT OF NAPOLEON'S DIVORCE, AND HIS ALLIANCE WITH A GRAND-DUCHESS.

(Note 23, Vol. I.)

101. Metternich to Stadion, Paris, November 30, 1807.
102. Metternich to Stadion, Paris, December 6, 1807.

101. I have had the honour to inform your Excellency, in many of my preceding despatches, of reports which have been spread about for some time of the approaching divorce of the Emperor. After having circulated secretly, it has been for more than two months the subject of public and general discussion. It is with these reports as with all which are not destroyed in the beginning—they are founded on truth, and would be very quickly stifled if they were not indirectly tolerated. But although a conviction of the fact exists, no one knows the details. The following inquiries, and some conversations with persons connected with the Empress, have procured for me information quite private, but which I do not hesitate to guarantee as certain.

The Emperor after his return from the army maintained towards his wife a cold and often embarrassed demeanour. He no longer occupied the same room with her, and many of his daily habits took a different course from what they did formerly. The rumours of the divorce began at that time to assume a more serious form; and reaching the ears of the

Empress, she determined to wait till they were confirmed by him in a more direct manner, without showing the least uneasiness to the Emperor.

The Minister of Police went to her one day at Fontainebleau, and after a short preamble, he said to her that the public good, and above all the consolidation of the reigning dynasty, requiring that the Emperor should have children, she would best comply with the wishes of the Senate, in which he joined, by demanding from the Emperor the most painful sacrifice for his heart. The Empress, quite prepared for this, asked Fouché with great calmness, if the step he had taken had been commanded by the Emperor. 'No,' replied he, 'I speak to your Majesty as a minister entrusted with the general surveillance, as an individual, as a subject devoted to the glory of his country.'

'I am, then, in no way bound to listen to you,' interrupted the Empress; 'I regard my union with the Emperor as written in the book of Fate. I will never explain myself except to him, and will never do anything he has not commanded.'

Many days passed without any mention of this between the Imperial couple, when suddenly the Emperor again began to occupy the same apartment as his wife, and seized a propitious moment to ask her the reason of the sadness which he had noticed for some time. The Empress then related to him the conversation she had had with Fouché. The Emperor repeated that he had never given his minister any such commission. He added, that she ought to know him well enough to be certain that he did not require any intermediation between them; he made her promise to make him acquainted with all she had heard about this affair.

Fouché, shortly afterwards, repeated the same demand to the Empress in a long letter, which is said to be a masterpiece of eloquence and of vigorous reasoning. She went at once to the Emperor, who received her with great coldness, and after many complaints and reproaches on her susceptibility and what he called her jealousy, he repeated what he had said before. He promised to reprimand Fouché, and the courtiers say they really saw some coldness shown by the Emperor to his minister.

His Majesty departed for Italy. The public were always busy with the reports, more or less well authenticated, which no one contradicted; when on the 23rd of the month the Commissary of the Government at the Bank of France called together the merchants assembled at the Bourse, to tell them that he was charged by the Minister of Police formally to contradict the report of the divorce which had been for some time current.

The mere account of what passed in private, taken together with the part played by Fouché, sufficed to prove that there was really something in the affair. No minister would dare to do anything here that was not ordered by the Emperor; above all, none of them would have risked a repetition. Therefore, it is clear that Napoleon does not wish to appear to have given orders.

But if this fact seems to me proved; if it is certainly confirmed, by the confession of several senators, that there is to be a *sénatus-consulte* to petition the head of the state, in the name of the nation, to assure a succession in the direct line; if it is so even by the anxiety and tears of the Empress, which she does not conceal from her intimate friends; it is the more necessary to discover the Princess upon whom the choice of the

Emperor will fall. The public have long ago named her, and my last accounts also mention her. But since Count Tolstoy assured me, in a most positive manner, that he is absolutely ignorant of the application of Napoleon for the hand of a Grand-Duchess, it is difficult to form an opinion of the real state of the negotiation.

It seems to me clear that there has been a question of this alliance between the two sovereigns since the conferences at Tilsit. To attempt to determine the mode, more or less direct, more or less definite, of the proposal of the Emperor of the French, is impossible ; it would be no less difficult to decide as to the manner in which Alexander has replied to it, if I did not know the character of this prince, and if I had not found facts to support my suppositions. I think, then, that the Emperor of Russia, too undecided at once to refuse all hope to Napoleon, has not decided the question ; but, escaping from the annoyance of a *tête-à-tête*, he hoped to withdraw from the affair by evasions, and that a feeling of dignity prevented him from saying anything on the subject to his ambassador.

I have come to know in a way which it is impossible to doubt, that General Caulaincourt is commissioned to make the formal proposal. Will it be refused, Yes or No? Your Excellency, who knows the ground at St. Petersburg much better than I do, is more in a position to solve this enigma. Here, all contingencies are prepared for ; the public expects a *sénatus-consulte* ; but if the divorce does not take place, all the rumours of it will be treated as idle tales, and we shall see nothing clearly till the moment when the Emperor is informed by his ambassador of the views of Alexander I. Probably this negotiation had a direct influence on the

choice of M. de Caulaincourt, and was one of the
reasons which caused him to be preferred to M. de
Laforest.

Metternich to Stadion, Paris, December 6, 1807.

102. The affair of the marriage seems unhappily to
gain fresh consistency every day. The rumour is so
general, the Empress herself speaks so loudly about the
divorce, that it would be difficult not to believe in it,
and equally difficult to suppose that the court would
tolerate the reports of an alliance if it had no more than
the hope of succeeding in the choice of a princess. The
Grand-duc de Berg is mentioned as likely to make the
formal demand. This affair, in one way or other, must
have the most important consequences. If it is proved
that alliances between sovereign families have hardly
any influence on their political relations in the long run,
it is no less true that this will have for the time more
influence on the course of the Russian cabinet in a
direct manner than any other proposal. If Alexander refuses his sister, we shall see complications arise,
the extent of which it is quite impossible to determine. It cannot be repeated too often that any rupture
between France and Russia will not be limited to a mere
interruption of their relations; the two Powers have
become contiguous since the disappearance of one of
the great intermediaries, and a state is organised under
the direct influence, even under the protection, of
France which involves our safety as much as that of
Russia.

NAPOLEON'S PLANS FOR THE PARTITION OF TURKEY.

1808.

(Note 31, Vol. I.)

103. Metternich to Stadion, Paris, January 18, 1808.
104. Metternich to Stadion, Paris, January 26, 1808.
105. Metternich's Notes of a Conversation with Napoleon, Paris, January 22, 1808.
106. Metternich to Stadion, Paris, February 26, 1808.

103. M. de Talleyrand, who now makes profession of attachment to the court of Austria, and who has latterly given me evidence of his desire to establish the closest relations between us and France, has had conversations with me on two consecutive days, and I shall convince your Excellency of their importance by merely sketching their principal features.

'The negotiation with England * may be considered as ended,' said M. de Talleyrand to me yesterday, on coming out from a long conference with the Emperor; 'the consequences which the obstinacy of the English minister must have are immense, and you will have to take one side or the other, and that as quickly as possible. Your relations with France are now on a good footing; you have played a great and honourable part; you must not rest in this, but you

---

* Prince Starhemberg was entrusted with the Austrian mediation between France and England, which, however, in consequence of Canning's opposition, came to nothing.

must join in the affairs which are coming on. Illusion
on your part would be more than dangerous, it would
be ruinous. The Emperor has two plans in his head : one
rests on real foundations, the other is a romance. The
first is the partition of Turkey, the second an expedition to India. You ought to be in both of them ;
French and Russian soldiers must not appear without
Austrian soldiers at the same time ; and the French, the
Austrians, and the Russians ought to enter Constantinople on the same day. What are your ideas on this
matter ? '

'My ideas are very simple,' said I.   'A great Power
must do all she can to avert the violent changes which are
not happy for anyone, above all in an age when so much
has already been destroyed. She has two means to
make use of—that of open opposition, and that of persuasion. In calculating for open opposition, all the
chances of war must be considered : in that of persuasion, the greater or less hope of success. The
moment when this Power is convinced that both of
these means are vain, she ought to decide to take a
decided part.'

'That is exactly my way of looking at things,' said
M. de Talleyrand ; 'you must take one side, for, do
what you may, you will not arrest the torrent : if you
put yourself in opposition, you will be crushed ; if you
remain passive, you will be reduced to the second rank
of Powers. You know that new revolutions do not
enter into my plans ; but in this respect nothing influences the Emperor, whose character you know. France
and Russia wish to divide Turkey between them ; they
ask nothing more than that you should remain quiet
spectators ; it is Russia especially which desires this,
and the two Powers are united by a calculation simple

enough, but not very honourable; but the shares would be smaller if made for three than if they are made for two.'

'You are going to send a courier to Vienna,' added he, 'and you will have a fine account to give to your court.'

The rest of the conversation ran upon the negotiation with England; M. de Talleyrand showed that the Emperor had made peace on the following conditions:

Both parties to put aside the question of right.

To guarantee to England the possession of Malta and the Cape of Good Hope. Sainte-Lucie and Tabago to be demanded for France.

To guarantee their present possessions to the Kings of Sicily and Sardinia.

To give up Hanover to England, and Pomerania to Sweden.

To give up the Braganzia to Portugal.

The fate of Surinam may be a contested point.

'I am convinced,' said he, 'that, peace once made, the Emperor would with great difficulty take up his arms again; now, nothing will make him lay them down.'

I do not allow myself to decide how far all these statements of M. de Talleyrand are true; and if the finishing stroke does not embellish them somewhat. The *Moniteur* of January 7 and 10 speaks in their favour, and M. de Talleyrand has latterly said to me many times, as well as M. de Tolstoy, that Portugal would not be a point of dispute.

We talked of Prussia. The result which M. de Talleyrand has arrived at is, that Prussia is lost beyond recovery. He maintains that the present moment adds to the ruin; but that the events of the war alone had reduced it to a hopeless condition, and that the finishing touch is being put to it by the fiscal system under which it is placed at this moment. 'You owe it to me,' said he, 'to have concluded the affair of the contributions at Presburg; and the Emperor has often since been angry with me about it; at Tilsit he shut me out of this arrangement, and if the military had meddled with it at Vienna, you would not have finished with it yet.'

I saw M. de Talleyrand again this evening. 'Well,' said he, 'have you thought over our conversation of yesterday? How do things appear to you to-day? Do you agree with me?'

'My principles,' I replied, 'do not change from one day to another, and I am ready to repeat to you all that I said yesterday.' 'Have you sent your courier?' he asked me. 'No; I lose nothing by waiting a day longer; perhaps we shall have news from England, and the company this evening will furnish me with some interesting data.' 'Do you think that at Vienna they agree with your views?' 'You ought to have found out long ago that we look at things rightly,' I replied, 'and we shall take the part suitable to our true interests; but you fall like a bombshell into my house, and I am going, according to all the rights of war, to send you out of it. Do you think that at St. Petersburg they wish to have a share of Turkey?' 'Yes, they thought of it long before we did, because our policy has latterly always been Conservative for the Porte,' replied M. de Talleyrand.

'Where do they desire it most? At Paris or at St. Petersburg?' 'At St. Petersburg, lately, but I believe they are about equal now.'

'Will they apply to us, if we say nothing?' 'No,

for the reasons which I mentioned yesterday.' ' But if we propose ourselves, shall we be accepted?' ' Yes, because they want you very much.'

' Are any bases of partition agreed upon?' ' No, but the first incision has been made, for even France will not succeed in making the Russians evacuate Wallachia and Moldavia.'

' Do you know Turkey well? and have you not a mistaken idea of the means necessary to overcome her?'

' I am afraid of that, and we are, perhaps, more ignorant than any other European Government of the Porte ; you know it better, but you are aware that no such consideration will ever stop the Emperor ; he will make its acquaintance on the spot.'

' Yes, I believe that we are better able to form an opinion on Turkey, because our judgment would be without partiality, and our only wishes would be for its preservation. The Russians look through Greek spectacles, and no spectacles are good in politics. Well! I reply to you, that the conquest of Turkey will cost three hundred thousand men in a few years, from sickness, brigandage, &c., and that in twenty-five or thirty years the country would still show no sign of civilisation, under any rule whatever.' ' I know it, but these considerations will not stop the Emperor.'

' What are your ideas on a possible partition? I see nothing which can tempt you in European Turkey ; I see, on the other hand, a great many things which tempt the Russians, and many others which in case of a partition would be absolute necessities for us !'

' The Morea, the islands adjacent, and Egypt would suit us. You will want the course of the Danube, Bosnia and Bulgaria. If the Russians do not get the

Crimea, Constantinople must be yours; in the present position of affairs, they have the most right to get it.'

' When do you think the execution of this plan will be commenced ? '

' As soon as possible, and therefore you should take your part quickly, for in a few months that may not be permitted which at this moment keeps you in the rank which is yours by right.'

Your Excellency will acknowledge that politics could not be discussed in a more laconic fashion, a vast empire be more easily divided, nor three or four hundred thousand combatants disposed of more quickly. But this is a true representation of negotiations in Paris; and every negotiator who does not go at this pace will in vain produce truth and right principle, he will die on the way for want of breath, without having been able to come up with his adversaries.

I slipped in the remark that the Emperor, our master, was the enemy of all revolutions, and that in this respect his system of policy had been lately misunderstood. 'It is not a question,' said M. de Talleyrand ' of a general *levée* ; part of your army will suffice, and you will have the more means of reorganising the remainder of it.' 'But how could you direct such a combined movement?' 'Can you suppose that the Emperor will give up this business ? He will manage all that from Italy.'

You will doubtless find matter, sir, in the present report to occupy you long and seriously; but it is only by setting aside all that is unimportant, and stating the matters in question precisely, that I can put my court in a position to see things from a positive point of view. Allow me, very shortly, to state my own.

It seems to me probable that the data submitted by M. de Talleyrand are quite in accordance with the views of the Emperor. Everything betokens some great movement, and the Senate was yesterday assembled for a new conscription. M. de Champagny read there a report which is said to have contained passages of great violence against England. The Senators were summoned to this meeting at night.

It seems certain that the great movements which were directed against Spain are no longer pushed forward with the same vigour; the breach with Lucien Bonaparte may have some influence on this object of ambition. The little value that seems to be attached to Portugal shows the great resistance which has been met with; it must now be kept, and consequently defended, but I believe that if the conquest had not been already made, it would not now have been undertaken. Marshal Bessières, who was to have commanded the 4th *corps d'armée*, assembling at Bayonne, makes no preparation for departure.

Turkey will therefore be attacked for want of something better to do, and because the Emperor has long desired to strike a blow at English commerce in those parts. Projects of colonisation and civilisation, great movements in short, are never matters of indifference to Napoleon. Egypt is to him a position which he has taken up, and must defend.

We must sacrifice much for the preservation of the Porte, but our real existence and political credit, the chief elements of the life of a great state, must put limits to our desires. We cannot save Turkey; therefore, we must help in the partition, and endeavour to get as good a share of it as possible. We cannot resist the destructive and invasive principles of the Emperor of the French, and we must therefore turn them away from ourselves.

I do not agree with M. de Talleyrand, with respect to the ambition of the Russians. It doubtless does exist, and is of old standing, but it has been much modified latterly. The Russians would gladly aggrandise themselves at the expense of the Porte, but they fear to divide the cake with persons of such good appetites, and they fear any sort of contact being again established between themselves and France. This fear, which I imagine the Russians possess, ought to lead them to seek us in one of those occasions when every timid and yet ambitious cabinet, like a timid and ambitious individual, must endeavour to procure the support of a friend.

I do not intend to communicate to Count Tolstoy any of the facts contained in this report; we have many times touched on the principles, and it is after these conversations that I think myself able to establish my argument on the desires of Russia. M. de Tolstoy does not seem to attach much importance to the conquest of the Morea by the French; he thinks, and not without cause, that this possession will absorb and consequently neutralise a great part of her strength, without any fruit for her so long as she is at war with England, and that all the arrangements formed by her would soon be overturned whenever new circumstances should occur in France itself.

If M. de Tolstoy should come to me with any overture, I should behave to him as I did to M. de Talleyrand, and we shall never be in so happy a position as when we are requested not to forget our own interests by two Powers friendly in appearance, but rivals in reality. Napoleon always begins by 'acting,' and every delay in taking a side seems to me exceedingly dangerous.

It would be very difficult to suppose that Constantinople would be assigned to the Russians; and it seems to me extremely probable that, of the three allied generals, France would have the most pretension to establish her head-quarters there. M. de Talleyrand, in our conversation of yesterday, said to me: ' It is necessary that we should become allies, and this benefit will be the result of the Treaty of Tilsit: however paradoxical this assertion may appear, nevertheless it entered my head even at Tilsit, but at that time the Emperor was not of this opinion. This treaty,' he continued, ' is only an expedient that they wish to pass off as a system; it puts you in the best of positions, because each of the contracting parties needs your services to watch the other; and if you take a prudent course, suitable to the spirit of the times, which neither you nor anyone else can change, you will come out of the combat, as a last result, more glorious than any other Power.'

Metternich to Stadion, Paris, January 26, 1808.

104. The Mayence courier having brought me the despatches from your Excellency on the 21st, I asked the same day for a private audience of the Emperor to deliver the letter announcing the marriage of our august master. His Majesty fixed an hour the next day, and I enclose the details of my long conversation with him (No. 105). This account includes three distinct points of view: that of the English negotiations; the question relating to the Porte, the prelude to which I have sketched in one of my last reports (No. 103); and the general relations of the two courts.

Your Excellency will see, from the first, that the

Emperor starts from the point that the present English ministry does not wish for peace. He repeated to me several times in the course of our conversation that peace could not be made till there was a change of ministry.

The Emperor made me plunge at once into the discussion on the fate of the Ottoman Porte ; and although I had seen a decidedly official tinge in the two conversations that I had had concerning this interesting subject with M. de Talleyrand (No. 103), I was not authorised to believe it would be approached so directly. . . . .

Our long discussion on the ministers of the Five Powers was conducted by the Emperor with extreme moderation in the expression and application of principles. I made my replies as candid as possible ; and I have since learned that Napoleon was quite satisfied with my explanations, and, on the whole, with all our conversation. . . . .

METTERNICH'S NOTES OF A CONVERSATION WITH NAPOLEON.

105. In handing his Majesty the letter announcing the marriage of our august master,* I added to the customary compliments that His Majesty should consider as a very good omen the formation of a tie made to ensure internal happiness at a moment when the friendly and satisfactory relations with France assured the external repose of the monarchy. The Emperor spoke much of the high opinion he had of the rare qualities of our new Empress. 'The Emperor Francis,' added he, 'has been very wise to marry again ; his simple tastes and habits, concentrated as they are in the happiness of those about him, cannot dispense with the domestic life offered by marriage. Besides the personal advantages of the choice he has made, it possesses that of not bringing the chance of foreign intrigues into his court ; internal intrigues are always less inconvenient and less dangerous. He told me that he had the honour of knowing the Archduchess (*mère*), and that to give his opinion about her would be only to repeat what the public voice has always proclaimed of the qualities of this august Princess. I also assured his Majesty that in no court and in no country is there less intrigue either foreign or domestic than in ours.

From this question the Emperor passed to the English negotiations. 'They do not desire peace,' he said ;

* With the Grand-Duchess Maria Ludovica von Este.

'if they had wished it, they would long ago have taken quite a different route to reach me.'

'The English are very cunning when they really desire to gain some object—in this respect I admire Lord Whitworth, who by the most secret paths, by the smallest and most unlikely openings, knows how to get at me. They have so many means of communicating with me that assuredly, when they do desire peace, they will let me know it without disputing over trifles. They know very well that I desire peace, and that is another reason for believing that in this last negotiation they have never really thought of treating. They are most foolish, for they will oblige me to show them that I have very powerful means to disturb even their internal affairs. What must they needs do? Assert in principle, and lay down as a first condition, the return of my armies into France. I have eight hundred thousand men—everyone knows enough of his own private affairs to know how much expense he can bear—I know that I cannot support such a number of troops, therefore I must disarm them; three years would be required to reorganise them; meantime I should place much of my capital in the navy, I should construct and prepare ships.' 'It seems,' said I, 'from my last accounts from England, that the ministry fears peace because it offers less favourable chances than war, affairs being as they are now.'

'They are wrong,' replied the Emperor. 'The chances of having for a long period nothing to fear from a French navy are certain; but the English have never known how to make a political calculation. They are always preoccupied by the question of the Pays-Bas, and will not believe that on the Continent nobody thinks of that any longer. If I were an English minister, I would make peace. I should for three or four years distribute many millions in Austria to bring up your finances, for without money there is no energy, and courage will return with prosperity. I should also give much money to the Prussians, to raise them in the same manner; and of course all this should be done in such a way that I should suspect nothing. At the end of the time they would be able to engage in a reasonable contest: reasonable it is not for them at present, for it cannot but terminate unfavourably for England.' 'To give money,' said I, ' its acceptance must be provided for, and at this moment I see but one common cause on the Continent, and I beg your Majesty to believe we really regard it as such; we have, besides, given undeniable proofs of it.' 'You know,' replied the Emperor, ' that I have no reason but to praise the course you have followed since the Peace of Presburg; in the last war you maintained the strictest neutrality; when you had no stores and refused them to me, you also refused them to the Russians; you made armaments, but you did not carry them to a point dangerous for me. If you would have made common cause with me, I should have been under very great obligations to you, and I should have been in a position to bestow on you great marks of gratitude. You would not do this, and I cannot complain; but my gratitude cannot be the same. I sent for General Stutterheim at once, when you sent him to Tilsit. The Emperor of Russia refused to see him, which was another reason for me to receive him and show my satisfaction at your thorough neutrality.'

On this I repeated to him all that on former occasions I had said to Champagny and Talleyrand.

He passed on to English affairs, and I now come to the interesting part of our conversation.

'How is it that the question of Constantinople does not enter into the ideas of the English Ministers?' asked the Emperor.

'Probably,' said I, 'because they do not think the existence of the Porte can be threatened by your Majesty, who of all the allies of the Porte have always the most loudly declared for its preservation! and after us perhaps no Power has so direct an interest in supporting her as France.'

'Our interest is more decided than yours,' replied the Emperor. 'You can only desire the preservation of the Porte since it has fallen into its present state of weakness; formerly you were and you ought to be rivals, but at no time in history have questions arisen in this way between France and Turkey. Imperative circumstances alone can force me to strike a blow at this Power, which I ought to sustain by every means. The English constrain me in spite of myself, and I must seek them where I can find them. I have no need of anything. I want no aggrandisement. Egypt and some colonies would be advantageous to me, but this advantage cannot equal the prodigious aggrandisement of Russia. You cannot see this aggrandisement either with indifference, and I see that what ought really to unite us very closely is the partition of Turkey. The day when the Russians,' he took himself up here, and recalling the word Russians substituted the phrase: 'When they are established at Constantinople, you will need France to help you against the Russians, and France will need you to counterbalance them. It is not yet a question of partition, but when it is a question of it I shall tell you, and you will have to join in it. Whatever may be the part which falls to you, you will have a very strong interest in having a hand in the affair, and you must have it. You have just and geographical claims on the course of the Danube.'

I replied to the Emperor that it was with real surprise that I found the question mooted of the destruction of an Empire in the preservation of which we were both so greatly interested. That, on the one hand, I could not but share his opinion on the results which would necessarily follow the fall of the Ottoman Empire. That if France herself abandoned that old ally, we doubtless should not have strength to sustain her alone; if it must fall to pieces, I added, in the nature of things we cannot be indifferent either to the choice of acquisitions made by the dividing Powers, or on the share which should come to us. 'Your Majesty sees,' I said, 'that I speak with the greatest candour. I can do so all the more because your Majesty must know that on a question so new, so unforeseen, I cannot have the least instruction from my court, and that all that I say to your Majesty can only be the result of the first effect produced on myself. Therefore I rest only on the following general statements :—That in Europe three Powers only exist; that these Powers have a mutual interest to take care of; that we, being placed between Russia and France, have a much more direct interest in being well with France, because she can do us more harm than Russia ; that France will always find it best to depend on our principles rather than on those of the court of St. Petersburg; that in the great questions which arise between France and that Power we cannot but be always very directly interested ; that, in fact, if a neighbouring Empire must fall, it is worthy of a great Power to sustain it, or at least to interfere in the questions which must arise from every revolution of that kind.'

'You are perfectly right,' said the Emperor, and he went off into declamations against the Russians, against their want of civilisation and of stability in their views and principles. He went over this question thoroughly with a full knowledge of the cause, and if he bases his plans on the co-operation of Russia, he will certainly not give up the conduct of them.

He came back to our affairs. 'There are many little questions,' said he, 'but they are nothing ; and, as I have just assured you, I have no matter of complaint against you since the Peace of Presburg ; if there are some little pin-pricks, we return pin-pricks.'

'Your Majesty doubtless refers to Count de Merveldt,' said I. 'I see that your Majesty thinks there is something there to complain of ; but if some slight mistakes may have been committed by him, they as little contradict the intentions of our court as they do the fine qualities which justify his master's choice. Besides, your Majesty must be aware that the Emperor had no intention of leaving him long at St. Petersburg.'

'I know all,' replied the Emperor. 'General Merveldt and M. Savary have had some conversations quite out of place on both sides ; Madame de Merveldt even was complained of.' Here he told me, with full details, the history of a dinner, and asserted that she gave her hand to the English Minister, refusing it to M. Savary, adding, 'If he had not been an Englishman it would not have been so much noticed ; perhaps, too, Savary came forward too quickly, but as my aide-de-camp he thought he was authorised to do so. However, that is nothing, and only proves what I am quite convinced of, that soldiers are of no use for diplomatic missions. You, too, have a man amongst you who is of no more use ; General Andréossy, like all his comrades, does not start from the one point of view worthy of a diplomatist, that of considering themselves simply as agents of peace, and woe to the ambassador who does not sacrifice everything to preserve peace, or who has to reproach himself with the contrary.' 'Since your Majesty,' said I, 'has alluded to General Andréossy, I will confess that I quite agree that soldiers are hardly ever suitable for diplomatic appointments; they think they fail in their duty whenever they work against what forms the true field for their activity; if they do not avow this principle, it secretly influences their actions and manners. General Andréossy gives daily proof of this fact.' The Emperor, whilst saying that military reports are bad, exaggerated, and bitter, recurred several times to the animosity existing in society at Vienna; and to his wish that the Emperor and his Minister should some day express their disapprobation of the feeling against France. He repeated himself over and over again for ten minutes on the influence which the sovereign exercises on the opinion of society. I showed him that there is a great difference between perfect civility and expressions of affection; that the Viennese public never failed in the first—the Government would not allow them to do so; 'as to love,' I added, 'history affords no example of a people not preserving some feeling of resentment against another with whom they have long been fighting, and it is very natural that those who have been beaten should have the most of this feeling; be friends for some time, and you will see even these slight traces of it disappear.'

'We are so,' returned the Emperor, 'and that in spite of what your society may think. At Vienna it was not believed that I should give up Braunau, after I had signed the treaty; I never break my word. Then

I think it is very natural that many of your nobles should feel some bitterness; when, like the Fürstenbergs, for instance, they have been sovereign princes, it must be hard, I allow, to belong to others less important than yourself; but this is the force of circumstances, against which it is ridiculous to fight. A word from the Emperor or a word from Stadion, spoken with energy, would put an end to all that. Andréossy is of no use, but I think there is some personal animosity between him and Stadion.'

'So little on the part of Stadion,' I replied, 'that on every opportunity he gives a real proof of abnegation in not showing to your Majesty's ambassador that he does not follow the line that we desire to see him take; let him observe and write, but let him observe justly and write truly—let him write history, in fact, and not romance, and General Andréossy will please Vienna better and be better pleased himself.'

The Emperor repeated himself on the impossibility of the Generals not being acrimonious in their relations. 'You see,' said he, 'there is General Tolstoy, a very brave and loyal man, whom I cannot but praise, and who serves his court well; but he too has had some conversations with the military men, which have ended by making some bitterness, and which are much out of place from people who have been beaten. You have succeeded here with me and with the public, because you do not talk, and people cannot quote any sayings of yours. Think all you like—thoughts are free, and no one has any right to interfere with them; but talk never advances anything.' 'Well, Sire,' I interrupted, 'order your ambassador at Vienna to act as I do, and we shall both be the better in consequence.' The Emperor spoke to me again of Count de Merveldt;

he assured me he had been much inclined to wish him well. 'I knew him very well at Montebello and Campoformio,' said he; 'he is clever, and we have always treated him well; if it had been wished to send him here, I should have accepted him with pleasure, but the misfortune common to most military men has ruined him.' 'General de Vincent,' said I to the Emperor, 'has, however, furnished a striking exception to this rule.' 'Yes, but they are very rare,' replied the Emperor. By this very preaching against the thing he proved to me that, though a sovereign, he still retained a strong dash of the military spirit which he condemned.

He spoke again of the war against the Prussians, the disorganisation of that state, the weakness of its ministry, and the duplicity of Haugwitz, who had offered to him twenty times, and amongst others at Brünn, the partition of Austria, and of this he authorised me to ask M. de Champagny to show me the proofs.

He had kept his luncheon and his attendants waiting for nearly two hours; we had walked up and down his room fifty times, when at last he said, 'I have nothing more to add, let us recapitulate our conversation.

'You will acquaint your court that since the Peace of Presburg not only have I had nothing to complain of in her conduct, but I have much cause to praise the strict neutrality which she has observed latterly; that there is at present no question of the division of Turkey, but that whenever there is you will not only be allowed, but called as by right to defend and discuss with us your interests and your views.'

I said to the Emperor that I would do as he wished, and left him.

Metternich to Stadion, Paris, February 26, 1808.

106. Your Excellency's despatches contain the most complete and precise instructions it was possible to give me on questions of immense importance. They show that I have had the happiness of proceeding in a manner which his Imperial Majesty thinks according to his interests.

The next day after the arrival of the courier I went to M. de Talleyrand and told him that this courier had brought a reply to my despatch containing the details of our first conversations. 'The answer is what I expected and wished,' said I. 'I am bidden to speak to you frankly, to tell you that nothing would pain the Emperor so much, or be so contrary to his principles, and his conviction of the true interests of his empire, as the destruction of the Porte. I am desired to bring forward all the good reasons which ought to prevent this desire, even on the part of France. They will support the Porte as long as possible; they will join in the partition only when it is impossible to arrest it, on the express condition, however, of the most perfect agreement between the three Powers.' 'The question seems to me rather remote. You have put yourself in the best position, and you will not find anyone more interested in your cause than I am. I hate the idea of the partition of the Porte. To tell you the truth, it is opposed to my political principles; but nothing can hold the Emperor back. Stand by this truth, consider it certain, and let your court look at it in the same light as I do. If I were Emperor of Austria I would say as Frederick II. did to the King of France, "Not a shot shall be fired in Europe without my permission." Then you would assert yourselves, then you would come out victorious from the combat in which so many others have fallen. When your courier left were the particulars known of your conversation with the Emperor?' (No. 105). 'No,' I replied, 'but those particulars will only strengthen the opinion of the Emperor Francis, which I have announced to you; they will prove to him, what you can now confirm, that the enterprises themselves are adjourned.' 'Do not say adjourned,' interrupted M. de Talleyrand, 'I said "only less imminent."' 'But do you believe that Russia shares Napoleon's views?' I asked. 'Heartily,' said he; 'the conquest of Turkey is one of the favourite ideas of the Emperor Alexander. He connects it with the glory of his reign, the pledge of his personal security. He has so expressed himself in many conversations with me.'

I asked M. de Talleyrand's advice, which seemed to me most essential, as to my conduct with regard to M. de Champagny. I informed him that my court had seen with pleasure that, up to the present time, I had treated the questions only in an unofficial manner; but he could not but see the false light in which I should be placed with the Minister for Foreign Affairs since my conversation with the Emperor, if he should have informed M. de Champagny of the particulars of our conversation. 'I have no doubt some excuse,' I added, 'for not hastening to mention a subject which is odious to us, but he must not think that I discussed the question unknown to him.' M. de Talleyrand assured me, not only that he was not aware that the Emperor had spoken of it to M. de Champagny, but he had reason to suppose that the secret was restricted to the sovereign, Talleyrand, and myself. I then agreed with him that I would wait till M. de Champagny spoke to me of himself, and that M. de Talleyrand should report to his master the details of that day's conversation.

You now see how things are at this moment in France. I avoid as much as possible showing either eagerness or anxiety. I take the attitude of an attentive listener, not putting myself forward to answer, and my part is taken from reasons so strong that it will depend on myself alone to make the most of my rights, and use them whenever I feel that the moment is come. These particulars correspond entirely with the wish expressed by your Excellency in the despatch of Feb. 8, 'only to use the data formerly given according to circumstances.' Accustomed strictly to follow the orders of my court whenever my part becomes an active one, I shall keep my full instructions to myself at present, when circumstances absolutely require perfect calm.

Two very important questions arise from all the data which I have given to his Imperial Majesty with regard to the great enterprise first announced to me by M. de Talleyrand, and since confirmed by Napoleon himself.

Does Russia agree with France on the general principle of the partition of Turkey?

Will France make use of our assent to make Russia enter into her projects?

M. de Talleyrand maintained the first of these statements, at least, as to the desire of Russia.

M. de Tolstoy positively denies the statement as to any actual stipulations. This does not, however, amount to a direct contradiction.

Since my conversation with the Emperor I take the second point of view—namely, that France wishes to make use of our consent to make Russia join in the projects of partition, which we dread. I see no fear of complication but in this supposition ; this, therefore, we must not lose sight of; it is of a kind extremely likely to be made use of by French policy ; they may, supposing that the cabinet of St. Petersburg is averse to the partition, represent us as having been the first to moot this question, and the only persons who desire it. We must therefore counteract this manœuvre, without committing ourselves in case it does not exist, the means to which end are ready to my hand.

I have already had the honour to acquaint your Excellency that I had, after the first overtures of M. de Talleyrand, mentioned to M. de Tolstoy the possibility of the destruction of the Porte, as a political dream of mine. I said to him that, after my conversation with the Emperor, this dream had acquired a certain degree of strength from a word of Napoleon's with regard to the necessity of dealing some blows at England, whenever the opportunity occurred, and that even the word Constantinople had fallen from him. He showed much curiosity as to the details which accompanied this expression. I did not tell him anything more, but confined myself to saying one day, ' Woe to you, if you do not find that word grave enough to excite all your attention and ours.' I tried to discover whether a similar string had not been touched with him ; this question made in twenty different ways brought me nothing but answers similar to the first made to me by M. de Tolstoy—' No ! and if they spoke to me of the partition of Turkey I should reply : Begin by carrying out the Treaty of Tilsit, and we will discuss the other question afterwards.' ' But,' asked I, ' shall you refuse when they insist, and will you make war to defend the Porte against French attacks ? '

The Ambassador declared that if the cake could not

be saved it must be fairly divided. It then occurred to him that, as they begin to know his sentiments here, perhaps M. de Caulaincourt was intended to make the direct overtures to St. Petersburg.

I took the opportunity of the arrival of a courier to tell Count Tolstoy, that being accustomed to ask instructions from my court long in advance, I had now received some with regard to my political dream, which was no longer a dream, since the word Constantinople had been pronounced. 'Well,' I said to him, 'these instructions are just what I had expected, and they will increase your confidence in my power of judging both my master and his minister. They will prevent it as long as they reasonably can ; they will act when they must act ; but what pleases me especially is the order to come to an understanding with you and to assure you that we look at this matter as one of common interest. This is what I shall say here whenever they tell me anything more precise, and this is what I authorise you to communicate to your court.' He made me promise to keep him thoroughly informed of all that is said here on the subject.

This is how matters stand with M. de Tolstoy. A courier, whom he had to send a few days after our conversation, carried the account of our conversation to St. Petersburg. The ambassador cannot have communicated anything but what I have just had the honour to state to your Excellency, and we may expect an answer from the Russian cabinet with respect to the communication, so decided as to its principle, but so vague in regard to its execution, of the overtures of France as to the fate of the Porte. It is now the part of his Majesty's ambassador at St. Petersburg to influence the answer M. de Tolstoy is ordered to give me.

Our position, then, seems quite what we could wish. This is generally the case with questions which are simply and frankly handled. You mention three, sir, in your despatch of February 1, which undoubtedly are of the highest interest :—

1st. Whether France has already made overtures to Russia similar to those which I have mentioned?

2nd. How they have been received, and from what point of view they are considered?

3rd. How far have the explanations between the two courts gone with regard to the plans of operation and of partition?

I have replied as far as I could to the two first in the present despatch. A great system of abandonment to the views of France springs directly from the Treaty of Tilsit; but I do not believe that the destruction of the Porte was stipulated there. Your Excellency will be convinced that I have every reason to suppose that this affair has not passed through the hands of M. de Tolstoy, and that it never will do so.

The answer must therefore return some day from St. Petersburg, if M. de Caulaincourt treats of it; and from this point of view it may perhaps be possible for our ambassador to furnish us with very interesting matter.

Supposing that the affair should be mooted in Russia, I see no reason to suppose that the military plans would be stopped. M. de Tolstoy assures me that they urge his court very much to an operation against the Swedes. It does not appear that his court wishes much to take it up, and if it does so, it will be as a pretext for reinforcing the army as much as possible. All my conversations with the ambassador, which I have twenty times turned on plans of operations against the Turks (if this scourge is unhappily forced upon us) prove that he entirely ignores the views of France and her plans of operation with respect to the East.

In these conversations the subject of the Servians was several times touched upon. Count Tolstoy has never denied the conditions under which he did not hesitate to sign a peace with the Turks—namely, the independence of Wallachia and Moldavia under the protection of the last treaty, and that of Servia under the protection and guarantee of Russia and Austria. One of the phrases which I see in the last despatches of Count de Merveldt shows me that the ambassador really ought to have his powers extended, so as to be able to advance or retard the peace negotiations. M. de Romanzow, at the beginning of January, seemed to be convinced that the negotiations were entered upon here. M. de Tolstoy has always refused the wish, which the ambassador several times expressed, that he should open the conferences ; he endeavours to show the court here France's want of faith towards Prussia. The little zeal shown by the cabinet of the Tuileries in the course of its mediation proves decidedly that it aims at the destruction of the Porte ; it never keeps a question open but with the intention of destroying the subject of it.

I believe it is urgent that, in the plan of operations, the clause should be expressed that it can only be executed by the three Imperial courts, with complete exclusion of the troops of the Confederation. Russia would have an interest equal to ours in getting rid of the active co-operation of small sovereigns, greedy of acquisitions and compensation for the expense of the war, which, in consequence of the present state of Germany and Prussia, could only be taken from Austria or Russia, cessions that your Excellency regards with reason as absolutely inadmissible under the point of view of ' no aggrandisements of any kind.'

The most frank and simple explanations on all these objects with respect to the two Imperial courts appear to me as agreeable to the true interest of the cause as natural in an occurrence where we only desire the preservation of a third Power; and where our co-operation in a sense opposed to our principles, far from being sought by us, will only be the result of the necessity in which every great Power finds itself of joining in what it cannot hinder without endangering its existence.

ON THE NECESSITY OF AN AUSTRO-RUSSIAN ALLIANCE.

(Note 31, Vol. I.).

107. Metternich to Stadion, Paris, April 27, 1808.

107. The catastrophes which overthrew the throne of Spain are assuredly made to fill the measure of the crafty, destructive, and criminal policy of Napoleon; a policy which he has never ceased to follow since his accession. Let us be thoroughly persuaded of this truth, let us get rid of all illusion, and we shall gain that strength which comes only in great crises. The overthrow of Spain is not, so far as regards principle, more than the reunion of Liguria, the present organisation of Holland, the hundred and one destructions that we have seen, and at which all the Powers of Europe have looked on with more or less good will, with more or less calmness. The shock of a great throne's fall is terrible; it resounds afar, and yet principle is not more violated than it is by the march of the squadron that tears an unhappy Bourbon from his asylum to shoot him at Vincennes.

The sceptre of Charles IV. has not been his for several years. He, the weak and feeble heir to the heritage of his fathers, and his unfortunate successor, are now summoned before a new and monstrous tribunal. A King who dare not abdicate in favour of his legitimate successor, and a son who dare not reign, except by the authority of a French ambassador, in reality reigns no longer. Your Excellency will see from the frightful article that I have marked in the semi-official Journal of April 24, that this tribunal does exist; Spain then has no longer a sovereign; the arbiter of the *Grand Empire* has in fact declared himself its master. He has long shown that he is master of all Europe on this side the Inn and the Vistula.

In 1805 and 1806 I cherished the dream of opposing to this Colossus a barrier marked out by the Weser, the Thuringian forests, and the western frontiers of the Austrian monarchy. Prussia has rejected the plans, which would save herself and her neighbours; she must necessarily be the victim of her selfish calculations, and not only Prussia, but all Powers who follow the same course, will be so.

This line, the only one which would cover our right flank, and relieve us from all anxiety in our rear, and which—since the Peace of Presburg and the loss of Venice (the principal and most precious of all the acquisitions that Austria can make), above all since the cession of Dalmatia—only leaves our left flank to be protected, can no longer be maintained. Prussia is effaced from the list of Powers; Turkey, whose weakness is even a benefit to us, is an immediate point of contact with France; we shall save her from total destruction by our geographical position alone. She cannot be attacked but by passing through us. To remain constant to old ideas, to old and impracticable plans, would be destruction; to have no plan would be ruin.

Austria and Prussia are intact; Turkey vegetates, but it exists. Spain will no doubt change masters, her fall will not alter our position; it adds nothing to the power of France.   Napoleon will return to his capital neither more strong nor less troubled than when he left it.   To hope that any time will be allowed to pass without movement on his part would be a mere illusion; to follow implicitly all his wishes would be to carry out his projects for destruction; to oppose him face to face would be to expose ourselves to be crushed under his weight; we can then only aim at modifying his plans.   We must enter into them to have the right to do this; we must have a firm and fixed plan to make this possible.   To this all my political calculations tend, and it seems to me that it is to this end we ought to direct all our efforts.

We should be very wrong to despise what is going on in Spain, but I freely confess that the fall of that throne is not a surprise to me; my despatches testify that I have long believed in the possibility of this catastrophe.   Napoleon only lifts the veil a little more—it is transparent enough—which covers his general intentions; he himself thinks he has done nothing extraordinary or new since his return from the Pyrenees.   Everything which is on this side the line of the Confederation seems to him so entirely under his good pleasure that the changes he has made in Spain seem to him hardly greater than the nomination of his brother-in-law to the government of Piedmont.   But as it is impossible that he should not look beyond the confines of what he calls his Empire, we shall no doubt be exposed to great complications in a short time.   We have still the power of looking forward, of determining our wishes and our course; we shall not have the time or the possibility of doing so when direct questions are put to us.   I am happy to feel convinced that our august master wisely occupies himself in determining the foundations of his future conduct. May he graciously permit me to touch upon some of the most threatening questions!

There remain three Powers which may furnish battle-fields to the man who cannot be satisfied without them —Austria, Russia, and Turkey. An alliance, however monstrous it may be, guarantees Russia for the time from a direct attack. Nothing points to any hostile views of Napoleon against Austria; all the measures he has taken for some time aim at the destruction of the Porte. It can only be saved by the firm will and close agreement of the cabinets of Vienna and St. Petersburg, by immediate peace with Russia, and by a successful war of these two Imperial courts against France. It will not suffice, for Turkey to avoid the blows which Napoleon is preparing, that we should stand on one side; our inaction would not save her, and it would ruin us.

All the Powers — I except England, who, having committed the mistake of signing the Peace of Amiens, did not make another by not preparing at once for a new war—have lost by attaching to the treaties they concluded with France the importance of a peace. Peace does not exist with a revolutionary system, and whether Robespierre declares eternal war against the *Châteaux*, or Napoleon makes it against the Powers, the tyranny is the same, and the danger is only more general. To believe that we can continue beyond a certain time quiet spectators of the changes present and to come in Europe, and to found this hope on the promises of France, would be strangely to deceive ourselves. If France invites us to rest, it should only be another motive to prevent us from confounding this offer with a state of calm and quiet, which must be renounced so long as Napoleon lives.

Turkey is threatened; she will fall, because this man has never threatened in vain, and because I see nowhere the necessary means of saving it. Therefore all the anxieties with which the complications resulting from this overthrow can inspire us, far from paralysing us, should stimulate our faculties. Shall we refuse to act in concert? they will act without us. Shall we refuse a passage to the French troops through our territory? we must then be ready to fight to stop them, or see them effect the passage against our will. It remains to discover whether our refusal would not suit Napoleon better than our consent.

Nothing assuredly can be more dangerous than to admit French troops into our territory; the recent example of Spain proves this sufficiently.

Your Excellency knows that I have always held that the salvation of Austria and Russia depends on their perfect agreement on all questions of common interest. Let us suppose that it is possible to establish this agreement, the order of things should be, that these two Powers should use all their efforts to dissuade Napoleon from the destructive projects against the Porte, but that they should end by taking common part in it, in case their efforts should be fruitless. It will then be a question of diplomatic and, above all, military measures, to guard the two Empires against the enterprises which the French may attempt beyond the lines which their troops must traverse. At that moment the Austrian and Prussian armies which are not destined to act in Turkey (and there would remain great masses) should be regarded as one and the same army, and take military positions strong enough to allow them to close the way behind the French armies. Supposing, on the contrary, that the cabinet of St. Petersburg continues to follow as imprudently as it does the impulsion it receives from France; that it even exaggerates it, as it has not ceased to do—in that supposition it becomes only more urgent to take an active part in projects impossible even to modify, if we do not enter into them immediately. If France and Russia agree to the destruction of Turkey, and ask of us a passage for the French troops, shall we refuse it? I suppose that we might refuse it, and that the interests the two allies would have in our not troubling their plans, or hindering their execution, would prevent them from insisting on this demand; but how should we oppose the return of the French army after having conquered Turkey?

Your Excellency sees that I here maintain the possibility that the French armies might arrive at Constantinople only by way of Albania and Ukrania. I do not know whether this possibility exists, but it hardly seems probable that, even in that case, Napoleon would long make the troops respect the neutrality of Galicia by taking them along the frontier.

I resume this long and doubtless too minute reasoning. It appears to me certain—

1st. That it is impossible to regard a state of peace with France as a state of repose.

2nd. That the return of Napoleon after his expedition to Spain will be the signal for fresh movements.

3rd. That the Western part of Europe being conquered, and having submitted to changes of dynasty and government which Napoleon has long meditated, he can only direct his activity towards the East.

4th. That everything indicates that the partition of Turkey is the first object to which it tends.

5th. That an alliance, offensive and defensive, between Russia and Austria, having for its object a successful war against France, alone can arrest Napoleon in his projects.

6th. That this alliance, considering the moral and physical dispositions of the two Empires, not being possible, it is essential to think of an agreement likely to guarantee their mutual existence.

7th. That if we cannot arrive at an agreement with Russia, by persuasion, to stop the destructive plans of Napoleon against the Porte, it would be necessary to take an active part in them; that even if Turkey could be protected from the danger which threatens it, it would be no less necessary to concert measures for opposing the restless activity of that prince.

8th. That if Napoleon does not renounce this attack, which he could scarcely undertake without us, it would be necessary to take diplomatic and military measures to prevent him from departing from the line of conduct agreed upon.

I should look upon this last enterprise as entirely chimerical, if the conquest of Turkey presented as few difficulties as that of Portugal, and if we were as isolated and as weak as Spain; if we had the *élite* of our army in the Baltic, a sovereign such as Charles IV., and ministers such as the Prince de la Paix. But it is in these important matters that the difference of our position from that of Spain consists. Our dangers are great—they are imminent; the fall of the last throne of the Bourbons does not augment them; it will have been an immense benefit if it arouses generally a feeling of indignation, and with us in particular the conviction that peace with Napoleon is not peace, and that we can only save ourselves by the wisest activity, and by the constant employment of our powerful resources.

FIRST SIGNS OF NAPOLEON'S WARLIKE VIEWS AGAINST AUSTRIA.

(Note 26, Vol. I.)

108. Metternich to Stadion, Paris, June 23, 1808.
109. Metternich to Stadion, Paris, July 1, 1808.

108. Your Excellency sends me reports from our military commanders which render it necessary to keep a watch on the movements of the French army. The remarks of these officers agree with the rumours heard throughout Europe; an imposing force is placed on one of our frontiers, furnished with everything necessary to enable it to cross it. At Paris and in Germany nothing is heard of but the approaching war with Austria; motives often the most ridiculous are alleged for this war. They are sometimes our pretended armaments; sometimes the petitions which they have made to us for the good of the Church and its visible head; sometimes a guarantee that they have demanded our neutrality in case of a rupture between France and Russia. Others say that the Emperor of the French will not any longer endure our Imperial title; that we wish to make war on the Turks and divide the spoil with Russia, or rather that we intend to conclude with the Porte a treaty against France. I make here a short *résumé* of the rumours which are circulated, giving a list of specimens; each day destroys those of the evening before, but only contradicts the motives of the war; the rumour of war continues, and nothing contradicts that rumour.

An immense responsibility would rest on the head of the man who should take upon himself to assert the pacific intentions of Napoleon. Your Excellency knows my way of thinking entirely. His Imperial Majesty has often deigned to appreciate my opinion; there is certainly in me no partiality for a man whom, I believe, I long ago judged more truly than many of his contemporaries. The great confidence of our august master, and that of your Excellency, authorise me to supply as soon as possible, by a reasoning which I have based upon facts, what is lacking in positive data on the great question. Does Napoleon wish to make war with us at the present time or not? Every sign answers in the affirmative. Our situation is different from what it was before the end of the last war with Prussia; we no longer go through the intermediate steps which formerly were necessary to precede the opening of a campaign. Napoleon has no preparations to make; he has two hundred thousand men in front of us, on our two flanks, and at our rear. He has not to pass the Rhine with the new troops to fall on us: he can enter Galicia before we know at Vienna that he has made war upon us; he might invade a great part of the Austrian kingdom, and the event would make no more sensation or noise than five or six years ago the arrival of a French squadron in the Margraviate of Baden would have done. Such is the situation of Europe—such is ours in particular.

We cannot, therefore, any longer stop at possibilities; we must simply calculate probabilities. Napoleon meditates our destruction; he meditates it because our existence is incompatible, as to principles, and as to the extent of our territory, with a universal supremacy, to which at this moment three Powers are opposed, Russia, Austria, and Spain on the part of the Bourbons. The two first up to the present time are but inert masses : the latter will succumb under the weight of the French power. Will Napoleon make war against Austria before having subdued Spain sufficiently to be able to abandon the King he has just proclaimed to his own forces? Will he make war on us without being certain of the side Russia would take on this occasion ? It seems to me that these are the two points to which all our calculations should be directed.

The different reports which I have added to my preceding despatch must have proved to your Excellency that the submission of the Peninsula will cost great efforts. It seems that the almost general rising was not foreseen by Napoleon ; we have never before seen him enter on a campaign without strong reserves : on this occasion he had none. We do not flatter ourselves that the devotion of the Spanish nation will prevent its fall ; it will succumb as all isolated efforts must ; but at any rate it will make a vigorous resistance : it seems susceptible of organisation and to necessitate strong measures ; besides, the season is advancing.

If Napoleon thinks his presence necessary for the subjugation of a people in revolt, there is all the more reason we should do him the justice to believe that he would not trust the management of an enterprise such as the annihilation of the Austrian monarchy to any other than himself. The affairs of Spain will not exempt us, except by some extraordinary chance, from fighting for our very existence. But I do not believe that Napoleon will try this adventure before having finished with the other, thus exposing himself to the probable miscarriage of a plan so long conceived, and with the success of which the fate of one of his brothers and the sort of prestige which up to this time has accompanied all his enterprises are intimately connected. Nothing offers less foundation for the calculation of probabilities than an insurrection; it may be prolonged indefinitely, it may cease to-day or to-morrow; but we are in the middle of the year, and I do not think this is quite the time he would choose by preference for the opening of a campaign which, although directed towards the South, may bring complications in the North.

Your Excellency has observed very judiciously the danger there would be in agitating officially questions which up to the present time have not been touched upon. This reflection would have always prevented my doing so, except by express command, even if the Emperor were in Paris. It nevertheless appeared to me very important to take a step which, without committing us, may help to clear up a few questions. I have after mature deliberation decided on the following, which, being very frank and loyal, must necessarily confuse the adverse party, a position always favourable to the cause one pleads.

Reports are circulated which succeed each other with a rapidity which prove direct machination. Whether Napoleon spreads them or tolerates them, the inference that we draw from the fact and the results are the same: he knows these reports. I went to the Minister of Police. I said to him that for a long time I had been tempted to speak to him of these things, but that I always despised common reports too much to be able to make up my mind. 'The case is changed now,' continued I. 'I receive news from Vienna which proves to me that these same reports are spread there; my letters from Germany contain the same; and there is

such similarity in the accounts, which contain too much
nonsense to have been invented in perfect agreement
in the four corners of Europe, that I cannot but see
them to be the result of machinations. I do not enquire
the source—that is nothing; but it is necessary that
you come to my help to combat these reports. The
pacific intentions of my court are known; personally
you know my way of thinking; it is not necessary
to prove to you that we do not dream of war—no one
even asserts it—but to reassure the Austrian, French,
and German public on your intentions with regard to
us. These are times when one cannot be silent without becoming an accomplice with those who speak;
for some time I have had no complaint to make against
your journals, but now give me an opportunity of praising them. Have an article inserted which will prove
to all readers that our relations are perfect; contradict
distinctly the intentions they attribute to you, and
which you allow them to attribute to you. On every
occasion here I pronounce myself a minister of peace;
furnish me with a good weapon to justify to my court
the opinion I have always declared of the sincerity of
the Emperor's intentions with regard to us.'

'I know all these tales,' said Fouché. 'I am
ignorant of their origin; but my reports to the Emperor have always been to the effect that you would
lose no opportunity of contradicting them and declaring
them to be completely false. You understand that I
cannot approach the political question. Does the Emperor wish to make war upon you, or not? He does
not tell me, and I have no right to ask him; if you wish
to know my private opinion, I will tell you that I believe
he neither wishes nor would do it. To-morrow I will
cause an article to be inserted in a journal in the sense

you desire; you understand that I cannot say all I
would wish, but I will tell the truth.   I detest rumours
of that kind.   Does the Emperor spread them?   He
allows them, there is no doubt, for he can stop them in
a moment.   Does he wish to occupy the nation, to dis-
tract its attention from a point which has not gained its
assent?   Does he wish to impose upon you?   Is he afraid
that you will seize this opportunity to declare war
against him?   Does he believe that you will not recognise the changes he is effecting in Spain, in consequence
of your rights over that crown?   I know not, but I am
too anxious for peace not to seize with pleasure an occasion for serving that cause.   All military men, officers,
generals, and marshals, are for war.   Since the latter
have been dukes, they wish to be archdukes, and so on.
I believe that a war with you would be not merely, as any
war would be, a misfortune : it would have the particular
character of dragging the universe into the waves, for
where would this scourge stop?   When war had been
made on you, Russia would remain, and then China.   In
short, I detest war, and the rumours of which you complain, for they will end sooner or later in leading to it.
No one knows better than I do how this concatenation
is brought about : all military men wish for war and
collect such rumours ; there is no wretched maker
of projects who does not bring his ideas to the Emperor ;
his agents and foreign spies, who are all rogues, make
their reports in that sense, to pay their court ; and the
Emperor ends by believing them.   To-morrow you shall
have an article as good as it is possible for me to make
it.'

I had no difficulty in agreeing with the minister's
opinions.   I observed to him that if the Emperor allowed
these rumours, with the intention of holding us in check,

he deceived himself altogether.   We can be won by
confidence, but are only estranged by the contrary.
'What do you say, for example,' continued I, 'of
the manœuvring of troops which has placed your
Silesian army in the most menacing position on our
frontier?   Why is each officer of that same army
allowed to spread the report that in a short time that
frontier will be free?   The Emperor Francis is animated
by one desire, that of peace and harmony between the
two courts ; he has never ceased to give proofs of this,
and his wish is based on the true interests of his
Empire.   Napoleon, and all the alarmists who surround
him, cannot suspect him.   It would be madness on our
part to provoke a war with France : it would be weakness not to repulse an attack with vigour.   Consider
our policy from this point of view, and you will know
the whole secret of our policy.'   Fouché interrupted
me to ask if the news I had just told him of a movement of the French army was in a public newspaper,
as in that case he would contradict it.   'No,' said I,
'all the reports from our frontiers bring it, and the
result has been a sudden fall in the stocks, which cannot
be indifferent to us.   We defend the same cause : why
should influence be used unfavourable to our credit?'
Fouché told me that the following day he would take
care to ascribe the fall of stocks to speculation.   He
spoke very frankly with respect to the publication
of a report of the death of the King of England *
by the Minister of Foreign Affairs, and used among
other energetic phrases the following : 'I am glad that
M. de Champagny has put his name to such an article
rather than I ; I never would have done it ; there is in

---

* Apparently a false report of the death of the King of England was
circulated at this time : he did not die till 1820.

the publication of a thing known to be false something unworthy of the master and his servant.'

It is impossible that Fouché does not know the real source of the disquieting news which was the subject of our interview. He asked me if I had written to Champagny. I told him no, and that if Champagny were here, I should have preferred to speak to him of a thing which I deplore equally as a friend to peace, as a cosmopolitan, and as Austrian Ambassador. 'I have no complaints to make,' said I to him; 'no question has been opened between the two courts, still less a subject of any discussion whatever.'

Fouché does not, then, oppose the Emperor's intentions, by slipping in articles of more or less tranquillising views. I have said above that it did not appear to me that it could be intended by the Emperor to subdue Spain and make war upon us at the same time.

A new point of view, which struck me the more inasmuch as I did not yet know the proclamation of Palafox, was that of our pretensions to the crown of Spain.*

Might it not be possible that this was the principal motive of all the reports, which Napoleon spreads and visibly maintains, to keep us, so to speak, at bay? A direct analogy comes to support this supposition. Your Excellency will remember that, at the time of my negotiation at Fontainebleau, there was a ridiculous vehemence in the demand for my recognition of the new King. The Emperor, who, more than anyone, sacrifices to his prejudices, believed that he could more easily obtain the cession of a province than the recognition of

---

* In the proclamation of the Spanish General Palafox, May 25, 1808, a reference was made to the Archduke Charles of Austria, nephew of Charles III., as King of Spain.—Ed.

the Kings, his brothers ; I am not astonished to find
the same fear in him at the present moment.

I hope your Excellency will treat the present report
with indulgence.   It is useless to tell you of the
singular position in which I am placed.   Deprived, since
the departure of M. de Talleyrand, of all means of contact, or connection, otherwise than by writing (the most
sterile of all), with the Government with whom I am
charged to overlook and defend our interests, deprived
even of all means of control in the official way, I am
alone, entirely isolated, crushed with an immense responsibility.   I should be an alarmist if I were credulous ; I
should be a quietist if I despised these same rumours.

I would rather risk falling into snares, such as those
which befell M. de Lucchesini, than lead my court into
error by not giving the alarm.   My reports have for
some time rather borne the impress of alarm than that
of extreme security.   It is not with the latter feeling
that, at this moment, I have the conviction that we
shall not be attacked by France immediately.   When
shall we be ? I do not know, but it is in the nature and
policy of Napoleon that it will be at the very first moment that appears favourable to him.   I do not believe
that he would prefer the present time.   But it may immediately become favourable, and it is with extreme
satisfaction that I see efforts made, by our august
master, well calculated for the good of his House and
his states.

Metternich to Stadion, Paris, July 1, 1808.

109. If it is difficult to know exactly what Napoleon's plans are, it is possible to understand them
to a certain extent by agreements which are much more
the result of a military arrangement than mine ; but data

furnished by an observer, however little instructed he may be, if he is impartial, are precious to the head of military affairs. They acquire much value when they are based on certain facts.

Your Excellency has for some time heard the formation of camps spoken of, which the French armies are to form in Prussia. The scarcity of food in many provinces, the total ruin of the inhabitants of the towns, serve as a pretext, and were perhaps the real reason of these assemblies. Camps are to be formed near Stargard, Berlin, &c.

Subsequent orders assign them a different direction. The troops of Davoust and De Mortier (comprising the Saxons and the Polonese, about a hundred and twenty thousand strong) have received orders to assemble in the neighbourhood of Schweidnitz, in Silesia. It is doubtless this movement which has thrown Bohemia into alarm.

The Marshals Soult and Victor, instead of remaining on the right bank of the Oder, are to form two camps near New and Old Ruppin and Rathenau. (Their divisions may be estimated at nearly seventy thousand men.)

An army of nearly twenty thousand men is to assemble at Merve, on the Vistula.

The idea is secretly being put forward, that the Prussian Government, to lighten their expenses in a moment of extreme penury, will include in the inventory to the French troops the fortresses in Silesia, which they have not yet occupied.

These measures, which I can answer for as exact, seem to be adjourned. The court is more able than I am to observe the movements of the French troops in Silesia, but it is the fact that a concentration there seems really necessary in consequence of the want of food in the provinces in which the troops are, who, after this movement, will encamp in the most fertile and best preserved part of the Prussian monarchy.

I hope his Imperial Majesty will allow me to submit to him a slight sketch which, bearing simply on the military operations, is perhaps on my part only a foolish dream. But I take the map in hand and calculate by analogy: all Napoleon's campaigns resemble each other!

Is it not easy to see in the army of Silesia the principal body, which would be destined to operate in a short straight line towards the centre of the kingdom? Penetrating Moravia, it isolates Bohemia, divides Galicia; it is sixty leagues to Vienna, and would penetrate Hungary as easily as Galicia.

Might not the camps of Rathenau and Ruppin be regarded as the reserves of the principal army?

The assembled army near Merve is obviously only for observation on the Vistula, and is strong enough to dispute some important passages.

Napoleon's movements are always concentric: he does not act from one point alone. The first control of this plan would be the certain connection of the different armies in country formerly Venetian; this would establish a basis of operations of which the extreme angles would be in Italy and Silesia. Austria and Bohemia would be conquered by the fact of the entry of the enemy into Moravia, or at least would find themselves so much beyond the lines that, their defence being impossible for us, their attack would be useless. The troops of Marmont would penetrate Hungary lower down, and any success on the part of the Italian army would immediately send us back into the centre of the kingdom. The Bavarian and Confederate armies would occupy in this manner without difficulty the provinces within their reach. We ought, then, to calculate our defensive measures as if we had a war to sustain against Prussia and France united. Are they not really united under one chief, with more powerful moral and physical means than those which they had formerly?

This plan is, no doubt, only practicable on the supposition of the most perfect impassibility of Russia.

Her army is composed of twenty-three divisions, of which six are in Moldavia and Wallachia, with from eight to ten thousand Cossacks; four in Finland; four in Courland, Livonia, and on the coasts of the Baltic; three never move from Siberia and the Caucasus.

There remain five divisions in the Polish provinces, to which must be added the greater part of the cavalry of the divisions, which are in Finland.

These five divisions, which may amount to about ninety thousand men, are then the only ones which, in the first moments of an energetic declaration on the part of Russia, we could count upon; but they would probably commence their operations by retaking Galicia, against which no doubt all the moral and military means would be used at first by the French. Could we indeed count, after the first defeat, on the help of a Power which was afraid to decide before the hostilities, and would not that help be so tardy as to destroy the chances a victory might offer?

I will sum up.

We have, then, an army of nearly two hundred and twenty thousand men, who can begin a campaign on our back and on our flank, in Silesia and in Prussia. This army has lately divided itself into a first line, a reserve, and a corps for observation on the Vistula.

The orders for this division of the army have not been carried out up to this moment.

There are, then, motives for this adjournment, and these motives are, no doubt, the efforts necessitated by the insurgent Spaniards.

This same army has not to wait for immediate reinforcements; all who can possibly be collected are transported in haste towards the Pyrenees.

The Emperor wished to call the conscription of 1810, but strong representations of the extreme youth of the individuals who would compose it have made him prefer to draw from the reserve of 1802, the only one which has not been employed, a measure which will make a great sensation, because it bears only on men established in homes of their own. I have no data of the number of men it can furnish, but we shall soon see it published.

The produce of the new conscription will no doubt, in the first instance, bear towards the coast of Spain, but as certainly will go to recruit the armies in Prussia the day the insurrection is put down.

We have at this moment to direct our means of defence against an army equal in number to our own, and which is disposed at all vulnerable points, not only of the frontier, but even of the interior of our Empire.

Does not this embarrassing position demand measures prompt, because fate has given us a moment of respite; energetic, because after them we can dispose of no more? Should secondary considerations prevent precautions which our welfare imperiously demands?

To provoke a war with France would be madness; it must therefore be avoided, but it can only be avoided by strong measures. Those which his Imperial Majesty has arranged—all the last military steps—have as-

suredly tended to put the army on the most respectable
footing ; but our army, however strong, good, and well
ordered it may be, is it in number sufficient to prevent
the final ruin of a monarchy attacked on all her
frontiers at one time, and deprived at the opening of a
campaign of her most precious resources and most
important provinces? It is, therefore, not in ourselves
alone that we must seek our safety ; it is as necessary
for our political intelligence as our military measures.

I look upon the present moment as the last in which
it will be possible for us to open up chances of preservation ; these chances are frail, because, according to my
calculations, they depend only on Russia.

It appears to me urgent, and, I should say, of the
last urgency, to explain ourselves very frankly, and,
above all, very directly with that Power. What can
there be of a dangerous nature in the following declaration, which a prudent and penetrating ambassador
would make, of the urgency of the case? He would
say to Alexander :—

'Our position becomes more embarrassing day by
day. Two hundred thousand men threaten to penetrate the interior of our kingdom. France herself
accredits the rumour ; she forces us to measures of
precaution, which she tolerates because she does not fear
them, but of which she will make a grievance the first
day she requires a pretext. We wish nothing from
anyone : we only wish for peace ; but we can only insure
it by uniting with you ; you owe your existence to our
preservation. Not to wish for peace is not to wish to
save your existence. Look at Spain. The day which
sees the reigning dynasty descend from that throne is
an appeal to all the sovereigns ; we would never allow a
proposal that you should descend from yours. What

will you say the day that proposition is made to the Emperor Francis? It is not in the nature of things that two Powers should come to an understanding at the time of a crisis, and even if they did, they would do more harm than could be conceived. We demand from you, therefore, a positive declaration of the course you will take when Napoleon, on his return from Spain, or regarding that conquest as certain, will turn his attention towards the East. There he will encounter Austria, Turkey, and lastly, Russia. Are you in agreement with him about the division of Turkey? We will put ourselves on one side: but he cannot amuse both of us with projects tending only to the removal from the centre of our empires of the strength necessary for our own defence. If he wishes to attack us what part will you play? Do you wish to prevent war? Then, pronounce against it with energy at Paris itself, and the odds are against Napoleon forcing it on us. Are you afraid to take this step, which the tone of conversation throughout Europe authorises you to take, the duty of which is even imposed upon you? At least let us agree about military measures; that in the first moment of hostilities we may regard your army in Poland as the right wing of ours, your armies in Moldavia and Wallachia as reserves. Let us combine a military plan on this principle, the only one which would make the French troops against us infinitely more feeble than ours. Let us, at any rate, base a plan of operation upon it. Tell us, in the contrary case, that you will leave us to our own resources, that you will allow the Galicians to rise without being afraid for your Polish provinces, and that you consider yourselves powerful enough to stand alone, while you are afraid to support us. It is necessary that we should have a prompt and precise reply on all these points, and we only wait for that to regulate our political and military conduct.'

In admitting the first proposition we should only be fulfilling our duty, a duty dictated to his Imperial Majesty by what he owes to his House and his subjects. We should have lost nothing by admitting the second, and we should, in one way or the other, have put an end to the state of uncertainty about our existence and means of defending ourselves against attack, which is often more painful than annihilation itself. Besides, none of the above reasons which I have put into the mouth of our negotiator in Russia is new to them. The Count de Tolstoy always spoke in that tone, and it is impossible that the evidence of facts should not end by a triumph over the apathetic security of that Government.

I submit this report to his Imperial Majesty as a proof of attachment and disinterestedness on the part of one of his servants; who, as to the first, will never change, and who proves the second by daring to give his views on military questions, which are beyond his province, for which he claims the indulgence of the enlightened men to whom they may be communicated.

OF THE NECESSITY OF A CENSORSHIP OF THE PRESS.

(Note 20, Vol. I.)

110. Metternich to Stadion, Paris, June 23, 1808.

110. I have a confused idea of having one day drawn your Excellency's attention to the editors of the Frankfort and Augsburg Gazettes.

There is a most urgent necessity to exercise some influence over newspapers in general, and particularly over these two, which never cease spreading lies, often of the most ridiculous nature, about us. It is from these that most of the articles are extracted which are found in the French journals. Why should not correct news be communicated to the different newspapers? Why do they not control their correspondents at Vienna, and why should they not refute these lies in the places where they are published?

A great fault which all the Governments, and particularly our own, have committed since the commencement of the French Revolution, is that they have regarded as useless, as beneath their dignity and that of the good cause, and indeed even as dangerous, to speak truth to the public, and to speak it incessantly. This fact is never more incontestable than when the French are concerned. They have the game to themselves; they have only occupied an empty place by seizing the desks of the journalists, and no one can reproach

them with silence; they have taken up the weapon we
have disdained to make use of, and they are now employing it against ourselves.

The use of a thing is confounded everywhere with
its abuse; the condition of a pamphleteer with that of
a political writer; the man who reasons, with the one
who simply relates correct facts! Public opinion is the
most powerful of all means; like religion, it penetrates
the most hidden recesses, where administrative measures have no influence. To despise public opinion is
as dangerous as to despise moral principles; and if the
latter will rise up even when they have been almost
stifled, it is not so with opinion; it requires peculiar
cultivation, a continued and sustained perseverance.
Posterity will hardly believe that we have regarded
silence as an efficacious weapon to oppose to the clamours of our opponents, and that in a century of
words!

Who can blame us if we will not allow the public
to be supplied with lies about us?

There is not one of the above-mentioned papers which
does not say under the heading of Vienna that we are
in full negotiation on important points, or which does
not publish lies about facts and individuals. The public
cannot distinguish if news is true or false. False news
has the air of being true if no one can be found to contradict it, and I place the Emperor Napoleon at the
head of the credulous public. There is a great difference between what he conceives and what is insinuated
to him; it would be found very difficult to change what
he wishes, but his credulity may be imposed upon.

I beg your Excellency to pay particular attention to
this subject. Nothing is more easy than to avoid the
official style in these publications, which have no merit if

they bear that impression. I speak to you from a place where, more than anywhere else, I can appreciate the success of the efforts of the Government to influence the public. The newspapers are worth to Napoleon an army of three hundred thousand men, for such a force would not overlook the interior better, or frighten foreign Powers more, than half a dozen of his paid pamphleteers.

ALARM AT THE AUSTRIAN ARMAMENTS.

(Note 26, Vol. I.)

111. Metternich to Stadion, Paris, July 25, 1808.
112. Metternich to Stadion, Paris, August 2, 1808.
113. Metternich to Stadion, Paris, August 2, 1808.

111. The courier Beck has brought me the despatches sent by your Excellency.

I send him back at once with the news which, according to all accounts, demands the chief attention of his Imperial Majesty. He will be convinced that we have arrived at the moment when the intentions of Napoleon toward us are becoming manifest. . . . *

The great question of peace and war is being agitated, for how can the remarks which are made on our military armaments be otherwise described?

Does Napoleon believe the moment has come to throw off the mask, and execute plans which he has long delayed?

Does he find the present moment suitable to his interests, and does he merely wish to be enlightened as to the organic measures which, by augmenting our real strength, might at any time be inconvenient to him; and which his suspicious nature may lead him to regard otherwise than in the defensive character they so clearly bear?

---

* The enclosures with this despatch are a letter of Champagny to Metternich, dated Bayonne, and the answer dated Paris. See Note 26, vol. i.

If we admit the first supposition, we can hardly avoid war ; on the second supposition we might do so, unless we directly provoke it.   Eight or ten days should suffice to discover what is Napoleon's real plan.

The course he has followed for some time resembles his well-known tactics, when he wishes to begin a quarrel.   In preceding despatches I have shown my way of judging of the warlike rumours which for some time he has himself positively encouraged ; by these rumours he provokes us to take measures for our safety, then he asks us why we are alarming our neighbours : such is constantly his manner of proceeding.   These same rumours have, during the latter part of the Emperor's stay at Bayonne, acquired great intensity among the hangers-on of the court, even in the Imperial family itself.   The Emperor gives no explanation.   I receive these facts from an absolutely authentic source.

From the same data which I have quoted, the conviction is forced upon me that the present moment is not the one Napoleon would choose for opening up complications with us, and that it will be only if we ourselves wish to make war that it will be made upon us.

If we reflect that Napoleon has but to say the one word—' disarm ! '—to place us in the alternative either of making war or of remaining in a state of weakness which would at once make us the victims of the least of his whims, we cannot deny that he has been moderate in the manner he has chosen to speak to us of our armaments.   Is not this the beginning of a discussion of which we now first get a first glimpse ?   Has he not wished to discover our decision, rather than retard it ?   In eight days we shall know what we are to believe.

I have maintained the sound principle that, our measures being permanent, they cannot be regarded as

offensive. I have compared them to the establishment
of the conscription in all the states subject to French
influence. If ever they ask us in a more peremptory
manner for a reduction, I should find in what has gone
before a text for all possible replies. France cannot
demand from us the revocation of an organic measure
suited to the spirit of the century, and provoked by her
own example, without coming to this demand, simple,
and explicit : ' I wish you to be weak, because I and
my allies wish to be strong, and remain so.' Such is
doubtless his real thought ; but it is not in the nature
of Napoleon to unveil himself thus. One can disperse
an assembled army, but one cannot alter constitutional
laws. It is therefore important to separate these two
things, and to prove that our military measures come
under the head of the last category.

Metternich to Stadion, Paris, August 2, 1808.

(Note 26, Vol. I.)

112. I send Count de Mier with the enclosed confidential note, which I received yesterday from M. de
Champagny, dated Toulouse, July 27. Your Excellency will find also the private letter to which I thought
I ought to limit my reply.

All argument ceases at the reading of compositions
such as those which M. de Champagny addresses to me.
Does the Emperor wish to make war upon us ?—does
he wish to sound our inclination to make war upon
him ? However improbable this latter supposition may
be, is it not nevertheless possible ? But neither one
nor the other can alter the part we have to take. . . .

Your Excellency will see that I have confined my
letter of to-day to explanations as frank as they are

simple—as void of oratorical phrases as they are strong
in reasoning and in facts. Nothing is left for Napoleon but the power of leaving it unanswered. That
is what he did with the one I sent on July 22; and
this it is that makes me desire to approach him as soon
as possible—a desire assuredly quite disinterested!

The present crisis is doubtless the most painful that
can occur to the Austrian kingdom. Its fate, its existence will depend on the part the Emperor determines
to take. To annul measures purely Conservative would
be to deliver itself bound, hand and foot, to the man who
has never yet rewarded concessions except by fresh
demands; directly to provoke war, and consequently
to depart from the system which his Majesty has so
wisely adopted, would be insanity. The question,
therefore, will be to find a middle course, which will
combine the safety of the Empire with the care required
more for our own preservation than our relations with
France, and will enable us to await the only end we
may reasonably hope to arrive at—that of retarding as
long as possible the explosion with which Napoleon will
never cease to threaten us.

I have indicated, in one of the reports last sent, a
plan for the union of one or more centres of troops, in
a position remote enough to be able to offer the enemy a
line of attack involving less risk than scattered bodies,
which might be cut off or turned—a manœuvre at which
he constantly aims. Would it not be possible to draw a
political advantage from a measure which would really
be military and Conservative, by taking upon me to
declare to Napoleon 'that, in order to give fresh proof
of his Majesty's intention not to act hostilely towards
any point whatever occupied by the French armies or
by the allies of France, and to silence the odious impu-

tations of calumny, his Majesty had ordered a retrograde movement of his armies?'　Is this possible, is it feasible in a military sense?　It is not for me to decide, but I believe it my duty to suggest to my court the best means of opposing facts to imputations, the most worthy, and consequently the strongest, measure which can be opposed to the whims of a man who is never so carried away by passion as not to desire to clothe the most odious enterprises with an appearance of right and reason, but unhappily too violent not to overthrow at the last any obstacle to his ridiculously gigantic views.

M. de Champagny, in his note, speaks of Russia; his assurance that she will never come to our assistance shows the Emperor's uneasiness.

He speaks of future arrangements in Europe; this can only refer to Turkey, for there is no need of our co-operation in those arrangements, which he reckons on establishing in states subject to his influence.　Such are the measures which, many persons assert, the States of the Confederation will soon be able to submit to him, to satisfy his views as to a new title with which he will replace that of Protector.

As to the march of troops from the interior of France towards the Rhine, this is for the moment nothing but a vain threat.　He can create a new army; we have, during the last twenty years, seen too many astonishing examples of such creations to doubt that with which he now threatens us, but it is a fact that he cannot at this moment send an army to the Rhine which would in any way deserve the name.

The Emperor must make a new conscription.　His armies in Spain require considerable reinforcements; he must have a reserve in case he should wish to make war upon us.　He has not too many soldiers, even supposing the contrary. Spain can no longer serve as a motive in the eyes of a nation indignant at the policy he has followed in that country. The *Corps Législatif* will soon re-assemble. It will be necessary to find a pretext for the *senatus-consulte*; they will make use of us to demand that, which the nation will agree to willingly.

Metternich to Stadion, Paris, August 2, 1808.

113. I had barely finished the preceding despatch when I received the enclosed note from M. de Champagny, dated July 30.*

The despatches being concluded, I send the documents, and your Excellency may sign without retouching them. You will see that the questions have, if not changed, at any rate taken a turn altogether different since the Emperor saw my letters to M. de Champagny, dated July 22.

There is nothing to add to Champagny's last note, which is evidently dictated by the Emperor himself. He does not wish for war at this moment, but he will make war upon us before very long. This is the result I extract from a composition containing a crowd of considerations which I cannot enter into, not wishing to delay the courier's departure. It is sufficient for me to declare to your Excellency that if we act adroitly, if we know how to turn to our own profit the weak side Napoleon presents to us, we can, with less charlatanism than he, derive great benefit from the present position of affairs.

We will not allow ourselves to be imposed on by grand words; all he has said of his armies and of their

---

* See Note 26, vol. i.

number is false.   If sixty thousand men can march towards the Rhine, what is the meaning of the embarrassment the affairs of Spain are causing him ?   The enclosed
sketches which I send to your Excellency are exact.   But
let us sacrifice some forms ; let us keep from the excesses
which he is committing ; let us organise our real strength
as far as possible without giving rise to complaints
which appear only due to the less essential parts of our
military organisation ; let us take him at his word, let
him withdraw his troops ; let him proclaim peace ; let
us in revenge punish the guilty, if any exist, at Trieste ;
let us yield to a pacific impulsion, if he will prove his
intentions by facts—and we shall have attained a
grand, an immense object, that of the adjournment of
the war.

I cannot send to your Excellency the reply I shall
make to M. de Champagny.   I shall—not to delay the
departure of the courier—be content with telling you
that I will write to him to-morrow, and that by founding
all I shall say to him on the constant desire of the Emperor to maintain peace, I shall leave the course open
to my court.

THE FAMOUS AUDIENCE,
AUGUST 15, 1808.

(Note 27, Vol. I.)

114. Metternich to Stadion, Paris, August 17, 1808.
115. Metternich to Stadion, Paris, August 17, 1808.

114. . . . All seemed to announce the near arrival of Napoleon. Public opinion was divided as to the place where he would dismount. Many people asserted that he would avoid showing himself to the Parisians, and go to Rambouillet. He completely baffled that calculation, and arrived on the 14th, at four o'clock in the afternoon, at St. Cloud. We received the same day, at eleven o'clock P.M., the announcement of a diplomatic audience for the next day, his fête day. If his hasty and unexpected arrival at St. Cloud may have been caused by the reports that the public thought he would not show himself in Paris on August 15, it may also have been caused by the desire of bringing about a scene unique of its kind and unlike anything that had occurred in diplomatic circles up to this time. He wished to speak to me, but not alone; he wished to do it in the face of Europe, and yesterday was on that account a day of very extraordinary interest.

After Napoleon had received the compliments of all the constituent bodies of the state, the *Corps Diplomatique* was introduced to the audience at the usual hour. The Nuncio not being there, I placed myself first. The

Russian Ambassador put himself at my right hand; the Dutch and other Ministers continued the circle. The Turkish Ambassador was the fifth or sixth in the line. All these details are of importance.

He commenced his round with me, and spoke to me of the heat of the past summer, of the health of my family, &c. He addressed questions equally insignificant to my neighbour; and after having hurried round very quickly, he returned to Count de Tolstoy, and said to him: 'Well, you have good news from Finland?' The ambassador having confirmed this fact, 'The English expedition,' replied the Emperor, 'has not been of much use to the King of Sweden; they have sent the troops to Spain who should have helped him. I am sorry that the English have not disembarked there fifty thousand men; they may remain there one, two, even three months, they will not remain four.'

Then, turning towards me, he said, with an air which did not usually announce the approach of a storm: 'Well, and is Austria arming considerably?' 'No, sire,' I replied; 'she is but carrying out the organic measures which, since the Peace of Presburg, she had conceived, but delayed. In doing that, she only follows the example of many of her neighbours, and maintains the position she ought to hold.' Seizing upon that, he said to me, with ample paraphrase, almost word for word what is contained in the note of July 30,* which was written to me evidently under his dictation by M. de Champagny. To repeat to your Excellency the replies which I made to him, would be really to copy my letters to the Minister of Foreign Affairs. I will content myself with gathering together here the facts and

* See Note 26, vol. i.

phrases, which will clear the ground still better than that correspondence.

The Emperor made no mention to me of the reserves; he only spoke of calling out the militia, and especially of the precipitation with which we had executed our military measures. 'Do you want to attack anyone,' added he, 'or are you afraid of some one? Has anyone ever seen such haste? If you had put it at a year, or eighteen months, it would have been nothing; but to order everything to be ready on July 16, as if on that day you were to be attacked! You have by that act given an impulse to the public mind which you will find it very difficult to set at rest. You see what has passed at Trieste: my consul has been insulted there. That fact alone was sufficient to have caused war, if I had wished it. I have treated Austria with much respect; she has not been deprived of any of her importance. I could demand fifty millions from Trieste; I have not done so. If ever I return there, I should have to burn the city! I do not wish for war; I do not want anything from you. The Emperor Francis, Count Stadion, Count Metternich, M. de Champagny do not wish it; no sensible men wish it; and I, who know the course of human affairs, I tell you that I believe we shall have it in spite of the wishes of sensible people. An invisible hand is at play; that hand is the hand of England. M. Adair * is again *en route* for Malta; he has left Vienna quite satisfied. England has gained fifty per cent. by your armaments—(what a good objection I could have made to him!); since she hopes to entice you again, this has

---

* Robert Adair, English Ambassador at Vienna from June 1806 to May 1809, was, as Napoleon hints, removed from his post at Vienna in consequence of a secret understanding between Austria and England.—ED.

made her more tenacious, more intractable than ever. You force me to arm the Confederation, to tell them to hold themselves in readiness. You prevent me from withdrawing my troops from Prussia, and making them return to France. What I had ordered, fifteen days afterwards I was forced by you to counter-order, withdrawing not less than a hundred thousand men. I am frank. You are ruining yourselves, you are ruining me. England can give you money, but not enough; and she gives me none. The States of the Confederation, already very unfortunate, are being ruined; and when all the male population of Europe are under arms, it will be necessary to raise the women! Can this state of things last? It must bring us to war against our will. What do you hope for? Are you in agreement with Russia? I do not believe it; but in that case you will present me a respectable line of defence! (These sentences were addressed as much to M. de Tolstoy as to me; that ambassador preserved the most imperturbable attitude.) But on the contrary supposition, what can you do against France and Russia united? And the first war with Austria will be a war to the death; you must either come to Paris, or I must make a conquest of your kingdom. Your armaments are equally displeasing to St. Petersburg. Do you know how this will end? The Emperor Alexander will tell you that he desires you to stop, and you will do it; and then it will be no longer you on whom I shall depend for the maintenance of tranquillity in Europe, it will be Russia. I shall not submit to you the future arrangements of many questions in which you are interested; I shall treat solely with Russia, and you will only be spectators.'

From that I could not doubt that he intended to speak to me of Turkey (the Turkish Ambassador being but three steps from me). 'See,' continued he, 'the conduct held by your minister at Constantinople. He does all he can to fan the discord with France. We know all; the Turks tell us everything. You have taken steps about the Servians by which they recognise you as their sovereign. Is it by your armaments that you hope some day to go halves with us in our arrangements? You deceive yourselves. I will never allow myself to be imposed upon by an armed Power. I will never treat with one who wishes to impose upon me.'

I denied strongly all these supposed facts and ridiculously false assertions. I denied emphatically the negotiation with the Servians. I took up the position that our chief end was that of maintaining the Porte in its integrity; and that far from desiring its fall, we should regard its preservation as a safeguard to our interests; that consequently the imputations made to M. de Sturmer,* concerning which I had already had full explanations with M. de Champagny, were either based on gratuitous suppositions, or, if these accusations were true, on a direct contravention to the most explicit instructions which that minister had received, instructions the less doubtful inasmuch as they were founded on the very principles I was here to establish as our own.

This conversation, in which I replied with extreme frankness and the greatest calmness (replies which, indeed, were only paraphrases of my last letters), lasted an hour and a quarter. The Emperor did not raise his voice a single moment; he never quitted the tone and expressions of the most astonishing moderation. He would certainly have said the same thing in a more energetic fashion if we had been alone, and I should have replied

---

* Austrian Internuncio at Constantinople; father of the subsequent representative of Austria at the Porte.

to him in the same manner; here we had the appearance of chatting, and of making a political discursion, including and maintaining the most immediate interests of two great Powers, touching on the intentions, the most secret relations past, present, and future, between these Powers, and concerning the whole of Europe. A conversation such as this, in which the Emperor agitated the question of the division of Turkey before the representative of that Power, is doubtless without example in the records of diplomacy.

It is superfluous to tell your Excellency of the effect which this long conversation produced on all who were present. Nothing else is spoken of in Paris: it was so extraordinary, and based upon antecedents of which those present were so completely ignorant, that the versions given of it and conjectures about it partake more of individual passions and desires.

The Emperor did not spare me some military discussions. He at first exclaimed about the uselessness of a national levy, then contradicted himself in declaring that measure useful under certain conditions; lastly, he blamed our excessive expenditure; a moment afterwards he said he had no objection to the provisioning of our fortresses, declaring it a measure of pure defence. He replied to the objection I made as to his armies on the march, we having opposed no assembly of troops which could in any way bear an offensive character: 'No, you have no assembly, but your troops are placed in such a manner as to be able immediately to form real *corps d'armées*. These are things,' added he, ' on which military men cannot be deceived.'

I said to him, *à propos* of illusions, that like Prussia we wished to make the most of our real forces. ' Believe me, sire, if you count our soldiers, we also

count yours, and we know exactly what your strength
is.' He replied: 'But you have three hundred thousand regular troops; you could have four hundred
thousand if you liked, and what more would anyone
have?' Alluding always to the levying of the militia,
having laid down a series of principles as to the political
views which Austria ought to entertain—very good
principles—and having added, 'You think the same,' I
said to him, smiling: 'Not only do I think the same,
Sire, but I feel as if I were debating our interests with
the Minister of Foreign Affairs of Austria, so true is
much that your Majesty tells me; and assuredly nothing
could less resemble a dispute between two Powers than
our present discussion.' The Emperor smiled in his
turn, and said to me: 'You see, too, how calm I am.'
I have since seen how important he considered it that
this shade in his conduct and proceedings should not
escape me.

Metternich to Stadion, Paris, August 17, 1808.

115. . . . M. de Champagny has many times
tried to discover the effect which my conversation with
the Emperor produced upon me. I confined myself to
the very summary assurance that I saw in that same
conversation a new hope for the preservation of peace.
He told me that such was the Emperor's wish. I assured
him that I could answer for the same intentions on the
part of my master.

'Yes,' said M. de Champagny to me; 'but intentions
do not suffice, facts are necessary.'

Seeing he had arrived at the point I expected, I
put off our conversation till the following day. This

fragment of conversation had taken place before dinner.* On rising from table, finding me in a corner of the drawing-room with the Ambassadors of Russia and Holland (my two nearest neighbours in the diplomatic circle), talking of the scene which occupied all the diplomatists grouped in the four corners of the apartment, the Minister of Foreign Affairs approached us and said : 'Well, how does the diplomatic committee decide?' 'It decides,' said I, 'that Europe holds a new pledge of peace.' He concurred entirely in this view, and dwelt much on the freedom and simplicity of the Emperor's explanations, and also on the proofs of the purity of his intentions. The two ambassadors agreed in this.

. . . The Ambassador of Russia, who never loses an opportunity of serving the cause which we have both so much at heart, preserved this morning a countenance quite suitable to the dignity of his position and to my wishes. He had opposed the most imperturbable *sang-froid* to all the overtures by which Napoleon had tried to make him give some sign in his favour. M. de Champagny gave him an occasion of serving us more actively. Having approached him, and asked his opinion about the Emperor's interview with me, Count de Tolstoy said to him, with that calmness and frankness which, if not necessary qualities in every man full of a good cause, was certainly the best of all manners to be adopted by the Russian Ambassador at Paris : ' I think the Emperor Napoleon has spoken well and that he is quite right. But I also am a military man ; I tell you that Austria cannot dream of making war against France and Russia united. If Austria ha

* M. de Champagny invited the whole *Corps Diplomatique* to dinner on the day of the great audience.

anxieties, they arise from your surrounding her with armies ; withdraw them ; according to the stipulations of the Treaty of Tilsit, we can send an army of a hundred thousand men to the confines of Galicia, and we will answer for the maintenance of the most complete tranquillity.' The Minister of Foreign Affairs, surprised, begged M. de Tolstoy to call on him the following morning to continue this conversation. . . .

Having repaired the following day to the minister at the hour agreed upon, I repeated to him what I had said the evening before on the contents of the last despatches of your Excellency. I told him at the same time that, sending a courier to Vienna, I thought it my duty to beg him to inform the Emperor that, in giving an account of the conversation we had had, I had given fresh guarantees of the pacific intentions of my court, which had given rise to his Majesty's explanations ; 'I believe by that,' said I, ' to have attained the end which his Majesty himself proposed.'

The minister received this assurance with evident satisfaction. ' The Emperor,' said he, ' asked me this morning if I had seen you, and what you thought of the explanations which he had with you yesterday ; I replied that, as far as you had allowed me to see, there seemed to be no doubt that you had understood them in a pacific sense. His Majesty seemed quite satisfied. You must have remarked,' added the minister, ' the complete justice which his Majesty is pleased to render to the intentions of the Emperor of Austria, to those of Count de Stadion, and to your own. The Emperor does not fear war, but he desires peace above all. He hopes that you will continue, as you have done up to this time, to employ yourself in this noble aim.'

' What,' said I to him, ' can all my endeavours do, if

the Emperor, in spite of his conviction that my master, that his minister, that all sensible men in the kingdom do not wish for war, never ceases to answer them with talk about Teplitz and Eger, the clamours of a drunken populace at Trieste, &c. ?   I did not come to you to-day to make any communications : I have told you that I had none to make before the return of M. de Mier ; but I desire to come to an understanding with you on some basis applicable to our future relations.   You assure me that the Emperor does not wish for war.'

'No,' said M. de Champagny, 'he does not wish for war.'

'Well,' replied I, 'what is the use of the stories with which he tries to amuse us, and which his conviction of the pacific intentions of my court should have imme-diately reduced to nothing ?   How can you expect good relations without reciprocity ?   I declare to you, then, that for each speech of an Austrian merchant I will reply to you with a letter from a French merchant ; that to the chattering of Teplitz I will bring that of Spa and Aix-la-Chapelle ; to the gossip about the warlike intentions of Austria I can oppose at least an equal quantity about the warlike intentions of France.   Shall we come to an end in this way ?   And whose fault will it be ?   Those who wish for peace should wish for the means of preserving it, and whoever does not wish for the means, consequently cannot wish for peace.   Let us begin by giving our word that we will pronounce judgment only on ourselves and our own actions.'

The minister, in his usual manner, without object-ing at all to the argument I had advanced, spoke to me of the people of Trieste, of so many letters speaking of war, of the impulse given to Austrian feeling against France by the proclamations of the Archdukes (the

Emperor is most annoyed, I do not know why, about those of Grätz and Trieste). 'Let us agree nevertheless,' said he, 'that if so many things do not prove the hostile intentions of the head of the Government, they prove the hatred of the public.'

'Ah,' replied I, 'give up the expectation of love from a foreign people : strength is scarcely ever pleasant. We, who have done little ill to the French people, have never aspired to be loved ; let us, then, on this point maintain the most complete reciprocity ; let our Governments be united, and our people will be friendly; let us commence with the one, and that will lead on to the other.'

M. de Champagny, without replying to my just observation, said : 'But it is necessary that the Emperor should be reassured on these points ; he has returned sooner than he intended to Paris, for the purpose of clearing up these questions, and to speak to you ; he wishes to be made absolutely easy on your account.'

'He never will be,' replied I, 'if he does not place himself at the point of view I have mentioned. You wish for facts? We furnish them in exact proportion to yours; if you do not wish for war, we do not wish for it ; if you do not fear it, neither do we. The Emperor has declared, in the last letter which he has made you write, many propositions to which he desires to bind himself. I cannot say anything decisive before I know the intentions of my master ; but I reply that if you proclaim we shall proclaim, that if you are quiet we shall be so, and that if you remain quiet so shall we. I have another request to make to you in my own name,' said I : 'that the Emperor for once will show that he desires peace by paying no regard to anything that may be done, said, or written with us before the arrival of my despatch of August 2 (Nos. 112, 113). I have seen with the greatest pain that his Majesty has not acceded to my just and pacific demand that he would suspend all operations till the return of my courier. What do you think our people at home must think of your demands and your acts? Do you think they are likely to reassure the Government and the people? Do they not impede the peaceful intentions of our Government?' M. de Champagny replied that my desire was extremely proper and that he would submit it to the Emperor, and it would certainly be granted by him. 'As to measures,' he added, 'they were ordered before I received your letter.' 'You see,' I replied, 'the inconvenience of the Emperor's journeys; he who is the centre, the pivot of European politics, is for six months of the year three hundred leagues from the representatives of the great Powers who are sent to his court because they feel the necessity of diplomatic relations other than those proceeding from inferior agents, who may be ill affected, and who, unhappily, too often write in a sense which, perhaps without cause, they think is that of their master.' M. de Champagny did not reply to this, and I do not think he could reply to so evident a truth.

It is important to observe everything, even shades of feeling, at a time like this. I am convinced that the Emperor does not think at the same time of the conquest of Spain and of war with us. One certain proof that he is tacking is the flattering promise he has made to Prince William of Prussia and Baron de Brockhausen * since his return from Bayonne, and those of the same kind M. de Champagny has made to M. de Tolstoy.

This ambassador came yésterday out of the minister's

---

* Prussian Ambassador in Paris.

room just at the moment when I was going in. The minister had addressed to Count Tolstoy the same question that he had asked me as to the impressions made by the audience; he asked him with evident interest whether he had seen me since yesterday, what I thought, &c., &c. M. de Tolstoy having told the minister that he and I were entirely of the same opinion that peace should be consolidated by frank discussions, and of one mind concerning the confidential and friendly form in which the Emperor had made these explanations, M. de Champagny begged him to write on this matter to Petersburg. Your Excellency has seen above that it was the Minister of Foreign Affairs who, at the conclusion of a court conversation, invited the ambassador of All the Russias to come and see him. The latter, after the reception given to his proposition the evening before, had reason to believe that the minister would bring back the conversation to a subject quite agreeable to the desires which the Emperor had expressed on the intervention of Russia in our differences. But it appeared— and the reason of it is clear—that M. de Champagny, having reported to his master M. de Tolstoy's words, had not been authorised to provoke the renewal of a proposal which tended to nothing less than the placing of a hundred thousand Russians on the flank of the French army. He did not mention the matter, and Count Tolstoy passed on to another question no less important, which is that of the carrying out of the whole Treaty of Tilsit, a question which interests us as much as it does Russia herself. . . .

The minister with many fine phrases insinuated that France would arrange her own affairs with Prussia. The ambassador then replied quietly and with dignity: 'Then the Treaty of Tilsit exists no more, for of what other interests did it treat than those of Prussia? You, then, in fact annul that treaty, and replace us in a state of war?'

M. de Champagny, thunderstruck, very hastily replied that he had not heard any but pecuniary matters between France and Prussia spoken of, details which he did not suppose would interest Russia, and he offered at the same time to make him fully acquainted with everything; and the conference ended by a formal promise being made by the minister that they would immediately proceed to carry out the stipulations of the Treaty of Tilsit.

Your Excellency can now compare all these different facts and statements. You will observe the position of affairs in Spain together with the threats used to Austria; you will doubtless trace the connection, which seems to me so evident, between the first overtures of M. de Champagny and General Andréossy with the return of the Emperor to Paris, and the call for a new conscription with the return of part of the army to France; you will see the motives which may lead the Emperor not to expose an immoral enterprise to the blame which always attends unsuccessful undertakings; you will calculate the military resources needed to enable him to support a disastrous war, while at the same time he would run the risk of a new war with Austria, in which he is far from being able to rely on the perfect quiescence of Russia; and I suppose that your Excellency will agree with me as to the possibility not only of our being able to avoid this war by wise and moderate conduct, but even to draw from the present complication a very great part for our political consideration. If the demon of war, if that invisible hand—which I do not believe to be so invisible as the Emperor asserts—in

spite of all our desires will wave the brand of discord so
as to force us again to a legitimate defence, is the present moment propitious for this defence? I do not
believe it, so true is it that the same measures which
the Emperor now condemns ought either to guarantee
us peace, or save us in a war; that, consequently, these
measures are good. But because they are so, they do
not suit the Emperor of the French. If I have the conviction that the Emperor does not at present wish to
make war upon us, if I have supported this conviction
on a number of the most valuable data, I am also
unhappily convinced that many people exhaust all their
powers to bring about war. All the smaller Powers, excited by the desire of obtaining some portion of the spoil;
all their agents, who think to serve the glory of what
they call their country, and who only aim at paying
their court to the Emperor; all the French agents, who
hope to rise a step in their master's confidence; all the
soldiers, who fear a civil war, in which they could neither
pillage nor gain glory from the '*bulletins*,' but might
meet their deaths; all the ambitious, all the speculators,
will move heaven and earth to provoke a war with
Austria. One of their constant means is to try to persuade the Emperor that we desire it; and that it is an
unpardonable imprudence to await the moment which
we think propitious to fall upon him. All these efforts
act like drops of water: they penetrate, they unite, they
swell, and too often end by carrying with them the
strongest wills; and the Emperor's will is never strong
when it is a question of opposing war.

NAPOLEON'S SPECIAL AUDIENCE, AUGUST 25, 1808.

(Note 27, Vol. I.)

116. Metternich to Stadion, Paris, August 26, 1808.
117. Metternich to Stadion, Paris, August 26, 1808.

116. The most mature deliberation on the orders of your Excellency, just transmitted to me, shows me that all my instructions are concentrated in the following passage, which I extract from your despatch.

' Your duty is to remove the remotest possible reason which the French cabinet can allege to justify an attack on Austria ; and at the same time you can and you ought to agree to all that does not lead to a revocation of the measures which we have executed, or a diminution or dispersion of our army of the line. These are the limits of your powers.'

Explanations on past accusations having nothing to do with the affairs of the day can only, as it appears to me, be referred to from an historical point of view, to show our perfect loyalty. But I must try to advance the present business as much as possible.

I went the next day, the 24th, to the Minister of Foreign Affairs. I informed him that I was desired to request an audience from his Imperial Majesty. To give here the conversation that I had with M. de Champagny would be to repeat what I said with more detail to the Emperor.

The Emperor received me yesterday at seven in the evening, before going to the play at St. Cloud.

I began by saying that the Emperor, my master, had expressly desired me to seek an audience; that the object of his Imperial Majesty in so doing was solely for the purpose of expressing, through his ambassador, the renewed assurance of his sentiments. 'I acquit myself of my august master's order,' said I, 'with all the more satisfaction that I can do so at a moment when I may regard the late discussions as entirely terminated. Your Majesty has promised me the retreat of your troops from those points which threaten Austria. I promise you, in the name of my master, the most strict accomplishment of all that was announced in the patents published by us in the month of May last. Our reserves will be, till September 1, all occupied in agriculture; the exercises of the militia will conclude with the fine weather. Has your Majesty been dissatisfied at the assembling of five regiments near Cracow? They shall be dispersed. We have no other measure to revoke, because no other measure has been taken in opposition to the threatening position of the French army and its allies.'

'Let us be neither Emperor of the French nor Austrian Ambassador,' returned the Emperor. 'I will speak to you as a man whom I esteem, and we need make no speeches, for we are not as we were the other day in the presence of a large audience. I look upon all as concluded: therefore there is no need to return to that subject. I have never believed that the Emperor or Count Stadion or the Archduke Charles wished for war. You are not on good terms with Russia; you cannot make war on me without her; but I feared that you might, by some false steps, be dragged into war without wishing it.   One ought not to put oneself in a position where a spark may decide one's fate.   Consider, one simple wrong word on your part personally, one single false step, would have provoked it.   I speak quite frankly.   You see how imminent the danger was.   I know what is required of our Government.   I am a soldier, therefore all that you may say will never make me look at your armaments and the present disposition of your army otherwise than as they are.   A Power that wishes to make war does not form camps.   It is quite possible to meet at a given point without camps previously made; they can be formed even in marching. Grant that it was the affairs in Spain which alarmed you; you already imagined your throne overturned, as I had overturned that one: which is not to be wondered at —the same thing was said by the public in Paris.   But what a difference!   Do you know why I made a change in Spain?   Because I want to secure complete tranquillity; because, since the famous proclamation at the time of the campaign in Prussia, the miserable Prince de la Paix himself had, what no one would believe, increased the army by fifty thousand men; because Spain, instead of putting her capital in the navy which I required to force England to peace,—she became daily more and more intractable,—spent it all in reinforcing the army, which could only be used against me.   I cannot blame them; I was too strong for them.   And then the throne was occupied by Bourbons; they are my personal enemies. They and I cannot occupy thrones at the same time in Europe.   The other dynasties have not that peculiarity.   I make a great difference between the House of Lorraine and that of the Bourbons.   Why believe in my extreme, immoderate ambition?   You see it is a prudential calculation of true political interest which made me profit by the dissensions in the royal House. It has been said that it was I who fomented them. That is not true. But I must have on the throne of Spain a prince who would have no anxiety on my account, and who on his side gives me none; the interests of Spain, even of America, demand it.'

I did not interrupt these speeches except by some observations to rectify the assertions of the Emperor about our armaments, which I declared have not, and never had, any other object but to insure the safety of the Austrian monarchy, and the internal and external consideration which it has a right to claim.

'What has annoyed me,' said the Emperor, 'is that at Vienna they denied the armaments.' 'How could they deny,' asked I, 'what has been done in consequence of patents printed, published, and circulated through the whole of Europe?' 'No,' replied the Emperor; 'Count Stadion denied them in his conversations with Andréossy.' 'He may have denied,' said I, 'what did not exist— that is, offensive and hostile intentions. He could not deny the very simple means of defence that we have adopted. Besides, I know the very words which M. de Stadion has used.'

The Emperor then passed on to a discussion which lasted more than half an hour on the want of friendliness in the relations of the two courts. He complained (while begging me never to mention such trivial matters to my court) that the Emperor and Empress, in the diplomatic audiences, never asked the French Ambassador after his health. 'Do you think,' said he, 'that when in every audience I ask you questions of this kind, I do it in order to be informed of what I know? No, it is only for the public, to show what good relations exist between the sovereigns. You see the footing on

which I am with the Emperor Alexander. We make
each other presents; these presents do not enrich us,
but they strengthen the ties between us. I had wished
to give a wedding present to your Empress, but she had
never pronounced my name. Do you not see that these
presents serve me here? Well, not one mark of attention on your part! Here we treat you personally better
than we ought, because we wish you well. With you,
never any little attention to my ambassador at Vienna
more than to those bestowed on an envoy of Bavaria
or Wurtemburg. Less attention is always paid to him
than to a Russian ambassador. You have seen the care
that is taken here to receive one of your archdukes
pleasantly. These little things are great when it comes
to results.'

I took up the question lightly, although it contained
very substantial truths, if not in its present application,
at least in principle. I said to him that if we had seen
the least advance on his part, that if we had not even
feared to involve ourselves by acting without meeting
any reciprocal action, we should have wished nothing
better than to put ourselves on a pleasant footing with
him, always much more agreeable than constant explanations. 'I reply to you, sire,' said I, 'that I should
be very quickly ordered to present some vases if they
would help to consolidate good relations between us.'

The Emperor replied: 'But I have given you such
good opportunities! At Tilsit I received a general
whom the Emperor Alexander had refused to see.
There has been no desire to take up the thread; your
people are so awkward! You might then have placed
yourselves on the same intimate footing as Russia; you
have not been willing to do so, and that must have been
a very great advantage to your finances.' 'Do you

desire an alliance?' said I, interrupting the Emperor.
'I am ready to agree to the bases, and I can assure
your Majesty that I could not advise my court of a
more flattering result to our discussions.'

'Preliminaries are necessary to such a state of
things,' said the Emperor; 'treaties are nothing, the
manner of acting is everything.'

'But I have seen none but the most bitter feelings
between France and Russia,' I replied, 'till the time of
Tilsit; they immediately gave place to the most intimate
relations, with all sorts of pleasant refinements.'

The Emperor did not well know how to reply. He
spoke of the personal character of the Emperor Alexander, of his extreme attachment to the prince, of the
proofs which they had given of their especial and
reciprocal esteem. He assured me that he should be
attached to him all his life, and that, in spite of what
might be generally thought, he considered him a wise
prince, firm in his government, and faithful to principles
once established. He added that the good relations
between France and Russia ought to be attributed to
him alone; that there was at St. Petersburg a great
party against France, &c.

After a conversation of an hour and a quarter, which
was much more like a quarrel between lovers than a
discussion between a sovereign and an ambassador, they
came to tell the Emperor that the play had been
waiting for him for an hour. He said to me, 'You
must take the blame of that to-day; but let us continue.
I understand, then, that by the 1st of September next
you will have brought back your reserves, raised the
camp near Cracow, brought the interior of the monarchy into perfect repose, and, finally, that you believe
your court will recognise the Kings. If they will not do

so, let them say so at once, or let them show some little good grace and say a civil word or two to the *chargé d'affaires* of Spain at Vienna. The Emperor Alexander did not wait for me to ask this ; he wrote a letter to me at once as soon as he heard of the changes in Spain. For my part, tell the Emperor that I consider everything concluded ; that I shall withdraw my troops from Prussia and the Duchy of Warsaw beyond the Elbe ; that I only wish for direct influence in Europe to the banks of the Rhine, and indirectly as far as the Elbe, the Inn, and the Isonzo. The thing is quite simple ; I think I am the stronger for not going as far as the Vistula, but keeping myself more concentrated. Prussia will become the strongest Power of the second order. She will always be your friend : your interest and hers make that necessary. I have nothing to object ; I do not desire to extend my influence beyond the natural line I have pointed out to you. Russia is at the present moment given up to her own political calculations ; she makes conquests in Sweden, she desires to grapple with Turkey, she does not evacuate the Principalities, and yet I evacuate Prussia ! I must have a conscription to reinforce the Spanish army, which will have to make great efforts. But for your attitude those efforts would have been small : now they must be considerable. I have armed the Confederation to replace fifty or sixty thousand men whom I take from my army in Germany. There is one point in Europe on which we both ought to fix our eyes : you see what is passing at Constantinople ; if you had taken a different line latterly, we should understand one another now ; but, things being as they are, in consequence of your attitude, I must come to an understanding with Russia. But in this matter I have only an indirect interest and little to claim from the Porte—some consideration, a change in some little things, may on their side lead to modifications in your favour. Explain thoroughly to the Emperor that it is not an ambitious motive which has directed me in the affairs of Spain, but simply the question of the Bourbons, and the incompatibility of their existence with mine, a principle which does not apply to any other reigning House in Europe; and tell him that I certainly consider everything between us as ended.'

I had asked Champagny to have Séguier * recalled, I now repeated the request to the Emperor. He promised this to me; he will not recall him at once, because he will not appear to yield to the populace of Trieste, but he will do it in obedience to the principle of never leaving an agent in a foreign country who is displeasing to that country. He said that if Séguier had talked in the way I mentioned, he was quite criminal.

The result of this conversation, which I can only consider the last scene of the discussion which has occupied us since the month of June, appears to me to be as follows :—

The Emperor Napoleon, being obliged to make great efforts for the conquest of Spain, does not at this moment think of attacking us. Austria having, on her side, attained the very great object of fairly completing her means of internal defence, can consolidate her forces; she has gained a no less important point by preserving an honourable attitude in the last discussion, such as becomes a Power of the first class, without fear or reproach.

Although I can only hope for the solution of a question which threatens many complications by the

* French Consul at Trieste.

efforts of a people on whose help one can never reckon, I think I can maintain the dignity of the court and the cause which I have the happiness to defend. The approval of our august master will be the best recompense I can desire.

Metternich to Stadion, Paris, August 26, 1808.

117. I suppose that your Excellency will have perfectly agreed with the conclusion of the preceding despatch. It requires no explanation, but it shows some favourable chances in its application to our future line of conduct. Austria has attained an immense end. She has profited by the only moment given her to heal her wounds, and step once more on to the theatre of Europe stronger and more powerful than ever. The most unforeseen events have come to her help; perhaps she could not have carried out what she had so wisely conceived without these same events, but these events taking place we have carried them out; let us only take care to establish them and profit by them.

The Emperor had really nothing to say to me yesterday, therefore he kept to trifles; but they are not trifles to him. We shall bring about better relations by little forms than by great concessions. If we one day wish for war, let us make it decidedly; wishing for peace, make it pleasant by the observance of small matters of form. Our position is too well established for us to fear committing ourselves by forms and ceremonies, however punctilious they may be. I said yesterday to the Emperor that these forms could only exist with the most perfect reciprocity. Let us feel our way, and stop if they do not respond to us in the same sense.

As to our military measures, let us start from the point of view that war cannot take place under a year; the conquest of Spain will be, whether impossible or quickly over, yet costly. It will demand great present efforts, and not smaller ones to maintain it. The Emperor will be occupied for several months beyond the Pyrenees; his best troops will go in that direction. He will raise a conscription; but he would not even if he could employ it entirely to fight against us. He respects us too much to attack us with raw recruits; he has just shown in Spain that recruits are only good when interspersed with old soldiers, or to give chase to a vanquished enemy. And what chances may not occur before the end of a year! The Emperor will day by day be less likely to risk the chances of a disputed war; such a war is odious to the public mind, and to bring back the armies of the Pyrenees towards the Inn is not the affair of a moment, and cannot be done for a mere whim.

I foresee that after the evacuation of Prussia (and the treaty is really ready to be signed) he will leave the army in Germany, and probably in Italy, to observe us: the merest prudence demands this. Let us not appear to see it; let us be calm and quiet, trust to our vast resources in case of danger, and show that we consider the present a favourable time for internal amelioration, quite exempt from all cause of anxiety from without.

This is how things appear to me, and therefore I do not hesitate to submit my views frankly to our august master.

I yesterday expressed my desire to accompany the Emperor on his first journey, being convinced that good relations between great Powers require to be ceaselessly cultivated. I told him that in case he did not grant my wish, I should request my master to allow me to go to Vienna, if it were only for two or three weeks. I expressed myself decidedly for one or other alternative, being convinced of the utility of the first, and failing that, to give me a chance of requesting his Imperial Majesty to recall me to Vienna, where I should regard my presence at a time of the greatest stagnation in affairs as perhaps useful by giving the opportunity for verbal explanations.

THE MEETING OF THE MONARCHS AT ERFURT.

(Note 24, Vol. I.)

118. Metternich to Stadion, Paris, September 14, 1808.
119. Metternich to Stadion, Paris, September 14, 1808.
120. Metternich to Stadion, September 22, 1808.
121. Metternich to Stadion, September 23, 1808.

118. An officer of the Guards, who arrived here the day before yesterday as courier from St. Petersburg, brought the Emperor the decision of the Emperor Alexander as to the time and place determined on for their interview. The two Sovereigns should go to Erfurt on September 27. The Emperor of the French should take the road by Metz, Frankfort, and Mayence, and reckons on returning here by October 15. The *Corps Législatif* is convoked for the 22nd of the same month, and his Majesty will go about that time to rejoin the army assembled at the foot of the Pyrenees.

Napoleon will be accompanied by MM. de Talleyrand, de Champagny, Maret, and Duroc; General Nansouty and two chamberlains will form the rest of the suite. MM. de Romanzow, de Tolstoy, and de Caulaincourt will accompany the Emperor Alexander. The Emperor Napoleon has hinted to M. de Tolstoy that he should invite him to accompany him. This ambassador has taken the Sovereign at his word, and assumed the fact in his subsequent conversations with M. de Champagny.

Convinced that on great occasions great measures must be taken, I yesterday presented myself to M. de Talleyrand, after much deliberation for and against the step I was contemplating. It was he who confided to me the details of his Majesty's journey, which I have just had the honour to communicate to your Excellency. He asked me if I had had any reply to the project of our august master's going to surprise the two Sovereigns at Erfurt; he insisted over and over again on the extreme utility of this step. He made an immense difference between the presence of our august master himself and the sending of one of the princes of the House, and thought the latter not of much use.

I then submitted to him the question whether there would be any difficulty in what I had in my private name suggested as to my being invited to accompany Napoleon. I attributed my desire to the nature of the relations which exist between Austria and France, and the importance which our intervention would have in the questions concerning a general peace, if such should be the object of the interview. I spoke of the embarrassment in which they placed themselves here by a refusal which showed us that, the presence of a man charged with the interests of Austria being unwelcome, the deliberations at Erfurt would be of a character which might endanger those very interests; and remarked to him lastly that a step taken in my private name, and with all necessary care, could not expose the dignity of my court, if, above all, I manifested my desire to prove to all Europe the real existence of good relations between our two Governments. M. de Talley-rand entered completely into my way of looking at things, and he approved my calculations and the conclusions I drew from them, and we agreed that I should make an advance to M. de Champagny in the way I had explained.

In fact, I went to see the minister just as he had

left the Vice-Grand Elector.   I turned the conversation
on the Emperor's journey.   M. de Champagny told me
that he had submitted to his Majesty my wish to be
informed of the time of his departure (a wish which I
had never expressed), that many of the members of the
Corps Diplomatique had the same desire, and that his
Majesty, who, however, had not given him any orders,
would no doubt enable him to inform me of it several
days beforehand.   I put some questions to M. de Champagny on the determinations of the Emperor Alexander
with regard to the choice of persons who are to accompany the Emperor of the French.   He only replied in
his usual manner in monosyllables.   'I do not know,'
said I, ' why I should ask you questions on the things
that I know.   But why does not the Emperor give to
Europe an evident proof of our good relations by admitting me into his suite ?   I take the same point of
view that the Emperor himself took in the last conversation I had with him on the subject of our good relations (No. 116).   From this the idea has come to me of
the real utility, both for our separate relations and the
cause of general peace, of my admission as the ambassador of a friendly and influential Power at the interview of Erfurt.'

M. de Champagny was embarrassed to reply, and as
he always in moments of difficulty chooses the least
plausible arguments, he said that I knew his Majesty
was not in the habit of being accompanied by the *Corps
Diplomatique* ; that this was nothing but a long-arranged
interview between two friends ; that I was quite right
to insist on the re-establishment of better relations
between the two courts ; and that he especially begged
me to believe that in the interview in question our
interests will not be in any way involved.

'If I could believe that,' I replied, 'I should not even mention the idea which has occurred to me; I should in that case regard my presence quite as useless to hinder the evil as in the contrary supposition it seems to me suited to assure the good. The meeting of the two Emperors bears a more serious character than that of a simple meeting of friends; they would not be accompanied by their ministers if great interests were not concerned, and what are those to which Austria can be indifferent? Is it a question of achieving a general peace? We are not less interested, and not less useful, than France and Russia. Is it a question of regulating the relations of the Continental Powers among themselves? Austria occupies there a too prominent place for an arrangement of this kind to take place without her. I believe I shall serve you,' added I, 'by furnishing you with so natural a means of attaining the great end that I suppose to be the only one which the Emperor Napoleon can propose to himself. I am besides quite at ease in speaking to you of all this, for the most that my court knows is that the interview is decided on; I am without orders and without instructions, and it is easy for you to calculate from the very dates themselves that I cannot speak as an Austrian ambassador, but merely as a private person.'

M. de Champagny then objected that the other members of the diplomatic body would be able to make the same claim. 'The Spanish and Persian Ambassadors will perhaps express the same desire.'

'It is not a question of claims,' replied I. 'I submit to you a wish for which there is good reason; besides,' added I, smiling, 'I cannot, either from a moral or political point of view, agree to your comparing an ambassador of Austria with the envoy of a

Khan of Persia ; we form a veritable diplomatic anti-
thesis.'

M. de Champagny, doubtless seeing that he was
treading on dangerous ground, told me that he would
communicate my idea to the Emperor. He agreed with
me on the terms to be used, which were quite in agreement with my wishes.

I am far from asserting that my project can be executed. It offers the double advantage of enabling me
to watch the French negotiators and influence the
Russian. This last point would be of great importance,
but the more favourable the chances seem to be the less
I allow myself to look at the possibility.

Be that as it may, I believe I have done my duty in
not neglecting the only step at my disposal, and especially in doing it so as not to commit my court in any
way, M. de Champagny having undertaken to sound the
ground before bringing a refusal upon me.

Metternich to Stadion, Paris, September 14, 1808.

119. It would be difficult beforehand to form a
correct idea of what may be the result of the interview
between the two Emperors. I believe even they themselves do not know. Napoleon knows what his intentions are and what projects he will bring forward.
Alexander believes that everything will be as he wishes.
The former wants all he can get ; the latter may agree
to far more than he wishes or intends to agree to.
There are events independent of all calculation : above
calculation when it concerns Napoleon ; below it when it
relates to a cabinet such as that of St. Petersburg.

The only foundation we can go upon is the position
of affairs at the time of the interview, the more or less
complications that Napoleon may take an interest in

bringing forth, the more or less courage which Alexander can bring to bear in this same position of affairs.

I send to-day to your Excellency communications of great interest, which will enable you to form your opinion on this position.

You will receive in No. 1 the *Moniteur* of September 5, which puts forth officially, on the very day of the sitting of the Senate, the point of view imposed on the public by the court with regard to the march of events in Spain.

In No. 2 the *Moniteur* of September 7, which contains the first published details of the sitting of the Senate on the 5th.

In No. 3 more details of that same sitting.

In No. 4 the remarks which have been made in several newspapers on the defection of General de la Romana and on the affairs of Spain and Portugal.

All these papers take us back by similarity of phrases and style to 1793. None of them present us with any fixed plan for the future. The Senate has decreed that the war with Spain is right, and founded on a system of sound policy ; the power of a Senate does not extend to eternal principles or the opinion of the people.

Rhetorical phrases are pushed to the point of supposing that the shades of Henry IV., Francis I., and Louis XIV. smile at the generous enterprise of Napoleon in overthrowing the throne of their great grandson. The shades of these princes cannot avenge the insult done to them.

Everything is overturned, principles, proprieties, and historical authority, to establish new principles of policy and the rights of men. Neither M. de Champagny, nor Clarke, nor the orators of the tribunes of 1793, will ever prove to the French people and the public of Europe

that the way to force England to peace is to furnish her
with new and immense means of making war ; they will
never make it believed that the existence of a feeble
Bourbon on the throne of Spain was more dangerous to
the well-being of France than the indefinite struggle in
which she finds herself engaged in the Peninsula, or than
the loss of America.

The levying of 80,000 conscripts, taken from the
reserves of the last few years, is justified by the obligation of sustaining the national honour, and they taunt
Austria with the calling under arms children of seventeen years; but the people are no more deceived as
to the real motive which endangers the glory of their
armies than as to the supposed intentions of Austria.

They pay some respect to us in the speeches of the
ministers, but we are reviled by the orators in the Senate.
The first are the manifestoes to the Powers, the last are
addressed to the French nation. The people of Europe
are no longer to be moved by these speeches; all
opinions are united in this fact, that the internal and
foreign position of Napoleon has sustained terrible
checks in consequence of his calculations as foolhardy
as they are false.

According to my opinion, Napoleon has sustained
reverses which he must repair, and the interview with his
august ally should furnish him with the means.

Does he wish to repair his failures on the same stage
on which he has sustained them, or does he not
rather seek another part of Europe in which to recover
what his own plans and the faults of his generals have
caused him to lose in public opinion? This question,
recently a very sensible one, exists no longer. There is
now no alternative. He must use every effort to terminate the work commenced. The march of his armies,

his last public acts, leave no doubt on the subject. The principal end of the interview must therefore be that of making himself easy against any possibility of annoyance and attack on the part of Austria and Russia.

Can he arrive at that end by complicating the questions between France and Austria? I think not.

Can he wish to breed dissension between Austria and Russia to attain this end? Two Powers which have neither the wish nor the motive to fight will explain to each other instead of fighting, and these explanations will lead too easily to their union for him to wish to give rise to them.

Will he make known to the Russian Cabinet all his projects for the future? Does he hope by that proof of confidence to bring it to declare itself implicitly an accomplice of his plans?

To make many insidious and vague overtures, to obtain formal promises in exchange, to caress the self-love of Alexander, to flatter the presumption of his minister and profit by it, to persuade Russia to hold us in check, to promise him the division and the greater part of Turkey, to guarantee him Finland—these are, no doubt, the things Napoleon will propose.

M. de Talleyrand will on his side do all he can to enter into a negotiation with England. That would be, for mankind in general, the happiest end of this journey.

What is, on the contrary, the part indicated to us by the present situation? Let us seek it in the military resources which Austria has so wisely displayed latterly; it is to those we owe our safety. A Power of the first rank can only sustain itself by its own weight. If France threw herself upon us with the forces of Russia joined with hers, we should run the risk of being crushed. The first does not dream of making war upon

us at this moment ; the second no longer dreams of it
at all. An Emperor who, according to the idea of M.
de Talleyrand, should appear in person in the midst of
the Congress at Erfurt, and should say, ' I put 400,000
soldiers, and all my people armed, in the balance of
justice ; I am ready to perish sword in hand if anyone
wishes to try to crush me ; I maintain that peace can
only exist with my assent ; I wish only for peace, but
in that peace a state of things suitable to the dignity of
my crown,' would very much embarrass the strength
of Napoleon and the weakness of Alexander.

A proof that questions eminently political are to be
discussed is found in the departure of many of the *employés* of the Department of Foreign Affairs. The chief
of division, La Besnardière, will go to-morrow morning.

One thing appears to me incontestable—that is, that
we cannot remain idle spectators of the conferences
which are now beginning.

Metternich to Stadion, Paris, September 22, 1808.

120. I hasten to have the honour of informing your
Excellency of the departure of his Majesty for Erfurt
at the very moment of his starting. He reckons on
arriving on the 26th of this month, and remaining
twenty days.

M. de Talleyrand has preceded the Emperor by four
days.

M. de Champagny left us yesterday. The Russian
Ambassador is in the immediate suite of the Emperor.

The evening before M. de Talleyrand's departure I
called upon him. He again expressed his wish that our
august master could resolve to take the personal step
he had advised formerly. ' All the Kings and princes
of the Confederation will repair to Erfurt,' added he ;

' the prince who is not there will have the appearance of being a neutral or an enemy. The Emperor of Austria cannot be in the first case, for nothing can take place in Europe without his offering either a hindrance or a facility. For myself, I would desire that at the right moment the Emperor Francis should arrive as a hindrance.'

He asked me if, in speaking at Vienna of this idea of the journey, I had made mention of it as entirely his own. I said ' Yes.' ' Well,' replied he, ' I hope your court will attach a little more importance to it ; in any case address whatever you may send to me at Erfurt. You may count on my care : I regard your interests as my own ; such is my way of thinking altogether at this moment of the greatest importance.'

Proceeding to M. de Champagny to take leave of him, I found his door closed to everyone except me. He came to meet me, and told me he hoped he had not been acting contrary to my wishes, by informing his Majesty of an idea I had expressed in our last interview. ' The Emperor,' added he, ' has expressly charged me to tell you that, if he consulted only his goodwill towards you individually, he would not hesitate a moment to invite you to accompany him, but it would not do on this occasion to make an exception in favour of the Austrian Ambassador. The Emperor has not admitted into his suite any member of the *Corps Diplomatique* except M. de Tolstoy, and he hopes that you will not see in that fact a mark of particular favour for him : he has an interview with the Emperor of Russia ; he brings with him his ambassador, because the Emperor Alexander is accompanied by M. de Caulaincourt; if he went to see the Emperor Francis he would propose to you to go with him, to the exclusion of all your

colleagues. The Emperor Francis came alone to Presburg on a very solemn occasion; no particular attention
is paid to General Andréossy. Believe me that the
Emperor has rendered to you a hundredfold any little
private attentions his ambassador has received at Vienna.
As things now are, the Emperor can carefully avoid
showing to another ambassador a preference over you,
but at the same time he cannot show a preference to
you over any other. You must see this case in the
relations of the Emperor with the Russian Ambassador;
nothing is done for him officially, while everything of a
private nature is returned to M. de Caulaincourt at St.
Petersburg.'

I said to M. de Champagny that my conduct must
have convinced his court that I knew very well how to
distinguish between private courtesy and official diplomatic favours; that the Emperor had an undoubted
right to receive into his suite and to take on his journey
whom he thought proper; that, on the other hand, I
could not admit that nothing had been done at Vienna
for the Ambassador of France. 'It would not be difficult for me,' added I, ' to prove that he has been treated
with marked and particular favour; we are now taking
the point of view of the most perfect reciprocity of all
the courts; although an ambassador is to be found at
Paris who has received attentions which are not accorded
to me, we should still be acting contrary to our general
rule in treating the Ambassador of France less well
than his colleagues. But we are not talking of a
thing which belongs in the least to etiquette. Your
Excellency will always find me taking the same course
—giving to both courts the means of understanding and
furthering their own interests by facilitating the means
of showing to each other reciprocal esteem and con-

sideration.   Such is my invariable aim.   The same point
of view makes me desire to accompany the Emperor.
It is a fact that in all which can or should be treated of
at Erfurt, Austria must have the greatest weight for or
against.   You wish only for peace, Austria only wishes
for peace; having then but one aim, we must wish to
attain it by the same means.'

'The Emperor,' replied M. de Champagny, 'has
expressly charged me to tell you that he finds in the
wish I have submitted to him on your part, of accom-
panying him to Erfurt, a new proof of the good spirit
which animates you; but the public attach a very
exaggerated value to an interview agreed upon for more
than eight months, put off from one time to another,
and which is, in reality, nothing but a meeting of two
friends.   It is expected to affect all the interests and
relations of the Continent; some reference will, of
course, be made to affairs, but that will be only a secondary matter.'

I interrupted the minister to tell him that I was far
from sharing the exaggerated opinions of the public, and
equally far from allowing my opinion and my calculations to be influenced by any reasoning whatever. 'I
know better than the Parisians,' said I, 'our strength
and our real weight.   I do too much justice to the position Austria occupies among the Powers of Europe
not to regard as vain and illusory an enterprise intended
to regulate the fate of the Continent without her concurrence.   I am perfectly easy on that head.'

Here the minister repeated what he had just said
about the object of the interview, adding some phrases
to assure me that the interview would contain nothing
which would involve the interests of Austria, and that
it was really principally to concert means to force Eng-

land to peace, which, indeed, must be done. 'You are not,' continued he, 'in a proper geographical position to influence England in that respect, and Russia alone united to France can force her to that result.'

I observed to M. de Champagny that if they wished to force England to peace, Austria could not long remain a stranger to the enterprise; that I was astonished to hear him say we had no influence over that Power, when the Emperor himself had said to me, before a number of witnesses, that the English funds had risen 50 per cent. from the simple probability that Austria might again enter the lists with France; that, on the other side, in calculating only the state of suffering in which we found ourselves in a great many respects, in consequence of our concurrence with Continental measures, I could but suppose that this same concurrence of Austria must have an equally powerful influence on the adverse party.

M. de Champagny, by way of reply, launched forth into protestations on the services we had rendered to the common cause by the measures we had adopted and executed. His principal object was to bring out tranquillising speeches for Austria, personally polite to me, but telling me in a manner meant to be gracious, but made awkward by the turn given to it by M. de Champagny, that they did not wish for us, and thought they could arrange alone with the Emperor of Russia.

Let us bring together all that is contained in my later despatches, that which I have now added, and what the Emperor said to me at the diplomatic audience of August 15, and at the private audience on the 25th of the same month (Nos. 114 and 116), and I find myself perfectly correct in what I took the liberty to submit to your Excellency in my despatch of the 14th of the month (No. 119).

Metternich to Stadion, Paris, September 23, 1808.

121. The Emperor's suite is composed as I had the honour to inform your Excellency. The Prince of Neuchâtel has left to-day with his Majesty. The Russian Ambassador went yesterday.

His Majesty's departure has been delayed one day, but the reason is not known. He sent the day before yesterday an aide-de-camp of the Prince of Neuchâtel to meet the Emperor Alexander, with orders to return as soon as he had joined that prince.

Thirty-two actors and *figuranti* of the Théâtre-Français have been sent with all haste to Erfurt. They compose only the *cadre* of the drama, and, excepting the two or three principal performers, more regard has been had to the persons of the actresses than to their talent. This circumstance, which has not escaped public malice, has amused the Parisians. This levying *en masse* of the drama is a very expensive piece of attention; each individual receives a thousand crowns for the expenses of the journey, the principal ones have eight thousand francs as a gift, and so on with the rest.

THE QUESTION OF THE RECOGNITION OF THE KINGS OF SPAIN AND NAPLES BY AUSTRIA.

(Note 24, Vol. I.)

122. Metternich to Stadion, Paris, August 23, 1808.
123. Metternich to Stadion, Paris, September 24, 1808.
124. Metternich's note concerning the recognition of the Kings of Spain and Naples at the Congress of Erfurt. September, 1808.

122. 'The Emperor has charged me,' said M. de Champagny, 'to beg you to come and talk of an object which he has very much at heart, and which will immediately put an end to all the explanations which have been going on between us for some time. You doubtless know that I am about to conclude an arrangement with the Prussian Minister at Paris which will terminate all the differences which still exist with that Power. The Emperor is sure that both you and the whole of Europe will acknowledge in the withdrawal of his troops beyond the Elbe a pledge of his pacific intentions. The camps in Silesia have alarmed you ; you will, therefore, find in the absolute evacuation of that province sufficient reasons for tranquillity. The Emperor desires, on his part, that you will give him—to him and to Europe—a pledge of your pacific intentions, and of the happy and intimate relations that exist between you and France ; he desires that you will recognise the new Kings of Spain and Naples.'

I replied to the Minister of Foreign Affairs that I would transmit with pleasure this wish of the Emperor

Napoleon to my court; that, without being able to reply officially to a new question, I did not hesitate to express my private conviction that his Imperial Majesty would seize with pleasure an opportunity which gave the Emperor Napoleon a safe means of baffling the calculations of all the malevolents in Europe, by withdrawing from our frontiers and from a friendly country armies whose presence alone led to a crowd of conjectures and interpretations.

'I may as well tell you,' interrupted the minister, 'that Russia has already recognised the new King of Spain. While we were at Bayonne, a courier from St. Petersburg brought to M. de Strogonoff* the order to recognise whatever Sovereign the Emperor Napoleon designated for the throne of Spain. The Emperor Alexander added that, the public voice naming King Joseph, his Majesty would have particular satisfaction in recognising him. King Joseph's accession to the throne,' added the minister, 'has taken place by virtue of treaties concluded according to principles in conformity with the rights of the public. The Emperor intends to communicate them to the Senate immediately.'

'The Emperor, my master,' replied I, 'has never needed any example whatever to guide him in his political career and in the friendly relations which he desires to maintain with France. The Emperor Napoleon will, then, find nothing more in the determination which the Emperor Francis will necessarily take than the simple desire to prove to France the sentiments which animate him towards her.'

M. de Champagny appeared perfectly satisfied with what I had told him. He asked if he might communicate the sense of our interview to his Majesty, and

* Gregor von Strogonoff, Russian Ambassador in Madrid.—ED.

said that he had addressed a short note to me, which contained the Emperor's wish in a very succinct manner. I authorised him to take the first step, and assured him that I would immediately transmit his note to Vienna. He ended our conversation by telling me that he had intimated to M. de Brockhausen * that the ratification of the arrangement which he had negotiated with him relative to the entire evacuation of the Prussian provinces would not take place till the return of my courier from Vienna, and consequently depended on questions opened between France and Austria.

To finish a question the same day as Napoleon raises it, is ordinarily to win at all hazards. It was with that view that, two months before the demand was actually addressed to me, I begged for precise instructions on this question, foreseeing not only that it would be made, but above all that the Emperor would attach to the recognition a value great enough for us to be able to derive a real advantage from it. What worse calculation than that of the Minister of St. Petersburg to recognise in advance, and implicitly, any disposition that prince would make! What a proof, among many, how little is known of the character of the Emperor of the French, and of the French character in general! The fact that no one has done the same, but the Prince Primate, is the most severe censure that can be passed on this proof of eagerness and submission from one of the first Powers in Europe.

Metternich to Stadion, Paris, September 24, 1808.

123. Nothing is more impossible to bring together than eternal and incontestable principles and a system

---

* Prussian Ambassador in Paris.—ED.

of conduct adopted and followed inversely to these same principles for a long series of years.

The elevation of King Joseph to the throne of Spain is incompatible with those principles; it is more so even than that of many members of the Napoleonic dynasty, inasmuch as the means used to place him on the throne are not justified by the pretext of a right of conquest. The crown was not vacant. Nothing could less resemble voluntary abdications than those of Ferdinand VII. and Charles IV.; they were not obliged, as I had the honour to inform your Excellency lately, to sign acts of renunciation for the younger branches, therefore there still exist imprescriptible rights to this crown among many members of the reigning family; they exist in the younger branches not less justly called to the succession; but these same rights form the indictment of all the Powers, which have recognised Napoleon in the place of Louis XVIII. That was the first, the grand usurpation; all the others are but corollaries. The Powers, by recognising that, have admitted that they have sacrificed the principles on which their own crowns depend to imperious and secondary conditions; but the principle has not the less been injured, and the conduct of the Powers put in opposition with that same principle. At the time of the proclamation of Joseph, I wished that my court would take its stand on a question common to all the Powers, but which had particular considerations for us. I then wished to know the side decidedly taken for or against the recognition, foreseeing, what has since happened, that Napoleon would make this demand one of those brusque incidents which are only too characteristic of him and his political career.

Measures on his part, as false as they were unhappy

in their execution, relieve us from the embarrassment in which we should have been found but for the noble effort of the Spaniards; but those same misfortunes lead him to address to us much more peremptorily the demand for the recognition. If he makes this demand a pretext to account for the recall of his troops from our frontiers, it is nevertheless true that this recognition has a value for him, which, besides its political importance, is worth a hundredfold more as a personal object. . . . Your Excellency will permit me to submit a calculation to you which the delay of the arrival of the courier from Vienna has enabled me to make. I have supposed that his Majesty, informed in the meantime of the approaching interview between the two Emperors at Erfurt, would have decided to send there a person of confidence; that this person would be charged to make the recognition of the new Kings a subject of negotiation; that he would put this demand in opposition to the exclusion of Austria from this interview; that he would do all in his power to make it advantageous for his side; that he would make this new condescension of Austria of as much more value as the attitude of France became more menacing. This step appeared to me more simple, as Napoleon had in the meantime withdrawn his troops, which he has done without waiting for what we were to do; but my calculation would have been wrong, because his Majesty was ignorant that the interview was decidedly settled; contradictory news have even been received from St. Petersburg in the probability of an event which unquestionably is a real political catastrophe.

The Emperor has gone: his minister is at Erfurt. M. de Vincent will be able to judge if our conditional recognition is not taken for a definitive recognition, if some advantage is not obtained by a manner more pronounced for or against. M. de Vincent, as negotiator on the spot, is, indeed, the only person who can obtain any advantage from all which he will be commanded to say. I, who am so far off, who can only write, and consequently can do nothing that would have any influence — I know too well the pace of affairs with Napoleon not to be convinced of my uselessness for the time being.

My Ideas concerning the Recognition of the Kings of Spain and Naples at the Congress of Erfurt, September, 1808.

124. The objects I proposed to myself in the month of September, 1808, were as follows :—

1. To put an end to all questions relative to our armaments.

2. To offer to my court, by the recognition of the new Kings, a way of commencing with France more amicable relations apparently; and, by putting delays in the way of the recognition, to furnish it with means no less certain of coming to a clear understanding on the general interests of Europe.

I have attained the first of these objects by Champagny's official Note, which declares that the Emperor is quite at his ease as to our intentions towards him, and which puts an end to all discussion on the Austrian armaments.

We are asked in this same Note for the recognition of the Kings, as a pleasure to be conferred upon Napoleon, who in this fact would find a sufficient guarantee of our intentions towards him.

I obtained an official and written declaration; I replied to the demand for the recognition of the Kings by verbal assurances of the amicable intentions of my court. I accepted as definite the assurance of the end of our discussions.

The Conferences of Erfurt were concluded at that time. An incident of so much importance ought to influence the determinations of my court.

It, too, can only keep three ends in view :—

1st. No longer to allow its armaments to be talked of.

2nd. Not to recognise the new Kings, without deriving some substantial benefit for itself and for the whole of Europe.

3rd. To be informed of the aim and result of the Conferences of Erfurt, and, if possible, not to be kept out of these Conferences.

It appears to me that these results might have been obtained if his Majesty, in sending General de Vincent to Erfurt, had entrusted him with an autograph letter to the Emperor of the French to the following effect :—

'It is with infinite satisfaction that I am convinced, by the official communication from M. de Champagny to my ambassador, that the explanations which I have caused to be given to your Majesty have sufficed to convince you of the pacific and amicable intentions with which I am animated for your person. Your Majesty has made known to me at the same time the desire that I should recognise the new Kings of Spain and Naples ; that wish which, at the time it was addressed to me, was only of importance as giving a new proof of my desire to do all I can to cement the most intimate relations between us, can now hardly be separated from the subjects to be treated of at Erfurt. I send you Baron de Vincent, bearing assurances that on this occasion, as on all others, I shall esteem myself happy in combining the best relations between our two crowns with the general interests of Europe, with which they are so intimately connected. The confidence which your Majesty evinces in me, and which must have a powerful influence on the cause of peace, my first desire, induces on my part the recognition which your Majesty desires, and which cannot but furnish you with a new proof of the real sentiments which animate me.'

Order to M. de Vincent :—

1st. To enter on no official discussion on our armaments, and to treat that affair as terminated.

2nd. To give official assurance that the recognition of the Kings will meet with no difficulty on the very day the Count receives the communication of the stipulations of Erfurt.

3rd. To say that the recognition would have met with no difficulties but for the incident of Erfurt.

The letter to the Emperor of Russia should contain explanations on our armaments, and the repetition of all we should bring forward as a condition of our recognition.

This conduct, without passing any criticism on that of Alexander, can only serve to induce him to make overtures on his part. The more rashness he showed in the recognition of the Kings, the more he would wish to make us sharers in his action.

OF *TALLEYRAND'S SITUATION AND PARTY.*

125. Metternich to Stadion, Paris, September 24, 1808.

125. It is necessary to be at Paris, and to be there for some time, to be able to judge of the real position of M. de Talleyrand.

In M. de Talleyrand one cannot but separate the moral man from the political man. He had not been, he could not be, what he is, if he were moral. He is, on the other hand, pre-eminently a politician, and, as a politician, a man of systems. As such he may be useful or dangerous; at this moment he is useful, and I do not fear to defend this statement, in spite of the powerful arguments contained in your Excellency's remarks.

Two parties exist in France, as much opposed one to the other as the interests of Europe are to the individual ideas of the Emperor.

At the head of one of these parties is the Emperor with all the military men. The first only desires to extend his influence by force; and it is to a degree of nepotism of which there is, perhaps, not another example —a sentiment at least as strong in him as egotism—it is, besides, to a warlike turn which long habit has given to his mind, and to the impetuosity of his character, that we owe all the violent changes which in a way contrary to all reason, contrary to all the calculations of a decided and healthful policy, he has attempted, and, unhappily, executed but too well. Napoleon sees nothing in France but himself; nothing in Europe, or in the whole world, but his family. When we see him, contrary to all prudence, isolating himself from all the members of his family, to place them on distant thrones, acquired at the price of much blood and many sacrifices; overthrowing the feeble princes who were entirely submissive to his will, even to his whims, to give these crowns to his brothers or relations on whom he exercises infinitely less influence—a fact seen day by day to his great vexation—we discover that even his ambition yields to his leaning to nepotism. The soldiers desire nothing but to fight, especially since those who escape death are sure of immense rewards. There is in France but one profession which opens the way to everything—fortune, titles, and the constant protection of the sovereign—this is the military profession; one might say that France is peopled entirely by soldiers, and by citizens created to work for them by the sweat of their brows.

The other party is composed of the great mass of the nation, an inert and unpliable mass, like the residuum of an extinct volcano. At the head of this mass are the most eminent persons of the state, and principally M. de Talleyrand, the Minister of Police, and all those who have fortunes to preserve, who can feel no stability in institutions founded on ruins, and which the restless genius of the Emperor only surrounds with new ruins. The war of 1806 and 1807 has strengthened Napoleon's resources; but the ill success of the enterprise against Spain in 1808 made this party (which has existed since 1805), and their arguments, popular; and what previous successes could not subdue, was consolidated by reverses provoked by the most disastrous and immoral calculations.   It is in the nature of things that two parties directly opposed cannot gain strength except at the expense of one another.   The reverse in Spain ; the destruction of several bodies of troops ; the return to the interior of France of troops which had hitherto been housed and fed at the expense of the foreigner ; the stagnation of a number of pecuniary resources : these facts, joined to a hundred other considerations, have enfeebled the destructive party, and consequently reinforced that of consolidation, which is composed of elements equally conservative for us.

M. de Talleyrand is doubtless more dangerous than an incapable minister, as he has proved during the twelve years of his ministry.   But what was danger as long as it was used in a destructive sense, turns to profit at the head of the opposition.

Your Excellency is mistaken if you attribute anything that seems more regular in the progress of affairs to the influence of M. de Talleyrand.   He can make no demand on the gratitude of the Kings.   That which at a distance takes the shape of prudence, close at hand is seen to be but fear.   Spain, and nothing but Spain, the disasters,* the destruction of a large and fine army— these are the great motive powers.   The only thing which I have no doubt is due to M. de Talleyrand is the exchange of the decorations ; but it is not at this moment dictated by the idea of disgracing, but rather of reuniting us.

Men like M. de Talleyrand are like sharp-edged instruments, with which it is dangerous to play ; but for great wounds great remedies are necessary, and he who has to treat them ought not to be afraid to use the instrument that cuts the best.

* This may refer to the capitulation of Baylen.—Ed.

NAPOLEON'S RETURN FROM ERFURT.

(Note 24, Vol. I.)

126. Metternich to Stadion, Paris, October 30, 1808.

126. The return of General de Vincent must have secured for his Imperial Majesty full information as to the Conferences at Erfurt and the turn which matters have taken there. I have the less hurried to send off this courier that I might be able to tell your Excellency of the return of the Emperor to his capital and his departure for Bayonne, for which place he started yesterday afternoon. . . .

I went to find M. de Champagny, who, by the manner in which he received me, showed at once that, if they were out of humour with us, they felt it their interest to conceal it. Our conversation, though turning on the Erfurt Conferences, is not worth relating. M. de Champagny merely repeated that nothing had occurred there contrary to the interests of Austria. He also spoke of the steps taken with regard to England without entering into any detail.

The diplomatic audience of the 23rd passed without any incident. The Emperor was extremely polite to me, and our conversation at the second turn—the critical moment in which he hurls his *oral* manifestoes—touched only upon the duration and forms of the Diet of Hungary—a dangerous subject, and which, while affording matter for comment, was probably started by the Emperor on this occasion to show his good temper. . . .

One circumstance is worthy of remark, because it shows how important it is not to allow oneself to be imposed upon by the assertions of the French, however emphatic they may seem to be—namely, that since the return of the Emperor here, neither he nor the minister have touched, even distantly, the subject of the recognition of the Kings, which was promised but not carried out. As I wished to ease my mind on this subject, I found an occasion quite naturally, when resuming the course of this negotiation, to establish the point of view from which we must now start.

'We have reorganised our military system,' I said to M. de Champagny. 'You have taken the alarm, and you have asked to be reassured. We have explained ourselves with the candour which becomes a great Power. The Emperor, after some discussion, has told me that all is concluded. He has officially declared that the recognition of the new Kings would be a sufficient guarantee on our part of the good intentions which he had never any right to doubt. I beg to inform you that the Emperor, my master, derives the answer to a question which is quite new to him from his friendly sentiments towards the Emperor of the French, and in the interests of the dignity of his crown and his people. The news of the Conferences of Erfurt arrived at Vienna at the same time as my courier. The courts of France and Russia have both since that approached the Emperor on the subject of the recognition of the Kings. My master, who could not do otherwise than leave in suspense a question concerning the general relations of Europe and the private relations of the two Emperors who met at Erfurt, had, up to the time of the departure of the courier, not been informed of anything that had passed there.

'I do not allow myself to doubt,' I added, 'that M. de Vincent has been put in a position by the two Sovereigns to whom he was sent, to enable his Imperial Majesty to judge of their views, and consequently of his own interests.'

'But,' said M. de Champagny, 'when the Emperor expressed a wish for the recognition of the Kings, he made at the same time a promise to draw back his troops to the frontiers.'

'You have withdrawn your troops,' I replied, 'before you knew whether we should recognise the Kings, and we could not but see that this fact proved the statement I have always maintained, that the Emperor Napoleon, whatever he might try to make us believe, was far from ascribing our military reforms to offensive intentions; all that he said to the contrary was nothing but talk; I have gained a fresh proof of this from the account of Napoleon's first conversation with M. de Vincent at Erfurt. The Emperor,' I added, 'had seemingly calculated that M. de Vincent might not know what he had said to me and what you had written to me, that our armaments were no subject of anxiety to him. As to our ignorance about the time of the Conferences at Erfurt, supposing that this secret was the result of a calculation on your part, it would show that you tried to carry off our recognition by surprise —and I cannot allow myself to admit this supposition.'

M. de Champagny, having nothing to say in defence of this statement, abandoned it at once, and protested that the interests of Austria had never suffered by the meeting of the two Emperors. . . .

One truth, very evident to me, is that the result of the Erfurt Conferences has not at all corresponded with the ideas which were taken there.

ON THE EVENTUALITIES OF A WAR WITH FRANCE.

(Note 28, Vol. I.)

127–128. Two Memoirs by Metternich drawn up in Vienna, December 4, 1808.

127. It is very necessary to begin a work of the nature which I propose by fixing the points of departure and the points to be arrived at.

I left Vienna in 1806, shortly after the Peace of Presburg. The Austrian monarchy, sapped in its foundations, only figured in the balance of Powers as an inert mass in opposition to France. Her military state disorganised, without confidence in herself, deprived of a great quantity of material resources, she awaited a new creation. Victorious France covered nearly the whole of the ancient Empire of Germany with armies intoxicated with a success as rapid as easily bought with but little fatigue, privation, or loss. The war of 1805 by its results had only served to double the military and financial resources of France; the military resources by new conscriptions and the union of new confederates; the financial by new imposts, for which the war served as a pretext, and by the possibility of keeping the armies for an indefinite time on the soil and at the expense of the foreigner.

It would be difficult to estimate in the same proportion the moral support which has been brought to Napoleon's aid. His views grew and increased by reason

U

of this extraordinary and unexpected support : his star made wise men tremble among his own people ; he appeared invincible.

It seemed to be proved in the eyes of all, that the foreigner's safety consisted in his following a course uniform with Napoleon's. Thirteen years of war, maintained with more or less equal chances, had not, till the campaign of 1805, made our strength at all doubtful, but only the right employment of that strength. It was otherwise with the Peace of Presburg : the last rampart of Europe's independence was undermined, it had fallen to pieces ; the public of Europe, France, and, above all, of Germany, even our people, no longer doubted that the only chance of safety for Austria was now to be found in the closest friendship with France, or, at least, in a system of the strictest neutrality.

Few statesmen in the quiet of their study guessed that friendship and neutrality are two words void of meaning to Napoleon, relating, as they do, to ideas impossible to be realised by any Power which cannot confound submission and ruin with friendship and neutrality. The end proves that their calculations were right ; but it was reserved to Napoleon himself to substantiate that truth.

Napoleon, who always prepared the ground for his future activity, whilst the public (and unhappily for too long a time the cabinets also) believed him to be solely occupied with the object of the moment (vast enough, no doubt, to absorb common powers), had, during the war of 1805, prepared for war with Prussia.

That war, more disastrous in its results in exact proportion to the difference between the real and intrinsic strength of Prussia and Austria, above all in exact proportion to the moral state of their armies, of

which one, proved by misfortune, and under skilful
guidance, was able to resist him, while the other was
impregnated with the poison of long inaction—that war,
I say, seemed to have been undertaken for the destruction of the partisans of the system of neutrality. If
in December, 1805, it seemed proved that it was impossible to succeed as an enemy of Napoleon, it was
decidedly proved in 1806 that the part of neutrals was
not more easy to sustain.

But we now come to a time when the last of the
positions in which a Power can be placed, with regard
to France, could not escape his attacks more than the
others. Napoleon, before the end of the war with
Prussia, prepared the destruction of Spain. The fall of
the oldest, the most tried, the most disinterested of the
allies, not only of Napoleon, but of all the preceding Governments of France (this is important to remark because
it overthrows the argument based on dynastic incom-
patibilities), must prove to the world that friendship is
unavailing to preserve any Power, if that Power crosses
the path of the Emperor of the French.

Neither enemy, nor neutral, nor friend —what part,
then, remains for a Power to take which cannot, like
Portugal, separate itself by the se from the scourge
which destroys Europe? It must preserve its own
identity, and the example of Austria shows that this
can be done when no time is lost in repairing the passing disasters caused by a permanent danger. Providence
determines the limits of every usurping Power. Spain
was called to save Europe ; yet these chances, too, would
have passed in vain, if we had waited for them to occur
before taking up the only attitude proper to us.

My reports for nearly a year past contain too many
facts on which may be founded a precise calculation

of the evil undoubtedly caused to France by the perfidious enterprise against Spain for it to be necessary
to repeat them here.   Admitting that Napoleon's resources against us were reduced by half (a very safe
supposition), and that our available resources are
doubled (an equally moderate supposition), the strength
of Austria, as compared with that of France in 1805,
will be quadrupled at the close of 1808.

This mathematical calculation rests on the following
data, impossible to estimate long before, but immense in
their results and in their influence on Napoleon's future
views, and on the possibility of his carrying them out.

It is no longer the nation that fights : the present
war is Napoleon's war—it is not even that of his
army.   He felt this when he announced to the assembled
representatives of his people that his inclinations and
taste drove him to throw himself into the whirlpool of
a war which had become a civil war.   He had wished
to gain the army by throwing himself into its arms.
Accustomed to conquer under him, the presence of the
head of the state is no doubt necessary to that army ;
but the sovereign who declares to his people that his
army is equally necessary to him reveals a fearful secret
—he is no longer the father of his people : he is the chief
of his army.

And such is in fact the relation between Napoleon
and the French nation.   It is only possible for a man
who is able on the spot to judge of the dispositions of
the nation, to ascertain the extent of the influence which
these last enterprises have had on the mind of the
French people.

But we will not endeavour to found our calculations
on the dispositions of a people as little friendly with
foreign nations, and more tolerant of the whims of its

rulers, than any other. The French people can and ought to be considered by us only so far as it offers less resistance to efforts which should tempt men drawn from its bosom and animated by a spirit of regeneration.

I have long since pointed out the existence of a party opposed to Napoleon's views of invasion. This party meditated, drew together, and increased in silence; it was reserved for Napoleon himself to give it force and consistency. Such will always be the result of an enterprise as false as was the expedition against Spain in both conception and execution.

Two men in France hold at this moment the first rank in opinion and influence—M. de Talleyrand and M. Fouché. Formerly opposed in views and interests, they have been drawn together by circumstances; I do not hesitate to say that at the present time their object and their means of attaining it are the same. These last offer chances of success, because they are agreeable to the wishes of a nation exhausted by a long succession of efforts, and terrified with the career which the present master of their destinies marks out for them—of a people as little disposed as any other to maintain, at the price of its blood and treasure, projects which are only personal to that master.

M. de Talleyrand has, since the campaign of 1805, opposed with all his influence, as Minister of Foreign Affairs, the destructive plans of Napoleon—a subordinate influence as to the political point of view of the Emperor, but powerful in the practical means of execution. We positively owe to him some more or less favourable aspects in the Presburg negotiation; he also opposed as long as he could the campaign against Prussia. The passion of the Emperor overcame on this occasion every consideration presented to him by his minister; but after the end of the campaign the latter was, under some brilliant pretext or other, dismissed, and his place was confided to a man whom Napoleon saw to be an instrument more incapable, but also more submissive.

In this new situation, M. de Talleyrand bethought himself of making friends with Fouché. A mutual interest united them. To consolidate the new order of things in their country ; to bring back the thoughts of the Emperor to internal affairs ; to labour towards a general peace—these were their objects. The choice of means was common to both. M. de Talleyrand could not hope, without the active assistance of Fouché, for any success in his plans, which were founded on the hope of keeping Napoleon within certain limits, and consequently of securing the new order of things established by him in France and in Europe on some sort of foundation. Fouché, on his side, yielded to the political conceptions of Talleyrand, whom we always see rise to the occasion. Means of maintaining peace between the Continental Powers must therefore be devised, to make it possible to hope for success to a plan which must be popular in its results. The course which M. de Talleyrand followed in his relations with M. de Vincent and myself, the different explanations between Fouché and myself contained in my despatches, agree with the point of view arranged between them.

It was at this period (shortly after the return of Napoleon from the Polish campaign) that the two intriguers wished to persuade the Emperor of the necessity of establishing the new order of things by a direct succession to the Empire. Fouché undertook to make this desire reach the Emperor through the voice of the public, necessarily easy to guide in that direction ; he even spoke of it to the Emperor. M. de Talleyrand seconded all his measures ; they wished to bring Josephine herself to seek a separation from her husband. She baffled all the calculations, all the manœuvres of her adversaries ; her part was easy in calling to her help the strong tincture of superstition really possessed by the Emperor ; she had besides only to combat projects of which the result would naturally be to fix the spirit of a man of restless temperament, and therefore of restless taste. The Grand-Duchess of Berg was let into the secret by the two ministers, her influence on her brother being very great ; from this period dates the estrangement between the two sisters-in-law which was never overcome.

The plan failed, and we come to a new era for Napoleon, France, and the whole of Europe.

The Emperor, absorbed by his plans of invasion in Spain, would listen to no remonstrances against a project as impolitic in conception as ridiculous and criminal in his means of carrying it out ! Guided by his own insatiable ambition, encouraged by the perfidious advice of Murat, who aimed at nothing less than filling the throne of Spain and of the Indies, all his measures were directed to one end. Misguided by the agents of the Prince of Peace, he believed the expulsion of the Bourbons easy.* It would have offered less difficulty without the revolution of Aranjuez, which put the succession to the throne into the most advantageous contact with the nation ; the strength of the armies intended for the invasion of Spain were only calculated on the scale of the resistance which a feeble Government had opposed, since the Peace of Basle, to the exactions of France. They deceived themselves : the short reign of Ferdinand had restrung a people full

* They had assured the Emperor that the only difficulty he would meet with in Spain would be the bad impression produced by his refusal to reign there in person.

of honour and spirit.   The Grand-Duke de Berg fired
on these people ; the expulsion and destruction of the
French armies was the necessary result of so many
false measures.*

The perfidious conduct of Napoleon towards King
Ferdinand resounded through all France ; the defeats of
the French army could not be concealed. The southern
provinces are in such close contact with those of the
north-east of Spain, the relations of people to people
are so intimate, that all the care, all the vigilance of the
police, the most active which ever existed, would not
have succeeded in allaying the unfavourable impression
regarding the head of the state which the nation drew
from the news of each day ; but this same police were
not active on this occasion.

Napoleon, partly to punish M. de Talleyrand for the
opposition which he had made to his projects against
Spain, partly tempted by the central position of Valen-
çay, established the Spanish princes in that place, where
they lived at the expense of the proprietor, till the day
when their House was restored. This was only one of
the many false measures which latterly darkened Napoleon's star ; but it would be difficult to say what may be
the consequences of this measure.

M. de Talleyrand, summoned to Nantes to be near
the Emperor, gained a new sphere of activity by this
new mark of favour. He returned to Paris, declared
himself without reserve protector of the Prince of the
Asturias, and his opposition to the past and future
calculations of the Emperor for the conquest of Spain
increased more and more.

---

* Napoleon was so mistaken as to the resistance he would encounter in
Spain that, at first, he only wished to send to that country the division of
Dupont.

It was at this time that the relations of this minister with myself took an entirely different turn. Deceived in his hope of holding Napoleon to the limits in which the plainest spirit of self-preservation ought to have kept him, as well as the desire of firmly establishing his dynasty and his institutions, Talleyrand's plans took an entirely new turn, and this turn was favourable to the independence of Europe, and consequently to ours. If I am here more explicit with respect to his views than I was able to be in my despatches, I cannot add anything to the details, which these same reports contain, on the course which he began to pursue, and which he followed till the return of Napoleon from Erfurt.

That journey, undertaken with the express object of persuading the Emperor of Russia to take active measures against us (a very natural wish on the part of Napoleon at a moment when a great part of his army was occupied at the foot of the Pyrenees, and when he wanted to devote the rest of his army to the conquest of Spain), offered a very different point of view to Talleyrand. Napoleon aimed at causing a quarrel to succeed the coolness which had reigned between us and Russia for some time. Talleyrand, on the contrary, sought to draw us nearer to that Power. The latter seemed to have succeeded in his enterprise at the expense of his antagonist, for thus we may regard the relations between the Sovereign of France and the first of his servants.

A man whom I have long pointed out as holding a memorable place in the scenes of these latter times, Count de Tolstoy, did not belie his character on an occasion of great interest for the safety of the world. This ambassador (dismissed from the Erfurt Conference by Count Romanzow and summoned by Napoleon), whom some very just prejudices had always held at a distance from Talleyrand, but who had the same object in getting admitted into Napoleon's suite, was to meet Talleyrand at Erfurt. This event, which I looked upon beforehand as a valuable control of the real intentions of Talleyrand, actually took place. The Ambassador of France in Russia was charged with the arrangement. It was he who, by acting as intermediary on this important occasion, gave us a proof of the claim which M. de Talleyrand had often made of having a boundless influence on the mind of M. de Caulaincourt.

The first day of his arrival Talleyrand presented himself to the Emperor Alexander, and said to him the memorable words : ' Sire, what are you going to do here ? It rests with you to save Europe, and you can only accomplish this by resisting Napoleon. The French people are civilised, its Sovereign is not ; the Sovereign of Russia is civilised, and his people are not ; it is therefore for the Sovereign of Russia to be allied with the French people.' *

The result of the conferences, which M. de Talleyrand announced to me soon after his return from Paris, may be resumed in his conviction ' that since the battle of Austerlitz the relations of Alexander with Austria have not been more favourable.' ' It only depends on you,' said he, ' and on your ambassador at St. Petersburg, to renew the intimate relations with Russia which existed before that event. It is this alliance alone which can save to Europe the remains of her independence ; Caulaincourt, entirely devoted to my political point of view, is instructed in a way to second all the steps of Prince Schwarzenberg.'

* He said to him at another interview : ' The Rhine, the Alps, the Pyrenees are the conquests of France. The rest are the conquests of the Emperor of France, and we shall not hold them.'

M. de Tolstoy, whom I found here, has confirmed entirely what M. de Talleyrand told me. The conduct of Caulaincourt at Erfurt, with respect to this ambassador, leaves no doubt of the extent of his devotion to the Vice-Grand Elector. Twenty explanations that I had with the latter, before my departure from Paris, never deviated from the following point of view : That the interest of France herself demands that the Powers which are able to make a stand against Napoleon should unite to oppose a barrier to his insatiable ambition ; that the cause of Napoleon is no longer that of France ; and, lastly, that Europe can only be saved by the intimate alliance of Austria and Russia.

We have, therefore, arrived at a period when allies seem to offer themselves to us even in the interior of this Empire. These allies are not vile and low *intriguants* ; the men who may represent the nation claim our support ; this support is our cause itself, our cause wholly and that of posterity.

It is certainly not without the strictest examination that it is possible to enter into the solution of questions of the nature of that which I have just stated. But what they ask ought to explain the true position of M. de Talleyrand and his friends. The first moments of our ambassador's stay at St. Petersburg, and those after my return to Paris, will determine our opinion irrevocably. But it is indispensably necessary, in order to attain this object, to establish our political point of view, and to be entirely at one amongst ourselves and in respect to the means to be employed.

Three objects of great importance now occupy the political theatre of Europe.

The victories or the defeats of Napoleon in Spain.

The rupture with England, or the entrance into negotiation with her.

The reconciliation between Russia and Austria.

What I have mentioned as to the aid to be expected from the political course of influential men in France cannot but enter into our calculations ; it ought not to be neglected.   But being favourable in all its aspects, I should not call the attention of my court to it if it were not a question when to commence a course which, above all things, should be fixed in principle.   It is then that it will be infinitely important not to lose sight of the necessity of reconciling, as closely as possible, our outward course with that which we follow in private.   One false step on our part might stultify, at one stroke, the good intentions of some of the heads of the administration in France ; one tergiversation would take away all their confidence : if, then, the general safety points to the necessity of having fixed immovable bases, not only for our political point of view, but also for the means of carrying it out, I believe I have fulfilled a great duty in bringing to the knowledge of his Imperial Majesty data too secret, too important, and too dangerous to have been confided even to a courier.

I join to the present memoir a paper (No. 128) giving some ideas on our present and future relations with Russia—by which I have not thought fit to interrupt this memoir.

These observations will determine, better than I can express, the immense difference between Austria's relations, internal and external, in the years 1805 and 1808— a difference which we owe to the energy which has been employed by the heads of the administration of our vast Empire during this period, and the uniform course which his Imperial Majesty has followed with regard to foreign affairs.

MEMOIR NO. II.

128. The war in Spain, which in my principal memoir I have considered from a moral point of view, is not less important to be explained in its military aspect. I find that the French forces are reduced one-half since the insurrection in Spain. This calculation is by no means exaggerated.

I believe that if on twenty occasions (often only too decisive) one is deceived by calculating the effective number of combatants that the French generals directed, on this or that point of attack, too low, one is not less often deceived in a contrary way, as to the total force of the national army; fatal errors, which cause us to despise the imposing masses whose marches and manœuvres—as bold as they were rapid—have placed them in presence of our armies, at the same time terrifying us by a national military condition which is infinitely below our calculations. The war against Spain divulges a great secret—namely, that Napoleon has but one army, his *grande armée*. This great army, the same that he organised before the war of 1805, on the coasts of the Channel,* and which fought under his command in the years 1805, 1806, and 1807, was not weakened by the first expedition against Spain and Portugal.

---

* This army was created by Napoleon *under the pretext* of an invasion of England, an operation of which he never thought. His real design was that of making war on us. Napoleon, in one of our conversations, made this avowal himself, which did not astonish me, my conviction having always been that such a rash and doubtful expedition beyond the sea had never been seriously contemplated by him.—(A. d. B.)

The greater part of the conscription of 1807 and 1808 was employed in the formation of new companies in the interior of France, to which the depôts of existing regiments served as a nucleus.

The conquest, or rather the occupation of the Peninsula (for to this the Emperor professed to limit this operation), was confided to the troops of the new levée. The first reverses of the French in Spain may be partly attributed to the crude formation of this army; but these same reverses are important to be observed, because they show that thousands of French conscripts, left to themselves, without support from older regiments of the line, were worth no more than raw recruits of any other nation, when not amalgamated with old soldiers.

It would be difficult to believe that of 89,000 men, who originally passed the Pyrenees, there still remained 20,000 at the opening of the campaign in November 1808. One of the most serious losses which this army sustained was that of nearly the whole Imperial Guard, which had been sent out to strengthen the French forces in Spain.

The political mistakes, military and administrative, committed by the French Government in Spain, having roused the whole French nation, Napoleon found himself forced to call his great army to his aid.

The questions which I propose to consider may be classed in the following manner :—

1st. What are the total forces of France and her allies at this present moment?

2nd. After deducting from the whole of these forces the number of men employed in the conquest of Spain, what number of effective troops could Napoleon bring against us?

3rd. What resources has Napoleon for carrying on

the war against Spain and against us at the same time?

Ad primum. I add to this present memoir a brief summary of the French armies, from which I learn their numbers (as far as they can be calculated) in the month of June last. I add to this estimate the two new conscriptions—namely, that of the reserves of the four last, and that of 1810. I have deducted the losses which the army has sustained since that epoch.

Ad secundum. Admitting that Napoleon employs at this moment 200,000 men in Spain, he could dispose of a force of 226,000 men to make war on Austria, and retain the necessary forces in the countries subject to his direct influence.

Ad tertium. On what resources does the Emperor of the French rely to maintain the war against Spain and against us? This question, of extreme importance in all our military calculations, appears to me decided by the last publications in France.

The later reserves (not called out by the last decree) were promised that in no case should they be called on for active service. The French, therefore, are living on anticipation, and an anticipation of two years offers already so many conditions in its disfavour that it would be difficult to believe that it could be extended. The conscripts of 1810 are seventeen years of age; it appears hardly probable that, even in an extreme case, they would, or rather that they could, put children of fifteen or sixteen years old under arms and make them take the field at once.

The summary of the military position appears to me to be the following :—

(*a*) Napoleon can fight us now with 206,000 men, of whom 107,000 are French, 99,000 confederates and allies.

(*b*) His reserves can after a time only be composed of conscripts below the age for service.

But I believe in the continuation of the war in Spain. This hypothesis leads me naturally to make some enquiries into the nature and means of feeding this war from one side or the other.

It is as difficult to estimate the Spanish people by the standard of other European nations as it would be possible to calculate the chances of the war in Spain by the chances of those which the French army have sustained up to the present time. If the national character has not since the earliest times been belied, several considerations are peculiar to this war. It is at the same time a national, a religious, and a commercial war.

It has become national by the conduct of Napoleon towards the reigning family and towards the assembly of the Junta at Bayonne.

No people wish for a foreign master or for foreign rule; every reform, however salutary it may be, becomes odious if it emanates from outside. Louis XIV., in placing his grandson on the Spanish throne, never lost sight of this important consideration. Far from committing the mistake of imposing on the nation laws made under his immediate authority and dictated by foreign influence, he pushed his scruples so far as not to allow the new King to be accompanied by one single Frenchman. Many errors were committed in consequence in the interior of the kingdom; intriguers played upon the credit of the King of France; and this consideration was not foreign to the national movement which imprinted such a special character on the War of Succession; but Louis XIV. would never have consented to sign a constitution for the Peninsula. The genius of Napoleon, which is not limited to military ambition, but which leads him to aspire to be a universal legislator, has made him commit faults which, more even than the change of dynasty, have influenced the nation, and placed it in the situation we now see. If ever a war was national, it is the present one.

The certainty of the destruction of the religious orders, the pillage of the churches, the total remodelling of the most opulent clergy in Europe, have rendered it a religious war. All the pains taken by the Emperor to enlighten the people will be fruitless, as long as all means of communication with this same people are placed at the disposition of the clergy.*

The geographical position of Spain, its immense colonies separated so long from the mother-country (whilst this latter made the most generous sacrifices in favour of the French system), and lost on the day when she first submitted to this system and to her conquerors, gives to the present war a commercial character. Thus, whilst honour, national sentiment, religion, pecuniary and commercial interests—all these powerful motives, unite under one banner 100,000 generous, brave, sober, and enduring men, Napoleon has entered upon a contest quite new to him. Germany and Italy have spoilt him. Composed of twenty different peoples, he had only to disunite what had never been united, to divide that which had long been divided. Such would have always been the essential difference between war south of the Pyrenees and that in the neighbourhood of the Rhine or the Alps; but the imprudent course which he followed in this affair has created fresh obstacles of an infinitely grave character.

---

* The Spanish peasant not being able to read, all proclamations and addresses must be interpreted to him by the clergy or by *employés,* all interested in the maintenance of the old order of things.

Calculations on military operations are so little in my line that I make them only with great reserve. But how can one refuse to see that in the present contest Napoleon will find considerable obstacles to vanquish? It is certain that in the War of Succession Turenne would have been embarrassed to make war in Spain with 50,000 men. Now 200,000 men are thrown upon a single narrow line of operations, and they advance into a country which offers neither provisions nor forage. The baggage-trains even must keep to the line of operations itself, without being able to deviate from it.

The geographical position of the Peninsula obliges the Emperor, on the other hand, entirely to change his system of war and attack. We have been accustomed to see him start from a large base and converge towards one centre. This manœuvre, which always made him arrive at the point he wished with masses infinitely stronger than those which the enemy could oppose to him on this unknown point, appears to me absolutely necessary when armies advance without supplies and live simply on requisitions. It is far different in the present war. Admitting that all the line of the Pyrenees can serve him as the basis of operations—a basis at any rate rendered very unquiet by the most warlike and most resolute people of the Peninsula—he must renounce the idea of conquering Spain entirely, or act on divergent lines. Of what use can requisitions be in a country where the traveller finds nothing but what he carries with him, where the peasant only cultivates the ground for the strictest necessaries for his family, and where the household deserts its hearth on the approach of the enemy?

If the genius of Napoleon is incontestable, if it is

fertile, immense, the difficulties that I have alluded to
are not less great, and the contest in which he has
engaged *de gaieté de cœur* certainly offers, under all
aspects, much interest to the political and military
observer.

Men of all sides and of all parties, who are cool
in their calculations and impartial in their judgments,
are united in the conviction :—

(*a*) That if, in spite of all the difficulties which it
presents, the *conquest* of Spain is not only possible, but
must be the necessary result of a long contest between
France and Spain, the submission of the Peninsula will
not be accomplished with ease.

(*b*) Even as to the conquest, all depends on the kind
of warfare which the Spaniards adopt. If they keep it
up in an active irregular manner, full of stratagems and
tricks—in a word, if they give it the character of a
civil and national war, Napoleon's embarrassment may
be great. If, on the contrary, the Spanish defence takes
a regular course, the conquest will be greatly facilitated.

One last question I must consider, and that is—
Can Napoleon abandon Spain in case of his wishing to
bring all his forces against us?

Such recklessness is not in Napoleon's character.
No doubt as a last resource, and as the sole chance
of safety, he would abandon the interests of his brother ;
but are not these interests his own ? Could he, under
the most favourable suppositions, dream of driving
back on us the whole of his forces ? Ferdinand VII.—
for he alone it is whom he would replace on the throne
of Spain—will he for certain be his friend, his ally, and
in consequence the enemy of England ? Will he deprive
himself of the resources which the colonies furnish, to
wait till Napoleon, after having finished his contest with

some one else, returns to take him up again? Would not propositions be made to Ferdinand VII. in a moment of great embarrassment to Napoleon? Will the young King, who may promise everything whilst he is in France, be able to keep these forced promises, when once he is restored to his people? I do not think it possible to believe this; one must therefore suppose :—

That, under the most fortunate circumstances—that is to say, in case of the pacification and conquest of Spain—the disposable forces of Napoleon will be weakened by more than 120,000 men necessary for the occupation of the Peninsula; one must further calculate other losses that the conquest would involve, a reserve for supplying this army, &c.

Thus the forces of Austria, so inferior to those of France before the insurrection in Spain, will be at least equal to them immediately after that event.

METTERNICH'S RETURN TO PARIS.

1809.

(Note 30, Vol. I.)

129. Metternich to Stadion, Paris, January 11, 1809.

129. The rigour of the season has delayed my arrival here till the beginning of the year. Though the rumour of the Emperor's return to Paris had less probability the nearer I approached the capital, I still continued my journey night and day, that I might lose no chance of being present at the first diplomatic audience, supposing that circumstances, which it was impossible to calculate, might have drawn his Majesty to Paris. I was convinced directly I arrived that there was still the most absolute uncertainty about the time of his return. Instead of the Emperor, I saw the Empress the very day of my arrival; she granted an audience on New Year's Day to the Diplomatic Corps.

My return here gave great pleasure to the court and to the members of the Government. It dissipated for several days the anxiety that the public had felt about the prolongation of my absence. The war in Spain offering fewer results every day, calculations on a speedy resort to arms in Austria seemed to gain more ground.

The Spanish war, the extravagance of the bulletins, the certainty of the rupture of the negotiation with

England, the strength and imposing attitude of Austria (quiet as she may be)—these are the subjects which I find occupying all minds here.   The eleven days which have passed since my arrival have not at all changed this aspect of affairs : the colours, in fact, have deepened since the day before yesterday, by the arrival of unfavourable news from Spain.

The day after my arrival I saw M. de Champagny. Our conversation was confined to small matters ; it could not be otherwise.   I began by saying that I believed I could announce nothing more agreeable to the wishes of the friends of peace than the fact that I had left my court as pacific in its intentions as I had found it on arriving.

M. de Champagny replied that France on her side only desired peace, as she had proved by withdrawing her armies from Germany.   'You know what are her desires,' added he ; ' she has explained them to you.'   I pretended not to understand to what this phrase related ; but M. de Champagny repeating it at every moment in the course of a conversation as vague on one side as on the other, I endeavoured to fix the question in the following manner.   'I found,' said I to him, ' M. de Vincent at Vienna.   He arrived from Erfurt a few days before me, and brought with him the general assurances of the good intentions which the Emperor Napoleon had given him.   True friends of peace might without doubt have desired that they should be more full, and more suited to establish relations of confidence between the two courts.   A very natural explanation, which M. de Vincent took to Erfurt, has been declared inadmissible by the Emperor.   Your ambassador has even been charged to declare the same at Vienna.   The Emperor Napoleon therefore evidently foresaw that circumstances independent of his will might place him in doubt as to the future fate of the Spanish monarchy. M. de Champagny expressed his astonishment that General Andréossy had made a declaration which he had not been authorised to make. I saw M. de Romanzow the same day, whom I found more than ever occupied about our recognition of the Kings. He furnished me with the true key of this anxiety on his part. 'The recognition of the King of Spain is my affair,' said he, ' entirely my personal affair. It is I who persuaded the Emperor Alexander to agree to it ; I look upon it as the foundation of peace for the continent of Europe.'

After having spoken to him in the sense of the explanations with which his Imperial Majesty had charged Prince Schwarzenberg at St. Petersburg, I made him understand that I felt the foundation of which he spoke a little shaken by the last despatches of Napoleon from Madrid. 'These are only words,' replied the Russian Minister. ' But the nomination of Joseph as Lieutenant-General of his own kingdom is a fact,' I replied, ' and a fact which may be followed by the union of Spain with France. Napoleon, who generally says less than he does, has not advanced this statement without some purpose. It may perhaps only arise from his desire to terrify the people of the Peninsula as to such a union, but it is not the less done to perplex the question of Joseph's capacity, and to defy Europe with respect to the new kingdom that the Emperor may destine for him in compensation for that of Spain, which would augment the power of France.' 'I cannot be uneasy about it,' said M. de Romanzow ; ' in a long course of centuries one cannot prevent a great genius like Napoleon's arising, and it is useless to wish to educate him. We must give him no cause for discontent, and must limit our policy to that end.' I did not find myself strong enough to combat this argument.

The most complete stagnation reigning here about affairs, I have had no further motive for conversing with the Minister of Foreign Affairs. Since our first interview, I have not seen him except in society. I know that in the report which he made to the Emperor of this interview he has removed the uncertainty under which I had been left. M. de Romanzow, for his part, imagined he saw warlike intentions in the fact that I did not bring here the recognition of the Kings. Your Excellency will find in these two opinions the most faithful picture of the relative position of the two ministers. M. de Champagny desires peace in the interest of his master ; M. de Romanzow desires it for himself. I have neglected nothing to persuade both of them of the reality of our pacific intentions, and I had many circumstances to urge in favour of my argument.

From the frontiers of Austria to the centre of Paris I have found but one opinion accepted by the public— that is, that in the spring at latest Austria will take the field against France. This conclusion is drawn from the relative position of the two Powers. Napoleon is seen to be occupied 600 leagues from the frontier of our Empire; the greatest part of his forces are directed towards that distant point, and are there busied in a grave and difficult task. The measures which he takes from a distance announce, on the other hand, that he casts an observing eye himself upon us ; in fact, everything, the designs which are attributed to him, the strength of Austria, the momentary but very real embarrassment of France, the state of decay of the Porte, the necessary tendency of Prussia to repair the losses which she has sustained, the journey of the King of Prussia to St. Petersburg, the general conviction that Russia will be forced by internal considerations to change her system, the rupture of the negotiation with England, the ferment which is springing up in the people of Germany and Italy—everything, I say, leads the public to make remarks and comments on the future.

But it would be superfluous to tell your Excellency how many passions, views, and individual interests modify these criticisms; how many are influenced by fear, hope, and anxiety. My position here has in consequence undergone a complete change. I was before aware of the interest which Austria's unhappy fate has lately excited everywhere : arrogance with some, compassion with others ; arrogance has given place to anxiety, compassion to hope. If in times past I showed to the politicians of the *cafés* and *salons* the most unalterable serenity, I do not now make the less profession of the most perfect calm.

NAPOLEON'S RETURN FROM SPAIN.

(Note 30, Vol. I.)

130. Metternich to Stadion, Paris, January 17, 1809.
131. Metternich to Stadion, Paris, January 25, 1809.
132. Metternich to Stadion, Paris, February 2, 1809.

130. I draw from a reliable source what I believe to be the true motive of the Emperor's return to Paris. My position becomes very delicate ; I am guided in all its details by the instructions agreed on at the time of my departure from Vienna.

I had yesterday a very long conversation with Talleyrand. He appeared absolutely ignorant of the Emperor's views, or rather he supposes them everything and nothing. Napoleon's interest is so clearly in direct opposition to any complication with Austria that he ought to avoid rather than provoke one ; but we do not see that he follows a line of conduct conformable to these same interests. All the French officials increase the irritation which is, and invent that which does not exist. The fears which they excite may lead to terrible results and to a choice of desperate means.

Let our eyes be constantly fixed on Poland ; surely here is a cause in common with Russia. On the other hand, one cannot sufficiently watch the army of Davoust. It appears to me that every position or offensive demonstration on his part should cause immediately very plain, prompt, but calm explanations on our part. In this way we may give the initiative to the warlike measures of France. Our conduct ought to put a limit to the world's misfortunes.

I do not know how to add anything to what I sent by my last courier about M. de Talleyrand. I see him, and his friend Fouché, always the same—very decided in seizing an opportunity, if the occasion presents itself, but not having enough courage to make one. They are in the position of passengers who, seeing the helm in the hands of a mad pilot guiding the vessel on to rocks, which he runs against quite merrily, are ready to seize the helm just at the moment when their safety would be still more threatened by doing so—at the very moment, in fact, when the first shock of the vessel would overturn the pilot himself.

The mere reading of the bulletins is sufficient to make us see the very difficult position in which the French army finds itself in Spain. Indeed, that position appears, from these data, infinitely worse than one had imagined. Commercial letters, which seem from time to time to undergo postal inquisition, always contain the most gloomy news. The Emperor's return proves more than all the rest. It is said (and it appears with truth) that the loss in the affairs with the English has been horrible.

Count de Romanzow dreams only of peace with England since the news of the probability of a Regency. He has delayed his departure indefinitely, convinced, he says, that he would not make three stages without being recalled to Paris. What a false calculation!

Metternich to Stadion, Paris, January 25, 1809.

131. The Emperor arrived here the day before yesterday. This journey has been very sudden. He

only took six days in travelling the distance from
Valladolid to Paris; he rode on horseback from the
first of these towns to Burgos.

I have the honour to inform your Excellency that
many of the reports of General Andréossy, of Marshal
Davoust, and a number of officials who for more than
two years have done nothing but alarm Europe on our
account, have appeared for some time to find more
credit with the Emperor. This anxiety has increased
since the journey of the King of Prussia to St. Petersburg, since the truce with Sweden, and certainly since
a number of reports from Germany, speaking of arrangements between the Northern Powers.

M. de Romanzow came to see me the day before
yesterday. I gave him a *résumé* of our political situation; which, I think, I ought to put before your Excellency, to make you thoroughly acquainted with what
I said.

'Austria,' said I, 'is the most central power in
Europe. France and Russia, after having been at war,
have become allies. What is the motive of this alliance? Does it tend to secure peace to Europe? It
will fail always in this object, if Austria is not allowed
to join. An alliance between the three Imperial Courts,
an alliance between Austria and Russia, or between
Austria and France, might ensure peace to the Continent.
The alliance between France and Russia, to the exclusion
of the intermediary masses, is against the peace of
Europe, because laws of the most simple prudence may
keep these same intermediate powers in a continual
excitement. Peace and anxiety are two entirely opposite
ideas.

'But France and Russia have contracted a separate
alliance. Austria has been repulsed on all sides; one is

driven to say to her, " Keep yourself quiet, if you wish
to be left quiet." There remains therefore for her only
to create means of defence equally independent of all the
world, to depend entirely on her own strength. At this
epoch the Emperor of the French turns towards Spain.
I was in the months of June and July last made personally
aware, if not of the pacific intentions of this prince
towards us, at least of the certainty that we should not
have war at this juncture. At Vienna they believed my
words, in spite of the clamour of all the French generals and officials. You yourself at this time believed in
war. Events in Spain then drew nearly all the French
forces from above the Pyrenees. Austria, in spite of
this, remained calm ; what further proof could she give
of the true intentions of her sovereign ?

 ' Napoleon now declares that the Spanish affairs are
settled ; and that he considers the kingdom as conquered. He seizes this very moment to load us with
injuries. He caused his return to Paris to be preceded
by diatribes directed against us, by appeals to our provinces not to serve in the cause of their master. He
returns : and all France, all the Confederation say, he
is going to advance against us. It is only, then, on the
guarantee of the Minister of Foreign Affairs for Russia,
that I can reassure my court with respect to Napoleon's
intentions, that I can again combat the general opinion,
believed and sustained as it is by the French officials
themselves.'

M. de Romanzow told me that it would doubtless
be difficult for him to guarantee the intentions of Napoleon ; that no one could guarantee them, but that
he, Romanzow, did not believe he had warlike views ;
he added that we had certainly brought these fresh attacks on ourselves by the refusal to recognise the Kings.

I maintained that the word ' refusal' appeared to me altogether improper. He withdrew it at once, and returned to the subject of the attenuation which he begged me to give to some articles in the newspapers. I replied that it was not possible for me to weaken the impression that probably would be produced upon my court and nation by the articles in these papers ; that this impression, at a moment when even the safety of the Empire was at stake, could hardly be influenced by a foreign minister ; all that I could take on myself would be to submit them to the consideration of his Imperial Majesty himself.

The Emperor received us yesterday at a diplomatic audience. The Prince de Kourakin delivered his credentials before the general audience. His Majesty took his two rounds as usual. All the Diplomatic Corps expected a scene between him and me. I foresaw the contrary, and I was not deceived. The Emperor does not care to amuse the curious ; he addressed me with some commonplace observations on his first round, and on the second he did not speak a single word to me. I shared this coldness only with the Prussian Minister.

Such are the facts. I do not accompany them by any explanation ; they speak for themselves ; they serve to show on which side the pacific intentions are ; they do more, they determine the question.

Metternich to Stadion, Paris, February 2, 1809.

132. The very day of my courier's departure there was an evening reception at the court. The Emperor, who generally treats me with the greatest attention, did not come near me all the evening, and avoided speaking to me. He confined himself to saying a few words to Madame de Metternich. Meanwhile the public journals are completely silent. Very reassuring ideas are spread amongst the public about the relations between the two courts.

These notions are very generally believed, and have a favourable influence on the funds.

The Emperor was present last Sunday, January 29, at a ball given by the Queen of Holland. The only foreigners who received invitations were M. de Romanzow, Kourakin, Prince Wolkouski, and his wife.

His Majesty took the two first into an adjoining room. There, in a conversation which lasted nearly three hours, the Emperor decided absolutely against us, and on the necessity he felt to take serious steps. He quoted two particular facts which have recently occurred at Trieste and on the Isonzo,* and added that he was obliged to give a great blow to Austria, that that Power was completely rotten, that she had no leader, &c. The Prince de Kourakin having observed that all he knew of Austria's designs had always been pacific, the Emperor spoke of our armaments, ridiculed our military arrangements very much, and maintained their complete uselessness ; he added, it was not possible to make war with soldiers who were *tout nus*.

M. de Romanzow, who in the course of this conversation objected to nothing, went away quite convinced that the part of the Emperor was decided, and that war was henceforth inevitable.

These details, which I believe I have gained from a reliable source, as well as all the facts which I can gather, appear to me to be of a nature to be presented, without commentary and without dispute, to the deep penetration of his Imperial Majesty. In a critical

* See Note 26, vol. i.

moment like the present, the faithful minister is he who abstains from all argument, and makes but few commentaries upon a subject on which often the fate of his country and that of the whole of Europe depends. If French officials at home and abroad had acted like myself, peace between our two Empires might not have been disturbed.

War will be the triumph of their conduct, a sad triumph for ministers of peace!

All that we see tends manifestly towards war. The apparent calm of the present moment is the precursor of the tempest. The Imperial Guard is arriving here from the Pyrenees. The corps which are in Dauphiné are under orders to remain; movements amongst the troops in Germany are talked of.

We have just heard that several marshals are recalled from Spain. I can speak certainly of the speedy return of the Duke of Dantzig. Marshal Davoust is also expected immediately.

All that is passing in the States of the Confederation (of which your Excellency is infinitely more capable of judging than I am) may serve to explain better than I can the questions of the moment. It is doubtless too easy to calculate Napoleon's course by former ones; there is now so much identity with that which he followed before the campaigns of 1805 and 1806 that a similarity in the results of this course seems to ensue very naturally. But what a difference between the position of Austria and Prussia in these two years, and that which appears now to place France in opposition to us! Austria in the most perfect calm, isolated by the Powers themselves, who appear now to consider it a crime that she reposes with dignity on her own means of defence—Austria, I say, unquestionably cannot be taxed with bringing on war : not to give herself up, feet and hands tied, not to expose herself to succumb to the first blow, cannot be a crime. And such is our position, the attitude which so disquiets a Power who asserts that she has five times as many troops at her disposal as we have. If war is made, one cannot too often repeat that it will not be we who have wished for it.

TALLEYRAND IN DISGRACE.

(Note 33, Vol. I.)

133. Metternich to Stadion, Paris, February 2, 1809.

133. The nomination of a new High Chamberlain is an event of the greatest interest to every observer of what is going on in Paris. Here is the course of this affair, as far as I have been able to learn it.

Last Saturday, the 28th, M. de Talleyrand visited the Emperor, with the Arch-Chancellor and the Minister of the Marine. The Emperor made a very lively attack on a party which he imagines to exist, at the head of which he places M. de Talleyrand and M. Fouché, and of which he asserts the aim is to impede his projects of government. He said they calumniated his ministers and wished to give him others; he declared his esteem for M. de Champagny, and that he would make him as powerful as M. de Talleyrand; that he esteemed the Minister of Justice and of Finance equally; that he knew if by chance he had perished in Spain, they would have endeavoured to place his brother on the throne. He passed from that to some political discussions, and specially spoke against the Peace of Presburg, which he called an infamous and corrupt business.

Some moments afterwards Marshal Duroc called on M. de Talleyrand to demand his seals of office. The nomination of M. de Montesquieu was declared on the evening of the next day, Sunday. He expected it as little as the public, who by this fact judged that M. de Talleyrand was in a kind of disgrace. The turn which his Majesty gave (in the *Moniteur* of January 30) to the nomination of the new Grand Chamberlain partly silenced the reports which were circulating amongst the public.

It appears generally that the Emperor, since his return, is irritated against a number of distinguished individuals occupying places more or less influential. It is announced as very probable that General Savary will be nominated to the French Government very shortly. This being a great extension of power, and General Savary being known as one of the men in whom the Emperor has so much confidence that on every occasion he is entrusted with the most secret and difficult commissions, the public draws the conclusion that his Majesty wishes to create a counter-police, in order to watch the party which he supposes to exist.*

---

* In an earlier despatch, of July 13, 1808, Count Metternich wrote to Count Stadion : 'The rumour of the disgrace of M. de Talleyrand has for some time spread amongst the public. M. de Talleyrand, since the campaign against Prussia, is in opposition to the Emperor's system of invasion. He expressed himself strongly against the overthrow of Spain. Indiscreet friends have spread the late minister's opinion; zealous enemies appear to have seized this pretext to malign him.'—ED.

ROMANZOW'S MISSION IN PARIS.

134. Metternich to Stadion, Paris, February 1, 1809.
135. Metternich to Stadion, Paris, February 9, 1809.
136. Metternich to Stadion, Paris, February 17, 1809.

134. I have been to see M. de Romanzow to-day.
There is nothing definite to be drawn from him. He
asked me what I thought of the war. I replied that I
thought that it was rather for me to address this question to him. He did not hide from me that he believed
the Emperor's course was taken, and that still more
prudence was required on our part. 'What do you
call prudence?' said I to him. 'If Napoleon takes an
offensive or even a distrustful attitude against us, we
must depart from the footing of peace on which our
army now stands. Do you wish that we should allow
ourselves to be surprised in our quarters?'

'I work hard to keep him quiet,' said Romanzow.
'I have a most trying task; but beware of involving
yourself; that might have incalculable results.'

'I suppose,' replied I, 'that the first news from
Prince Schwarzenberg will be of a nature to show that
the Emperor, my master, was right to make him his
Envoy. One cannot do the Emperor Alexander the
injustice of believing that he could ever be found on
a course hostile to us.'

'That depends on the position,' replied M. Romanzow. 'There might be very embarrassing anterior engagements.'

'Embarrassing in case of the aggression of France,

replied I ; ' the question from which side the war comes should be more clear to you than to anyone else.'

'When once the guns are heard,' said M. de Romanzow, ' it is very difficult to decide from which side the aggression is.'

'War does not date from the first shot,' replied I ; ' a moral war precedes that of arms. Suppose that we are disturbed to the point of being compelled to take the attitude of repelling force by force, and that you were then told, "You see it is they who make war on us," would you believe that version?'

M. de Romanzow lost himself in phrases which sometimes led to the conviction that it was not possible to avoid war, sometimes to the hope that he might succeed in quieting Napoleon ; spoke of the necessity for our being very prudent, said that we should be on our guard, that we should not arm ourselves, &c.

On my visit to this minister all my energies were directed to proving, as decidedly as possible, that it is not we who put ourselves in a state of hostility.

Metternich to Stadion, Paris, February 9, 1809.

135. Romanzow is more and more convinced that war is inevitable ; he draws this conclusion from the silence which the Emperor preserves about us when with him. He continues to do all that he can to persuade the Emperor. Nevertheless, it appears to me that he should neglect nothing in explaining at St. Petersburg, step by step, each attempt, each measure that we take ; the essential point is to keep that court acquainted with the French initiative ; the passion of Napoleon furnishes us day by day with proofs in support of this idea. It is said that many French troops are marching towards Savoy. People who know the available re-

sources of France have much difficulty in following the
calculations of the Emperor.　Nevertheless, it is certain
he is not ready, because if he were so he would already
be in the field; let us observe things from this point of
view, and we shall not be deceived.　He said yesterday
to Romanzow : ' Everything has failed ; my calculations
prove that I lose more by the present state of things than
by war.'　What hope is there, then, of the Russian
Minister being able to persuade him of the contrary ?

Metternich to Stadion, Paris, February 17, 1809.

136. M. de Romanzow left us the day before yesterday.

This minister's sojourn here appears to me to have
been perfectly useless.　Always vacillating, sometimes
confident and sometimes discouraged, his desire of
making a maritime peace has not been crowned with
more success than, unfortunately, he appears to have
had in preserving the continental peace.　I have seen
enough to judge of him in his relations with his own
court as well as with that of France.　A great change
which has come over him is that of the conviction—if
this word can be employed of a man who changes daily—
that Russia has not employed the true means, or rather
that she could employ others, to preserve peace.　He
did not appear to me lately adverse to the idea of
establishing a union between the three Powers which
would lead to a general arrangement fitted to maintain
peace.　This is the extension which just at the last he
gave to his idea of a guarantee.　He could make no
objection when I remarked to him that this project
would not have been chimerical had it been made at
the Peace of Tilsit, or even at the time of Erfurt, by
extending this interview to the three Emperors, or at

least by summoning an Austrian minister. It appears to me useful to add here the fact, which I learned from a reliable source, and which serves to fix opinion irrevocably as to the side which has desired the continuation of a state of tension very easy to change into a state of war : Alexander at the time of the interview at Erfurt desired that Austria should be summoned to the conclave. Napoleon refused this.

I repeat, if Russia wished, she might maintain peace in Europe; if, instead of being caressing to France and menacing towards Austria, she had acted with the most perfect impassibility, with the most impartial justice, the *rôle* of mediator, of armed protector of the peace, war might have been avoided. But the cabinet which is contemptible enough in its actions to menace those whom it ought to reassure, and on the contrary to cajole the Power which for some time had prepared and brought on the actual state of things, could by its representative only offer me the habitual incongruities which I encountered in him continually.

In the last conversation I had with M. de Romanzow he constantly insisted that he feared my court had been led into error, and that it believed he, M. Romanzow, wished to encourage us in war. I reassured him completely on this question ; and I cannot better conform to his wishes than by expressing here my firm conviction that no one regrets more than this minister the explosion which he foresees as only too likely, and that no one is more pacific than he ; but though his wishes equal ours for the maintenance of peace, unfortunately he is deceived, and will always deceive himself about the means of maintaining and assuring this peace, so much desired by him and by us.

M. de Romanzow, at the last hour of his stay, fur-

nished me with a proof which irresistibly supports my
assertion at the beginning of the present despatch of
the entire uselessness of this minister's stay in Paris.
He told me that there were twenty motives to keep him
here; but that the wish to labour for the preservation
of peace between Austria and France led him to hasten
his departure for St. Petersburg. I could not hide
from him my conviction that he would have difficulty
in finishing, at a distance, that which even on the spot he
had not been able to begin; and I pointed out to him
the four weeks which he would pass on the road as
the critical moment of the crisis. He could not deny
this; and the fact of the Russian Minister of Foreign
Affairs leaving Paris, with the idea of conducting affairs
better by taking the post of courier, certainly offers
one of those political phenomena to which lately the
impartial observer has become only too well accustomed.

The private conversations which M. de Romanzow
had almost daily with the Emperor had much influence
on the versatility of the political views of this minister.
He told me one day, for instance, that the real cause of
the Emperor's irritation against us was the uneasiness
that our armaments caused him. It was not difficult
for me to prove to him that the Emperor of the French,
impregnable on his own hearth, having the Confederation as an advanced post against us, and Russia as a
support in case of attack from us, merely mocked Austria when he pretended to be uneasy about her measures
for defence—measures to which a Power finds herself
forced when placed in the middle of the Continent in
a veritable state of political siege. I could understand
that our preparations for defence might not be agreeable to him if he had the intention of dividing Austria;
but if he wishes for our preservation, the organisation

of our forces should rather satisfy than annoy him. M. de Romanzow replied that certainly the French Emperor could not fear us, but that the attention which we compelled him to fix on us prevented him from attempting anything serious against England. He wished to prove this to me, by a number of reasons, which he said he had gathered from his Majesty himself; that but for our armaments, the Emperor would have attempted an invasion of England, and an expedition to the Mediterranean. It was not more difficult for me to refute this second argument, than that of his uneasiness. How, said I, would the Emperor, without entirely exhausting his resources, think of sending all his armies into the interior, supporting them at his own expense, and both make war on Spain, and at the same time, a large, new, and above all, maritime armament? If war breaks out, it can only be because France desires it— and the Emperor of the French does desire it, because he needs more or less virgin soil to explore, because he has need to occupy his armies, and to entertain them at the expense of others. M. de Romanzow did not dispute my argument.

He came to visit me two days after this conversation, and repeated, nearly word for word, the arguments which I had made use of on my visit to him, as if he had been inspired with them that morning in a long conversation he had had with the Emperor. He wants money, said he—he does not hide it; he wishes for war against Austria to procure it; but when he has finished that, he will come and seek it from us.

Just at the moment of his departure, M. de Romanzow was informed by the Minister of Foreign Affairs of the conclusion of peace between the Porte and England. M. de Champagny wished to persuade him to put off his journey. To this he did not consent.

THE PEACE BETWEEN ENGLAND AND THE PORTE, AND THE AUDIENCE OF THE DIPLOMATIC CORPS WITH NAPOLEON.

(Note 31, Vol. I.)

137. Metternich to Stadion, Paris, February 23, 1809.

137. My last reports have informed you, sir, of the great sensation that the certainty of the conclusion of peace between the Porte and England has produced here. It is very natural that they make a grievance of it with us. At a moment when they seek to pick a quarrel with us about everything, this was too good an occasion to be lost. There would be, in any case, so many cries of ' well played! ' on our part that, independent of considerations relative to Russia, it would be rather a sentiment of modesty, the desire not to meddle with what is absolutely foreign to us, which might lead us to take exception to the honour that is done to us in one of the most important events of the present time.

The correspondence between M. de la Tour-Maubourg and our *Internonce* appears to me to show as much impudence on the part of the first, as meekness on the part of the second.* Who would not acknow-

---

* The cause for this violent correspondence is laid to the following: Count La Tour-Maubourg expressed, in a note (dated March, 1808) to the Austrian *Internonce,* his displeasure that the latter had not given official information to the Porte of the rupture of diplomatic intercourse between

ledge that, whilst rendering a French official his due, one must not hesitate to repulse an insult by a most decided and energetic attitude? If M. de la Tour-Maubourg had addressed the letter to me which he dared to write to a man whose public character is so much respected as M. de Stürmer, he would have been very much embarrassed in producing my reply.

It is for this very reason that I regret not having been commissioned to carry a formal and official complaint against this *representative*. The very day of the arrival of the courier who brought the important news of the conclusion of peace, I went to visit M. de Champagny. I told him that I had seen the courier that evening. 'He tells me that which you have known for two days, and which has not caused less astonishment at Vienna than at Paris—the peace between the Porte and England. This question does not concern us ; but our embassies at Constantinople have just had a disagreement, which certainly does.'

'M. de la Tour-Maubourg,' said M. de Champagny to me, ' actually speaks of an altercation which he has had with M. de Stürmer, but he does not enter into any details, and promises to send them to us by the first courier.'

Austria and London, but had left it to be gathered from the public papers. ' I will not dissimulate, sir,' writes the French representative, ' that the language of persons who speak to the minister in your name is a subject of astonishment to me. The system which has just been adopted at Vienna cannot have good effects, nor give to Europe a speedy and solid peace, unless it is followed by the other courts of Europe. It appears to me, in consequence, surprising that, instead of supporting and encouraging the Turks in the war which they have with England, and reminding them that this Power has only withdrawn from this war with shame, the persons who speak in your name only occupy themselves in suggesting to the ministers imaginary fears. This conduct, so little in harmony with the sentiments which his Majesty the Emperor of Austria publicly professes, appears to me so singular that I am obliged to make it known at my court.'—ED.

'I am not astonished at it,' replied I ; ' they would hardly boast of proceedings such as these. I am not only instructed to speak to you about this, but I have even been furnished with documents having relation to this inconceivable affair, with the intention of enabling me to reply to any questions which may be asked. It is not, therefore, the Ambassador who speaks to you, but Count Metternich who hastens to furnish you with a fresh proof in support of his old theory that it is your foreign officials who in great part cause the misfortunes of Europe ; they it is who, animated by I know not what evil spirit, seek to embroil matters as much as they can.   You believed you had grievances against one of our Ambassadors : it pleased the Emperor, my master, to recall him ; he gives you now a proof of moderation, of which I avow I should not have myself been capable, in not addressing to you a very peremptory demand for the recall of M. de la Tour-Maubourg.'

I read the correspondence to him. M. de Champagny could not advance anything in the least to serve the cause he defended.

He told me he should perhaps be instructed to complain to me, about the part that it was said our *Internonce* had taken at the pacification between Turkey and England.   I replied that if ever he brought me such a complaint, I should reply that the part of the *Internonce* had been so circumscribed that, when the peace was already signed, he wrote to Vienna that the negotiation on the Dardanelles would without doubt remain suspended till the issue of that of Jassy.   He asked me if I knew anything of the conditions of peace? I told him that our ignorance on this subject was a fresh proof of our complicity.   It is a fact that here as little is known as with us.

We have just received notice of a diplomatic audience for to-morrow. I foresee the possibility that the Emperor may question me about the event of Pera ; all my coolness may perhaps not suffice, in this case, to avoid an explanation to which I do not feel myself drawn by any political motive.

We went the day before yesterday, Sunday, at eleven o'clock in the morning, to the Tuileries. My appearance there now always makes an excitement. We were introduced to the audience. The Emperor approached me and asked for news of Madame de Metternich's health, a phrase which he always makes use of with me when he wishes to say nothing. I replied that she was 'much as usual ; ' and with this small, very small incident, the crowd of spectators and gossips had to be content. He made his round, and on his return asked the Minister of Bavaria, in a low voice, if the Bavarian fortresses were in a state of defence, and especially Passau ?

He approached the Prussian Minister a second time, and spoke to him in the most friendly terms about his master's journey into Russia.

He asked the Marquis Almenara if he had not left Turkey in open rebellion ? The Spanish Minister replied in the affirmative.

He then said to the Russian Ambassador, ' You know what has passed at Constantinople between the Imperial *Internonce* and my representative ? ' Prince Kourakin replied, ' Yes, sire, but it appears to me that we must wait for the details.' The Emperor, without considering this observation, uttered these remarkable words : ' They wish it then ; very well, they shall see what it is.'

The Emperor did not speak to me again, and finished the audience. He has since told several persons of his household that he had treated me badly, but that he could not do otherwise, because his ambassador had been treated in the same manner at Vienna.

CAUSES OF NAPOLEON'S DELAYING THE WAR.

(Note 31, Vol. I.)

138. Metternich to Stadion, Paris, February 23, 1809.

138. It would be very difficult to submit to your Excellency a well-grounded opinion upon the actual position of our affairs. My last despatch contained several ideas about the calm and silence which the Emperor preserves both in private and public. But this calm, this attitude which he maintains, and which are the most certain proof that his decision is made, on what do they rest? I did not dare to admit in my last despatch the possibility that the Emperor had actually deceived himself about our true position. I shall not ever admit it, and suppositions similar to those in the article marked in the journal enclosed, called the *Publiciste*, of February 22, 1809, could not be advanced but for the idlers in the interior of France. In excluding the possibility of a complete illusion about our means of defence, the Emperor must admit as the first line of his calculation—

That the means of Austria will be exposed to the extravagant chances of the campaign of 1805, or rather,

That there exists a party in the interior of our empire very decided in favour of France; that it can reckon on Hungary (I do not mention Galicia); or

That the noise which it makes in Europe will terrify us, and we shall give in—that is to say, we shall consent without a blow to make such a modification in our political and military relations, in our very existence, as he would impose upon us ; or, in short,

That his military forces, not being ready, nor yet arrived at the points which he judges most favourable for an attack, he hopes to keep us in a state of uncertainty which will permit him to assemble, to augment his forces, and to convey them to those points which, in his military operations, he looks on as cardinal points —in a word, we shall let favourable opportunities slip from us, and await those which will be favourable for him.

I do not hesitate to speak decidedly upon this last hypothesis. It is in the character of the Emperor. He will seek explanations, he will assure us by all possible means that he does not wish for war ; he would be at the head of his army if it had arrived where he expects it ; but, as he does not reassure us, and is not yet at head-quarters, the present moment is not yet his. This theory appears clear to me because it is simple. No doubt the Emperor reckons on our want of energy, on our habit of neglecting the moral and military means which, in preceding wars, we never called to our aid. He hopes, perhaps, that the known manœuvres of General Andréossy and of many subaltern officials in the interior of our country, and above all in Hungary, will excite revolt or a refusal of help to our Government. But as it depends on us not to repeat old mistakes, as our resources are as substantial now as they were hypothetical in 1805, I can only give a secondary place to the calculation of our mistakes in favour of the enemy, and I do not believe at all in the bad moral tendencies of the interior of our country— always excepting Galicia. Napoleon, who, up to the beginning of the affairs in Spain, had always calculated justly, can but separate the question of the commencement of the war which he wishes to undertake from that of its continuance. The first battle, the first moments of the campaign appear to me more worthy of being weighed by him on the present occasion than on any other. He must know the general feeling of minds in Germany and Italy. Even here we are able to gather too many notions about this last country to have any doubt about the effect which the beginning of an unsuccessful French campaign would produce there. He needs, therefore, more caution, more prudence in the question which he now approaches than in any former one; and here, I cannot doubt, is the explanation of what even in Paris appears problematical in the present conduct of the Emperor to all those who do not look upon articles in the gazettes as also articles of faith. These persons oppose to the folly of the assertion that we have not 146,000 men and not 100 guns the very simple question, 'How can a Power in such a state of decay cause disquiet to the Sovereign of France, the ruler of two-thirds of Europe and the ally of the rest, with the exception also of this Austria, so despicable and so despised?' It is, therefore, only a desire for general destruction, for universal dominion, which can lead him to wish to strike off the surface of the Continent this Power, already too independent. Assuredly, admitting this supposition, there was never a defence more legitimate than that of Austria, and does not the Emperor himself force us to it?

For several days the most pacific rumours have been spread abroad. These rumours are carefully circulated by the police, and by persons who are near the Emperor. It is said that Count de Mier has carried to

Vienna proposals for a very satisfactory arrangement; they pretend not to doubt that we could remain at peace by means of some slight concessions. This game is as simple as its design is evident. All Napoleon's tactics at this moment tend to gaining time, and after having provoked a very just alarm amongst us, and military measures suggested by this same uneasiness, he looks upon our means of defence as so many steps against himself. But if Austria wishes for war or enters into it (terms of the Erfurt Treaty), Russia can and ought to be invited to fulfil the engagements which she has made. This incontestable truth should prevent us from being duped by a state of apparent calm, and enable us to express ourselves as frankly as possible at the court of St. Petersburg. Convinced that in important times exceptional measures are necessary, and not being able to separate the force of a measure from extreme simplicity, I believe that nothing would be more out of place than to address the question, of how he regards the present state of affairs, to the Emperor of Russia, or to take account of the embarrassment in which France places us, far less to notice the provocations of France, but to ask him simply, Yes or No, if he looks on our military measures as free, or as imposed by a foreign impulse and beyond our province. This question decided, this Yes or No pronounced, would serve as a basis for all our future relations with Russia. I do not see that the latter could refuse to answer questions of fact, and in no wise hypothetical questions, which, above all, far from troubling the state of quiescence over which Alexander watches, would furnish him with the means of preserving it in his own empire.

ON THE QUESTION OF GUARANTEES.

(Note 31, Vol. I.)

139. Metternich to Stadion, Paris, February 27, 1809.
140. Metternich to Stadion, Paris, March 16, 1809.

139. Prince de Kourakin has just given me a fresh proof of his wishes for the preservation of peace by speaking to me of the guarantee which Austria could obtain.

Doubtless nothing would be more happy than a state of things which from its stability, its reciprocity, its political and military convenience, should enable the Powers to reduce their means of defence. Call this condition guarantee, peace, equilibrium : the name matters not. No doubt a reunion of the three Imperial courts could attain this end. It is that which the political principles of M. de Kourakin make him consider as the most desirable of all. Who aspires more than Austria to such a state, who solicits it more, and finds itself more united in intentions and wishes with this minister ? I believe that one could not better determine Napoleon's intentions than by addressing to him the following demand very promptly : Austria wishes for peace because she has always wished it, because it is for her interest. The idea of the guarantee has fallen through; it appears to be desired that she should diminish her means of defence. Without doubt it does not enter into your ideas, if you aim at a state of repose infinitely desirable and generally useful, that Austria has less means of defence than the other Powers have means of attack, taken in proportion. Austria wishes to reduce her army; how much would you reduce yours?

I do not think a single objection to a demand so simple, and so just, can be found by anyone. It is thus that the questions should have been proposed by Russia; they could be so still if Russia was not seven hundred leagues from the volcano which consumes Europe. Your Excellency without doubt agrees with me on the only interpretation which the word guarantee can have. I have on every occasion, and according to my firmest conviction, explained it in this sense to Prince Kourakin, and I cannot let this opportunity pass without again assuring the Emperor of the purity of this ambassador's views. All his endeavours tend now to avoid an explosion which would without doubt be very disastrous. The ambassador of a Power who is friendly to Austria, bound to her existence by his own interests, cannot undertake a more noble enterprise. But the difficulty, the impossibility perhaps of succeeding, does it not prove, better than all the arguments in the world, who troubles the peace of Europe, who troubles it by inclination and principle, and who in consequence will always refuse the establishment of an order of things which would not produce war, or the possibility of making it to-day or to-morrow?

Metternich to Stadion, Paris, March 16, 1809.

140. The Minister Champagny invited me on the 13th to visit him. M. de Champagny, in a long conversation, did not cease to protest that the Emperor desired to preserve peace with Austria. He added that his master wished nothing from us; that our integrity pleased him; that, in spite of the chances of success

which his position offered him, he was far from wishing
for new conquests—that they would embarrass him;
that he did not aim at all at general dominion. I protested as strongly the pacific intentions of my court;
I supported my argument by the evidence of facts, by
proofs furnished on many occasions by our august
master of his amicable and pacific intentions towards
France. M. de Champagny quoted as proof of the
intentions of Napoleon towards Austria, the retreat of
the French troops from Germany. I found my proofs
in the strict neutrality of Austria during the campaigns
of 1806 and 1807 (neutrality which turned so much to
the disadvantage of Russia that from this epoch date the
reproaches that that Power has cast on us); in our perfect tranquillity during the months of October, November, December, and January last, when a great part of the
French troops had actually left Germany, and when our
state of peace was as complete as in February, 1809.
It was with this discussion as with all the others : each
party stuck to his opinion and his proofs. M. de Champagny himself made this remark : ' Our two masters are,
then, animated by the same spirit, but their armies do
not the less find themselves in opposition.'

The minister had on a preceding occasion pronounced
the word guarantee ; having asked him then what he
meant by guarantee, he said he could not give me any
explanations, not being instructed to speak to me about
it. This same phrase having been made use of in our
conversation yesterday, I insisted again on some explanation. M. de Champagny replied that he supposed
that M. de Romanzow had spoken to me of it. I could
not but tell him that this minister had actually on several occasions made use of the same phrase, but that all
the explanations which I received were equally limited

to the assurance that he was not authorised to give me any, this idea being merely a personal one.

Knowing the wishes of my court, the extreme care which our august master has taken for a number of years to preserve the most amicable relations with all his neighbours, all the ineffectual efforts on his part to establish between Austria and France relations conformable to the general interests of Europe—interests which certainly are concentrated in a state of general peace—I repeated to the minister that on every opportunity I should endeavour to convey to my court any idea which the Emperor of the French could suggest for the establishment of a state of affairs in conformity with the wishes of the Emperor my master.

I concluded from several of the minister's phrases, accompanied by the remark, several times repeated, ' that in any contest which might occur Russia would be on the side of France,' that the courts of the Tuileries and St. Petersburg might well guarantee Austria reciprocally, and that the latter, in compensation, would reduce a part of her military forces. I defined the question more by expressing my doubts to M. de Champagny that a real guarantee could exist without the most perfect reciprocity; and in adding that I could not believe a Power of the first rank, and who herself can offer a reciprocity of guarantee, could find in a perfectly passive state a proper security to reassure her in all future cases. I added that the existence of a great Power should be settled and strengthened both by its diplomatic relations and by its military force. How would it be possible to replace this true and only equilibrium between Powers of the same order—these proofs, these pledges of their reciprocal independence ! Apart from this principle I could not doubt that, if ever there was a question of the reduction of the military forces of the Austrian Empire, she would find herself in perfect harmony with that which would equally please France, Russia, and the States of the Confederation. The minister did not hide from me that France, being at war with England, could not think of reforming her army, but rather of a more active employment of it against this Power, and that she could only leave in Germany the necessary number of troops ; that the military state of the Confederation, being determined by the federal act, could not suffer any modification.

This point led us to speak of the war with England. M. de Champagny told me that the war with Spain was as good as ended, and that it no longer required to employ the same number of troops in that kingdom. He spoke of the very true idea, that England will always find, in the hope of war breaking out between the Continental Powers, a pretext, perhaps even a reason, for not agreeing to a maritime peace. I could not help reminding him that since the interview at Erfurt, and at the time of the overtures which were made at its conclusion to the cabinet of St. James's, I established and defended the same point in favour of the admission of Austria into a union which alone will ensure the peace of the Continent and, if possible, maritime peace. I founded on this truth another motive for desiring that it were possible to establish an order of affairs in Europe which, by forming honourable relations between the three Imperial courts, would not be less useful to all the Powers who feel the need of peace and repose, at the head of which I do not hesitate to place ourselves.

.

THE LAST DESPATCHES OF THE AUSTRIAN AMBASSADOR AT PARIS.

(Note 31, Vol. I.)

(Extract from a Memoir of Metternich's.)

141. I can but regard the present despatch as the last that I shall be likely to address to your Excellency. I do not betray any private judgment on the conduct which is shown to me here. If it is painful for me individually, I add this sacrifice with pleasure to those which an ambassador to the Emperor at Paris is daily obliged to make in his service. The more the enemy permits direct violation of the right of nations, the more he renders his cause a bad one, and the more he furnishes proofs of his humour on the true position of matters, humour which never exists with Napoleon without fixed motives. He preserved up to the last moment gentleness in his relations with Prussia.

I allow myself, after the course which affairs have taken, and the effect they have upon myself, to admit all the chances, even the least probable, in consulting the most common laws of the rights of nations. I should not be at all astonished if they refuse my passports at the moment when I receive the order to demand them.

The Emperor probably not being in Paris, they will act as with my courier passport. I shall ask, and no one will reply. If they stop my couriers, I shall not even be in a position to make a demand. I have several ideas already in support of my supposition. They do me the honour of supposing that my presence might be of some use at Vienna from the knowledge which I have of places, and, above all, of individuals. I believe that, whilst enduring this separation from my country, I fulfil a sacred duty in placing here in the hands of his Majesty my wishes and my feeble counsels on the general character to be impressed on the course of affairs.

Napoleon, by his passionate disposition and by his excessive ambition, has provoked these present complications. He believes in the chances of success ; on the other hand, he is not deceived about the nature of the contest in which he engages with us, or our real means of resistance. He founds his hope of success on his military genius, on the spirit which animates his generals and soldiers. For the first time he begins an immense contest with inferior resources ; he hopes to double these by extra mobilisation. He founds his hope on the slowness of our movements, on the repose that we might take after the first success, on the discouragement and weakening of our moral forces, as well as the paralysing of our physical forces after the first defeat. The Emperor said lately to some one : ' The Austrians make a tremendous beginning ; I may have the disadvantage at first, but I shall regain it.'

This certainly can only be calculated by the insufficiencies of our moral forces. Peace or war do not depend on us.

Let us be prepared for strong blows, and, above all,

unexpected ones ; let us oppose the utmost activity to
his ; let us follow his principles, not regarding ourselves
as conquerors till the day after the battle, nor as
vanquished till four days afterwards.

Do not let us be disconcerted by these enterprises,
however bold, however hazardous they are. Once the
first cannon shot fired, do not let us give up the advantages of the attack ; let us have the most determined will, let not our wishes be confined to this or
that success, let us be ambitious on all points. Let us
hold always the glove in one hand and the olive branch
in the other ; always ready to negotiate, but only negotiating whilst advancing. Here is Napoleon's system ;
may he find enemies who will carry on war (undoubtedly provoked by himself) as he would carry it
on himself!

The military resources are equal, the feelings of the
people are on our side, why should not success also be
for us ? If Napoleon has no illusions, do not let us
have any either. If he has chances of success, so have
we ; if a total defeat would sap the foundations of the
Austrian monarchy (a defeat not very easy, in spite of
all that has been affirmed), defeats would sap the very
existence of Napoleon. It appears to me that at
Vienna, ever since the new dynasty has reigned in
France, an erroneous point of view has been taken in
contrasting France with Austria or any other Power.

France, since the Peace of Luneville, no longer
makes war. It is *Napoleon* who makes it with French
supplies ; it is now, in the present moment, *Napoleon*
who makes war on Austria. One man must, according
to the plainest calculations, run at least as much risk
as an ancient and formidable Empire. We cannot
but admit this point : to base our calculations on the

opposite supposition, to admit that it is France and all her allies who rise against Austria, would be to fall again into the very error that I undertake to combat.

I regard it as so much the more dangerous as it impresses a character on the management of all measures of the war opposed to that which alone can serve us. My opinion has the more weight as Napoleon does not make war on the Austrians, Bohemians, or Hungarians; he makes it on the Sovereign who unites these nations under one sceptre. The contest which engages him is the challenge of Napoleon to Francis I. The people of our Empire all press round the throne of the august House which has secured for them centuries of prosperity and happiness. I am far from seeing the same devotion here. The contest is, therefore, not equal : it is entirely to the advantage of our august master. These advantages cannot be annulled but by cowardice, moral weakness, or treason. May Austria sustain her ancient glory in sustaining her Sovereign; may the Sovereign grant to his people the means of employing usefully the force of his will, by placing according to principle questions as this ought to be, and by impressing on the entire machine a course conformable to these principles !

Bohemia should be warned that it is known from French publications that there is a design to make of her country a tributary state like Bavaria; Austria should know that some French marshal is perhaps destined to govern her with the title of Archduke. Hungary need not flatter herself that she will remain united as a nation. The French Government does not hide its intentions : let us profit by them. In a word, let us fight the enemy with his own weapons, let us send him back his own balls; let us, in short, destroy this prestige, this gentle illusion which up to the present time has served the cause of the French Government. We must destroy this illusion or we shall cease to exist. It is not we who have placed these points thus—it is the opposing party itself.

The history of the last campaigns furnishes the ordinary observer only with extraordinary French victories; it furnishes to the enlightened observer— opportunities lost by both parties—causes abandoned in moments of the enemy's greatest embarrassment — hazardous, irregular enterprises of Napoleon — cowardly, feeble, contemptible resistance of the allies. Let us never forget that it is in the way we profit by the first fortunate blow, and in our perseverance, that we can alone look for the general welfare. Any individual who is not penetrated by these truths will only serve the enemy's cause; and he will serve that of his master in a moment, perhaps the present one, when the whole nation proves that his cause is her own. If unfortunately the Government itself—and everything proves the contrary —is not convinced of this, if it can have a single doubt about the true views of Napoleon, or the necessity of making war and peace in the same way as he does, a frightful gulf would open before us. The die is cast, it has been against the will, against the dearest wishes of the Emperor; but those alone who have done this may at last prove victims of their foolish and immoral enterprise. We shall not attain this end except in fighting our enemy, without a moment's intermission, with his own weapons and resources. We are, for the first time for some years, strong in ourselves : let us be so altogether, let us take advantage of our strength, and never forget that the year 1809 is the last of the old, or the first of a new era.

It is no doubt unnecessary to recommend all the commanding officers of the army never to enter into the least *pourparler* with the enemy; that every envoy shall be sent back to head-quarters. Napoleon has never begun *pourparlers* except to gain time or to cause alarm; he is silent except when he aims at one or other of these ends. A great difference must be made between the sending of simple regimental officers bearing letters, or the sending of a Savary, Duroc, or others—the first being always that which needs a reply; the second comes only to spy, surprise, deceive. The commanding officer after a repulse or after a victory should follow no direction which has not come from the commander-in-chief. They should always test the news which the enemy gives them, as it often bears the character of the greatest probability, being, or not being, true. It appears absurd to give a warning so simple; but all absurdity vanishes when one can convince oneself on the spot of the daily course of the French cabinet, of the character which it displays with a perfect uniformity in all occurrences. The entire machine rests on that, all its actions must then on every occasion respond to the first and motive power.

Metternich to Stadion, Paris, April 11, 1809.

142. The present war affords three chances.

1st. It may have a speedy and fortunate result for France.

Austria, in this case, is swept out of the list of Powers, her vast states are dismembered. Europe undergoes a complete reform. A central and oppressive Government weighs down feeble tributaries solely occupied in dragging on a miserable existence and riveting their chains. Spain is subjugated; the

Ottoman Porte banished to the Bosphorus; the frontier of the great Empire stretches from the Baltic to the Black Sea; Russia in a few months driven back to Asia. Napoleon's fixed plan is executed. He is the Sovereign of Europe : his death will be the signal for a new and frightful revolution; many of the divided elements will try to reunite. New princes will have new crowns to defend; dethroned sovereigns will be recalled by old subjects; a real civil war will establish itself for half a century in the vast Empire of the Continent the very day when the iron arm which holds the reins shall fall into dust.

2nd. The war may go on slowly : its results may be favourable to Austria.

These two last chances are entirely in our favour. The consequences of having to sustain a war for several months are incalculable for Napoleon. What might have been the consequences of a delay of the battle of Austerlitz?—I do not speak of its loss—and let us compare the position of Napoleon in the month of December, 1805, with that of the moment when he enters the field in 1809 !

The war against Austria in 1805 was unpopular in France; that of 1809 is still more so. The treasury of the state was then full; now it is emptied in a great measure by the Spanish war. Napoleon then employed his whole army; it was composed of old regiments, intoxicated by former successes; fresh successes, and of a kind of which history hardly offers any example, had led it almost without striking a blow to the centre of the Austrian monarchy. Now the greatest part of his army is occupied in Spain; the resistance of the people of the Peninsula has broken the charm in the eyes of all the European nations; bloody defeats have to be effaced by future successes. Conscriptions are to be anticipated, reserves to be put in motion. For some time Napoleon has lived on anticipations; the reserves are destroyed. The Head of the old German Empire, in 1805, had only enemies in Germany. Now the cause of Austria is that of all nations up to the banks of the Rhine.

In 1805 (and this consideration appears one of the greatest to me) we submitted to the counsel of a cabinet which, facts proved only too well, could not govern itself; at present we are guided only by our own proper calculations. Our position is, therefore, no doubt better; it is far beyond what the boldest wishes could have formerly imagined. If we succumb, it will only be from our own fault or from delay.

3rd. If Austria, though not having a prodigious success here in the autumn (and why should she not have it?), has no great reverses; if she sustains the contest with equal chances, what will be the situation of France, or rather of Napoleon in France, at that epoch? I defy a politician the most versed in knowledge of the character of the public mind, and in that of the true position of affairs, to decide this question.

Metternich to Stadion, Paris, April 18, 1809.

143. The Emperor, informed on April 12, at ten o'clock in the evening, by telegraphic signals, of the Austrian army having crossed the Inn, started five hours afterwards for Strasbourg, where he arrived on the 15th at five o'clock in the morning. The ordinary gathering at the court had been announced for the 13th. The Empress, awakened by the noise which she heard in the apartments of the Emperor, went to him, and having entreated him to allow her to accompany him

immediately, her Majesty started with only one attendant.
The household followed several days afterwards. The
Queen of Holland and her children will also go to
Strasbourg in the course of this week.

The Senate was assembled on the 14th. M. de
Champagny read a report there * which, as it appears
to me, only contains the account of the conversations
between him and me, and the communication of the
French notes. The report of the meeting having been
sent the same day to the Emperor, it will not be published for two or three days. The Emperor has asked
for, and the Senate has granted, a fresh levy, 40,000
conscripts, of which 20,000 are to be charged on the
earlier reserves, and 20,000 on those of the year 1810.
This measure is in direct contradiction with the promise
made last year to the old reserves that they were never
to be called to active service, and the rumour of it
which has reached the public has not produced a
favourable impression. It appears that they also intend
to put the National Guard on active service.

M. de Champagny invited me to visit him on the
morning of the 15th. He told me that I ought to know
that all was at an end between us, and he asked me if I
had no news. I remarked that, as my couriers had
been intercepted, it was hardly possible for me to have
any. He told me then that the Emperor, who held
himself prepared to start at any moment, had not gone
till after we had declared war. He took a paper from
his bureau and begged me to read it, to convince me of
this last fact. It was the letter addressed on April 3
by his Imperial Highness the generalissimo to the commander-in-chief of the French army in Bavaria. I

* Published in the *Moniteur* of April 25, 1809.

remarked to the minister that this paper proved clearly the existence of a declaration of the Emperor my master to the Emperor of the French. M. de Champagny said that he did not know of it; that he knew of a declaration addressed to the Powers. 'One does not exclude the other,' replied I; 'but that to the Emperor Napoleon is doubtless earlier. It is possible that by intercepting the couriers you have deprived Europe of a last and precious means of preserving peace between the two Empires.' M. de Champagny said several sentences to which I could attach no meaning. There appears here to be a singular difference between the Emperor and his minister. The first told all the world that he intercepted three couriers, two coming from Vienna and the last that I sent from here. Champagny assured me that only one had been stopped, coming from Vienna, and that this courier could not have arrived here till April 10 or 12, therefore after the passage of the Inn. He had assured me three or four days before that none had been intercepted. I therefore give the preference to the version given by his Majesty himself.

M. de Champagny, in consequence of the request I made to him that I should not be less well treated than my predecessor, to whom in 1805 at least they delivered open despatches—a hope which the minister did not entirely gratify—told me that the Emperor, finding that after the rupture it would be inconvenient for the ambassadors to prolong their stay, had authorised him to return me my passport.

He added that his Majesty had nevertheless charged him to express to me the complete satisfaction that my conduct had given him during the term of my ambassadorship; that, to give me a proof of the same, he made me the offer, if it suited my private convenience, to leave my family here as long as I wished ; that his Majesty himself would be responsible for their safety, and that Madame Metternich should have the necessary passports whenever she wished for them, and for any route she wished to take. I replied by the assurance of my extreme gratitude for the personally flattering sentiments which the Emperor expressed to me by his deputy ; that as to my passports, I did not consider myself authorised to demand them without definite orders from my court ; but that, the Emperor being without doubt in a position to limit the duration of my stay here, I begged him to tell me if his Majesty had fixed a day for my departure.

M. de Champagny replied he had not, but that the Emperor hoped that it would not be delayed. I foresaw then that if he gave me my passports willingly I must make use of them during the week. I asked at the same time if M. Dodun had received orders to quit Vienna ; he replied in the affirmative.

I have since been informed that M. de Champagny was embarrassed in explaining to his master the duration of my stay up to the beginning of the following week, the time which I had fixed on. I therefore resolved to hasten my departure, and I intend to start next Friday, the 21st of the month. Having asked M. de Champagny if the Emperor had fixed any route for me to travel by, he informed me that, knowing there was uneasiness at Vienna on my account—a reason which added to his wish for my speedy return to my court— the Emperor would take as an insult any *détour* that I might make to avoid his armies. I shall therefore travel by the Strasbourg route straight to the headquarters of his Imperial Highness the Archduke Charles. I shall be accompanied by Prince Esterhazy, MM. Mier,

Lefevre, and d'Ugarte. M. de Floret will follow me in a fortnight. Not knowing by what route to send my family to avoid the annoyance of armies or popular tumults, of which rumours, true or false, are spreading here as if coming from the north of Germany, I have decided to leave them here till, having arrived at the Imperial court, I may be able to make some other plans. M. Neuman remains with them.*

Critical Remarks on the French War Manifesto, April 25, 1809.

144. The epoch of the war with Austria must be determined by two causes—by great success or great defeats in Spain.

The division of Europe into Powers, of which the strongest would not have more than three or four millions of subjects, has for some time been in Napoleon's plan. All his enterprises, all his military efforts, aim only at this end, above all since Austria's unfortunate war in 1805 facilitated the execution of this plan.

To create a vast empire, to become chief and protector of twenty or thirty small states, such was the design at which Napoleon aimed ever since that time. He did not dread the frightful convulsions which Europe would necessarily experience before the realisation of this plan ; he was not held back by any moral principle ; nothing could, therefore, counterbalance his unmeasured ambition and the effects of the low flattery of those who surrounded him, who never worked but in the way they knew would be most agreeable to the secret wishes of their master. To extend this division up to the

---

* Metternich's residence in Paris was prolonged till May 26. He was treated as a prisoner, and subsequently exchanged at Komorn. The reader will find a full account of these events in the Autobiographical Memoir.—ED.

borders of the Niemen, Borysthene, and to the confines of Hungary and Turkey, to make use of the short-sighted course of the cabinet at St. Petersburg for the destruction of the Ottoman Porte, then to fall with all the power of ancient Europe upon Russia, and drive her back into the steppes of Tartary and behind the Volga—such is the plan of universal dominion which Napoleon dreams of, and in which his confederates frankly support him. They and he cannot hide from themselves that up to the present time he has done nothing in his own country to settle his dynasty on such a basis as to secure the rule even of his immediate successor. Plunged by taste, by the need of moral and physical movement, into the vast career of conquest, it is no longer in France, in the attitude of the sovereign of this vast empire towards his subjects, that Napoleon and his confidants seek their security and that of their descendants—it is in the weakness of their neighbours and in the destruction of ancient Europe. 'It is we who place princes on the thrones created by us,' says Napoleon's party.

None will be powerful enough to put themselves at the head of a coalition against the chiefs of this league; the jealousy of colleagues, the military depôts and police spread by France on all the surface of the great federation, will discover schemes and annul them before they can be tried. The Emperor of the French, if he were even feeble and without strength of character, will maintain order solely by his position, by the need that the entire federation will have of him and of his authority.

Woe to the state who sees at the head of its administration men so narrow and so corrupt as not to acknowledge the truth of this design or the dangers of its realisation!

Napoleon, after the Peace of Tilsit, had the choice between the overthrow of Austria and that of Spain. He preferred beginning with the second, because he believed he could accomplish it without striking a blow. Nothing would have been less popular in France than an immediate war, after the sad and disastrous campaigns in Poland. The *grande armée* itself, weary and dispirited, longed for repose. Napoleon did not doubt but that he should show Europe the novel spectacle of the fall of one of the first thrones without a blow being struck. These are the only true motives of a course which appears enigmatical to an observer who does not possess the means of verification, and one from which the interested partisan of the Napoleonic system endeavours to draw the conclusion that the Emperor did not wish for a war with Austria, or he would have made one in 1807 or 1808. If, on the contrary, it were possible, at this moment of truce, to draw any other conclusion than that Napoleon was deceived in his calculations about the Spanish revolution, it would certainly be that the Emperor was perfectly convinced that Francis I. would not make war until he was forced to it, and that in consequence the moment of the explosion was entirely in his own hands. I have before shown that the submission of the Peninsula or great reverses there would infallibly serve as a signal for a war with Austria.

To penetrate into the real course of Napoleon's policy is sufficient to convince one that the destruction of a Bourbon throne was merely a pacific interlude between the war of 1809 and that against Austria, the principle of which he signed at Tilsit. The day when the new King quietly seated himself on the throne of Spain and the Indies served as the signal of war with Austria.

But every chance turned against the destroyers of this throne. Napoleon, shut up in Castille, his armies threatened on all sides, destroyed, or on the verge of being so, was compelled to think of a pretext for leaving a kingdom in open insurrection without appearing willingly to abandon his brother to all the dangers of his position, or to abandon an enterprise as unfortunate in its execution as it was criminal in its design. He made war on Austria. This decision was taken the day when he signed at Valladolid the order to the Confederation to keep their armies in readiness.*

He ought by this determination to attain one of the following ends—either to make Austria succumb in this critical moment to his immense military forces, and to conquer her easily without means of resistance, and consequently without further efforts on his part than the 60,000 French and 80,000 confederates and allies in Germany; or to prevent an attack on our part, to which we might have been tempted for some months by the necessity of employing our forces, and by the general feeling of European nations. One or other of these alternatives would draw him from Spain, and might with success turn either to his future or present advantage. Such is the war of 1809, and such were the wishes of Napoleon.

The preservation of the Spanish throne appears to be at variance with the plan of division which I mentioned. But the division of the Peninsula was no less decided on than that of the rest of Europe. The French domain extended to the Ebro, took away from the

* In Champagny's report to Napoleon, which had to serve as a war manifesto, it says: 'Your Majesty wrote from Valladolid to the Princes of the Confederation, to request them to prepare their contingents—a measure of simple precaution called forth by the fears which they have long felt for your Majesty and which your Majesty realised on returning to Paris.'—ED.

Spanish crown its most powerful bulwarks, and Portugal would have formed one or two distinct states. The Spanish colonies were not left out of Napoleon's views, and he hoped to recover on the American continent rich compensations for the loss of the old French colonies.

The Spanish insurrection thwarted a plan which was given up on the first indication of a popular movement in this kingdom.

FROM THE PERIOD WHEN METTERNICH WAS
PRIME MINISTER.

1809—1810.

145. The events which befel the great army on the 5th and 6th of July resulted in an armistice which, from its extent, exercised a decided influence on the political and military relations of the monarchy.

Not to accept the armistice was impossible on account of the state of the army at that time. Your Majesty, therefore, ordered your brother to carry it out. There remained but two things to be done—to use the interval for negotiation, and to place the army so that it should support the negotiation, and in case of the renewal of hostilities, be turned to good use.

Your Majesty has made use of the preliminary conferences of Prince Liechtenstein with the Emperor Napoleon to inform him of the nomination of peace negotiators. It is to be supposed that the opportunity was taken. These were necessary instructions, and in relations like the present can only proceed from your Majesty.

It is not to be supposed that Napoleon would agree to the *status ante bellum.* These conditions had to be signed without hesitation, since the true end of the war was unattainable by reason of the reverses our arms had sustained. But it was not to be expected that, as Napoleon declared to Prince John Liechtenstein, Austria would be ready to lose as she did by the Presburg Peace, not less than three or four million subjects.

This supposition must be founded on the idea that our position is the same as it was at the end of the campaign of 1805. But it is in no way the same, either in military or political respects.

At the end of 1805 our forces were quite crippled, nearly destroyed. Now, on the contrary, we have still two hundred and fifty thousand men to present to the enemy, and a campaign behind us in which this army covered itself with honour, and went near to utterly destroying the enemy.

On the other hand, in the year 1805, our rear was quite secured by Russia, while our flank was protected by the whole strength of Prussia; we entered into negotiations at Presburg and had to make cessions which diminished the state, but did not destroy it. We had, behind us and on our right flank, faithful allies. The Emperor of Austria was still a German Emperor. France's influence in Germany was still usurpation.

Now Prussia is destroyed, Russia is an ally of France, France the master of Germany. Austria also stands alone, without any support but in herself. Our political situation is also beyond comparison worse than that of 1805.

The cessions which then took place might weaken, but now there are hardly any which do not bring ruin to the empire.

In the year 1805 a faithful servant of the state might still advise; now he must limit himself to laying before your Majesty a statement of the position of affairs. To the monarch alone is it reserved to choose between many difficulties and dangers. In the idea of choice there still remains an available resource. But for this there would only be capitulation or moral and political death.

I venture to maintain the truth of the assertion that every cession now strikes at the very life of the state. From the day of the signature of a peace negotiated by means of cessions, our existence depends on blind fate.

It cannot, however, be concealed from your Majesty that if a fresh blow should unhappily fall, or a happier chance not be properly used, the present united states of Austria would be in danger of being entirely dis-united.

It is possible that Napoleon might be got rid of by the cession of Salzburg, the circle of the Inn, and part or the whole of the Littorale and of Galicia. Such a demand—joined perhaps with the disarming of the population and reduction of the army to forty or fifty thousand men—is surely only to be answered in the negative.

Perhaps, and probably, he would make only part of these demands : Salzburg and the circle of the Inn, or Salzburg and the Littorale, or Salzburg and Galicia.

These different cessions seem to me to react on the monarchy in different ways. From a military point of view Salzburg has the greatest, West Galicia the least value. Financially considered, the Littorale has the first position. I confess I do not see that it is possible to relinquish the Littorale.

If, then, Napoleon insists on cessions, and if your Majesty prefer some concession to open combat, it is necessary to decide beforehand what cession and to what extent shall be fixed by your Majesty as the ultimatum. The reduction of the army is a question connected with that of cession. This seems to me, however, of less importance. As soon as peace is concluded we must reduce the army from financial reasons. These reductions are in reality only nominal so long as the *cadres* are carefully maintained. Napoleon and our finances both lay down the same law for us in this matter.

It is different with the reserves and *landwehr* system. On these points very little can be conceded.

Napoleon will require contributions for three reasons : he requires money ; by taking it he injures our finances, and by extravagant demands keeps the quarrel open.

Different opinions exist in the Finance Department as to the possibility of bearing the contributions of money. Count O'Donell denies the possibility ; Count Pergen thinks a contribution of even twenty millions could be easily borne. I share the opinion of Count O'Donell, as also does Count Stadion.

The guarantee for the Austrian loan in Holland, which seems to have been taken by France, leads one to fear fresh complications. This point must receive special consideration.

The retaining of the Imperial title by your Majesty must not be called in question. I could never agree to the relinquishing of this, for Napoleon connects with the Imperial dignity the idea of supremacy and independence.

These are the chief points on which instruction is needed.

In another paper I will give my views of the

present position of the monarchy after the conclusion of peace.

In conclusion, I entreat that more prompt and vigorous military measures may be adopted. Your Majesty's firm will alone can save the state. If two hundred and fifty thousand men cannot obtain a bearable peace, what prospect of support has the monarchy from an army of fifty or a hundred thousand men? And even if the present demoralised condition of the army makes an unhappy peace preferable to the chances of war, yet it is not a question of capitulation. The first will only be possible if your Majesty endeavours to centralise the forces and remove the unhappy influences of divided powers. No one but your Majesty has the decision of peace or war.

Metternich to the Emperor Francis, Komorn, August 10, 1809.

146. In the former report (No. 145) I considered the chances of peace and war ; in the present one I will confine myself to the conclusion of peace.

After the Presburg Peace we were not only permitted, we were summoned to work for the restoration of a general peace in Europe. Our object must be to seek security for this in the emancipation of our independence. What means we have to attain that end depends on the condition of our army.

Whatever the conditions of the peace may be, the result will come to this, that we shall find our safety only by accommodating ourselves to the triumphant system of France. That this system, being entirely contrary to all sound principles of policy—being opposed to every great union of states—is most unsuitable for us,

I need not repeat to your Majesty. My principles are unchangeable, but to necessity we must yield. If the present war, with extraordinary means, is unsuccessful, to repeat the attempt with reduced strength against a stronger adversary would be an act of insanity.

From the day when peace is signed we must confine our system to tacking, and turning, and flattering. Thus alone may we possibly preserve our existence, till the day of general deliverance. Without the assistance of Russia, opposition to the universal pressure is not to be thought of. That vacillating court will awake more quickly if it finds that nothing more is to be gained by its miserable policy. Always in contradiction to itself and its principles of yesterday, it will perhaps serve as a support to us when it finds an eager rival cross its path. For us there remains but one expedient, to increase our strength for better days, to work out our preservation by gentle means, without looking back upon our former course.

One of the first conditions will be the closing of the harbours against England. We must also join unconditionally in the general continental system, objectless as it is.

The recognition of the Spanish usurpation is the second consequence of the peace.

We may be asked for active assistance; but never would I consent to an action so degrading both morally and politically.

One question, which touches on the inner life of the states, is that of the subjugation of the Roman See. If it can be passed over in silence, so much the better. But should it be discussed, the incorporation of the States of the Church, with the recognition of all the changes of recent times, without expressly touching on ecclesiastical questions, would be the preferable modification.

The truce which has been concluded has made it impossible to escape entirely from contributions. The various opinions of those versed in financial usages amounts to this, that the last-made contribution should be accepted as the maximum. An attempt, however, should be made to apply to the contribution the four-and-twenty millions which, by the Peace of Presburg, were to be paid to France. Austria's demand on France would merely be to be left alone. The retreat of the enemy must take place immediately after peace is signed.

Metternich to the Emperor Francis, Komorn, August 11, 1809.

147. The negotiation which is to decide upon the proximate and the remote condition of the monarchy remains where it was. I have been honoured by your Majesty with the conduct of this negotiation.

It is scarcely possible that the minister should not be judged exclusively by the results of his work. In conflict with all parties—in conflict, alas ! with the principles admitted to be true—he undertakes a work occasioned by necessity and temporary complications. Everything which in the usual course of things turns to the advantage of the negotiator, everything which in this case, too, is in favour of the negotiation (the great amount of our resources), increases the responsibility of the negotiator in the eyes of the nation and of all Europe. . . . . .

The conviction, the profound consciousness of having stood by the monarch in the time of danger, of having to the utmost of my power served him to the sacrifice of myself, to the disregard of every subordinate consideration, without courting the favour of anyone, can alone support me in the work which I undertake at your Majesty's command. I start early to-morrow for the place which has been fixed upon for the negotiation (Altenburg). On July 20 I had the honour to submit to your Majesty my first note on the future negotiations. Appended to this your Majesty will receive a second, which confines itself merely (No. 146) to a general sketch of the peace, and to the future state of our political relations, as seen in the peace itself.

It only remains for me to ask your Majesty for definite directions upon our present labours.

Resolution of the Emperor Francis, August 14, 1809.

148. The principles upon which the negotiation must proceed are the following :—

With the forces which the monarchy still possesses it is not forced to capitulate. There can only be a question of an acceptable peace which does not undermine the existence of the Empire, and which will not lead to its certain destruction.

Resting on these principles, the negotiators will endeavour—since it requires time to bring the armies into the field—to gain time till the end of August, and to use this interval to discover Napoleon's views, whether he means an acceptable peace, or whether he means to make demands which would bring about the destruction of the monarchy or new wars, when it would be our duty to take up arms to avert the mischief.

In the meantime, the views of Russia must be discovered, and we must hold ourselves ready for action.

Although, apart from extraordinary and unexpected events, I should regard every peace with Napoleon as extremely dangerous for the monarchy, on account of the consequences which would spring from it, yet there might be cases where such a peace would be necessary —such as our relations with Russia, and still more the views of the greater part of my subjects.

I should regard the following as inadmissible conditions :—

The reduction of the army before the evacuation of all my provinces by the enemy.

The abolishing of the *landwehr* and reserve system, or of any like institutions under other names.

The payment of exorbitant contributions.

The payment of debts to foreign Powers of a similar kind.

The cession of sea-coasts, to the commercial ruin of my monarchy.

The subjects of negotiation are, the exchange of West Galicia for Tyrol, or for Istria and Dalmatia.

Compensation of my claims on France.

In all cessions and exchanges my approval is always previously to be obtained.

Proposals to be made for the provisional suspension of contributions, and for the destiny of Tyrol and Vorarlberg . . . . the best provision is to be made, as an affair on which my honour depends.

Also the utmost possible care must be devoted to the interests of allies, such as the King of Sicily and Sardinia, and of those of my servants who have suffered much from their fidelity to my interests.

FRANCIS.

THE ORGANISATION OF A SECRET STATE-OFFICE.

(Note 43, Vol. I.)

149. Metternich to the Emperor Francis, Totis, November 11, 1809, with the Decree of November 14, 1809.

149. May it please your Majesty! The sketch is with great deference enclosed of a plan of organisation for a Secret State-Office, specifying the business to be transacted in each department and the officers required in each.*

* This is omitted as being entirely without interest, as well as unintelligible to English readers.—Tr.

THE MARRIAGE OF NAPOLEON WITH MARIE LOUISE.

1810.

150. You desire, my Prince, to receive precise directions on the intentions of his Imperial Majesty relative to a question which may immediately come before us. If Napoleon's divorce takes place, it is possible that you will be consulted as to an alliance with the House of Austria. I know there is a party in Paris which will exert itself directly in favour of this idea, the same which for a long time tried to put limits to the violent changes in Europe. My reports in 1808 contain very exact notions on this subject. If the divorce of the Emperor Napoleon did not take place at that time, the motive of the delay was the impediment which he foresaw in the development of his political system by an alliance with one of the first Powers of Europe. If the divorce of the Empress was certain, the same calculation might keep him from thinking of the daughter of our august master; the fact of the demand itself might furnish you with a ground on which to calculate the extent of his destructive projects against us, and the time more or less distant which he fixes for their execution.

The Emperor, our august master, has on all occasions proved that the safety of the state is his first law. What sovereign has sacrificed to this principle more opinions, just resentments, and private happiness? If the deepest feelings rise in the heart of any father against the mere fact of an alliance with Napoleon, how much must these feelings be increased when this father finds himself the sovereign of a great empire? Nevertheless, his Majesty, to whom nothing is repugnant which can contribute to assure the well-being and tranquillity of the state, far from rejecting this idea, authorises you, sir, to follow it up and to refuse no overtures which may be made on the subject. It is, nevertheless, only possible that you can approach the question with the following restrictions :—

1st. Every overture should be received by you in a non-official character ; and your Highness should only undertake the affair by showing your personal goodwill in feeling the ground with us.

2nd. You will assert as a private remark coming from yourself, my Prince, that though no secondary consideration, no prejudice will ever influence the decisions of the Emperor, there are laws to which he will always submit. His Majesty will never force a beloved daughter to a marriage which she abhors, and he will never consent to a marriage which would not be in conformity with the principles of our religion.

3rd. You will also try to determine as far as possible the advantages that France would offer to Austria in case of the conclusion of a family alliance. The personal character that you will maintain in these first overtures will greatly facilitate their conclusion.

Such are the directions which at this moment I have the honour of transmitting to your Highness, and which alone suit the general position of affairs, and ours in particular.

I ought to inform you, my Prince, that, before his departure, M. Alexandre de Laborde, whose part in the last peace is known to your Highness, came to see me, to sound me on the possibility of a family alliance. He discussed the marriage of the Prince Imperial with the daughter of Lucien, as well as that of the Archduchess Louise with Napoleon. I hardly left him hope for the first, and expressed myself about the second in the sense of the instructions which I have the honour of forwarding to you to-day.

Laborde, who lately has been directly employed by Napoleon in his relations with us, will not fail to prepare the ground in this sense, and I make it clearer for your Highness by informing you of this circumstance.

Countess Metternich to her Husband, January 3, 1810.

151. To-day I have some very extraordinary things to tell you, and I almost believe that my letter will form an essential part of the transaction.

First, I must tell you that I was presented to the Emperor last Sunday. I had only mentioned it verbally to Champagny, when I received a letter from M. de Ségur, which informed me that the Emperor had fixed on Sunday, and that I must choose some lady of the court to present me. In my wisdom I chose the Duchess of Bassano, and after having waited with twenty other ladies, amongst whom were the Princess d'Isenbourg, Madame de Tyszkiewitz, and others, from two o'clock till half-past six in the evening, I was introduced the first, and the Emperor received me in a manner I could hardly have believed. He showed real joy at seeing me again, and seemed pleased that I had remained here during the war. He spoke of you, and said : 'M. de Metternich has the first place in the monarchy; he knows this country well; he can be useful.' This phrase struck me particularly in connection with what follows.

The next morning Madame d'Audenarde came to visit me, and told me that the Empress much wished to see me. I went to Malmaison the next day, which was yesterday. When I arrived the Vice-King, who is indeed the best of creatures, was the only person in the room—he is the Queen of Holland in man's attire. He spoke much of you, and in the middle of our conversation the Queen came in, who was much pleased that we had so quickly renewed our acquaintance ; then, taking me aside, she said, 'You know we are all Austrian at heart, but you will never guess that my brother has had the courage to advise the Emperor to ask the hand of your Archduchess.' I had hardly recovered from my astonishment when the Empress entered, and after having spoken to me of all the events which had just happened and of all that she has suffered, she said, 'I have a plan which occupies me entirely, the success of which alone could make me hope that the sacrifice I am about to make will not be a pure loss ; it is that the Emperor should marry your Archduchess. I spoke to him of it yesterday, and he said his choice was not yet fixed ; but,' added she, 'he believes that this would be his choice, if he were certain of being accepted by you.' I said everything I could to assure her that for myself individually I should regard this marriage as a great happiness ; but I could not help adding that it would be painful for an Archduchess of Austria to establish herself in

France. She said, ' We must try to arrange all that ; ' and then expressed regret that you were not here. ' It must be represented to your Emperor that his ruin and that of his country is certain if he does not consent, and it is perhaps the only means of preventing the Emperor from making a schism with the Holy See.' She told me that the Emperor would breakfast with her to-day, and that she would then let me know something positive. This very moment I have received a note from Cochelet, telling me that the Queen expects me to-morrow morning ; we must therefore wait and hear what she has to say.

I have not seen the Queen of Holland again, because she is ill. I have therefore nothing positive to say to you on the affair in question ; but if I wished to tell you of all the honours with which I have been overwhelmed, I should not finish so soon. At the last reception I played with the Emperor. You can well believe that it was no trifling matter for me ; nevertheless I came out with glory. He commenced by praising very highly my tiara of diamonds and my *robe d'or*, and then questioned me a great deal on my family and all my relations ; he would have it, notwithstanding all I could say to him, that Louis Kaunitz was my brother. You can hardly believe what an effect all this had. When the game was over I was surrounded and courted by all the great dignitaries, marshals, ministers, &c. I had opportunities for philosophical reflection on the vicissitude of human things.

Metternich to his Wife, Vienna, January 27, 1810.

152. It was with great interest that I read the information contained in your last letter about the interview you had had with the Empress. That prin-

cess has lately shown a strength of character which ought very much to increase the feelings of veneration which for some time France and the whole of Europe have evinced for her.

She has spoken to you with such freedom as to enable you to reply in the same way to her, and I desire very much that you will seek an opportunity to do so. There are some questions which are so delicate that they cannot be approached too carefully. The Empress placing herself before you with that nobleness which characterises her, you should respond candidly to the flattering proof of confidence she has given you. It would be superfluous to mention twenty considerations which may come out of questions such as those which the Empress touched upon to you.

I regard this affair as the greatest which could at this moment occupy Europe. I believe the choice which the Emperor has made will prove as conducive to the general interests of the numerous class who, after so many and such frightful revolutions, long for peace, as to the private interests of that prince. This consideration led me, from the first moment I was informed of the probability of a divorce, to turn to the princess who might be called to take this part. There were many reasons for the Archduchess presenting herself to my mind ; I believed it my duty to assure myself of the disposition of my master, so as to prevent any hint of a proposal if his consent had proved impossible to obtain. I found the Emperor on this occasion, as on all others, without prejudice, fair, loyal, strong in principles and will ; I found him both the sovereign of a vast empire, and the tender father of a daughter who merits his love by every attraction which can be found in a child.

I saw at once that I might make my calculations

with confidence ; your last letter has proved, to my great satisfaction, that they are entirely agreeable to the wishes of the Empress Josephine. Two obstacles nevertheless are present to my mind : the first, the most insurmountable, that of religion, seems no longer to exist ; but the Archduchess is ignorant, as is only right, of the views concerning her, and it is not from the Empress Josephine, who gives us so many decided proofs of her confidence, from her who to so many qualities unites that of a tender mother, that I should try to conceal the crowd of considerations which will necessarily present themselves to the mind of the Archduchess Louise when they speak to her of her establishment. But our princesses are little accustomed to choose their husbands from affection, and the respect due to the wish of a father, from a child so good and well brought up as the Archduchess, makes me hope that there will be no obstacle on her part. I shall then consider myself authorised to bring forward this question the same day the views of the Emperor of the French call upon me to do so, and there is no reason why you should not reply to the Empress Josephine's proof of confidence in you by confessing this secret to her.

Metternich to Schwarzenberg, Vienna, January 27, 1810.

153. It is with very great interest that his Imperial Majesty has learned the details which you sent him by the last courier with regard to the marriage of the Emperor of the French.

It would be difficult to draw a precise conclusion from the different data we have received. There is a certain official character in the explanations, however vague they may be, between your Highness and the Minister of Foreign Affairs. The proceedings of M. de

Laborde, the talk of so many persons attached to the Government, show all the same wish ; above all, the direct overtures which have taken place, on the part of the Empress and the Queen of Holland through Madame de Metternich, would lead to the supposition that the Emperor has decided, as the Empress says, if our august master consents to grant him the Archduchess. On the other hand, the proposals which are generally said to have been made in Russia do not agree with this supposition. These questions should, in any case, be made clear soon after the arrival of the present courier, if they are not before that time. We cannot suppose, after all they have said to us, that it has not entered into the intentions of the court of France to ally itself with the Imperial House of Austria. Following a very simple calculation, and referring to the great publicity which has been given to the demand said to have been made in Russia, and the secret ways that are followed with us, one might perhaps be authorised to suppose that the direct views are now on our side ; but all calculations are useless in a transaction of this kind with Napoleon, and we can only follow a calm and uniform course, the result of which must, in one way or another, turn to our advantage.

Your Highness has seen, by the former instructions I have had the honour to address to you, that his Imperial Majesty, to whom the good of his people will be always the supreme law, will not hesitate to make his august daughter a guarantee of relations which will ensure the repose and prosperity of his monarchy.

The religious question removed, there only remains that of the consent of the Archduchess Marie Louise. The well-known sentiments of all the members of a House which only exists for the good of its subjects do not permit us to doubt that her Imperial Highness will consent to an alliance which certainly offers very important points for her consideration.

I cannot see any good reason for doubting the success of the project, but it is necessary to determine its existence without committing ourselves, and to prepare to turn success or failure to advantage.

After the many hints of which your Highness' last despatch gives an account, we cannot doubt that it is expected in Paris that by the present courier you will receive instructions which will enable you to reply in an unequivocal manner to the questions which have as yet only been agitated, as well as to those which may be addressed to you more directly.

The most decided overture having been made by the Empress and the Queen of Holland to Madame de Metternich, his Majesty believes it to be no less his duty to follow this unofficial course, and to let his real intentions be known to the Emperor Napoleon. I have the honour to enclose to your Highness a copy of the letter which I addressed to Madame de Metternich on this subject. You would do well to hold a similar language to M. de Laborde, and if the question should be put directly by the Duke de Cadore, to that minister himself.

We believe, by so sincere an attitude, we shall establish new claims to the esteem of the Emperor of the French. This should be of use to us, even in the supposition that this prince will contract other ties. The reproach, so often put forward, of a private prejudice nourished by our august master and his cabinet against the Sovereign of France, must certainly fall before such evident proofs. His Imperial Majesty on every occasion sacrifices private resentments, unhappily too often provoked, to the important consideration of the repose and well-being of his people.

The Emperor commands me to declare to you, my Prince, his complete satisfaction with the steps you have taken in the conduct of an affair so delicate as the present, and in the manner in which you have placed the question, thus binding the evident interest of the Empire to the consent of the Emperor and his august daughter, and you will do well, my Prince, to continue to pursue the same line.

Metternich to Schwarzenberg, Vienna, February 14, 1810.

154. The courier Laforet brought us on the 7th of this month the despatches from your Highness of January 31 last. Their contents prove that the calculations which we made in the despatches sent from here on January 27 are confirmed.

The last overtures which have been made to you, sir, in the affair of the marriage, authorise us to suppose that the explanations, precise but unofficial in form, which the courier Renard brought to you, will bring you more direct proposals on the part of the French cabinet.

In considering the ordinary course of the Emperor of the French, from the time that the first notions relative to the marriage were agitated, we have thought right to put your Highness in a position to reply to any hint that may be made to you.

Our last despatches will have shown that our august master, having only the well-being of his people in view, would not refuse to give the Archduchess to the Emperor of the French. But as her Imperial Highness was not, at the time of the departure of the last courier,

informed of a question which for some time has occupied the whole of Europe, I was not able to speak positively of her consent. I have now the satisfaction to
tell you confidentially that, however, when her august
father opened to her the possibility of Napoleon seeking
her hand, the Archduchess Marie Louise only saw
another opportunity of displaying the most absolute
devotion to her beloved father. She feels all the
force of the sacrifice, but her filial love outweighs
all secondary considerations, and her consent may be
regarded as certain, whenever his Imperial Majesty
thinks right to ask it. This state of things allows us
to wait with calmness till the official proposal of the
Sovereign of France be actually made. If the last explanations, which the Emperor commanded me to make
at the very source, through Madame de Metternich,
and which your Highness has been authorised to support, have not led to more direct overtures before the
arrival of the present courier, there is nothing to prevent your Highness from making use in a quiet way of
the important fact I have communicated to you, without pressing it too eagerly, which might deprive us,
when the official demand is made, of bringing forward
many questions of the highest importance.

No doubt the measures of Napoleon against the
Head of the Church are embarrassing at this moment.
The hints of the Empress Josephine to Madame de Metternich, and those which have since been made to your
Highness, tend directly to bind the cause of the Church
to the arrangement of the marriage. If the manner
in which, on principle, we have advanced the questions
relative to religion has contributed to reveal the
religious views of the Emperor of the French, it seems
to us not less evident that, with circumspect and skilful

management, it may be reserved to our august master
to play an important part in the arrangement of the
affairs of the Church, even profiting by the embarrassment which these cause Napoleon. You cannot be
too much impressed with this point of view, as the occasion for making use of it may occur at any moment.
We cannot lay too much stress on the necessity that
the Emperor, our master, should receive, on placing
his august daughter in a foreign country, the most
complete guarantee for the repose of her conscience,
and what we could not obtain recently for the Holy
See might perhaps be secured when the Emperor of
the French becomes convinced, by the opposition he
daily encounters on the part of his own clergy, of the
difficulties presented by the destruction of religious
peace.

There are many other questions of greater interest
which we will reserve to the time when the formal
proposal arrives. We are far from thinking an alliance
with a prince whose system is daily only too evident
a sufficient compensation for the sacrifice made by the
head of the first sovereign house of Europe in acceding to this arrangement. To obtain as much as possible by the sacrifice must be our first consideration,
and the views of the Emperor, always benevolent and
moderate, aim in the first place at the safety and future
tranquillity of his people.

Metternich to Schwarzenberg, Vienna, February 19, 1810.

155. It is impossible that the important event
which is about to be consummated should not spread
great uneasiness in many states of Europe; it will
be received with joy in other parts of the Conti-

nent. Russia, Prussia, and the Ottoman Porte, will see more or less, in a family alliance between the two Emperors, an entire abandonment of Austria to the French system. The court of St. Petersburg, calculating our policy from her own point of view, will discover a system of conquest to indemnify us for our losses. The other two Powers will be afraid that certain parts of their dominions will excite our covetousness.

The wishes of his Majesty are limited to the hope of being able to gain, by the immense sacrifices he has made, some years of repose, and the possibility of healing many wounds caused by the constantly renewed struggles of the last few years.

We are far from deceiving ourselves as to the very great distance there is between the marriage with an Austrian Princess and the abandonment by the Emperor Napoleon of the system of conquests; but we do not despair of turning to profit the moments of repose which necessarily would begin for us, in order to consolidate our internal affairs and temper the views of the Emperor of the French. The very fact of his marriage with one of our princesses is an impediment to the rapidity of his destructive progress, since the people subject to the authority of Napoleon believe they see in it a pledge of peace. But if our ambition confines itself to a pacific attitude, we do not the less believe it ought to be shared by our neighbours. We undertake to reassure Prussia and the Ottoman Porte. The retreat of the troops from Germany and the Illyrian Provinces serves us to this end, and we are anxious to make it valued as the first consequence of our present attitude. Your Highness should, in your despatches, make this explicit with the missions of these two Powers.

We have adopted a very different plan with Russia. We are informed by the last despatches from M. de Saint-Julien of his uneasiness with regard to our pre-sumed connection with France.

The effect that this supposition must produce on a cabinet as feebly conducted as that of St. Petersburg is not to be contradicted ; since it began to fear us, it has sought every possible means to establish its former connection with us, and we believe we could not be placed in a better position, for attaining this end, than by preserving the most perfect impassibility and showing without temper the contempt we have lately felt for its conduct.

At a distance it would be difficult to judge of the sensation generally produced here by the news of the marriage.   The secret of the negotiation had been kept so strictly that it was only on the very day of the arrival of M. de Floret that the thing reached the public. The first effect on the exchange was such that the rate would have been to-day at three hundred, and even less, but that the Government had interest to hold it at a more advanced price ; and it was only by buying in the space of two days a million of specie that it was able to fix it at three hundred and seventy.   Few things have ever obtained a more universal assent on the part of the real body of the nation.

The diplomatists suspected nothing either, and the Count de Schouvaloff was terrified at the news.

The preparations for the fêtes now occupy both the court and the public.   I have had the honour to send to your Highness, by the last courier, the programme for the few days to be disposed of.   His Imperial Majesty has commanded that here, following the strict-est etiquette and the protocol which was used at the time of the marriage of Marie Antoinette, nothing must be spared to give the greatest possible *éclat* to the ceremony. Your Highness will do well to explain this, for we know by experience how much the Emperor of the French thinks of these details.

AT THE TIME OF THE SPECIAL MISSION IN PARIS.

1810.

METTERNICH'S ARRIVAL IN PARIS, AND HIS INTERVIEW WITH NAPOLEON IN COMPIÈGNE.

(Note 46, Vol. I.)

156. Metternich to the Emperor Francis (Report), April 4, 1810.
157. Metternich to the Emperor Francis (Report), April 4, 1810.

156. . . . I met, on entering Paris, Prince Schwarzenberg and Madame de Metternich on their way to Chalons, going by invitation of the Emperor to meet her Majesty the Empress. I did not stop, and on arriving at the capital, I wrote to the Minister of Foreign Affairs, who had been since the previous evening at Compiègne, to ask him the place and time when I could give to his Imperial Majesty the letters of which I was the bearer. He invited me to repair to Compiègne on the following day. I was told at the same time, by a letter from the Grand Marshal of the palace, that his Majesty the Emperor had assigned me an hotel at Paris, where I should be lodged at the expense of the court.

Your Majesty's ambassador, undertaking to mention in his despatches everything relating to the stay we

made at Compiègne, I am bound to bear witness that it
would be difficult for this court to be more refined in
its conduct to us than it has been.

The Emperor received me on the day of my arrival,
before dinner. I gave him the letters from your Imperial Majesty. He received me with evident marks
of satisfaction. He did not hesitate to express what
he felt as to the conclusion of the affair which exclusively occupies him at this moment; he entered into
all the details on the progress of that same affair, and
always returned to the theme, that we had neglected
nothing to render the happy event as pleasant and
agreeable as possible to him. He spoke of the entire
oblivion of the past, of the happy and calm period we
were coming to, of the impossibility of anything henceforth disturbing the natural connection which would
be established between us, &c. &c. I expressed to him
my desire to be authorised to arrange during my sojourn
at Paris many matters of great importance for us, and
of common utility for the two empires. He received
my request with gratitude, and told me that he would
immediately give orders to the Duke de Cadore concerning my proposition. The ecclesiastical question in the
affair of the divorce led us in our conversation, which
had already lasted nearly half an hour, to speak of the
quarrel with the Holy See. The Emperor entered into
many details. The result of this first interview was the
assurance that he would consider an interview between
the Holy Father and himself as a very happy occurrence. In proportion as I saw that he looked upon our
good offices as useful for himself, I diminished my
eagerness to intermeddle in a discussion so delicate,
and I put the question in such a way as to leave him
in no doubt that, if we undertook to carry words of

peace between him and the Holy See, we should establish certain rights to his gratitude.

Dinner being announced, we broke off our conversation, which, besides the conviction that the first moments the Emperor had passed with the august daughter of your Imperial Majesty seemed to have given him an assured pledge of domestic happiness, convinced me that my journey here will not be without utility for the interests of the monarchy.

Invited to dinner the following day, on rising from table the Emperor engaged me in a conversation which lasted more than three hours, and in which we touched on nearly all possible questions, both private and general.

I will not take up too much of your Majesty's precious time by retracing the details of our interview ; I confined myself to determining the most essential points, and especially those which have been developed as I expected.

We are called upon to carry out our mediation between the Holy See and France. The Emperor desires that we should send some one to Savona, and he appears to me not unwilling to come to an arrangement on any basis but that of Rome. I have not entered as much into the question as I should desire, not having yet received the help promised me by the Archbishop of Vienna, whose previous knowledge seems to me very necessary, so as not to venture on subjects from which it would be difficult to withdraw.

I have every hope that I shall be able to negotiate the loan required by the finances of your Imperial Majesty.

I shall regulate the commercial relations. I do not allow myself yet to prejudge the question of Fiume.

The Emperor—than whom no one could have been more flattered by the honour which your Majesty has conferred upon him by granting him the hand of your daughter—calculating the happy results which this union must have for him in many ways, convinced till the last moment that the consent of your Majesty would never be obtained, is at this moment in the best possible disposition to render himself useful and agreeable to Austria. There are few branches of the internal administration of our States which we did not touch upon in our conversation. He knows all their machinery, and appreciates them at their proper value. He renders full justice to the character and intentions of your Imperial Majesty. The Emperor spoke to me of two projects he had conceived to ruin us, supposing that we had continued the war without success. 'I had ready three hundred millions of notes of the bank at Vienna,' said he to me. 'I would have inundated you. On the other hand, I would have guaranteed the Hungarian Constitution.' I replied to him that in the first measure I saw only a means of putting us at our ease, and of discharging your Majesty's conscience on the bankruptcy which would have been inevitable in the above-mentioned supposition. I assured him that I did not attach any value to the guarantee of the Hungarian Constitution, a vain measure in case of success on our side, and adding nothing to our misfortunes in the contrary event. The Emperor began to laugh, and said: 'I shall send the false notes to you, and I wish to show you that it is necessary you should begin to think of reforming Hungary, without which you will never be really strong.'

I showed great anxiety to be put in possession of the notes and said that as to his ideas of reform in Hungary, we were entirely of his opinion, but that your Majesty could not wish for a thing without the means of executing it, and therefore had never declared yourself on a circumstance so important. We spoke of the last war. Many very interesting confessions escaped the Emperor: ' I should have been lost,' said he, ' if at the renewing of hostilities in the month of September you had beaten me.' Seeing that he had said too much, he corrected himself, and replaced the word *lost* by that of *very much embarrassed.* I would not let him off, and assured him that I should hold to his first expression, and that this conviction had much strengthened me in my attitude at Altenburg. I thanked him personally for having refused me at the time of the negotiations of Vienna, and assured him that *I* never would have made the last peace there. ' Well,' interrupted he, ' and what would you have done?' ' I should have made a peace much more suitable,' said I, ' to our real strength, and consequently much better, or war.' ' You would have been wrong to make war upon me,' replied the Emperor. ' I was difficult to dislodge from Vienna, but you would have made a better peace. Well, you sent me very feeble negotiators.'

The Emperor told me that he had received news from St. Petersburg which showed him that his marriage had produced a very strong sensation there. I told him I had no doubt of it, but that I was not without uneasiness as to the results of the new position of affairs. The height of our wishes is peace and tranquillity; it cannot, therefore, enter into our views that Russia should involve herself. ' What do you mean by involving herself?' demanded the Emperor. ' Russia acts only from fear,' said I ; ' she fears France, she will dread our connection with that power, and anxiety

upon anxiety will go far to move her.' Upon that he
entered into many details of his relations with Russia,
which all confirmed what I had but too much reason
to fear—that things have come to a point which will
need all the wisdom and all the calmness of your
Imperial Majesty's policy to avoid a quarrel. The
Emperor seized this opportunity to speak to me of
M. de Romanzow's * last stay here. He spoke strongly
with respect to this minister, whom he taxed with
want of judgment and character, and of sacrificing
everything to his own fancies. If I had not known the
Emperor, I should have been astonished to hear him
maintain the theory, so often defended by me and attacked by him—that it was to the feeble conduct of the
Russian Minister that we owed the last war.

The Emperor spoke to me of Prussia with very
little caution. ' What a country and what a Government!' cried he. ' If they are to be pitied,' said I, ' it
is certainly the Emperor of the French alone who can
save them or crush them. The former appears to me
infinitely more in harmony with the interests of the
whole of Europe, and more worthy of your Majesty.'
' But to whom would you that one should speak in that
unhappy country? They have neither sovereign, nor
people, nor minister, nor money. I do not wish to
crush Prussia, but she must fulfil the engagements she
has undertaken.'

I broached the question of the negotiation with
England. I knew that frequent conferences had taken
place between the two Governments; I said so to the
Emperor. His Majesty did not deny this, but expressed
his conviction that peace would not be possible unless
Lord Grenville was at the head of the British Ministry.

---

* See the Romanzow Mission (No. 134–136).

He believed Lord Wellesley little fit to follow a negotiation, because the interests of Spain and Portugal have
become his own cause, and, so to speak, that of the name
of Wellesley.   I submitted to the Emperor whether it
would not be in the natural order of things that the intervention of Austria—the only Power of the first rank
entirely removed from all questions of maritime legis-
lation, and consequently the only one essentially neutral
—should be claimed on an occasion so important for the
welfare of the whole world.   The Emperor made no
objection to my idea, which he even admitted to be quite
natural ; ' but,' added he, ' it is not necessary to think
of a negotiation at this moment.   The ministers are too
much occupied with their own affairs and with supporting themselves against the attacks of Parliament
for it to be possible, for some weeks, or, indeed, before
the end of the session, to begin seriously and with hope
of success any negotiation whatever.   We will talk,
then, of France and Austria.'

These, Sire, are the principal features of a picture
which I am the less able to fill in as the negotiation
I am beginning now with the Minister of Foreign Affairs
can alone clear up the questions and place them in their
true light.   The principal impression made upon me
in the course of my long conversation—an impression
which no one is more able than myself to appreciate
from the comparisons that I am able to make with
former epochs—is, that Napoleon has a very decided
feeling at the present time that our existence, far from
being incompatible with his own, may serve him as a
shield.

This good feeling will permit me perhaps, during
the short sojourn which I make here, to bring about
happy results for the monarchy.   I shall clear up many

questions, and shall place many others as they ought to be; and lastly, I shall communicate several important and really useful results to your Majesty.

Metternich to the Emperor Francis, April 4, 1810.

157. The despatch which I respectfully take the liberty of addressing to your Majesty by the present courier will only acquaint you with the most important points of our present attitude. It is not at the moment when I am trying to reunite the scattered elements, to make them serve as a basis to an edifice on which our existence may rest, that I should permit myself to form a judgment on any question. I have always had the hope that my journey to Paris would be really useful: I am now convinced of it. The direct news from St. Petersburg which arrived here the day before yesterday proves that they are beginning to be in better spirits there. Count de Romanzow, always careful for the true interests of his country, now appears to wish to press on his court the course of action to which he nerved himself. It had proposed a convention relative to the affairs of the Grand-Duchy of Warsaw which the Emperor of the French has not ratified. The Russian cabinet is uneasy about this refusal; uneasiness with the feeble and presumptuous often takes the form of arrogance and menace. This will certainly happen at St. Petersburg, and, foreseeing the blow, I believed it my duty to prepare and propose the questions to Napoleon as I have done. Your Imperial Majesty will condescend to convince yourself by my preceding humble despatch (No. 156). Our manifesto is published; we wish for peace and tranquillity. I have declared your Imperial Majesty the apostle of this noble cause. Nothing will prevent you from holding the same language on every occasion, as well at Paris as at St. Petersburg ; and your Majesty will have the glory—following a course worthy, upright, and calm—of being the mediator of the destinies of Europe.

Maréchal Kalckreuth arrives here to-day.   The King sends him to compliment the Emperor on his marriage—a feeble expedient at this frightful crisis.   The fate of Prussia is in the hands of Russia.   If she quarrels with France, Prussia will be the first victim.   I have, however, no doubt that the frank and loyal conduct of your Imperial Majesty to the cabinet of Berlin has produced there the best effect.

The attitude of your Majesty's ambassador at Paris is now the same as that of the Russian ambassador before the last war.   Everyone pays him attention, and the French public, always following the impulses given by the court, give them a colouring on the present occasion which did not exist formerly.   It has less the appearance of following a foreign impulse than its own.   A general enthusiasm reigns, which increases every day among all classes of people.   The cause of peace and of general order, consequently that of Austria, has made many allies.

METTERNICH AS MEDIATOR BETWEEN PIUS VII. AND NAPOLEON.

(Note 47, Vol. I.)

158. I have decided to send M. de Lebzeltern to Savona in two days. He will go there under the ostensible and natural pretext of treating with the Holy Father of things which concern our affairs. He will enter on these general questions in such a manner as not to complicate them more than they are already, and not to throw the odium of a refusal on the Pope in the case, unhappily too probable, of his not acceding to any arrangements.

The Emperor, with whom I have debated the religious question a great deal, is so much committed to it, and so certain of not being able to bend the Pope to his will, that he will not press some of his ideas if his Holiness will on his side give up some points which, however, could only with great difficulty be abandoned by the court of Rome. I believe that it would not be impossible for a skilful Sovereign Pontiff to return to Rome, under certain modifications, but saving the essential rights of his dignity. Unfortunately, the Pope has spoken on several points in a manner which he will be obliged to retract, and his position is therefore much complicated. If the attempt does not succeed, your Imperial Majesty will yet have played the best part, a part the most worthy of the first Christian Prince.

Not till the next post can I have the honour of submitting to you, Sire, the details of the instructions I have given to M. de Lebzeltern. Wishing to move safely, and to run no risks with his Holiness, I have insisted on the Emperor communicating to me his views in writing. But foreseeing that this kind of declaration would not pass the most narrow limits of what he would be ready to grant, and not wishing to deprive the head of the Church of the possibility of obtaining more, I have informed his Majesty that I should only regard these as preliminary ideas to which on neither side should be attached any precise value. I thus attain the object of not placing your Imperial Majesty in an attitude unfavourable to the part of a mediator, by appearing to have decided in favour of one of the parties. So to arrange matters has not been the least task that I have had to fulfil. The Emperor has made the affair drag on up to the present time, in the hope that he could bring me to take his view ; he has never ceased to insist on the utility of our adopting similar points of view, sufficiently decided to be presented as such to the Holy Father. I was firm, and I flatter myself I have avoided a rock very dangerous for the interests of the Church and for our own cause.

Metternich to the Emperor Francis, Paris, May 6, 1810.

159. My last very humble despatch (No. 158) has informed you, Sire, of the first conversations that I had with the Emperor on the subject of the relations with

Pius VII. They have proved to your Imperial Majesty that this prince, whilst seeking our mediation, does not the less aim at complicating us in his previous measures. I have defended our independence of opinion and attitude with the greatest warmth, and by never ceasing to maintain that the part of mediator is the only one suitable to the Sovereign of Austria, and that this part can only be sustained by consideration of all the past events. I have at last persuaded Napoleon to entrust me with a memoir which, without any official value, leaves every latitude for reconciliation.

I have the honour of submitting to your Majesty the enclosed instructions which I gave to the Chevalier de Lebzeltern (No. 160). The original French memoir (No. 161) is one of the enclosures in this budget. M. de Lebzeltern started yesterday for Savona, and will return here on May 23rd, or 25th at latest. Your Imperial Majesty will see, in reading the memoir (which M. de Champagny has returned to me) of my instructions to Chevalier Lebzeltern, that the first part has been drawn up by the French cabinet, as one might have foreseen, in a sense infinitely more strict than it was in the private conversations which I had with the Emperor. I did not hesitate to base my instructions on the conclusions to which I have actually arrived. I have too many opportunities of judging of the real embarrassment in which the Emperor finds himself, of his desire to get out of a quarrel whose duration even embitters him, not to be convinced that if the Sovereign Pontiff was able to accede to these arrangements (which at the same time are impossible if he does not consent to some modification of his temporal power), he could attain what I have shortly pointed out in the document which I have sent to M. de Lebzeltern.

Whilst giving a certain publicity to the despatch of the embassy's counsellor with the object of regulating our own ecclesiastical relations with the Pope, I have aimed at not making things worse, in case his journey should prove fruitless, and should not lead to any result favourable to the general cause of Christianity. It appeared important to me, in the first instance, to avoid allowing the Pope to compromise himself by a direct refusal (unfortunately, only too probable), to agree with such an arrangement. I flatter myself that your Imperial Majesty will deign to honour with your approbation my mode of acting. I have endeavoured to be worthy of it in the whole conduct of this affair. The private acquaintance that I have made here with the *Sacred College*, the inconsistency which I remark in the conduct of its members, the isolation of the Pope, several measures on his part which it would be very difficult for him to retrace—all these conclusions unfortunately only make me fear for the success of the holy enterprise of your Imperial Majesty. But if we do not succeed, we shall have done no harm, and you will not be the less able to enjoy perfect satisfaction in the efforts you have made to hasten the moment of the triumph of Religion, and to re-establish on the most desirable footing the relations of the Holy See with the Catholic Powers.

Instruction for Herr Ritter Lebzeltern, Paris, May 6, 1810.

160. It is necessary in the first place to explain the question of the moment. The Emperor of the French has embarked in an enterprise which in principle does not appear to present any difficulties to him. Moral force has again sustained its rights against purely

material force ; the Holy Father, in resisting Napoleon's
desires, while sacrificing some precarious advantages,
has retired into impregnable entrenchments, and the
discussion between the adverse parties has necessarily
ceased since the open violence to his person has placed
the Pope in a perfectly passive attitude. Things are
come to the point when the intervention of a third
party can alone smooth a difference which, if it still
subsisted at the death of the present Pope, would
lead indubitably to a schism in the Church. I cannot
stop to speak of the difficulties without number
which, for some time, have resulted from the actual
position of things for all the Catholic states ; they are
such that the Emperor of Austria would see himself
without doubt called to play a most glorious part, if he
could succeed in obtaining by his good offices that which
appears as if it could only be obtained through him.

Napoleon desires an arrangement with the Holy
Father. It is to be supposed that if he still had the
choice, he would not undertake what, after the experience he has just had, cannot but present insurmountable obstacles. He has, on the other hand, made
a great advance. He has laid down certain principles ;
he has incorporated Rome with his Empire : so many
false steps would appear impossible to retrace if we had
not seen the French Government continually retract
principles and facts previously advanced and established. A skilful Sovereign Pontiff, ready to seize the
weakness of his adversary's position without disgracing
him, and resting on the idea that in great political
crises one must trust much to the future, would doubtless be able to restore many matters to a good footing. M. de Lebzeltern should undertake the task of
putting this possibility before the Holy Father.

M. de Lebzeltern will go to Savona under the ostensible pretext of obtaining from the Pope several concessions desirable for the ecclesiastical administration of Austria.

In the conversations which he will have with the Holy Father, he will speak only in the general sense which I have taken care to use in my letter to the Pope, of our august master's desire to see a reconciliation take place between him and the Emperor of the French. He will rest his motives on the advantages which would result to the Pope by his re-establishment on the Papal throne, even in a condition modified in its temporal relations. The inevitable evils which would be created for the Church in the case of a vacancy in the first office of Christianity are also points which should be noticed by the negotiator.

But there is another important consideration which cannot be too explicitly set forth, and by which it would be difficult not to be struck.

If the Emperor of the French is unquestionably compromised in a question which it will be very difficult for him to bring to an end by force alone, it is not the less true that the obstacles which he has encountered up to the present time, in the opposition of the clergy subject to his domination, will diminish every day. As dispute excites minds, nourishes hatred, strengthens motives, so a state of stagnation cannot but turn to the disadvantage of the weaker party, and we cannot but see that the crafty conduct of the Sovereign of France has placed the head of the Church in this last situation. The evangelical spirit is dying out in the dioceses for want of instituted bishops; the canonical spirit grows weaker in the Universal Church for want of a head. The Holy Father should not confound the present time with the middle ages, when the affairs of religion were in everyone's eyes the first affairs of the State, and when a disagreement with the Sovereign Pontiff affected the general interests. Millions of men will soon forget, in our times of quietism, even the existence of the Pope ; the clergy will end by supplying his place, and the grave questions which will be agitated after the death of Pius VII. will be no more than a subject for discussion between cabinets whose interest it will be not to let them depart from the diplomatic line. Napoleon understands this fact so well that, at the present time, he aims at reinforcing his opposition by ours, and at changing our part of mediator into that of an ally for his own cause.

Our most constant care must be to avoid this rock. I have determined our attitude ; I have marked it out with Napoleon in such a manner as to prevent his making us deviate from our course—the only one which can lead to a salutary end. He gave me the enclosed memorandum (No. 161), which contains only summaries of facts, and has been expressly declared to have no official value. As I do not wish to prejudge questions which it may not be possible for us to arrange, I confide a copy of this memorandum to M. Lebzeltern, only for his private information. The following conclusions, which I have been able to draw up after several conversations with the Emperor, are the only ones proper to guide us in case of the Holy Father wishing to come to terms.

1st. I am convinced that the Emperor has entirely given up the idea of fixing the seat of the Catholic Church at Paris, which would cease by such a translation to be that of the Universal Church.

What the memorandum says of contrary intentions is only from Napoleon's pen a means of negotiation.

2nd. The memorandum barely touches the question of the return of the Holy Father to Rome. The Emperor went much further in his conversations with me. I do not believe it impossible to re-establish the pontifical chair in that ancient capital of the Christian world, if the Pope would accept some modifications concerning his temporal power over the patrimony of St. Peter.

3rd. The Emperor will not oppose any of the Pope's external forms of independence, such as the reception and sending of ambassadors, couriers, &c.

4th. I have no reason to doubt that he might secure an independent revenue for the Sovereign Pontiff, as far as the idea of independence can be allied to the supremacy which the Emperor of the French exercises over all the small states of Europe.

5th. The Emperor is ready to renounce the oath which, after the last *Senatus-Consulte*, the future Popes were bound to take about the Gallican Church.

M. de Lebzeltern can only make these ideas the subject of verbal and entirely confidential communications. If the results which they have in view are to be attained, it can only be by a course as skilful as pliable on the part of the Holy Father. Would he risk compromising the moral height on which he is placed at present? Will he be convinced of the advantages which may result for the Christian cause from a skilfully calculated compliance on his part? The more difficult it is to judge these questions in advance, the less reasonable it would be to extend the mission of our ambassador beyond that of a simple observer. M. de Lebzeltern is not charged with a negotiation, but simply with introductory *pourparlers*, not compromising either party, and capable of leading to a negotiation the success of which we should consider a very happy circumstance.

The Chevalier Lebzeltern will doubtless encounter great difficulties from the isolated situation of the Pope. All that I have been able to obtain from the Emperor, after reiterated representations, has been an agreement that if his Holiness should desire a Council, he might choose such persons as he would consider suitable, the Emperor refusing the assembly of all the Sacred College.

Supposing that M. Lebzeltern's journey led to no other result than some private arrangement for the Austrian Church, it will not be less useful for him to sound the Pope in order to know if the permanent presence of an Austrian envoy near his person would be agreeable to him—the Emperor having consented to this.

OBSERVATIONS BY THE EMPEROR NAPOLEON.

161. I. It is for the interest of France and Austria to be of one accord and to prevent schism. The similarity of religion between Vienna and Paris has always been one of the points of union. It is an advantage which these two courts have had for many centuries over other courts.

II. The Emperor Napoleon will make no schism in spiritual matters. He has quite decided to remain in the religion of St. Louis, which the school of theology in France has professed since the time of that sainted King till that of Louis XV.

III. To judge by the *Senatus-Consulte* and by other measures, one might believe the Emperor's wish to be, whilst preserving the denomination of the Roman Church and the bishopric of Rome to the Pope, to make the Pontiff reside at Paris, where he would be nearer Madrid, Vienna, and Lisbon, and more in the centre of the Catholic Church, and because a residence in that city, where there is more movement amongst men and affairs, is likely to give him more influence amongst those whom he ought to direct. What proves that such is the Emperor's idea is :—

1st. The meeting of the members of the Sacred College; it appears that he had wished to have them assemble in Paris, above all in the event of the Pope's death.

2nd. The arrival at Paris of the archives from Rome,

the *Daterie* and *Pénitencerie*, which have already passed the Alps.

3rd. Several millions devoted to the enlargement, decorating, and furnishing of the archiepiscopal palace, a number of the surrounding houses being already demolished to make a garden for it.

IV. On the other hand, Rome has been united to the Empire, all the monks have been sent away, the Code Napoléon published, and everything in that country has taken a French aspect. The Pope is at Savona; he is well treated; from thence he manages, when he wishes it, all Christendom, through the Bishop of Savona. He receives freely everything that is addressed to him. His style and dignity are placed on a much higher level than they were at Rome.

The Emperor no longer seeks the Pope. He has obtained what he wanted. His clergy are united in doctrine, which is that of the Gallican Church; his bishops are devoted to him.

Two difficulties may still be raised: the first, on the subject of dispensations; but the bishops lend themselves to it, and the Code Napoléon not exacting the intervention of priests to secure the civil effects of marriage, this object has not more importance than it had formerly.

The second difficulty is caused by the refusal to institute bishops. It is known that Napoleon has called together a council of fifteen of the principal doctors of the Church, who have declared that if the Pope should continue to refuse the institution of bishops, the Emperor could call a council which should provide for their institution. The Emperor, then, has this means of instituting bishops, which would result in diminishing the prerogatives of the Pope; but one may suppose that the Emperor will not give himself this trouble. What does it matter to him who governs the dioceses, provided they are governed? According to the sacred canons and the usage of the Church, the chapter appoints vicars to fulfil the functions of the bishop, and this nomination is submitted to the Emperor. A very good spirit animates the French chapters; the vicars nominated by them are entirely devoted to the Emperor. Thus the Emperor obtains a double advantage, that of nominating the bishop and influencing the nomination of the vicars; and if these last are not bishops, they have not the less the administration of the diocese.

This state of things may last twenty or thirty years; the Papal system alone can support it, and it would only be a feeling of discontent with the Pope, and not necessity, which might lead to the assembling of a council.

Thus the Emperor has no need of the Pope. Twenty bishops on their own account have just written to the Pope in the strongest manner, to make him understand that if he refuses their canonical institution they know how to procure it. This measure, taken without the knowledge of the Emperor, has been produced by the indignation excited by the conduct of the Pope, who is seen to sacrifice the interests of religion and to place the Church in a state of suffering—simply for the sake of temporal interests.

V. Such is the situation of the affairs of the Pope and of France. The Emperor has no advances to make with regard to the Pope; he has no need of him. Everything is arranged for getting rid of him, and the Emperor, having a new organisation all ready, has not any dangerous consequence to dread from the present state of things. The Pope is in quite a different

position : it is for him to take the first step. He has
need of the Emperor, whose power can extend or
diminish the Pope's influence as he chooses. He ought
to take this step as a reparation of the wrong and also
of the ridicule which he caused when he tried to excom-
municate the Emperor ; and in what manner ?—by an
act which almost provoked assassination. The Emperor
has all the merit of generosity and good manner in
this matter. By the conduct of Charles V. and other
princes in similar circumstances, one sees what he might
have done, and can recognise his moderation and
nobleness.

VI. What is the interest of Austria and the other
Catholic Powers ? It is to free themselves from the
Papal authority while making use of their Church ; or
to insist in a firm and loyal manner on an arrangement
between the Emperor and the Pope. If Austria, the
first of these Catholic Powers, prefers the latter, she
ought to make the Pope understand what he does not
suspect—the true situation of affairs in France—and
convince him that in the interests of Christianity he
ought to make an arrangement. Does he wish to return to Rome ? He cannot do so without renouncing
his ancient sovereignty heartily, and sincerely acknow-
ledging the union of that city with the empire. Does
this acknowledgment wound his pride or his delicacy ?
It may be thought that this return of the Pope to
Rome would be contrary to the true interests of
Christianity, from the difficult position of the Holy
Father—on one side exposed to regrets, on the other an
object of suspicion—which might lead a second time to
the scandalous catastrophe which so profoundly affected
the Emperor, and obliged the Pope to be again removed
without any order from the Emperor, because his

presence appeared to menace public tranquillity. If these inconveniences are seen, then Austria should insist on the Emperor Napoleon renouncing his project of bringing the Pope to Paris, and arrange for placing him at Avignon. There he would be treated as a spiritual sovereign, and in a manner suitable to his dignity. He could have envoys abroad, receive the ambassadors of foreign courts charged only with the spiritual affairs of their country. The envoys and ambassadors would enjoy all the privileges of their titles, and would send and receive their couriers. All Christendom might contribute to augment the revenue of the Pope. The position of the Propaganda and the Cardinals would be determined, the number of these for each country being determined according to its population. Cardinals' hats might be attached to certain sees, but always leaving those to remain which have already been settled by the concordats for dispensations and the institution of bishops.

VII. These arrangements would be in conformity with the interests of France and Austria. If the Pope were settled at Avignon, France would have no interest in exacting from the Pope a formal renunciation of his ancient sovereignty. It would suffice if he agreed to make no law contrary to the rights of France. He would be also dispensed from the oath not to violate the rights of the Gallican Church. It would be taken for granted that such is his intention, and, moreover, the *Senatus-Consulte* does not impose this obligation on Popes except at the time of their accession.

Such an arrangement seems to unite all advantages, and to be the most easy of execution.

Austria is the Power best placed for mediating in this affair, for if she assembles a Council in her States when the Emperor assembles one in his (which comprehends all Catholicism), the influence of the Pope would be much compromised. He would be in danger of losing his best prerogatives, and Austria can make him fear this danger.

VIII. Perhaps these observations may not give the ideas of the Emperor exactly ; perhaps the Emperor may not be so compliant as is supposed. His position is so good that in a few years the Pope will end by doing all that the Emperor wishes. The course now followed by the Emperor and the ulterior measures that he may take are nothing new in France. They have always been indicated by parliaments and bishops, but the court of France has often been stopped in this course by the influence of the King's confessors and by the intrigues of the court of Rome.

Lebzeltern to Metternich on the Audience with Pius VII., Savona, May 15, 1810.

162. My audience yesterday evening with the Holy Father lasted an hour, and I was not deceived in my anticipation that, on seeing me again, he would show an emotion of which I received the most flattering and unequivocal proofs. . . .

The Pope, faithful to his attachment for my court, told me how very sensible he was of his Majesty's attention, of the professions of sympathy which I transmitted to him in the name of my august master. He was surprised at the complaisance of the Emperor Napoleon in consenting to my mission, and struck by my assurances that that sovereign—yielding readily and with the best grace—had not opposed free access to the head of the Church and showed real pleasure in the faithful addressing their petitions to him. He appeared sincerely to interest himself in the details which, in the course of our conversation, I gave him about the august marriage, which would offer the most certain guarantee of a lasting peace, and which, while securing domestic happiness to his Majesty, had gained the approval of all the people. The Pope appeared to forget for a moment his grievances and troubles, and to take a real and sincere interest in that event. He said to me : ' Would to heaven that this unexpected event would consolidate the peace of the Continent! No one desires more than I that the Emperor Napoleon may be happy, and I desire it with all my heart. He is a prince who unites in himself so many eminent qualities. Would to God that he would discover his own true interests! It is in his power, by reconciling himself with the Church, to confer the greatest blessings on religion, to draw down on himself and his family the benedictions of nations and of posterity, and to leave a name glorious to it and to them.'

Soon afterwards, some bitter memories and reflections coming across this outburst of enthusiasm, which he freely expressed with his habitual candour, his isolation and other disagreeable subjects were discussed . . .

When I spoke to the Holy Father of the embarrassment of our bishops, of the imminent dangers which menaced the Church if it remained in its present state of inaction, he replied : ' I have felt this a great deal ; it is the only thought which occupies me. This interruption of every relation with the foreign clergy, the difficulty of communication even with the French bishops, is a subject of profound grief to me. Although detained here, without free correspondence, without any news except the very vaguest which I can gather from some numbers of the *Moniteur*, which the General has the kindness to send to me, I well know what must be the embarrassment of the bishops. I have not ceased to complain of my situation under these circumstances; a real schism is established *de facto*. I ask nothing for myself from the Emperor; I have nothing more to lose; I have sacrificed everything to duty; I am old, without wants; what personal consideration, therefore, could deter me from the path which duty and conscience have prescribed for me, or make me desire the least thing for myself? I do not want pensions or honours; the alms of the faithful will suffice; there have been other Popes poorer than I, and I think of nothing beyond the narrow walls where you see me; but I ardently desire that my communications should be restored with the bishops and the faithful. It would suffice if the petitions of the latter could reach me freely, and I might have the means of exercising my functions. I am always repeating this to the General. And they ought not to leave me without assistance (this they have carried so far that I have been obliged to raise a servant, whose writing is legible, to the post of secretary), nor prevent me from performing my spiritual functions for want of people absolutely necessary to me, and the difficulty experienced by the faithful in gaining access to my person. I have done what depended on myself, having, without assistance, sent off more than five hundred dispensations, and coming as far as I possibly could to the assistance of those bishops of the French Empire whose entreaties have reached me; but, besides that physical strength fails me, there are matters which ought to be examined and discussed, and there are forms to observe which, *bizarres* as they may be, are yet necessary although I understand nothing about them.'

I assured him that I could not doubt that the Emperor Napoleon would consent, if the Pope desired it, that he should have the necessary assistance in so laborious a task ; I showed him that he would have done better to speak or do something to show his wishes to the Emperor. 'He knows how perfectly isolated I am. The repeated complaints and entreaties which I have addressed to the Préfet and to the General must be known to him. You cannot imagine,' added the Pope, 'the consolation that I feel in seeing you charge yourself with affairs relating to my clergy. This is the first channel which opens before me.' I seized this occasion to assure him that the Emperor, far from opposing his fulfilling the duties of his high mission, left him quite at liberty, and I profited by the happy mood of the Holy Father to beg him to give as much latitude as possible to the favours asked of him by our bishops. He promised me to do his part, and repeated that the bishops of the Church would always find their spiritual head a tender and indulgent father.

Among the subjects which greatly annoyed the Holy Father, he took much to heart the detention of Cardinal Pacca and his nephew at Fenestrelle. 'He may,' said he, 'have done some bad offices with regard to his Majesty, but he cannot make them a matter of personal offence. He was my State Secretary at an unhappy time, and he is the innocent victim ; but,' added he, 'that cannot be his fault in the eyes of the Emperor. You know, like all the world, that I wrote my protestations myself ; that in order not to involve anyone I took my own defence entirely upon myself ; it was necessary for form's sake that the Secretary of State should

lend his name.' The other causes of the Pope's annoyance are : the summons of his cardinals and ministers
and their stay in Paris; the deportation of many bishops
who literally followed his instructions; and, lastly, that
he had not obtained leave for Monsignor Minocchio, his
confessor, Monsignor Devotis, his secretary, Monsignor
Testa, another secretary, and some copyists to be sent
to him.

The Pope did not say one word concerning his temporal affairs or his sovereignty in Rome. He, however,
alluded to this in the following words : ' When opinions
are founded on the voice of conscience and on the feeling of our own duties, they become immovable, and
there is no physical force in the world which can long
contend with a moral force of this nature. What I
have pronounced through my See on these sad events as
they have occurred was dictated by similar sentiments,
and consequently cannot vary, whenever I may be
obliged to declare myself.'

I thought the Pope somewhat aged, but looking
well ; calm as usual, and not speaking with the slightest
bitterness, even when he touched on those subjects which
he must have felt most deeply. He seemed to me, too,
firm in his opinions. There are certainly some which
will never change, and cannot change ; every attempt
to move him in this respect would be vain, and to touch
on certain questions will never produce any other effect
than to excite long theological discussions, on which
both sides have already exhausted everything they have
to say ; after many repetitions, each one will remain of
the same opinion and even follow it. This applies just
as much to our court as to that of France. Provided
that the Pope tolerates certain laws, and that the sovereigns carry out what they think to be the interest of

their states, what would be gained by exacting the formal recognition of principles which the Holy Father cannot approve? Constant use makes these laws daily more valuable, and much more so when they are not brought under discussion.

But I hope that your Excellency will allow me to reserve my judgment as to the Holy Father's state of mind. I have only sounded the way. I have even avoided, in this first interview, giving my opinion on many subjects, and it will only be when he has eased his mind of a weight augmented by long restraint, that I shall really know what he thinks, and therefore how he will act. Many little matters, however, not unfavourable to our views, will not escape your Excellency's penetration and observation.

If the Emperor Napoleon thinks proper in his generosity to liberate the Cardinal and Monsignor Pacca, and to do some little personal kindnesses of this kind, I am certain they would make a deep impression on the heart and mind of the Holy Father, having observed how much he has already felt the circumstance that his Majesty has facilitated my mission to him. I have never seen anyone more easy to touch by such attentions than his Holiness. This shows the qualities of his heart, and during my long administration at Rome I have always worked in this way with great success.

The Pope praised very much the manner and attentions of the Prefect and Count Berthier. Up to this time he has constantly refused to leave the bishop's palace, where he lives, and only walks in his room and in a very small garden. The flow of people brought daily to his feet by devotion does not at all diminish. The Prefect, Count de Chabrol, and the General, are on their side well satisfied with the great circumspection of the Pope and his kindness to them.

Metternich to the Emperor Francis, Paris, June 12, 1810.

163. I most respectfully take the liberty of submitting to your Imperial Majesty in the present report the whole of the negotiation with Pius VII., as carried on by M. de Lebzeltern.

When our envoy arrived at his destination he found some difficulty in approaching the Holy Father. The Duke de Cadore had, in following out a system which I knew to belong to his character of a trifler and a bungler, omitted to let the military authorities at Savona know of the mission of M. de Lebzeltern. The firmness shown by the latter to the French general enabled him to triumph over this unforeseen obstacle before the arrival of an express order from the Emperor, which I got him to send as soon as I knew of the difficulty. . . .

M. de Lebzeltern brought me the letter (No. 164) which I have the honour of enclosing to your Majesty. This was written in answer to the letter which I had sent him by our envoy.

The *résumé* of the verbal report made to me by M. de Lebzeltern since his return shows me :—

1st. That the Holy Father had not expected a step of the kind just taken by the court of Austria and sanctioned by the French Government; that he was extremely flattered by the former, and from the second gathered some hope of its return to principles more suited to the interests of Christianity.

2nd. That his Holiness, left quite without help and support, urged in the first place the obtaining of a Council.

3rd. That, from a religious and proper principle,

his Holiness would devote himself to the full exercise
of his spiritual functions, in any place, if he were supplied with the indispensable means to do so, and if the
Emperor of the French showed, by some actions, a
willingness to approach him, and if he did not, on the
other hand, exact, as a *sine qua non*, the express renunciation of his temporal rights.

4th. That, on the contrary supposition, the Pope had
decided to leave the defence of his Church to God
Himself, and that, strong in his conscience, the Holy
Father would wait without capitulation the end of the
persecution.

These are the points to which I believe the questions may be reduced, and I will later on submit to
your Majesty a fuller report of the different conversations that M. de Lebzeltern has had with the Holy
Father, and which he is at this moment occupied in
writing down.

The Emperor having sent for me to Saint-Cloud on
the 8th of this month, I had a very long conversation with him on the affairs of the Church. I was unhappily soon convinced how little he was disposed to
enter into the conciliatory views of your Majesty, and I
had only too many causes to congratulate myself with
having, from the first beginning of this negotiation,
followed a line of conduct persistently impartial. The
Emperor began the conversation by saying that the
Pope did not desire a reconciliation ; that since the
arrival of Chevalier de Lebzeltern, he had addressed a
letter to Cardinal Fesch which contained threats and in-
vectives against him—Napoleon ; that, on the other
hand, he did not cease to excite, by all spiritual means,
the people of the Roman states to resistance and revolt ;
that the priests at Rome refused to admit to the Sacra-

ment those of the inhabitants who were inscribed on the list of national guards, &c.

I expressed to the Emperor my surprise at conduct so contrary to the effect that our envoy thought he had produced on the mind of the Holy Father ; and from the style of the letter which I had received from his Holiness himself, I thought I could not be wrong in assuring the Emperor that there must be some mistake of dates in his charges. He said this was not the case ; but I am since convinced that I was right. The letter mentioned as having been sent to Cardinal Fesch was sent to Savona the day of the arrival of M. de Lebzeltern, and the conduct of the Roman authorities was founded on the instructions the Holy Father had left at home, before he left his country.

The Emperor continued to say that the paper which I had communicated to M. de Champagny showed that the Pope did not think of a reconciliation ; *that he was not yet ripe* ; that he, Napoleon, would go on with the business, and that the Holy Father would one day repent of having let slip so favourable an opportunity as the present for submitting to the force of circumstances.

I observed to his Majesty that it appeared to me that the Holy Father had seized the opportunity which was offered to him as far as he could in his isolated position. I added that when his Holiness expressed to me his wish to come to an understanding with the Emperor of the French, he could not have deceived himself as to the character of the overtures made to him through me :—That M. de Lebzeltern had been ordered never to take the attitude of a French negotiator ; that he had expressed the wish of the Emperor, his master, to serve the interests of religion with a prince who had become his son-in-law, but that he had not prejudged, nor even indicated, the nature of those interests of which the Pope himself must be the best judge. That the Sovereign Pontiff, by calling for a Council, evidently showed that he was ready to reply to the overtures which might be made, or to make them himself.

'But,' interrupted the Emperor, 'how could you wish that I should take the initiative, and grant to the Holy Father to surround himself with a Council which he will make use of against myself?'

'I foresaw this objection,' I replied. 'To avoid your Majesty having to take the initiative, we as a Power friendly to both parties ask for this Council. If your Majesty fears to grant it, your Majesty must feel conscious that your proposals will not be acceptable.' The Emperor was astonished at my reply, and could not make any objection to it. He asked me if I thought that the Holy Father would accept a Council which he would compose. It was not difficult to show him that a Council, whose members were to be chosen by an adversary could never fulfil the Pope's object.

Our conversation always returned to the ecclesiastical question, and I left the Emperor, after going over the questions and reducing them to the simple proposition to grant the Pope a Council to be chosen by him.

In the morning I went to the Minister of Foreign Affairs, to whom I gave an account of my conversation with his Majesty, and I thought I ought to repeat my request in an official manner, begging him to transmit it to his Majesty. I did not conceal my personal conviction that the Emperor had no intention of a reconciliation with the Holy Father, and I asked him to rectify the date of the letter to Cardinal Fesch. The minister undertook to report to his Majesty all I had just said.

This, Sire, is the state of the question with regard to the Holy See. Your Imperial Majesty will deign to believe that in the present position of affairs the part you have taken is the most worthy of you; the attitude of the Holy Father is strengthened by the embarrassment of the Emperor of the French in having to refuse the just demand of a Council; and if, as is too much to be feared, Napoleon persists in views destructive of all ecclesiastical organisation, your Majesty will have no less employed your good offices in a cause which is only compromising to those who attack it. I shall regulate my subsequent measures by the reply which the Emperor makes to me, and in the very probable supposition that he will not consent, I shall remind him of his promise not to oppose your Majesty's placing an agent near the person of the Holy Father.

M. de Lebzeltern must have convinced himself, during the journey which he made in Italy, of the impression produced in that country by the violent changes introduced by the Emperor of the French, and above all, by his conduct to the Holy Father. All eyes are turned upon us, and the arrival of an Austrian diplomatist at Savona has made a sensation, and has aroused universal hopes. If, as is too probable, they are not accomplished, many minds will be still more stimulated against the oppressive government under which this unhappy country groans.

Pius VII. to Metternich, Savona, May 21, 1810.*

164. *Dilecte Fili*—Salutem et Apostolicam Benedictionem.

* Translated from the Italian.

Signore Cavaliere Lebzeltern has delivered to us
your most gracious letter, in which you make mention
of the profound sympathy which your august sovereign
takes in our distressing vicissitudes, of the desire he
cherishes of contributing to our help, and of the prayers
which without ceasing he addresses to Heaven for the
well-being of the Catholic religion in its present low
estate.   Although we have never doubted of these
religious sentiments of his Imperial Majesty, which become not only his piety, but still more his duties as a
prince by birth the protector of the Church, we must
nevertheless confess that this has been for us a supreme
comfort amid all the great afflictions which wound our
heart, and with the consciousness of which we are continually imbued.   God knoweth how greatly we desire
to re-establish the good harmony with his Majesty
the Emperor Napoleon, to whom we have given on
many occasions the clearest proofs of our special love,
which, notwithstanding our calamities, we still preserve
towards him undiminished.   But since this harmony
might induce us to make conditions not suitable to the
dignity of the Holy See and to the Vicar of Jesus
Christ, we, constant in our desire not to be wanting
in our duties, have at last lost the hope of attaining
this so desirable end.   Notwithstanding if ever Heaven,
from whom all good things do come, should bless
the religious efforts of his Imperial Majesty, and these
should succeed in bringing the Emperor Napoleon
to recognise the justice of our cause, we need not say
how great would be our gratitude and satisfaction, nor
how abundantly God would recompense you for all
that you have done for an object which so greatly concerns religion.   We have expressed ourselves in similar
terms to Signore Cavaliere Lebzeltern, reposing in him

that perfect confidence which his personal qualities have inspired us with, and feeling towards him that esteem with which we have always regarded him.

From the same Signore Cavaliere Lebzeltern we have just received the note on the powers which we are asked to grant to the bishops of the Empire of Austria. In consequence of this we have delivered to the above-mentioned Cavaliere a letter to our Nuncio, whom we commission in the first place to thank his Majesty for all the assurances made to us in his name, and then to place himself in correspondence with the Archbishop of Vienna, who in his own name and the name of the other bishops has preferred the like petition, so that the wants of the faithful may be aided, in furtherance of which we have renewed powers which were soon to be extinct, so that bishops, in cases where it would not be easy to have recourse to us, might grant dispensations of the second degree of consanguinity, and of the first and second degrees of affinity. We are therefore persuaded that his Majesty will not cease to demand for his subjects the right of free and open communication with the head of the Church. Though deprived of all the resources necessary for the due exercise of our office, isolated, without being able to consult with anyone on the most important affairs, we shall nevertheless not fail to devote ourselves to all the petitions which reach us, and this we shall continue to do, whilst God gives us health, and so far as we may be permitted.

As long as we continue in this destitute and isolated condition, his Imperial Majesty will do us the justice to allow for the physical impossibility which prevents us from making provision for the bishoprics vacant in Germany; and the Emperor may be assured that we shall occupy ourselves without delay with these matters, as soon as we shall be surrounded by our ministers, the consistory of cardinals, and the other means which are necessary for the due despatch of business so important. In the meantime, it is requisite that the administration of the vacant dioceses should be provided for by capitular vicars, in the manner prescribed by the canons, as had been done under Pius VI. of glorious memory, and also in other similar circumstances for a still longer period.

Lastly, we must profess our true esteem for your venerable person, our especial satisfaction for the exact manner with which you have signified to us the dispositions of his Imperial Majesty, and the desire which remains with us to find some occasion to give you a distinguished mark of it. Meantime we pour on you with our whole heart our apostolical blessings.

Given at Savona, May 21, 1810,

In the eleventh year of our Pontificate.

THE FORGED VIENNA BANK-NOTES.

(Note 52, Vol. I.)

165. Metternich to the Emperor Francis, 1810.
166. Metternich to Champagny, 1810.
167. Champagny to Metternich, 1810.

165. Councillor Raab, who was sent here by the Department of Finance to see to the destruction of the Vienna bank-notes manufactured in Paris last year, came to see me immediately on his arrival. I had told him that, having just obtained from the late Minister-General of Police information on the fate of the notes, &c. &c., I had reason to believe that the destruction of these things had been ordered by the Emperor, in spite of my repeated demands that they should be delivered up to us ; I nevertheless took the opportunity offered me by the arrival of an *employé* of our finances to bring out the facts, and the same day I addressed the note a copy of which is enclosed (No. 166) to the Duke of Cadore.

The next day the Emperor kept me in his closet after his levée. He told me that the Minister for Foreign Affairs had submitted my note to him ; that he hastened to reply directly with the assurance that the things which I claimed no longer existed, and that he had ordered the immediate destruction of them as soon as he was informed of the abuse which had been made of some of the notes. I expressed my regrets that his Majesty had not preferred to act on his first idea of delivering to us the *corpora delicti*, which, in spite of the confidence that we might have in his promise, would certainly have had a much better effect on the finances of your Imperial Majesty in a question which exacts a quite mathematical certainty. The Emperor said to me: 'Reassure the Emperor, your master; give him my word that nothing remains of all the fabrication, and that he can never hear anything more of them. Let there be no longer the least anxiety about it with your people.'

Your Majesty will please to observe that all insistance being useless in a matter beyond our control, it only remains for me to keep the Emperor to his personal engagement, and I repeated his words to him. Seeing my persistence, he laughed, and said : ' It seems to me that you have not too much confidence in me. Well, give my word, as sovereign to sovereign, that nothing of all that now exists.'

A few days afterwards I received the note (No. 167) enclosed from the Minister of Foreign Affairs, which treats of the same subject.

There remains nothing to object, and I therefore send back to Vienna Sieur Frappart, who was sent here some weeks ago, charged with the first inquiries which took place on the appearance of the forged notes.

Councillor Raab, being charged to procure several patterns from the *Département des Monnaies*, will leave Paris as soon as he has done so.

Metternich to Champagny, Paris, June 19, 1810.

166. Shortly after my arrival in Paris the Emperor did me the honour to speak of a great manufacture of Vienna bank-notes. His Majesty declared that this measure was intended for a quite different period from the present, and led me to hope that the mass of false notes would be sent to me.

Since that I have told your Excellency of the giving out of a sum equivalent to nearly two hundred million florins by these same notes. Search made by our administration to discover the distributors has been seconded by the French police ; several guilty persons have been arrested in Paris. The inquiries ordered on this occasion by his Majesty are a new proof of his friendly sentiments towards the Emperor, my master.

His Majesty has just ordered me to make known his desire that the French Government would tranquillise the Austrian finances with respect to the possibility of an even involuntary abuse, by causing the false notes, dies, &c. &c., to be sent back as things of no value to a friendly Government, and which a strict watch may not always preserve from an abuse such as we have just experienced.

I beg your Excellency to submit this desire to the Emperor, and to remain, &c. &c.

Champagny to Metternich, Paris, June 28, 1810.

167. I have received your Excellency's letter of the 19th inst. concerning the fabrication of Vienna bank-notes which has taken place in Paris. When the Emperor found himself master of the city of Vienna and of a great part of the Austrian provinces, and consequently of a great part of the funds and revenues which formed the mortgage on the notes of the bank, it occurred to him to use the right that this possession gave him by issuing notes on the bank, especially when similar notes were daily fabricated in Hungary and circulated. The manufacture had been ordered at Paris, but could not be quickly executed. The first notes were only ready after peace was declared. Thanks to this circumstance, none of these notes have been circulated by the Government.

His Majesty the Emperor authorises me to inform you that these notes have been destroyed, and that none now exist. Your Government ought to have no uneasiness with regard to issues arising from the trickery of subordinate agents employed in the matter.

By making this communication, I hope I have satisfied the desire expressed by your Excellency in your note of the 19th instant.

ON THE RELATIONS OF RUSSIA WITH FRANCE.

(Note 53, Vol. I.)

168. Metternich to the Emperor Francis, Paris, July 9, 1810.

168. I have taken in hand, before leaving Paris, to gain an insight into the present relations existing between the French and Russian cabinets, and the views of the former with regard to Turkey. I will undertake, Sire, to give you a most circumstantial account of the result of my observations.

Some time ago a difference arose between the Emperor Napoleon and the court of St. Petersburg on the subject of a convention signed by the plenipotentiaries, to which the Emperor of the French refused his ratification. The Russian cabinet, very uneasy about the Emperor's plans with regard to the re-establishment of Poland, wished for a written engagement. The French plenipotentiaries adhered to the form drawn up by Count Romanzow, which contained the promise, on the part of France, *that Poland should exist no more.* The Emperor stumbled at this phrase, and refused to ratify it, at least unless replaced by the promise, ' that France would not contribute either directly or indirectly to the re-establishment of Poland.'

If Count Romanzow showed the nature of his politics by attaching a particular value to one phrase more than another, the Emperor Napoleon showed, by the way he held back, that he only sought some idle pretext to refuse to bind himself even by a single phrase. I shall be able to return to this subject later on.

Shortly after the Emperor's return from his journey to the coast, I took an opportunity to sound him on the Turkish question. The Emperor, without entering into many details, told me that we owed to Erfurt, and to our refusal to recognise King Joseph, the promise which the Emperor Alexander had obtained that he (Napoleon) would not oppose the reunion of the two Danubian Principalities with Russia. I observed to the Emperor that this fact seemed to me too intimately allied to French policy for it to be possible for me to believe that any secondary consideration influenced him in this determination. The Emperor passed to another subject, but I was certain he would return to this point on another occasion.

He did, in fact, begin the conversation a few days afterwards, by asking me if I had no news from the Turkish frontiers. On my reply in the negative, the Emperor said that it seemed that the campaign was about to commence. His opinion, which he discussed at some length, was, that the Turks would be forced to cede the Principalities. ' It is,' added he, ' a great affair for the Russians and for you. I do not think the Porte will lose much ; the Principalities have long been more Russian than Turkish ; but this aggrandisement of Russia will one day form the basis of the reunion of France and Austria. The Danube is an immense interest for you. Look at the map : those countries ought to belong to you rather than to the Russians. In the possession of the latter, they will be a constant subject of jealousy to you.' He then returned to the Erfurt conferences, and seemed to regret having been forced out of his course, which, added he, is much more favourable to the interests of Austria and the Porte than to those of Russia.

I seized on this last point in order to repeat to his Majesty what I had before said as to my doubts. Secondary considerations cannot have any influence on a question of so much importance. I asked if there was no means of arranging the whole in a manner which, according to the Emperor himself, was for our common interest, by trying to re-establish a state, even if modified, which would approach the *status quo ante bellum*, and which would not attack the Porte in the foundations of its existence. I thought the time was too favourable not to mention Servia, and our desire to see that province return to order and obedience to her legitimate sovereign. I did not conceal from the Emperor how impossible it would be for us ever to consent to an extension of Russian domination over Servia, either all or in part. 'Servia,' said the Emperor, 'must necessarily belong to you some day, and you risk nothing on the part of the Russians, for when I engaged at Erfurt not to oppose their aggrandisement by these Principalities, I expressly stipulated that they should never pass the Danube. They are too much afraid,' added he, 'to risk involving themselves. The Emperor has good intentions, but he is a child. The Count de Romanzow is always in the clouds. What can one do with a man who knows no better means towards safety than waiting for an opportunity?'

The Emperor, who on many occasions has used the same language to me in speaking of the Chancellor of the Empire, has been directly provoked by an affront which the Count de Romanzow had offered to Caulaincourt on the refusal of the French ratification, and of which the Emperor has been informed. I knew that he had summoned Kourakin, through the Minister of Foreign Affairs, to express his surprise at the language of the Russian cabinet, which, he said, he neither could nor would confound with the real intentions of the Emperor.

'The Servians,' repeated the Emperor, 'have already wished to submit themselves to you.' I replied that in truth this unhappy people, fearing to see themselves given up without help to private vengeance, bound to us by daily connection and many interests, had often asked our support. 'We have given on these occasions,' said I, 'unmistakable proofs of our conviction that one of our first interests is the preservation of the Ottoman Porte. We have never ceased to play the part of mediator between her and the Servians.' I added that, as I have since known, the chiefs of the insurrection had in like manner claimed the support and intervention of France, but that it was necessary to distinguish between the wishes of the nation and the private interests of any one of her chiefs.

The Emperor returned to the conquest of the Principalities by the Russians, and repeated many times that that conquest would necessarily establish the basis of an alliance between France and Austria; 'and it is the only natural one,' added he. 'I believe I have acted against my own interests by aiding in the aggrandisement of Russia, who has played her game well by turning to advantage the time when I was occupied with you. But I had no choice: you wished for war; it was therefore necessary to make the best of it, and one of my means was to paralyse Russia. Do not think that I am under an illusion. The Russians would have fallen on me if I had been beaten, but I should have had to be well beaten. I had made a promise that I would not oppose their conquest of Moldavia and Wallachia; nevertheless I should regard all idea of conquest on their part on the right bank of the Danube as a breach of their engagement with me.'

The Emperor then spoke of the fear which the Russian cabinet had of his intentions, as much with regard to Turkish affairs as to those of Poland. He used the very words which your Imperial Majesty will have found at the commencement of the present despatch, and which indicate the dispute that has arisen between the two courts on the subject of the satisfaction of the Polish Convention. 'I will never agree,' said the Emperor to me, 'to that which the Count de Romanzow demands. I should need to be God, to decide that Poland should no longer exist! I can only promise what I can fulfil. I will do nothing for her re-establishment; but if ever in the course of time Lithuania should rise and espouse the interest of Poland, or if on an opportune occasion the Varsoviens should seek to aggrandise themselves at the expense of Russia, why should I make any opposition, if the cabinet of St. Petersburg found itself engaged at that time in a cause which differed from mine?'

I observed to his Majesty that the reasons for which the Duchy of Warsaw must be maintained in a subordinate position appeared to me, looking at it from a French point of view, to derive their force principally from the independence which this same Duchy would acquire, by French influence, in aggrandising herself.

The Emperor told me that this motive prevented him from contributing to that aggrandisement, or he would have made the engagement willingly; 'but,' added he, 'I will never make an engagement the accomplishment of which would be beyond my power, and I will not ratify it.'

The courier sent from Vienna on the 17th June brought the despatches to us in the morning of the 4th of this month. I found the news from the frontiers of Turkey of such importance that I made a resolution immediately to repair on the following day to Saint-Cloud, and having been prevented from going earlier, I found the Emperor going to bed and very busy. His Majesty dismissed everybody, and made me go into his room.

Being furnished with an extract of the news from Bucharest, I read it to his Majesty, who went to look for a map, in which we followed the operations of the Russian army. The inspection of this map proved to me that the Emperor had followed all the movements of the Russian troops. He immediately pricked it with pins, according to the information I had brought him, and I found him strongly impressed with the prompt and, as it seemed to him, decisive successes of the Russian army. It was Varna especially which appeared to occupy him most. The Emperor, after having spent more than a quarter of an hour in examining his map, rose, and, taking me by the arm, said to me with an altered accent and in broken sentences: 'This is peace! Yes, it is peace! The Turks are forced to make it!— Well, it is as I told you lately: the alliance between France and Austria; our interests are common; now you must think of repairing your losses—the moment has arrived—the loss of the Danube is odious to you. Is the Danube more easily ascended from below than above?'

On this occasion, as on all preceding ones, I allowed the Emperor to speak without engaging myself in a discussion with him. I contented myself with saying that we had, for a long time, regarded the relations of friendship with France as agreeable to our interests; that these same interests were served by the preservation of the Porte as a quiet and peaceful neighbour; that from the first we regarded the possession of one of the banks of the Danube by the Russians as very prejudicial, and that this loss must make us look upon the return of commerce to the Adriatic as infinitely more precious still.

The Emperor said to me: 'All can be restored; these points are not worth a hair to me; even the Carniola has no value.' And he returned always to the same thing: 'Yes, here is a real alliance between us. An alliance based on common interests, the only durable one: such an alliance does not yet exist between us; a family alliance is certainly something, but it is not everything. Romanzow, in his fancies, believes that a family alliance is nothing; that, on the contrary, it might bring back a coolness—that if I quarrelled some day with the Empress I should naturally quarrel also with her father. He does not know that the Emperor Napoleon will never quarrel with his wife; that he would never have quarrelled with her even were she infinitely less *distinguée* than she is in all respects. Yes, a family alliance is a great deal, but it is not everything.' . . .

I laid hold of the family alliance; I pointed out to him all its advantages, and did not touch more than on previous occasions the chord of more intimate political relations, convinced of the necessity of not venturing too far, or of forcing him to develop his ideas. I also seized the opportunity to beg him to terminate my affairs as soon as possible, so as to enable me to rejoin your Imperial Majesty. 'Political questions are becoming too important,' said I to him, 'for the minister to be away from his master.' The Emperor promised me that he would immediately put the work in hand, so that I might leave.

Your Imperial Majesty must have direct information of the details of late events in Sweden.

Shortly after the death of the Prince Royal, the King sent a courier here to the Emperor Napoleon to inform him that he had resolved to propose to the Diet Prince Christian, brother of the deceased Prince Royal, as his successor. The Emperor assured me, on learning this news, that he had nothing to say against the choice, and that he approved of it as the wisest course. 'The son of Gustavus,' said he, 'would have been a more legitimate choice, but his extreme youth is a real inconvenience.' I have nevertheless since heard that the Emperor had, on the pretence of an invitation from the Swedish nation, thought of giving this kingdom to a prince of his own family. He had thought of the King of Naples, and intended Naples for Jerome and Westphalia for Louis. All the members of the family having protested against the crown of Sweden, he thought of Berthier or of Bernadotte. Wishing to be enlightened on this extraordinary question, I seized the moment when we were speaking of Polish affairs to say that the Russians did not fear only the Duchy of Warsaw, but that there was some uneasiness at St. Petersburg about an understanding which seemed to be established between him (Napoleon) and Sweden. The Emperor replied without hesitation: 'The Swedes absolutely throw themselves at my head. They now wish me to give them one of my marshals for a king. They speak of Berthier or Bernadotte. Berthier will never leave France, but Bernadotte is another thing. They desire one of my relations: but there is an insurmountable obstacle—that of religion. A marshal would not mind that so much. I will show you my correspondence with the King of Sweden.' And he called his private secretary, Meneval, to demand these papers; after having searched for them, the latter came to tell us that they were in Champagny's hands.

Not seeing the letters, I asked the Emperor if the King shared the wish of the nation. 'He has not spoken to me,' said the Emperor; 'my correspondence from Copenhagen tells me nothing either, but it is the Swedes who came here lately who torment me.'

I did not conceal from his Majesty that the choice, even admitting the most perfect unanimity on the part of the King and the nation, seemed to me infinitely more a French and Russian question than a French and Swedish, and I asked him what he intended to do. 'I shall leave it to the nation,' said the Emperor, 'and will do what it wishes, without influencing its opinion. If the Swedes take a marshal for king, it is to reconquer Finland; if they take the Prince of Augustenberg, they wish for peace. If a marshal mounts the throne of Sweden, I shall find myself in natural complications with Russia, which I am far from seeking, but which, perhaps, I shall not be able to avoid.'

The Emperor dismissed me after a conversation of more than two hours; and this, Sire, is how things appear to me in the great and critical moment to which we are hastening:—

The Emperor, when he guaranteed the Principalities to the Emperor Alexander, only considered his own interests, and acted according to his usual impulse, which leads him to place all the Powers in a dependent attitude, and consequently quarrelling among themselves. The end of the war between Russia and the Porte did not suit him. The prolongation of a quarrel in which Russia makes great exertions, and which, by presenting to us prospective results injurious to our interests, keeps us in suspense all the while, must suit him in all respects, and it is with this view that he continues to fan the discord both at St. Petersburg and at Constantinople. But the moment has come when he sees a Russian army placing itself in a threatening position for him. He must fear that with the feeling of strength returning to Russia, will come that of independence. He wishes and must wish to turn to profit the combinations of the moment to attach us to his interests; and it is in this consideration, so natural and so simple—in this consideration, which belongs to the very nature of things—that lies, in my opinion, the great political fault of the Russian cabinet, a fault for which acquisitions sure to have been made at some other time cannot compensate.

No doubt Russia does not dream of complications with France : she cannot wish to provoke them, after the sad experience she had in the campaigns of 1806 and 1807, without counting the reasons which arise from the well-known character of its sovereign ; but she would wish to turn to profit the results at which she has arrived. To enjoy peaceably her immense conquests, to concentrate her military forces in the provinces most threatened by the spirit which reigns there, to live in peace with us, to cajole France, even to maintain the remains of the Ottoman Empire—such would be her most probable political system. Can she put it in practice? Can she arrive at the peaceable enjoyment of conquests which impose a great many

privations upon us, which sap the foundations of the
Ottoman power, and, by allowing the Russian Empire
to advance in all directions towards the centre of
Europe, provoke by the force of circumstances alone a
thousand complications? I cannot but doubt it. I
could decide the question if things were going better
for France in Spain and Portugal. Napoleon would
never have allowed the present results of the opening
of the Russian campaign but that he encountered a
greater opposition than he could possibly resist. But
if he cannot oppose as entirely as he wishes what he
regards as contrary to his interests, he can not the less
leave everything in suspense, and harass the Russians
with continual uneasiness—uneasiness which, as I know
on good authority, gains daily in intensity at St. Petersburg.

But what should be our line of conduct at this
important moment? We cannot flatter ourselves that
we can swim between two waters, or play a part
altogether neutral in questions so important between
two Powers which encroach by turns either on our
property or our interests. We are called upon to play
a great part. We are, I dare to affirm it, in spite of
appearances to the contrary, the strongest. It is we
who are sought by both sides : the side which is reinforced by us will acquire an immense preponderance.
The moment has come when, with wise and circumspect
management, having in view a fixed and stable aim, we
shall be able to attain immense results from the present
and future combination of affairs.

But it is essential in the first place to understand
exactly the plans of the Emperor of the French. The
path I am now following must bring us soon to this
result : and I think I shall be able to give your Imperial

Majesty in my next despatch all the information necessary to establish your political system on a sure basis,
founded on a perfect knowledge of the views of the Sovereign of France. His method of acting is too grave in
its results for simple suppositions to suffice. My principal aim at present will be attained if I am able to keep
all these questions open to your Imperial Majesty—
questions in which the French cabinet will be so far
advanced that they will be no longer problematical,
but certainties which may guide us in our political
calculations, without in any way constraining the future
development of your Majesty's views.

THE DANUBIAN PRINCIPALITIES AND SERVIA.

(Note 53, Vol. I.)

169. Metternich to the Emperor Francis, Paris, July 28, 1810.
170. Metternich to the Emperor Francis, Paris, July 28, 1810.

169. His Majesty, the day after his return from Rambouillet, detained me after the levée, and asked if I had no news from Vienna. Having replied that I had none, the Emperor told me that the public in Vienna appeared very uneasy at the progress of the Russians against the Turks. I replied that nothing was more likely. 'Everything which resembles war,' said I, 'is unwelcome to us; and the happy period having just arrived when our people were made easy about the western frontier of the Empire, it must be very painful to them to see complications arise on the opposite frontier. The smallest trader,' continued I, 'calculates more or less the extreme importance of the course of the Danube. The loss of this stream will be so grave that it will be felt in the most remote channels of our national industry. Besides, our public has been forced to become political: it has been occupied with great questions too long not to be able to estimate the present one at its just value.'

The Emperor said that this was very natural, and repeated on this occasion almost all he had said to me in the last conversation I had with him on the common interest between Austria and France in the affairs of the East. 'I have,' continued he, 'just sent a courier to

Caulaincourt to order him to inform Count Romanzow that, faithful to my engagements at Erfurt, I cannot
oppose the union of Wallachia and Moldavia to the
Russian Empire, but that I will suffer no encroachment
beyond that. The occupation of strong places on the
right bank of the Danube, and the protectorate of the
Servians, must not take place, and I will allow neither
one nor the other.'

I replied to his Majesty that I believed this declaration would suffice to keep the Russian cabinet within
the limits of the Treaty of Erfurt. 'I wish to believe
so,' replied the Emperor, ' but appetite comes with
eating, and I will not allow myself any longer to follow
the calculations of Count de Romanzow. I myself have
too little faith in the Russians keeping within their engagements with us to speak officially of measures to be
taken in case my expectation should be deceived.'

' Servia,' continued the Emperor, ' must belong to
you some day. I do not believe it my interest to provoke the fall of the Ottoman Empire ; its destruction
would be no advantage to you. If you wish to occupy
Belgrade, I shall not oppose it, so that the Porte makes
peace with the Servians, and gives them a prince of
their own nation, and that this prince is under your
guarantee and protection. I shall have nothing to say
against all that, but I can neither admit a hospodar
under Russian guarantee and protection, nor the least
usurpation of that Power on the right bank of the
Danube. If she wished to guard one single strong place,
I should look upon that as the conquest of Constantinople. The Danube is a great obstacle ; the passage of
this river has, up to the present time, stopped the progress of the Russian armies ; but an inch of land on the
right bank in the hands of the Russians would be, in

my opinion, equal to the complete destruction of the Ottoman Empire.'

I said to the Emperor that I was very pleased to hear this declaration from his own mouth; that although I perfectly agreed with him on our common interest of preserving the Porte, I could not so easily understand how he had allowed Russia to sap its very foundations.

'Ah,' interrupted the Emperor, 'it is you who are the cause; I was obliged to think of the main chance, and that main chance was to paralyse Russia.' (He then repeated again all which is to be found in my last reports of the motives and the progress of the negotiations at Erfurt.)

'As to Belgrade,' replied I, 'that place would doubtless be of great utility to Austria, but two considerations have up to the present time stopped us from the pursuit of any active measure in Servia: the first, not to hasten the fall of the Turkish Empire; the second, not to provoke complications with France, whom we could only regard as a tranquil spectator of any such attempt. This last consideration having ceased, we are then called upon only to occupy ourselves with the first.'

'It would be necessary to try,' interrupted the Emperor, 'to take the place by storm, or to make the Servians themselves replace you. Commence by taking it *en dépôt*; once within, they could never get you out. Servia under your protection has nothing but advantages to offer; in your possession, you would one day lead the Servians to battle against me; it was thus necessary to adjourn the conquest till a time when we were forced to these general arrangements about the Porte, arrangements which at this moment I can only regard as neither for your convenience nor mine.'

I left the Emperor in the most complete uncertainty as to my opinion on the occupation of Belgrade, and I kept strictly to the sense of the reply which I have inserted above. I know the Emperor too well to express unreservedly my opinion on a first proposition, which he has twenty times seemed to put before me as a sort of advice, and which is very often only a way of sounding the ground, and making himself certain on an important and general question.

The Emperor, in an interview which lasted more than four hours, often returned to the same subjects, and discoursed the rest of the time on a number of measures to be taken in our internal affairs, on the necessity of establishing a Council of State, on many financial measures. The whole of his discourse bore the mark of real interest in the prosperity of the reign of your Imperial Majesty.

He often referred to the Russian cabinet, and especially to Count de Romanzow, with whom the Emperor is much annoyed. ' I have never seen such men as they are,' said the Emperor to me, among other things ; 'they are always complaining ; as for me, I never complain. I leave complaints to women, and I act. They, on the contrary, are always weeping, always demanding a remedy for something or other. Help thyself and God will help thee ! that is all I can reply to a great Power.'

The day after this interview the Duke of Cadore asked me to come to see him, to read his counter-projects of convention on one of my subjects of negotiation. On entering his room he told me he had received news from M. Otto,* who informed him that there was a great deal of uneasiness at Vienna about the progress of the Russian arms. I made the same reply to him as I had made

---

* Count Otto, French Ambassador in Vienna.

to the Emperor the evening before. M. de Champagny observed to me that, according to his letters, it appeared that the Austrian cabinet shared the uneasiness of the public. I showed him the extreme importance of the subject, and I purposely used a phrase a little more accentuated. 'You understand,' said I, 'that if one of our neighbouring Powers wishes to overthrow the Porte, we shall oppose it with all our might ; if we cannot succeed, we shall join in the partition against our will, and contrary to our utility and convenience.' M. de Champagny asked me if we were ready to oppose the Russian conquests on the right bank of the Danube ?

'We cannot allow them,' replied I ; ' but are you decided to regard the left bank as lost ? '

' The Emperor has made engagements on the subject,' replied M. de Champagny ; ' if you do not wish to allow ulterior encroachments, you should take the initiative of the question with us.'

' The Emperor,' interrupted I, 'has saved us that trouble. He has assured me that he will never allow the extension of Russian influence over Servia, and much less the occupation of territorial positions on the right bank. Have you sent your courier to St. Petersburg with orders to Caulaincourt to make a declaration to this effect ? '

M. de Champagny regarded me with that air of uneasy surprise which he so often wears, and asked me if I was aware of the news by this courier from the Emperor.

On my replying in the affirmative, he told me that the courier would leave in the course of the day. This all proved to me that the minister wished to sound us, and that the project of a convention had been a simple pretext to procure an interview with me.

The courier Liepscher, who arrived here on the 25th of this month, brought instructions to Prince de Schwarzenberg on the line to be taken by him in Turkish affairs, and an order to sound the French cabinet on these same questions. Having conducted the first steps in this negotiation, I begged Prince de Schwarzenberg to leave the further care of it to me. After having translated the last despatch of our agent at Bucharest, and communicated it to the Minister of Foreign Affairs, I went yesterday morning to the Emperor's levée. His Majesty not having yet received the despatch, I did not remain with him, and returned to St.-Cloud in the evening.

The Emperor detained me, dismissing everyone else. He thanked me for the communication I had made to him, and informed me that a courier had been sent to your Imperial Majesty with the announcement of the pregnancy of the Empress and the reply to your Majesty's last letter.

I desired to employ the evening in settling the Turkish questions, and I put them in the following manner :—

'The Emperor,' said I to his Majesty, 'not being sure that the courier who arrived yesterday would find me still in Paris, has sent me no orders. But I have seen, by the despatches addressed to Prince de Schwarzenberg, that the uneasiness as to the fate of the Porte, and in consequence of the encroachments of the Russians, is increasing with the successes of the latter. It appears to me, then, essential to draw a very precise line of conduct between your Majesty and my court. The last courier whom I sent to Vienna has informed the Emperor of three extremely interesting questions. I have made known to his Majesty :—

'1st. That the Treaty of Erfurt stipulated in favour of Russia the tolerance by the French Government of the acquisition of the left bank of the Danube.

'2nd. That France will not allow the extension of Russian conquests on the right bank of that river.

'3rd. That she will not allow the Russian cabinet to meddle in the affairs of Servia; that, on the other hand, Austria will be free to interpose in these same affairs.'

'I return to these three subjects,' continued I, 'and at a time of such imminent danger for the Porte I can take upon me to put these questions more directly, so as to enable us to take a side immediately. I therefore ask the Emperor :—

'1st. If he has decided to maintain in all their integrity the engagements he contracted at Erfurt, or if he will agree to make common cause with us, and take a step at St. Petersburg which may save the Principalities.'

'I have contracted engagements,' replied the Emperor, 'which I have no reason, nor even a pretext, to violate. These engagements are extremely onerous; I foresee in them real injury to France, but you know what actuated me at the time. To act now against these engagements would be to furnish Russia immediately with a direct motive for war; that would not answer my purpose, and would deprive me for ever of the right to be believed in any of my engagements. What guarantee could I give one day to yourselves if I break an explicit engagement for the simple reason that, circumstances having changed, I have less need of conciliating the Power with which I have contracted it? If you wish to make war on Russia, I will not prevent you; I will make an engagement with you to remain perfectly neutral. But can it be for your interest to spend a great deal of money and lose many more men ? I do not think so, and I should be far from giving you that advice.'

' 2nd. Is the Emperor opposed,' continued I, ' to the extension of Russian conquests on the right bank of the river ; would he regard the pretension of comprehending in the Turkish cessions the mouths of the Danube, and of fixing the frontier between the two Empires at the bend of this river, called the " *Trockene Donau*," as contrary to engagements contracted by him at Erfurt ; in short, what would be his line of conduct supposing that fresh reverses had forced the Turks to sign a peace more onerous than that foreseen by this same treaty ? '

' I have already explained myself,' replied the Emperor, ' on the principal question, and I have not only sent a courier to St. Petersburg about this subject, but I have also had a direct explanation with Prince Kourakin (the Home Minister, brother of the Ambassador). I have declared at St. Petersburg, and I have repeated to Prince Kourakin, that I will never allow the acquisition of an inch of territory on the right bank of the Danube ; neither will I allow the preservation of strong positions under the pretext of arrears of contributions. I limit my compliance to the " *Thalweg du Danube*," and I will pay no regard to any stipulation contrary to these principles. If then, which I do not suppose, the Russians should aim at making such a peace, if they should wish to break our engagements by exceeding them, I shall believe myself free, and you may count upon me in every respect.'

' 3rd. I admit in the third place the possibility that the Turks, forced to peace, might perhaps consent temporarily, or for the future, to the independence of Servia under Russian protection.'

'I will not recognise any other stipulations than those. Arrange the affairs of Servia; place the country under your direct influence, and I will support you. I have lately explained this subject to you at too great a length to go over it again.'

The Emperor finished with this sentence: 'All that I have said to you necessitates a written treaty. If you have ulterior views, or rather if it should happen that the Russians were mad enough to quarrel with us, which would cost them Finland, Moldavia, and Wallachia, which they have acquired under cover of their alliance with me, you know that you can count on me, and you will then communicate your ideas to me, as I shall communicate mine to you.'

'Send some one to Constantinople,' added the Emperor; 'make known at the Porte the interest you take in her; advise her. If you do not wish to fight for the Principalities, let them go; interfere in the affairs of Servia: these are my ideas, for I cannot see any use in your making great preparations to no end at the present moment.'

I repeated to his Majesty that I had put these direct questions in my private capacity, but that I was anxious to send his own words to your Imperial Majesty as nearly as possible.

The Emperor, in the course of our conversation, told me that the last courier who had arrived from St. Petersburg had brought the assurance that Russia was not thinking of making any acquisition beyond the stipulations of the Treaty of Erfurt—that is to say, beyond the left bank of the Danube; that, on the whole, he had been the bearer of satisfactory communications;

the Emperor only desired peace with the Porte in order
to have it in his power to act with more vigour against
England, and to have troops at his disposal for that
object.   He confided to me that he was going to recall
Caulaincourt ; that the ambassador had been spoiled
at Petersburg by the flattery he had received ; that he
had been wrong in not rejecting at once a complaint
made by the Count of Romanzow as to the way in
which it was alleged France had, at Constantinople, in-
stigated the Porte to refuse consent to an arrangement
with Russia . ' All nonsense,' added the Emperor, ' originating in the peevish disposition of the Count of
Romanzow.'

I reserve for a separate communication (No. 170)
my observations on the contents of my present report,
which offers conclusions worthy of grave consideration
on our part.

Metternich to the Emperor Francis, July 28, 1810.

170. My official despatch (169), most respectfully
submitted to your Majesty to-day, places in the clearest
light the relations in which France at present stands
to Russia, the Porte, and ourselves.   On it a system
may be built up which may serve to guide our political
conduct through one of the most important epochs of
our more recent history.   I think it necessary to examine the question which we have to take into consideration, from the double point of view of Austria's
present position in Europe, and that of her special and
individual interests.

1.—Austria's present Position in Europe.

The greatest and most decided advantage—the one
most difficult to calculate on account of its magnitude—

that we are justified in drawing from the marriage of a daughter of your Majesty with the French Emperor, is that of having changed our condition of entire and hopeless confusion, both internally and externally, into a state of peace. Under these circumstances the chief efforts of the Government must have for their aim the regulation and restoration of vigour to our internal energies, and the accumulation of these energies for all possible emergencies in the future.

It would be a great mistake to estimate this future altogether according to the standard of the first year of the reign of the Emperor of the French. In his marriage with an Archduchess there is a guarantee for Austria which could be supplied by no other event. It would, however, be no less a mistake to attribute to this fortunate union an influence which should extend to all Napoleon's plans, or which should even be able to modify them as a whole. The tendency of that monarch to despotism is part of his nature : it may be modified, it may be curbed, but it can never be totally destroyed.

If without this support the state of Austria might perhaps already have collapsed, or have been on the verge of doing so, it is not less true that, in spite of the marriage, periods may occur when we shall have to summon all our energies to avert or resist the threatened danger of subjection.

Even without this belief, which in me amounts to a conviction, I have no doubt that it would be necessary for us to oppose openly, and with all our strength, the disastrous usurpation of Russia with regard to our best and most trustworthy neighbours. However convinced I may be that the smaller danger must ever yield to the greater, however certain it is that we have

at all times more to fear from France than from Russia,
I yet feel myself obliged to advise your Majesty to make
common cause with France in order to save the left bank
of the Danube !

But if France, with regard to this object, merely
promises to be a quiet spectator, if we have to expend
much military power on her Eastern frontier without
any security on the west and south, if the conduct of
France is to be simply neutral, in this case it seems to
me that any waste of our strength would be in the
highest degree rash.

I could not advise a war against Russia with the
Porte as our only ally, even did there not exist in the
relations of Russia with France and of the Porte with
England inexhaustible material for complications of
which Russia would very easily make use to our disadvantage.

2.—*The individual Interests of Austria*

demand that, in case the two Principalities cannot be
saved, further mischief shall at least be prevented, and
our influence on Turkish affairs be extended as much as
possible.

In this the declaration of the French Emperor offers
us support.

Should Russia—which is, however, highly improbable—decline to concur in the declaration of this
Government, the case would then undoubtedly have
arisen when we must render active assistance to the
Porte. The alliance of Russia with France would be
disturbed; Russia would have no alternative but to
unite with England, and the choice of our own course
would admit of no doubt. That Napoleon intends to
leave to us the exclusive protection of Servia I do not

believe; his character would not allow him to do so. It is nevertheless certain that we must endeavour to gain the most direct influence over that province. Having been entered into at his request, the greatest weight can now be given to our negotiations with the Servian leaders. Regard to the natural jealousy of the Porte should alone tend to moderate our steps in this matter, as in the occupation of Belgrade.

My humble opinion would be, then, that we should make a confidential communication to the Divan to the effect that Austria would never permit Russia to extend her conquests to the right bank of the Danube; that the recovery of the Principalities must remain an object for Turkish bravery; that Austria is now ready to come forward publicly as mediator between the Porte and the Servians; and that the interests of Austria demand this course of action with the double view of at last obtaining peace on her frontier, and of preventing any further action of Russia in those provinces.

As it is equally improbable that the Servian nation will return under Turkish dominion as that the Divan intends to relinquish its right to the province, it is only open to us in the first instance to propose mediation. This may lead to our occupation of Belgrade, which we can represent to the Porte as the result of our wish to establish our influence on the Servian negotiation by anticipating the designs of Russia. In any case Belgrade must only be taken over by us provisionally.

In the course of the negotiation its ultimate form will gradually develop of itself. Whatever its result, our influence in Servia must be established by it, and we may look on this important province as our own under all future circumstances.

This is my humble opinion on this momentous question. Much will depend on the way in which the affair is opened. The expedition to Constantinople must take place immediately, and a negotiator be sent with equal despatch to· the Servian frontier. . . .

In Russia every attempt to establish our exclusive influence in Servia will, of course, cause great excitement. . . .

I consider it still less in accordance with our own interest to advise at Constantinople the cession of the provinces, to which the Emperor Napoleon alluded during his last conversation with me, as we have in the promise of that monarch decided reason to doubt the further progress of Russian conquest.

From my behaviour towards the French Emperor and his minister, your Majesty will be pleased to understand my intention to keep ourselves aloof from every possible unnecessary complication with Russia, room for which would easily have been given to the cabinet of this country by less guarded conduct. The principal aim before us was to place the intentions of France in the clearest possible light, and in this I flatter myself that I have succeeded.

The key to Napoleon's greater forbearance towards Russia as well as ourselves lies in the disastrous direction taken by Spanish affairs. Without this his course would have been widely different to what it is at present.

THE AUSTRIAN LOAN IN PARIS.*

(No. 52, Vol. I.)

171. Metternich to the Emperor Francis (Despatch), Paris, August 23, 1810.

171. A detailed report from the banker Eskeles to the Finance Department will give your Majesty the fullest information as to his negotiations since his arrival in Paris.

Anxious to assist him in every way from his first arrival in this city, I have been fortunate enough to effect a prolongation of the last three terms of payment, and a rate of instalments, the former of which will extend to eight months, while the latter is arranged in exact accordance with the suggestions of Eskeles.

I had several conversations with Eskeles respecting the business of the loan, before I allowed myself to be persuaded to take any decided steps in the matter.

The loan rests in my opinion on two distinct and equally important conditions :—

1. On the active concurrence of the French Emperor.

2. On the condition of our credit.

The first of these conditions seems to me beyond

* The Austrian Loan of 35 to 40 million gulden (20 gulden currency) was to be opened in Paris, Geneva, and Amsterdam. As Napoleon passed through Brussels on his journey to the Netherlands, whither he was escorting the Empress Marie Louise, he himself announced to the authorities of that city that he had consented to the raising of a loan by the Emperor of Austria.—ED.

doubt, after the renewed assurances of readiness to assist and daily tokens of real friendship on the part of this Government in an affair hostile rather than favourable to their private interests, and I therefore consider it as settled.

The credit of our Government is, however, unhappily very low. We are reproached with not having fulfilled former agreements. This feeling operates principally in Holland. Much distrust exists as to our financial measures for the future ; this distrust is universal.

I thought it right to introduce Eskeles to the present head of the Périgaux house. The banker Lafitte enjoys the entire confidence of the Government as well as of the public. He is one of the directors of the bank of France, head of the most important banking house, and fully informed of the intentions of the Government : therefore no one could give us better information than he can.

I take the liberty of respectfully laying before your Majesty a statement given to me by him. Banker Eskeles sends a copy of the memorandum with his remarks upon it ; I therefore leave it to him to give his views on the financial side of the question, and confine myself to making a few additions of a general and political nature.

Lafitte starts from the assumption that without the most express and decided consent of the Emperor no loan would be possible, either in France or in Holland (now part of France), or in the confederated states. I have already declared myself equally decided on this point.

He asserts as the result of this fact that a loan opened in Paris, of which the shares would be constantly quoted in the 'Exchange List' of that city, and its terms published in the French official papers, would bear the stamp of a guarantee that in the present position of affairs could be afforded by no other means. He further declares that the Dutch, who, it is hoped, will be the principal sharers in the loan, would prefer to supply the capital in Paris to doing so at home, as they are all timid, and in the first case would appear under a false name, while in the latter they would be afraid of betraying a degree of prosperity which might prove injurious to them. This question can best be decided on the spot by Eskeles.

The scheme of the house of Périgaux-Lafitte is really little more than a rough sketch, and contains among others one point which it seems to me impossible to accept. The proposed appointment of a French commissioner at Vienna for the security of the creditors, in addition to the commission entrusted by Government with the management of the loan, must certainly be rejected ; the harm which would spring from it would, in my opinion, by no means be counteracted by the appointment of a corresponding commissioner in Paris.

The following is a point which deserves some consideration.

It seems that the Dutch deputation, at present in Paris, contemplates a proposal to come to some agreement with the French Government as to the previous Austrian loan in Holland. The exact object of this proposal, according to what has come to me at third hand from some members of the deputation, is to relinquish to the French Government all the claims of the Dutch money-lenders, and to take for themselves five per cent. commission.

This intention on the part of the Dutch was repre-

sented to me as a threat to be averted by direct negotiation with Austria. I confined myself to representing
to my informant that it was impossible for me to enter
into a negotiation on a subject entirely strange to me ;
and while I expressed my doubt that the French
Government would entertain such a proposal, I remarked that in the event of their doing so, no serious
results would be likely to ensue for us.

I confess that I consider the first of these points as
only true conditionally. At a moment when it might
be important to the French Government to involve itself
with us, and on the distinct supposition that the Dutch
would give up their claims on Austria at a considerable
reduction, a transaction of this kind might possibly
succeed ; but in my opinion, on these suppositions *only*,
and the Dutch seem up to the present time to have no
idea of making any reduction.

I think, however, that the nature of the affair demands that it should be brought to the knowledge of
your Majesty and the finance department, particularly
at a time when it is important to know the state of
feeling, in every respect, of a whole class—and that perhaps the most important one—of those who it is hoped
will take part in the new loan.

I cannot sufficiently express my satisfaction at the
very favourable attitude of the Emperor as regards our
financial designs. Any plan made by our financiers
will certainly be supported by the French Government.

In spite of all my efforts, I have not been able to
bring my remaining subjects of negotiation to a conclusion. Though we have agreed on all the principal
points, smaller difficulties have been continually placed in

my way, which left me in no doubt that it was the intention of the Emperor to make me prolong my stay here. For this I found sufficient grounds in the course of events in the East.

Your Majesty will have had the goodness to convince yourself, from my last very minute report of the conversations which I had with the Emperor on Turkish affairs (Nos. 169 and 170), that in case of any important advance of the Russian army, the Emperor's mind is made up as to his course of action, while his intention is equally firm to oppose no obstacle to the war, should its operations be confined to the defence of the banks of the Danube. Were the power of Russia to bleed to death from day to day, this would fit in perfectly with Napoleon's plans.

Since the last reverses of the Russian arms, and the more vigorous measures taken by the Porte, the Emperor considers that the danger which threatened the latter has been removed, and I made use of this opportunity to ask from the Emperor my farewell audience.

I am now convinced that I was not wrong in my calculations. The Emperor has not fixed the day for my audience, but he has let me know that it is not far distant, and the Minister of Foreign Affairs has received commands to wind up all business with me.

In consequence of this, I am now on the point of signing the remaining articles of negotiation, such as the convention relating to our transit-trade and the formation of branch establishments and depôts, as well as that relating to the general removal of sequestrations. Both have been laid before his Majesty to-day for the last time, with very slight alteration, and I flatter myself that I have in both cases fully satisfied your Majesty's expectations. As soon as these conventions shall have been signed, I hope to forward them for your Majesty's ratification by a special courier, as I proposed, particularly for the one relating to the sequestrations, a very short term, because the interests of so many people in distress were bound up in it. By the same courier I shall have the honour of announcing positively the day of my farewell audience, and also that of my departure.

One most difficult point is that of the relations of Frenchmen in our service towards their former country. All the Emperor's ideas of government are bound up in this question. I summed up my last report on the subject in a *note verbale* which I gave to the Minister of Foreign Affairs, and to which he has to-day promised me an answer. Though I see good grounds for indulging in hope, yet I cannot look for more than the silent permission of the Emperor that the individuals who, according to the Code Napoléon, never cease to be French subjects shall be allowed to remain in our service, without ever setting foot on French territory.

The principles and ideas of the Emperor regarding this question, which, after the outbreak of the last Austrian war, were still in many respects political, are now altogether abstract and administrative, and on the first ground especially difficult to combat. As for the rest, I beg to assure your Majesty that I shall earnestly seek to press on a subject which, for reasons of so honourable a nature, is near to your Majesty's heart.

I must reserve till my return to Vienna the honour of laying before your Majesty my verbal and written reports on all political and other subjects.

I feel assured that your Majesty will be perfectly satisfied in every respect, and this conviction alone consoles me for the fact of my stay having been protracted so much against my will and inclinations.

CONVENTIONS ON THE TRANSIT TRADE OF AUS-TRIA, AND ON THE REMOVAL OF SEQUES-TRATIONS FROM THE PROPERTY OF FORMER FEUDATORIES OF THE GERMAN EMPIRE.

(Note 51, Vol. I.)

172. Metternich to the Emperor Francis (Despatch), Paris, September 5, 1810.

172. I have the honour to submit the two enclosed conventions for the gracious ratification of your Imperial Majesty. That on the subject of transit across the Illyrian provinces, and on the formation of a commercial establishment at Fiume, has been drawn up in a sense agreeing with the wishes expressed by the Aulic Chamber of Finance. These were limited to the possibility of establishing commercial branches. In obtaining permission to have an agency composed of Austrian subjects under the direction of an Austrian Consul, I flatter myself that I have surpassed the hopes that had been formed.

The important station of Trieste has not been granted by the Emperor, that unhappy town being destined to become an exclusively military post, or, what is the same thing, being destined to ruin. Superior considerations in favour of Venice have led the Emperor to this determination, against which all my pains and efforts have proved unavailing.

. . . The convention on the removal of sequestrations is much more complete than could have been expected. It is entirely exhaustive, and will demand on our side several measures, my ideas on which I shall on my return take the liberty of respectfully submitting to your Imperial Majesty.

The terms of the convention have been accepted by the Emperor exactly as expressed by me. I was careful to prove in a manner which should admit of no mistake that it is to your Imperial Majesty, and to your Majesty's urgency, that so many unfortunate families owe their happiness. The beginning of Article II. fully accomplishes this object.

While I venture to hope for the gracious approbation of your Imperial Majesty, I beg your Majesty to believe that it would have been impossible to obtain more in either matter than I have the honour of laying before your Majesty to-day.

Nothing less than the general position of affairs at the time, and the extreme patience with which I have conducted my negotiations, was required to obtain for us conditions which offer in every way more advantages to us than to France. The experience of a long series of years ought to have convinced the most incredulous of the difficulties presented by this undertaking.

THE SWEDISH THRONE.

173. A courier, who arrived here two days ago, brought the news of the nomination of the Prince of Ponte-Corvo as successor to the throne of Sweden. It is said that the formal application will be made by a deputation empowered to solicit from the Emperor permission for the Prince to quit his service, and from the latter his acceptance of the crown.

This event materially affects the Russians. They cannot fail to see, in the choice of a French marshal, a virtual compact between the future sovereign of Sweden and his people to undertake, at some future time, the reconquest of the provinces lost in the last war. The influence exercised by France over that choice proves to them that the relations between the two Empires are exposed to very evident risks.

On the other hand, the calculations of the French Emperor can only be followed with difficulty.

The election of a marshal cannot fail to disquiet Russia. Is it to Napoleon's interest to irritate her just now? Has he not twenty different means of effecting this object without running the risk of obliging the cabinet of St. Petersburg to choose that moment for a rupture which may least suit the circumstances of France? It is beyond doubt that the French party in the Russian cabinet must be placed in the greatest possible embarrassment by this event. Is it to the interest of Napoleon to overthrow that party? I do not know, but it is certain that for some time all his measures seem to have been devoted to that object.

The example of the elevation of a simple marshal to the royal dignity appears likely to place too great a temptation before his colleagues not to cause serious difficulty to the Emperor eventually. The removal of Bernadotte, who has always been disliked by the Emperor, does not seem to compensate for the discontent of the other marshals, and the complications which it would cause.

Finally, the elevation of Bernadotte to the royal dignity finds many objectors in the Imperial family, from consideration of the moral wrong done to the dynasty of Napoleon by increasing the number of *parvenus* who have been raised to the throne.

These considerations, which have all been submitted to the Emperor, and which he has discussed with his relations, as well as with persons enjoying his confidence, and even with myself, as your Majesty will graciously have perceived from my previous despatches, have not arrested him in his course. One word of disapproval on his part would no doubt have ensured the failure of the intrigues in favour of the Prince of Ponte-Corvo. It is now proved that he encouraged them in every way.

I have just learned that the election of the Prince of Ponte-Corvo was only decided by a weak majority of seven votes.

Prince Alexis Kourakin left Paris two days ago, a few hours after the news of the election of Marshal Bernadotte. His Majesty had granted him his farewell audience more than a fortnight ago, but had kept him waiting the rest of the time for a letter to his master.

I may add that the election of Bernadotte, according to the political principles lately unfolded by Russia, is not an event unfavourable to us. The new Sovereign of Sweden will form a more or less powerful counterpoise on a vulnerable side of that Power; and I am not afraid that the cabinet of St. Petersburg, oppressed by the weight of apprehension and by a compromising war, would be in any hurry to bring about complications which must also be in every way disagreeable to us.

Notes of a Conversation of Metternich with Napoleon, Paris, September 8, 1810.

174. The Emperor entered upon the subject by observing that the election of the new Prince Royal tended to create difficulties and embarrassments for himself.

'*I.*—Your Majesty has foreseen them, and it would seem that they have entered into your Majesty's calculations; otherwise they might have been avoided.'

'*Napoleon.*—I allowed the nation to do as it pleased. I even gave a cold reception to Baron de Rosen, who brought me the King's letter announcing the fact. I did not conceal my astonishment at the course pursued towards me by that prince. Indeed, his last letter but one expressed his desire that the Prince of Augustenburg should succeed his brother; the last informs me of the election of the Prince of Ponte-Corvo.

'I said to M. de Rosen that the King might have consulted me earlier on the subject; now it is too late, I can no longer refuse. The choice of the Prince of Ponte-Corvo is displeasing to me from two points of view; it endangers my relations with Russia, and by raising a private individual to a throne, a wrong is done to existing Sovereigns.

'Nor is the question of the change of religion unimportant, and I judge of it by the effect produced on the Empress by the news. "What!" she exclaimed, "does the wretch give up his God for a crown? None of my friends would ever have consented to such a thing." I had offered the crown to the Viceroy of Italy, who refused it, at once.'

'*I.*—As your Majesty speaks to me with so much openness of these things, with equal frankness I shall not conceal that I share your Majesty's views; and I consider, too, that the precedent of a marshal being raised to the throne must exercise a bad influence on his companions. Your Majesty will soon be obliged to have one of them shot, in order to moderate the lofty ideas of the rest.

'I agree most sincerely as to the undesirability of increasing the number of private individuals placed on thrones, and I think that your Majesty should consider it a great advantage to remain the solitary instance.'

'*Napoleon.*—You are right; that consideration which is personal to me and my family, has often made me regret having placed Murat on the throne of Naples. It does not do to think of all your relations and cousins. I ought to have appointed him Viceroy, and as a rule not give thrones even to my brothers; but one only becomes wise by experience. As for me, I ascended a throne which I myself had newly created; I did not enter on the inheritance of another. I took what belonged to no one. I ought to have stopped there, and to have appointed only Governor-Generals and Viceroys. Besides, you need only consider the conduct

of the King of Holland, to be convinced that relations
are often far from being friends.

'As for the marshals, you are so much more in the
right, as some of them have already had dreams of
greatness and independence.

'But I will prove to you that in the Swedish affair I
remained perfectly neutral.'

The Emperor rang for his private secretary, and had
all the correspondence with King Charles XIII. brought
to him.

After reading these documents to me, the Emperor
said that Russia had behaved very foolishly in exercising
no influence on the choice of the Prince of Sweden. 'I
asked nothing better,' he continued, 'than to see the
Prince of Augustenburg elected. I would never have
consented to the choice of the Prince of Oldenburg;
but the Russian cabinet should have acted in the same
manner, from similar motives, with reference to Marshal
Bernadotte. And this is what is gained " *au bénéfice
du temps*," as M. de Romanzow says! I hear from
Stockholm that the Russians did nothing at all, no doubt
trusting implicitly to their fortunate star.'

'Do you know Bernadotte well?' the Emperor
asked me; 'and what do you think of him?'

'*I.*—I am acquainted with him only in the ordinary
intercourse of society, and I am not, therefore, able
to form any opinion of him.'

'*Napoleon.*—He has plenty of brains. I have always
found this to be the case; but I foresee he will have
a good deal of difficulty in maintaining his position.
The nation expects everything from him; he is the
god from whom they demand bread, but I cannot see
that he has any talent for government; he is a good
soldier, and that is all. For my part, I am delighted

to have got rid of him, and I ask nothing better than
his removal from France; he is one of those old Jaco-
bins with his head in the wrong place, as they all have,
and that is not the way to keep on a throne. If you
see him again, sound him a little, and your opinion will
be the same as mine; in any case I could not refuse my
consent, were it only that a French marshal on the
throne of Gustavus Adolphus is one of the best possible
tricks that could be played on England.'

METTERNICH'S FAREWELL AUDIENCE WITH
NAPOLEON AT THE TUILERIES.

175. Notes by Metternich, Paris, September 24, 1810.

175. The Emperor has charged me to convey from him to the Emperor, my master, the most positive assurances of his friendship and of his most constant affection. ' Let the Emperor be assured,' he said to me, ' that I desire only his happiness and prosperity. Let him dismiss any idea of encroachment by me on his dominions. They ought to be enlarged and increased by an alliance with us. Assure him that anything that may be said to the contrary is false. It is more agreeable to me to have him on the throne of Austria than it would be to have any of my brothers there ; I no longer see any cause for disagreement between us.'

I then touched again on Article III. of the secret Treaty of Vienna.*

' I warned you, Sire,' I said to him, ' that I should not quit Paris without having obtained from your Majesty the revocation of that article, which is odious from the fact of its existence, and in reality useless. Your Majesty was of my opinion when I mentioned it to you for the first time. Your Majesty acknowledged that, should we resolve to make war on you, we should not be stopped by that stipulation; while during peace it is equally useless and humiliating. Your Majesty

* Article III. of the secret treaty limits the strength of the Austrian army to 150,000 men.—ED.

avowed that the article was only inserted as it now stands in a moment of displeasure against the Austrian Government; it was yourself, Sire, who told me that in its original form it would have afforded to France a means of control, while, by its actually existing terms, it offers nothing but simple degradation. I therefore have now to request the fulfilment of your promise to me that it should be annulled.' I asked the Emperor if he wished me to address a note to Champagny on the subject, to which he should reply in the sense agreed upon, or if he would have a sentence inserted in the letter he was to give me for my Imperial master, expressing the same thing.

'I should prefer the last method,' replied the Emperor; 'I cannot remember much of the wording of that secret article.'

I had foreseen this difficulty, and had provided myself with a copy. The Emperor read it, and said :—

'The thing is quite easy. I shall write to your master that, having been informed by you of his desire to see the article in question annulled, and having thus learned the satisfaction which the Emperor would feel at this being done, I shall charge you to acquaint him with the anxiety I feel to give him this fresh proof of my friendship and confidence. Do you approve of this mode of expressing myself?'

I declared myself satisfied, and asked the Emperor when I might reckon on the letter? His Majesty replied that he would send it to me in the evening. The following day the Emperor took his departure for Fontainebleau. I saw the Minister of Foreign Affairs, who told me that he had been charged by his Majesty to apologise for his not having sent the letter which he had promised me, but which he would make a point of writing immediately on reaching Fontainebleau. The Duke de Cadore further added that he would remain a day longer in Paris on purpose to be able to give it to me himself.

A courier despatched by the ambassador, on the very day of my departure from Paris, brought me the letter enclosing the one I was expecting from the Emperor Napoleon.

SCHOUVALOW'S TREATY OF ALLIANCE.

(Note 58, Vol. I.)

176. Metternich to the Emperor Francis (Despatch), Vienna, October 31, 1810.

176. Count Schouvalow was with me this morning, and gave me the first sketch of the proposed treaty with regard to which my father recently submitted a preliminary report to your Majesty during my journey into Styria.

I was able to draw him on ; and at last, after a long conversation, I became most fully confirmed in the conviction I had previously formed, that the whole of Schouvalow's proposal only pointed to a defensive alliance between the two courts.

After much circumlocution and many protestations as to the desirability of a union between our sovereigns, and the dangers of an uncertain future, the General told me how much the Emperor Alexander wished to prevent the latter by means of a candid explanation of our mutual intentions ; he added that many other points still unsettled between us might easily be settled at the same time.

I replied to Count Schouvalow that the Emperor Alexander could not well feel any doubt as to your Majesty's sentiments ; that your Majesty's principles are too well known and tried to allow of the most remote supposition of any possible future deviation from them. I was able to declare that the wishes of your Majesty

were entirely in accordance with the interests of your
Majesty and of all Europe in pointing to one object—
namely, the preservation of peace. I added that,
in consequence of this, I should have no hesitation in
giving to him (Count Schouvalow) for the satisfaction of
the Russian cabinet, the same assurance which the
Emperor Napoleon had granted to the Russian Minister
of the Interior, Prince Alexis Kourakin, in his farewell
audience, and had recently repeated to his brother,
the Russian Ambassador at Paris, that between your
Majesty and France there exists neither an offensive
nor defensive, but only a family alliance; that the latter
has already had the most beneficial results for the present, and secures the peace of Austria for the future,
thus making every political alliance superfluous, and
promising to your Majesty the blessings of a real independence, in so far as such can be imagined in the
present state of Europe, against which your Majesty
has so long struggled.

Count Schouvalow remarked that there were questions still existing between our courts which required
mutual advances and mutual agreement. He mentioned the mistakes which thus far have arisen from the
union of the Principalities. He touched upon the mediation between Russia and the Porte as an idea which
seemed to prevail here more than in Russia, but held it
up as a result which might possibly ensue on an agreement as to our far more important general interests.

I replied that your Majesty must, of course, wish
for a speedy peace with the Porte, since every movement which tends to produce unforeseen difficulties
endangers your Majesty's general interests, and any
alteration of the present state of the territorial position
of the Porte, and particularly the government of the

Principalities, would stand in direct opposition to those interests. That your Majesty attached no importance to mediation in its proper sense I knew for certain, since unarmed mediation is in itself worthless; if, nevertheless, your Majesty's friendly intervention between the two Powers should succeed, your Majesty would feel the greatest satisfaction in employing it. We cannot, however, I added, contemplate any speedy termination of the war, which would leave the government of the Principalities in the hands of Russia.

I let fall a few words as to the return, at least nominally, of these provinces beneath Turkish rule.

Count Schouvalow assured me that the Emperor Alexander would never abandon the hope of annexing the Principalities to his empire, but that we might secure important advantages from them for the future as the result of a general agreement. He here touched upon the proposal of exchanging Little Wallachia for some parts of Poland, a proposal which had been made not long ago, but which, from some causes unknown to him, had not been accepted.

As he was not to be turned from this subject, I told him that I could not form any exact idea as to the intentions of his court. It did not appear to me that a political difficulty could be foreseen so long beforehand. As to our mutual wish to prevent it, no special agreement was needed. Every negotiation, and especially every formal treaty, must be founded upon some basis, which in the present case it was hard to find, as the whole conduct of Russia of late had rendered it quite impossible for us to understand the intentions of her cabinet. We should therefore gladly receive any information and listen to any proposals as to these; the initiative did not rest with your Majesty, and it seemed to me plain that a treaty framed on sentiments admitted on both sides must be dangerous from its very existence.

Count Schouvalow assured me that the existence of a renewed treaty would never come to the knowledge of France; for this he pledged the Emperor's word of honour. 'How can you,' I asked the Count, 'reconcile the idea of an alliance with Austria with your present relations to France? Is your alliance at an end?'

Count Schouvalow replied that the relations of Russia to France remained unaltered; but that the alliance with that Power had reference only to the contingency of our being the aggressive party; as this was now, however, altogether out of the question, there was no difficulty in reconciling with that stipulation a treaty which should ensure to our two countries mutual help in case either one or the other should be attacked by France. At least it was of the greatest importance to be able to reckon beforehand on the part we should respectively play in such an event.

I hinted to Count Schouvalow at our very different situations, according to which Russia stood in definite political alliance with France, while we, agreeably to the assurances I had given already, were perfectly free from any engagement of that sort, a freedom which your Majesty was well able to prize at its real worth. As to your Majesty's entertaining no schemes of conquest, Russia might find security for this in your Majesty's universally acknowledged moderation, and in your distinct conviction that at times when self-preservation is a thing of such great difficulty, attempts at conquest are seldom carried to a successful issue.

Count Schouvalow remarked that I was avoiding the question of the alliance, and returned to that of the

Principalities, endeavouring to place most distinctly before me the interest we must have in obtaining conditions favourable to ourselves.

Your Majesty will entertain no doubt from my despatch that Russia's sole design in her present negotiation is her own security.

Threatened by an ally to whom the Emperor Alexander had sacrificed all other considerations and obligations, he turns to your Majesty for help against the approaching danger. Involved in a war which is directly opposed to your Majesty's interests, Russia will nevertheless give up none of her designs against the Porte— but Austria is to serve her as a bulwark against which she would be able, undisturbed, to carry out, perhaps in the only way possible, her plans of conquest.

There is no doubt that in entering into such an alliance your Majesty would become a sharer in all the burdens it might involve, without any prospect whatever of advantage, and with evident danger of complications with the only Power Austria has to fear. I therefore solicit your Majesty's commands whether, in the probable event of the Russian minister returning to the question, I may act upon the policy which I have propounded in this report, and, accordingly,

I. Continue to evade the treaty of alliance, on the grounds which I have just stated ;

II. And insist on the separation of that question from the remaining subjects of negotiation, for the reasons also given above.

DESPATCH ON THE RESULTS OF THE MISSION
TO PARIS.

(Note 57, Vol. I.)

177. Metternich to the Emperor Francis, Vienna, January 17, 1810, with the Emperor's Resolution on it of the same date.

177. I should not have delayed laying before your Majesty, immediately on my return, a report of the general political results of my stay in Paris, but that such a proceeding, before I had made myself again familiar with the state of our internal affairs, would have rendered it impossible for me to represent to your Majesty in one paper the true position of the state in the present political system of Europe.

Every glance abroad without due regard to the power of the state, and, again, any estimate of the latter without weighing all our foreign relations, is not only useless, but actually dangerous. I shall attempt to give your Majesty, in as condensed a form as possible, a comprehensive view of the present position of affairs, free from all self-deception and prejudice. On this foundation alone can a political scheme be built. How necessary it is to form this at a time when it still depends more or less on our own calculations, when we are able to throw into our behaviour shades of difference which generally determine the direction of the whole, we are taught by the experience of all, and especially of recent times. Finally, that we are almost the only European

Power to whom the possibility of a choice still remains,
I now undertake to show.

A remarkable combination of strength and weakness, of struggles for organisation and confusion, of subjection and the consciousness of an insufferable yoke,
strikes the impartial observer in France and in the confederate states.   The certainty that the first and inevitable result of Napoleon's death—he alone is the centre
of all power—would be a revolution, is general.   It is
exactly this feeling that Napoleon makes use of to carry
out his plans, and perhaps nothing could be more useful
to him.   In the conviction which is shown by so many,
both rulers and subjects, that the yoke under which
they sigh is only temporary, lies, in my opinion, the
true cause that has made it possible for one single
individual to carry out so many gigantic and destructive schemes; the height on which that individual
stands, however lofty, would never have been sufficient
to realise all that we are witnessing day by day.   Napoleon alone lives and acts in the present.   The nations of
Europe all live in the future, and so he is able to unite
the final ends of the chain without their perceiving it.
Secret in their origin and early development, the schemes
of the French monarch remain his own exclusive possession till the time when, by being put in practice, they
at last excite general attention and can no longer be
concealed.   But by that time he has already accomplished what to the world appears to be only in its
beginning.   Things had been only outwardly the same :
beneath, all was undermined, demolished, created anew ;
and when the slight veil of deception is raised, the work
bursts into view in all its completeness.   Each step he
took had all along been part of a whole.   Each, however apparently isolated, leads to the objects he has in

view.   How mischievous and productive of bad consequences any error as to these objects would be, how
disastrous any misconception of the true state of affairs,
requires no explanation.

France is very far from being happy.   Under an
iron rule, an unexampled finance, a tremendous load of
taxes, and entire destruction of commerce, the idea of
their internal condition would be intolerable to the
French if the idea were not softened by what appears
like a calm after prolonged storms, in comparison with
other nations and their heavier burdens.   What a
pledge of internal repose is contained in the self-reliance
of the French citizen, who, himself experiencing no
shock, sees one shock after another fall around him,
and exactly in proportion to that repose fancies himself
happier than any other European nation.   The state
coffers are empty : those of the sovereign are full.   The
latter, by the establishment of a ' *domaine extraordinaire*,'
which receives all foreign contributions, has made it
possible for him to grant extensive assistance in any
state emergency, apparently from the private resources
of the crown.   France is undeniably the richest state
on the Continent, and can bid defiance to any other
from a financial point of view.

Thus there is no possibility of any agitation in the
old kingdom of France.

The feeling of the confederate states must be divided
into that of the princes and that of the people.   Both
share the hope for a happier future ; but the princes,
separated by private motives and by ever-increasing
compromises, are no longer to be brought into union
against France, as they were in former times.   How far
the feeling of the German people was productive for
itself is proved by the last twenty years.

The Spanish war has recently taken a turn which leaves France little hope of a favourable termination. The latest information speaks of the very serious situation of Massena's army in Portugal. That Napoleon will never quite relinquish the undertaking admits of no doubt to anyone acquainted with his character; but what modifications he may be likely to make in his plans, in case of any important defeats, is all the more difficult to decide in advance as the position of his affairs in the Peninsula is new to him, and still more so to a foreign observer.

It seems to me that two conclusions may be drawn with certainty in the event of decided reverses to the French arms. One is, that defeats in Spain would at any time be the signal for fresh disturbances in other directions. The other, that in the present position held by France, even supposing the most marked success on the side of the Spaniards, the war beyond, or even on this side of, the Pyrenees must only be regarded by any other threatened Power as a partial diversion, scarcely affecting the main course of affairs : a diversion which could only be of real military value at the moment of great and important advantage to a Power engaged in war with France.

England is in a very critical condition. However certain it is that the Continent bears the primary and heaviest burden of this prolonged war, it is equally certain that the state of affairs reacts upon England. No one can foresee which of the two Powers will vanquish the other by endurance; but it is certain that the supplies which England would have to send to the Continent on the outbreak of another war can be but very limited. The extreme difficulty of transmitting subsidies would prove of no small importance. Russia, placed by her late unfortunate policy in a position which renders her dangerous to all her neighbours and powerless against France, without money, without cohesion in her component parts, finds herself obliged to seek assistance, without being able to give any in return.

Prussia is no longer to be reckoned amongst the Powers.

After these preliminary observations, I may approach more closely to the object of the present statement, and consider the two great questions :—

1. What plans has Napoleon next in view, and what means has he of carrying them out?

2. What must Austria's next step be?

Whenever I have had the honour of laying my views before your Majesty, since I first entered the diplomatic career, my estimate of Napoleon's views and schemes has never varied.

He has held, and still holds, the monstrous idea of ruling alone over the whole of Europe. By admirable coolness in the conception of expedients, and a most rapid and happy application of them on every occasion, both small and great, Napoleon has at length reached a height where he may indeed set bounds to his own ambition, but where none can be set by any human Power, with reasonable prospect of success.

To examine into the reasons *why* this alarming state of things was brought about, at a moment when we should alone consider the present and the future, would be outside the aim of the present statement. The history of the last twenty years shows an uninterrupted succession of moral, political, military, financial mistakes made by all the European Powers. Not one is free from reproach ; not one worked for her preservation with means suited to the object, or in a way likely to lead to the wished-for goal. But all the fault does not lie with the Powers themselves. The appearance of a great Power rising from her ashes in the midst of Europe, with fresh and tremendous energies, was too wide-reaching, in its daily results, to be universally grasped, and thus turned to general account. If a temporary unity of purpose in the preponderating Powers of our time should occur, their paths would speedily diverge. The unavoidable weakness of coalitions would increase and develop with each undertaking, and experience unhappily shows that France knew how to appropriate the victories of the allies. The highest triumph of French policy was the Peace of Tilsit. By it Napoleon crowned the efforts which for years he had been making without result against the Russian cabinet. That which had been undone by the death of Paul I., all that had only been touched upon in the unfortunate Franco-Russian mediation of the year 1804, was accomplished by Napoleon at Tilsit. Since the year 1807, scarcely anything stood in the way of the completion of his work. The two great Powers who *united* were invincible—Austria and Russia—were separated. All the events which have already taken place since Tilsit, all those which probably would develop themselves only too quickly in the future, are, and will be, nothing but the results of this system of isolation.

In the years 1808 and 1809, the Russian cabinet acted with unexampled blindness. Unmindful of the last inevitable reaction on Russia herself, Count Romanzow gave to the policy of his sovereign an entirely wrong direction. Alexander was to come forward as a conqueror by the side of the greatest conqueror who had appeared for many centuries. As subjects for aggrandisement, Romanzow selected the states belonging to peaceful neighbours who had never been the objects of fear, and instead of thinking of self-preservation, he destroyed Russia, and assisted ever since the Peace of Tilsit in the destruction of one after another of the bulwarks of her security. The fall of Austria was resolved on in Napoleon's mind at the time of the outbreak of the last war.

All the proclamations of the Emperor and his generals, his personal attacks and the deliberate indignities offered to members of the reigning House of Austria, attest this fact, even if I had not far more cogent reasons for representing it as certainly true. Compare the course which the French monarch pursued for years towards Austria and Russia, simply with a view to the dismemberment of actually existing kingdoms, with that maintained at the same time towards Russia, and no doubt will remain that Napoleon intended to advance over the ruins of Austria and Prussia to the work of driving Russia back into the deserts of Asia.

The marriage of the French Emperor with the illustrious daughter of your Majesty gave, however, to the whole a new and unforeseen direction. I think I ought now to examine this event from a point of view which is generally not sufficiently considered—the only one from which it can be represented in a light that enables us to judge of its consequences.

In every instance where he has been engaged in the work of demolition or annexation, Napoleon speaks of guarantees. This expression, in its usual sense, can in no way be reconciled with his mode of action. A guarantee depends usually on the state of the political relations of one Power with one or more others. It is not so much the political side that Napoleon values in a guarantee : he aims at something tangible, some actual security. In this way even mere usurpation becomes to him either a guarantee of his own strength, or of that of his dynasties. In this sense of the word he assigns a 'guarantee' as the reason for the fall of a fresh throne. His intention in the choice of this word is to give (at least in sound) to the most unjust and grasping measures, the appearance of a right grounded on self-preservation or self-defence.

By a marriage with your Majesty's daughter, Napoleon found, in his sense, the guarantee which he formerly, in fact just before this new plan presented itself to him, intended to find in the overthrow of the Austrian throne.

In this idea of a guarantee consists the substantial alteration that has taken place in the position of your Majesty towards the French Emperor. This altered position was not foreseen by Russia ; and at the time of the marriage, a time so important for all Europe, Count Romanzow gave a fresh proof of the distorted view he takes of affairs. In the event in which your Majesty sought and found support, in the enormous sacrifice made to her country by the daughter and descendant of so many Emperors, who by this act will ever live in the memory of posterity, he saw materials of dissension between France and Austria originating in petty family and conjugal relations, having no foundation in Napoleon's own character—dissensions which, without perhaps giving occasion to an open feud, would nevertheless leave Russia for some time in a position to aggrandise herself at the expense of her neighbours, and to complete, unperceived, the work she had begun. From these facts I am convinced that the Austrian political alliance, without the family union with France, would not have withstood the unavoidable pressure till the year 1811, and that but for the family alliance, even if we had preserved our existence, we should have been on the brink of dissolution.

If it be undeniable that the family alliance with France removed your Majesty's possessions out of danger from Napoleon's first attacks, it was still easy to foresee that, in the event either of the very successful or very unsuccessful course of the Spanish war, the French Emperor would in the first case find materials for renewed activity, and in the latter compensation from new complications in an opposite direction.

My stay in Paris was prolonged under various pretexts by the Emperor, until the time when he could give a definite account of the immediate future. This time came at last, after the election of the Swedish Crown Prince, and after the English had shown signs of a vigorous resistance in Portugal.

Directly I arrived in Cilli, I took the liberty of laying before your Majesty two *Précis de Conversation* with the French Emperor.

The *first* of these, concerning the Swedish affairs, affords the best historical account of the course of Napoleon's policy in these affairs, and of many important events in the history of the present day (Nos. 173, 174).

The *second* contains, in a compressed form—possibly more compressed than it might have been under other circumstances—the outlines of the present state of affairs.*

Your Majesty will condescend to observe that the

* See the Conversation with Napoleon of September 20, 1810, vol. i, p. 138, and the remarks on it *note* 55, vol. i. p. 139.—ED.

following great, all-decisive questions lie open before us :—

I. Can Austria prevent the outbreak of a fresh Continental war ?

II. What must our political course be, and what position should Austria take on the outbreak of a war between France and Russia?

To the *first* question, from my innermost conviction, I give a decided No !

The *second* deserves the most mature, the deepest consideration. On the decision which your Majesty forms rests the possible future welfare, or the certain, perhaps the rapid, dissolution of the monarchy.

Far from imagining ourselves in a more favourable position than we are, I believe that we are on the point of a complete financial collapse, of a reduction of the army caused by this, of a thorough prostration of strength constraining us ; and that our whole external policy of the present moment must be limited to every possible avoidance of any catastrophe (and any fresh war would lead to one). I negotiated with this intention in Paris ; my reports during last summer, my behaviour to the Emperor Napoleon and the Russian Envoy in France, bear witness to this truth. Your Majesty condescended to authorise me in this opinion under all circumstances, giving to the St. Petersburg cabinet an undoubted proof that Austria, contrary to Russia's late political course, was free from any alliance with France ; in this sense, finally, we must move forward to the furthest limits of possibility.

I before stated the fact that Napoleon reached his final goal by isolation from Austria and Russia.

Does there not lie a means of deliverance in a fresh alliance with this Power ? Shall we not be liable to well-founded reproach if we do not offer a hand to Russia's much-desired alliance?

This question is certainly a most natural one, and offers, from a superficial point of view, many different aspects. For the observer who overlooks the whole, Napoleon's policy and his means of attack—the policy of the Russian cabinet and its means of defence; our own geographical, military, and financial position, certainly can leave no doubt to an observer from this point of view that Napoleon would not give up this isolation, with the wishes of the Powers, unless they were founded on actions arising out of the actual position of affairs.

If we receive as an apparent truth that our active policy must be directed to the gaining of time, and the delay of any outbreak of war, we cannot hide from ourselves that, though your Majesty's disinterested noble line of conduct may stave off in some measure the stream of destruction, it does not lie in our power entirely to keep it back.

In the present state of things, your Majesty can meet the war which Napoleon has determined to carry on against Russia in the first instance, only from the North, thus exposing Austria to the first attack, in the hope that Russia may recruit her strength within her territories. There is not the most remote prospect that we can successfully carry on this conflict. Napoleon offers us, as your Majesty would graciously observe in the second supplement, a fresh field for the deepest reflection. The position is new to us. We have to make a choice!

Napoleon puts three proposals before us: Austria united with Russia; Austria actually allied to France; the neutrality of Austria.

The *first* alternative appears impossible from my point of view. Your Majesty's active forces are crippled even before they enter the field; the enemy is in the capital of the kingdom; Galicia in a condition to place 70,000 men under arms in case of a reverse. And under these circumstances the so often dreamt of, but never accomplished, general arming of the people is not to be thought of. What help your Majesty might expect from Russia's co-operation may be learned from the history of the former war. If one were to take Prussia into account, past experience and the certain knowledge of the fixed determination of the King to ally himself with France as the only means of preservation, in case of an outbreak of war, would prevent any favourable conclusion.

Only two possibilities therefore remain: Austria actively allied with France; Austria's neutrality. Any alliance of Austrian forces with those of any other Power, whose exclusive design is the destruction of the present order of affairs, and whose plans are aimed at dominion, would be a war against holy immutable principles, and against Austria's direct interests. The peculiar characteristic of Austria's position is the moral height from which the most adverse circumstances ought not be able to displace her. Your Majesty is the central point, the only representative left of an old order of things founded on eternal unchangeable right. All eyes are fixed on your Highness, and in this character lies that for which nothing can compensate.

On the day when Austrian troops fight in the same ranks with French confederate troops in a war of destruction, your Majesty will have laid aside this character. In a moral sense we should lower ourselves to the baseness of the confederates, and in a political, to all the late faults of the Russian cabinet. To such a part we could only be compelled by the actual impossibility of doing otherwise.

Neutrality, in its strictest sense, according to Napoleon's very precise representation (in his conversation of September 20), offers certainly many dangers, without even one advantage. It is undeniable that there lies a danger for us in the too great weakening of the Russian power, and no lesser one in the possession of Galicia after the restoration of the kingdom of Poland. By a strict neutrality we avoid neither the one nor the other.

If once peace is concluded with Russia, and the result of the war declared against Russia, a strict neutrality could give us no claim to any respect on the side of France : we could expect only the strongest reproaches from the Russian cabinet.

The means of unravelling these very difficult questions, in any practical way, seems to me contained in one single idea, and that idea is Galicia.

If we would not deceive ourselves, there remains nothing left but to take this subject into our earnest consideration (without any prepossession either for or against it), and that of the Emperor Napoleon's arranged object of compensation—Illyria.

Napoleon has initiated us into his plan of operations against Russia. He first pronounced to us the word Poland, and in this word lies my firmest conviction of the palladium of the future French war against Russia.

Many somewhat cool observers, whose insight into the peculiar condition of affairs in Europe is rather limited, believe that the beginning of a war against Russia must, in the popular feeling at the present time, be the signal of a general disturbance—also the fore-runner of Russian victory.

Napoleon—as little acquainted with the feeling of the people as we are—would not undertake a new war if he must carry it on with his own resources alone.

But, faithful to his long-tried policy, he appears in this war at the head of eighty or a hundred thousand Frenchmen at most, and occupies the countries between the Rhine and the Oder with his other troops; whilst 200,000 confederates and Poles, united to the 80,000 of his own men, spread the fire of insurrection to the furthest point of the old frontiers of Poland. The last and all preceding campaigns show that an Italian insurrection is not to be expected without the help of a foreign Power—and that help cannot come from Austria. The 300,000 Frenchmen whom he has left in these countries will more than suffice to hold Germany and Italy in check, and stifle every popular movement in its birth, or prevent the possibility of its becoming troublesome.

How the possession of Galicia will be maintained, during and after the revival of the kingdom of Poland from its ashes, may be easily imagined from the most superficial observation of the temper of this nation; and I do not think that I am venturing too far when I limit the real question to this : ' Shall we lose Galicia without any compensation, or shall we surrender it for a due equivalent?'

There can be no doubt that it would be most difficult to find an equivalent for Galicia. The whole province of Illyria, the ceded portion of Carynthia, as well as Krain, Croatia, the Hungarian Littorale, and Dalmatia, offer an adequate compensation neither in population nor in revenue.

In political and commercial respects they are undoubtedly to be preferred.

Politically, because by means of the possession of Illyria we approach once more the natural line of our political relations. The advantages of a frontier adjoining Italy and Tyrol, and direct intercourse with the lands given to us, stand in no comparison with the frontier towards Russia.

We have latterly been forced out of the European political system : now we shall again enter it in the same degree.

As regards our commercial interests, the entire northern and eastern coasts of the Adriatic Sea decidedly offer advantages which Galicia does not possess.

Yet I should not venture, on the strength of these advantages alone, at a time of such general revolutionary changes, to contemplate alteration in the territorial condition of Austria, were not the danger imminent that at the close of the Russian war we may lose Galicia, the object of our present deliberations, without obtaining anything whatever in exchange.

I put aside all considerations of the advantages or disadvantages to Austria if the re-establishment of the kingdom of Poland presents itself as a huge and powerful body by the mere word of Napoleon. He does not need any co-operation from us to secure the success of his undertaking.

If we had, in this time of France's weakness, merely to speak a submissive word in this entirely Russian or Austro-Russian question, and to make no important sacrifice in order to the restoration of Poland, I should really find advantages for us in the re-establishment of this ancient kingdom.

I allow myself to make this reflection *en passant*, as

I am very far from confounding what is unavoidable with any considerations of what is beneficial or disadvantageous.

A remark naturally arises from the juxtaposition of the proposals for territorial exchanges, made to me in Paris by the orders of Napoleon, with the plans always attributed to that sovereign. The impartial observer is justified in enquiring, ' How can Napoleon wish Austria to approach Italy again, and be disposed to sacrifice his direct communication with the Porte?'

This point of view offers most assuredly a subject for the most careful investigation. It may be disposed of, however, by a consideration of the usual political course of this monarch. He is always accustomed to sacrifice the smaller to the greater; and there can be no doubt that the restoration of Poland will necessarily be his first important object on the day when the war with Russia is brought to a close.

But, even granting this, there is the strongest cause in the affairs, the strongest possible ground for the most cautious conduct on our part, and for the avoidance of any precipitate development of our plans.

After this examination of the present position of affairs founded on existing facts, which I have now placed before your Majesty, I venture, most gracious sovereign, at this moment of critical importance to the state of Austria and the Imperial House, to offer you respectfully the following sketch of our political course. My humble opinion as to the line we ought to take is the following :—

(1) Your Majesty to contribute towards the maintenance of peace between France and Russia what is always only attainable by means of diplomacy. I consider as the means of negotiation :—

(*a*) A policy towards France excluding any idea of the extension of the present limits of the monarchy.

(*b*) The maintenance of the present demeanour towards Russia, endeavouring to remove all unfounded fears as to our political relations with France, and every vain hope of a practical union with Russia.

(2) Should war, notwithstanding your Majesty's efforts, still prove unavoidable; if we are fortunate enough to reach the moment of the outbreak without special pressure on the part of France, your Majesty might then seize the first opportune moment to enter into negotiations for the cession of a portion of Galicia, to be decided on with due regard to military and financial considerations, in return for adequate compensation elsewhere.

(3) If Napoleon proposes as compensation the whole of the existing province of Illyria, the following points seem to me desirable :—

(*a*) Illyria, including Dalmatia, the Quarnero Islands, and Venetian Istria as far as the Isonzo frontier ;

(*b*) Upper Austria, at least the ceded portion of the Hausruck district, and if possible the former Inn frontier ;

(*c*) A portion of Silesia ; this compensation, however, only to be conditional, and in the event of the dismemberment of Prussia—to my mind a certain result of the impending war.

(4) A quiet unobtrusive preparation for securing these different objects, by which alone it will be possible to secure an adequate consideration of our claims to compensation. Should your Majesty approve my proposal as to the basis of our present political requirements, I shall be prepared to submit to your Majesty

the working out of the different subjects arising there-from in a separate report.

METTERNICH.

Resolution.

After a consideration of the clear exposition of our present position contained in the above report, I have to lay down the following principles as the basis of our political system :—The utmost possible care to avoid and to prevent all political complications as far as this can be done without damage to ourselves ; and in case of political complications proving unavoidable, the observance of a strict neutrality and the attainment of the greatest possible advantage therefrom, so far as can be accomplished without any violence to the principles of justice and honesty. Should it be necessary, for the avoiding of a greater evil, to consent to the exchange of Galicia, the greatest care must be taken that such an exchange be carried out at least without detriment to my monarchy, on which account you will be careful (in a manner not to attract notice) to inform yourself of the nature of that province, as well as of those which would be suitable for us in exchange, and to furnish me with a detailed report, which shall embody all that is to be suggested and prepared in accordance with the principles which I have now laid down, and which you will put before me for my examination and sanction.

FRANCIS.

Vienna, January 17, 1811.

THE PERIOD BEFORE AND AFTER THE RUSSIAN CAMPAIGN.

1811—1812.

1811.

RESPECTING THE POSITION AND BEHAVIOUR OF AUSTRIA IN THE IMPENDING WAR OF FRANCE AGAINST RUSSIA.

(Note 61, Vol. I.)

178. Metternich to the Emperor Francis (Report), Vienna, March 26, 1811.

179. Metternich to the Emperor Francis (Report), Vienna, April 25, 1811.

180. Metternich to the Emperor Francis (Report), Vienna, November 28, 1811.

181. Metternich to the Emperor Francis (Report), Vienna, January 15, 1811.

182. Schwarzenberg's Audience with Napoleon, December 17, 1811.

178. Everything seems to indicate that the Emperor Napoleon is at present still far from desiring a war with Russia. But it is not less true that the Emperor Alexander has given himself over, *nolens volens*, to the war party ; and that he will bring about war, because the time is approaching when he will no longer be able to resist the reaction of the party in the internal affairs of his empire, or the temper of his army. The contest between Count Romanzow and the party opposed to that minister seems on the point of precipitating a war between Russia and France.

I can scarcely longer hope that the outbreak of this war is to be avoided, if this result could be attained only through concessions on the part of Napoleon, of which we have as yet had no example; and I have every reason to suppose that the Russian cabinet would take every concession from France as evidence that the present, or a very early, period would be most favourable for Russia to assume the offensive.

The policy of France towards us is evident. We are to lead the way and to quarrel with Russia under cover of Turkish affairs. That France should reserve herself in order to support one or the other at a suitable time seems to me not probable. In the present state of affairs, Napoleon's views can only extend to a pretence for going to war with Russia, by an operation undertaken apparently in our behalf.

Russia attempted long ago to engage us to take an active part on her side. This attempt failed, and it appears from its later declarations that the Russian cabinet is at present bent on securing an absolute neutrality. The possibility of French proposals for an exchange of territory in respect to Galicia has naturally attracted its attention. To become acquainted with this secret, and to give the means of doing so, the appearance of a plan promising the aggrandisement of Austria, is evidently the object with which the Emperor Alexander wrote his last autograph letter to your Majesty. It appeared to me necessary that, to answer these designs of Russia, sometimes apparent, sometimes concealed, a verbal declaration should be made to Count Stackelberg, and instructions of a similar nature to Count St.-Julien : namely—

1. That your Majesty is ready to exert yourself to the utmost for the maintenance of peace.

2. That in the event of war actually breaking out, your Majesty would assume a neutral and independent position as far as may be consistent with the manifold interests arising from the geographical situations of your Majesty's dominions.

3. That, as Russia itself must see, any active co-operation on our part in her favour is quite impossible at a time when friendly relations subsist between your Majesty and the French Government, there being no grounds for any complaint against that Power, at a time moreover which requires the exertion of all the power of the government to avert serious internal difficulties.

I cannot conceal from your Majesty that the above explanations may prove far from satisfactory to the Russian Government; and if we consider the well-known overbearing temper of that court, it is by no means impossible that we may be exposed to difficulties of a peculiar kind.

Count Stackelberg was with me yesterday, and showed me a letter entirely in the Emperor Alexander's own handwriting, from which he read me the following passage :—'You will correspond with me directly, and will address your letters and send the couriers on important occasions to M. de Kascheleff, who enjoys my entire confidence. The Chancellor will know nothing of their contents.'

He added verbally that the Emperor would before now have dismissed the Chancellor, but that such a step would have been equivalent to a declaration of war against France. In the course of our conversation I remarked several expressions which gave me the im-

pression that, at some time, and under certain circumstances, the occupation of Galicia might take place in
expectation of our consent.   The eccentric tendencies
of the Russian court, only too well known to us, of
which the conduct shown towards Prussia in the campaign of 1805 affords a notable example, justifies us,
it must be admitted, in regarding such an *apparent impossibility* as *possible*.

I feel compelled, therefore, to request authority from
your Majesty to take a suitable opportunity, in the
course of friendly conversation, of giving Count Stackelberg to understand, in an unmistakeable manner, that
every violation of the frontier of your Majesty's
dominions would be regarded as a declaration of
war.

I might also take the opportunity of making some
representations respecting the concentration of Russian
troops on the frontier of Galicia and of Bukowina.   It
would be easy to convince Count Stackelberg that such
accumulations of troops must necessarily lead in time to
movements of our army, and that Russia might thus be
bringing about a state of things which would be at the
same time opposed to the mutual wishes and interests
of both countries.   I shall be in a position to judge
from the nature of the answers which M. de Stackelberg may make to these representations, whether any
and what measures may be necessary on our part; but
this point is so intimately connected with questions of
our general policy, that I must reserve the discussion of
it for a later despatch.   METTERNICH.

I have already given my sanction to your proposals,
and authorised you to act accordingly.
                                             FRANCIS.

Metternich to the Emperor Francis, Vienna,
April 25, 1811.

179. The despatches of Prince Schwarzenberg afford us a very distinct view of the real objects of the Emperor of the French as to the immediate future. It were greatly to be wished that this future itself became more clear ; but at the present crisis the question of peace or war depends so greatly on the mind of Russia that it is impossible, before the arrival of the next courier from St. Petersburg, to pronounce with any certainty as to the probability of war breaking out or of this danger being averted.

In the meantime, as the Emperor Napoleon has himself lifted the veil, we may without danger either to the general advantage, or to our own interests, continue to maintain that attitude of absolute neutrality which we have hitherto observed. It would be most desirable in your distinct instructions to your Majesty's ambassador at Paris to observe the greatest caution, not only as to his conduct, but as to the language he may hold to the Emperor. . . .

In my report to your Majesty of January 17 (No. 177), I have already spoken of the case which has now arisen ; the language of Napoleon to Prince Schwarzenberg was much the same as he addressed to me last September, with, however, one very important exception, that he then proposed only a conditional neutrality : he now appears to desire our active co-operation. The principal motive urged by him for the policy to be followed by us was then, as now, the insecurity of our possession of Galicia after the re-establishment of the kingdom of Poland ; but in his conversation with your Majesty's ambassador, the Emperor added also new and important considerations to the arguments he had formerly used with me. He represented the possibility that in the course of the internal war insurrections might break out even in our portion of Galicia, which in the interests of his allies, the Poles, he might feel himself obliged to support, and we might thus ourselves be involved in war with him.

I have already, in my report of January 17, expressed so fully my humble opinion on the question of the exchange of Galicia that it is unnecessary at present to do more than refer to it very briefly. As Napoleon has himself taken the initiative in the matter, our position is now materially improved, and we must make the most of this advantage. The maintenance of absolute reserve respecting the part which we shall finally take in the event of a Franco-Russian war, affords us a great advantage in our negotiations. We may very properly, however, look more closely into two equally important questions arising out of the present state of affairs :—

1. What does Napoleon understand by an equivalent for Galicia ?

2. What would be the position of Austria, if the war should end to the advantage of France ?

We most assuredly have an absolute right to an equivalent for Galicia, if we remain neutral.

In case of our active co-operation with France, we have a claim to new acquisitions of territory. This might be deduced from two considerations, the increase of the power of France and her confederates : and the right to be indemnified for our own efforts.

I have therefore, no hesitation in recommending that Prince Schwarzenberg be instructed :—

1. To represent again to the Emperor your Majesty's

unqualified desire for the maintenance of peace. The expression of this desire would be the more emphatic were the assurance at the same time given that your Majesty would be prepared to make similar representations at St. Petersburg.

2. To raise distinctly the following questions :—

(*a*) What is the equivalent in territory, population, and revenue which the French Emperor proffers to us for Galicia?

(*b*) What indemnity does his Majesty propose to assign to his confederates? In what direction are we to receive ours?

(*c*) What are his Majesty's plans, and how far would they extend, in a war with Russia? Are they confined to the re-establishment of the kingdom of Poland?

By this course we shall obtain more precise information whether Napoleon really wishes for war or whether it would in effect not fall in with his plans.

We evade the pressing question as to the part we propose to take in the war, and endeavour to postpone the answer to a time when more light may be thrown on the probable course of the campaign.

It is my full conviction that this is the line of conduct which we can observe consistently with our interests. The Emperor Napoleon himself has not yet expressed any desire for a formal treaty. He has merely mentioned the subject in a confidential way to Prince Schwarzenberg; and our communications in their turn must be made in a similar manner.

Should your Majesty vouchsafe to approve this outline of the instructions to be addressed to the ambassador, I would venture to submit that a statement should be appended, showing the present territorial position of Galicia

METTERNICH.

I approve your suggestions ; and desire that everything possible is to be attempted for the preservation of peace.

FRANCIS.

Metternich to the Emperor Francis, Vienna, November 28, 1811.

180. The time has come which Napoleon has long calculated on, in which the final struggle of the old order of things against his revolutionary plans is unavoidable.   Whether he gains or loses in the struggle, the whole position of affairs in Europe is altered.   Russia, also, has brought on this fearful crisis in the most unpardonable manner.

The dangers which threaten Austria in this position proceed from taking too superficial a view of the objects and plans of France and Russia—Powers equally to be feared by all others, whether they are allies or enemies. To place these dangers in the clearest light, it is only necessary to remark that France, without taking any account of Austria, has completely destroyed the old order of things, and that Russia, apparently, even in restoring this order, believes that she can do without Austria.

Before I pursue an inquiry into the future course which it may be necessary for us to follow, as the only possible means of preserving our existence, I beg respectfully to lay before your Majesty a short summary of the present state of the relations between the European Powers.

France is preparing herself for a gigantic struggle in the North, without being hindered in her energetic measures by the continuance of the war in the Spanish Peninsula.

The force which the French Emperor can unite under his command is more than sufficient to support his undertaking properly. His own army will at the end of the year on the Elbe, the Oder, and the Vistula, number at least 120,000 to 140,000 men; the Saxon-Warsaw, at least 50,000 to 60,000. He might besides, from the confederates, place 25,000 to 30,000 men in the field. He can, therefore, open the campaign with 200,000 or 230,000 men, a number which is more than sufficient, as from the distant boundary of the Baltic to Wallachia certainly not more than an equal number could be raised by Russia.

Prussia finds herself in the hopeless position in which any aggressive course of action could only lead to a too probable dissolution.

Your Majesty has been made fully acquainted with the present indecision of the Berlin court by the treaties with the ambassador Baron von Jacobi, and Count Zichy's last despatches. In the unhappy situation of having only a choice between two equally great evils, two opposite parties, each in their own direction, are struggling against each other to overcome the characteristic irresolution of the King.

Baron von Hardenberg is certainly inclined to a new coalition. He joins those men who believe that they see in the signature of a treaty of alliance with France the loss of the King's independence; but yet he has a leaning to the opposite party, who in a declaration for Russia see the certain dissolution of the state. From this doubtful position Prussia desires to be raised by a union with Austria, and there can be no doubt that Prussia would not attack the party which unites its interests completely with ours. How difficult the part of Austria now is will be shown by what follows in this humble despatch. If the Berlin court should—which is still possible—join with France, the French arms would receive an increase of not less than 20,000 men. Prussia, on the contrary, could place in the balance in the favour of Russia upwards of 100,000 men ; for on her union with that Power all those forces would be set free which are now occupied in Prussia and the Silesian fortresses.

Denmark in the next war stands quite on the level of the German confederate states. France certainly cannot expect military help from this Power, neither can she fear a demonstration in favour of Russia.

Sweden appears provisionally to have taken a neutral part. To this part she is incited by her almost complete isolation, at the same time tempted by possible conquests in Russia and Denmark. It would be difficult to determine what course her Government might take at the moment of the breaking out of the approaching war, whether she would remain true to the system of neutrality, or whether, in case of an issue of the war unfortunate for Russia, she would cast her eye on Finland : if unfortunate for France, on Norway. In either view, Sweden stands quite out of the line of our calculations.

The Porte is still at war with Russia, and will probably not end it unless the conditions are made tolerable for her. That the peace is not yet signed shows that the negotiations were not begun in great distress ; each hour that the conclusion is delayed is, in regard of the Turkish Government, gained. The approaching outbreak of the Franco-Russian war only affords to the firm mind of the Sultan a means for delay. Will Russia proceed from strongly-asserted pretensions to important conquests ? This question I find myself little able to answer decidedly, as the course of Russia's policy towards the Porte is inexplicable.

Russia has given in these last few years every proof of a quite peculiar policy. This very policy—which in the beginning of the eighteenth century, guided by a great ruler, raised her from a scarcely recognised Asiatic Power to one of the most imposing European Powers, which, under the government of some great women, strengthened this new position—might probably, under the feeble rule of Alexander I., drive Russia back again to the steppes of Asia.

No Power has had a sadder experience of these political principles than Austria. I might almost think that only one other yet remains to us—the experience of the game by which Russia threatens the ruin of her European relations, and in case of a French or Russian victory, the measure of our unhappy position is ready to be filled up. Since Peter the Great the eyes of the Russian cabinet were only directed to the western frontier of the huge empire; all Russia's conquests since that epoch were made at the expense of Austria's friends or allies. Russian influence supported Prussia's ambition when it threatened us with danger, and this state dissipated under Russian co-operation what might have been useful to us. Russia destroyed Poland, and with this kingdom all idea of true European policy, and established in its stead a system of destruction and robbery which found only too faithful an imitator. But for your Majesty's perseverance in an opposite policy the Porte would long since have fallen a victim to Russian attacks. The former German Empire was overthrown in the year 1803 by direct Russian intervention, through intentional breach of the Imperial word, and uprooting of all the foundations of a thousand years' Constitution.

These, out of a crowd of obvious facts, are in the most unfortunate harmony with the political attitude of the Russian cabinet in its direct relations with Austria. Who could count the endless mistakes, often quite unavoidable, which were caused by the one-sided, unaccountable, vacillating, and always arbitrary conduct of this Power in the wars of the last twenty years? These reflections are of the greatest importance in a moment when Russia, for the first time, is left to herself, and begins to prepare alone for the great struggle in which, formerly, she had looked on Austria and Prussia as protectors of her own states. If, after the active co-operation of Alexander I. in all Napoleon's plans since 1807, this monarch only cherished the idea of destroying the edifice he had so richly endowed; if we see that terrible Russia, who twice already had abandoned her allies to their fate when she saw her own frontier threatened, now ready to take up arms within these boundaries; how necessary is the inquiry whether well-calculated resources and the consciousness of her own strength, or mere self-conceit and dangerous self-deception, lie at the bottom of this conduct. That it is not principle which now actuates the Russian cabinet is shown in the most unmistakeable manner by her conduct in the years 1800, 1803, and since 1807. That the unnatural alliance between France and Russia must change to an open feud was to be foreseen at the time of its conclusion.

Already in September, 1810, the French Emperor was occupied with the design of a breach between the allied Powers. I declared on my return from Paris that war would break out in the North at the beginning of the year 1812. My anticipations in this matter have been fulfilled. Judging from former experience

I never reckoned on any steadfast political system in Russia. The steps of the Russian cabinet and their incoherence have even outstripped my expectations, and given the most undoubted proofs that the Emperor Alexander, on the present occasion, as in former times, follows the impulse of a party, without taking into consideration the dangers of an undertaking which even to a superficial observer appear enormous. Remaining true to your Highness's fixed principles, I have endeavoured to direct my attention to the removal of complications. Already at the beginning of the present year I even maintained that it lay in our power to postpone, if not to prevent, a fresh Continental war. We have now reached the utmost limit of this delay, and the choice no longer remains of taking an aggressive part in this unavoidable war.

I could also appeal to my former report of January 17 (No. 177), if there were not new and weighty reasons which were not then taken into account—reasons the least of which touches the existence or non-existence of the Austrian confederation. That the year 1812 will lead to greater disturbances than any of the former ones must be apparent to the most superficial observer. The proclamation of a kingdom of Poland is Napoleon's next step. Russia appears not to wish to take the aggressive part. Napoleon will the more certainly open the campaign at the most favourable opportunity for himself. If his arms are successful, all Russian Poland is gone, and the loss of this very considerable territory, Russia's only European possession, will be unavoidable. With it also disappears the Prussian power. At the probable approaching outbreak of war we stand surrounded by enemies, in the midst of this horrible federation which leaves us no peaceful frontier except that of Turkey. If Russia is victorious, if she gains one or two fortunate campaigns, the designs of this pertinacious war will not be lessened. Napoleon once said to me : ' The Powers never calculate sufficiently, at the beginning of a war, that a man in my position can conclude no peace if he is beaten and cannot revenge himself.' These words are only too true, and are the more so in a war with Russia, whose preponderance by victory would increase to such enormous proportions that France under her present, or any other ruler, would be compelled to oppose it.

At this moment of the probable outbreak of war we find ourselves in the position which at the beginning of the present year I expected, though not so soon.

But the year 1812 was destined to place us in financial difficulties ; plans of every kind were proposed for arranging these important matters. We have reached the last month of the year, and stand close to an abyss whose depth can hardly be measured. I carefully remove from this humble despatch everything which has reference to present or future measures of the home government ; but unfortunately in these inner relations lies now the greatest danger for our political situation.

Your Majesty convinced yourself, even at the beginning of 1811, that the choice for us lay only between two courses, either that of the strictest neutrality or of an agreement with France during the Russian war. The political conduct we have maintained during the year still leaves the choice open to us. What advantage either one or the other course affords may be learned from a few concise words of Napoleon in his conversation with me on September 20, 1810.*

* See Autobiographical Memoir, p. 136, vol. i.—ED.

'It will be necessary at this epoch (that of the war between Russia and France) either to ally yourself with France, to keep a good position with Russia, or to remain entirely neutral. The last course will lead you to nothing ; it will be the means of recovering nothing, and if you preserve a simulated neutrality, in order at the end of the contest to range yourself on the strongest side, this will be so little to your taste that you will gain little profit from such a course.'

In my despatch of January 17 (No. 177) I proposed the following questions :—

1. On the impossibility, in the coming war, of appearing as Russia's allies.

2. On the desire to go to the help of France only in extreme necessity.

3. On the desire to maintain a modified neutrality, which in a time of great pressure, such as always precedes a war, may leave the possibility of opening negotiations for the exchange of Galicia, so as to ensure the monarchy from the risk of a subsequent loss of such an important province without any compensation.

Your Majesty has deigned to grant your royal decree in the sense of my report. Nothing remains to me, then, at the moment when Prince Schwarzenberg must be provided with more definite instructions, but to seek your Majesty's pleasure with respect to them.

To relieve your Majesty in this very difficult question (if relief is possible in a matter which may result in the entire overthrow of the monarchy), I take upon myself to explain the said instructions to Prince Schwarzenberg.

1. Our internal relations are not only in a perplexed condition, but in the most critical of all positions.

The great financial reform concluded in January

1811 has gone forth without receiving its full execution.
One-half of the monarchy still opposes the system itself.
Our coffers are empty ; the present Hungarian Landtag
is not to be depended on for any material help in the
future ; at the most we may receive a subsidy from it,
which we must endeavour to make as large as possible ;
but even to attain this end it will be necessary for the
Government to make the most anxious efforts.

The adoption of no political party in the impending
war must, according to my firm conviction, lead to
the sure and unavoidable ruin of the monarchy. Your
Majesty would in that case be greatly compromised
without the possibility of corresponding benefits. The
insurrection in Galicia so probable in case of French
successes ; the very possible movements, encouraged
perhaps by Napoleon himself, in Illyria and the provinces on the frontier still belonging to your Majesty,
will serve him as an excuse to use the first moment of
peace with Russia for the destruction of the Austrian
states, deprived of all means of self-defence.

If, however, your Majesty can take a part, whether
it be that of neutrality or that of active co-operation,
we shall need a mobile army corps of at least forty to
fifty thousand men, and, to all appearance, a reserve,
also mobilised, of at least an equal number.

I do not conceal from myself the difficulties of carrying out this scheme ; but when it is a question of the
existence of the state, means for carrying it out must
be found.

2. The present position of Russia is in every respect
dangerous for our interests. If the arming of these
states leads to a closer union with France, Prussia will
make great claims for compensation, and will gain a
great advantage over us ; her activity, indeed, destroys

the only excuse for the passive attitude which, in the present reduced state of our finances, we might have wished to maintain, since the resources of Prussia are beyond comparison smaller than ours, and that Government already shows what energy may do in the production of military resources in situations to all appearance desperate. If France nourishes views dangerous to Prussia, and the Tugendbund forces the King into the arms of Russia (and the former seems to me as probable as the action of the allies in the latter sense is certain), these states will be overrun by the French army. The conqueror will then hold the fate of Prussia in the balance, and the fragments will probably fall into the hands of the allies.

In my last reports I took Prussia to be an ally of France in a general way without any especial manifestation of strength on her side. How essentially this differs from the true point of view I need not point out. This touches on one of the most important questions, on that of the possible dissolution of the union of the whole Russian states ; it threatens to place Silesia in the hands of a Power quite foreign to our interests, although this province not only lies conveniently for us, but in case of the re-establishment of the kingdom of Poland is indispensably necessary—thus robbing us of the possibility of any compensation for the loss of Galicia.

I. If your Majesty desires to maintain a strong neutrality it will be necessary—

1. To draw a *cordon* along the frontier of Silesia as far as Bukowina. Whether Prussia throws herself into the arms of France, or whether it is overrun with French hostile troops, this cordon along the Silesian frontier will be equally necessary.

2. To establish a corps which shall dominate Galicia

as well as support the *cordon* at any place threatened by
a hostile Power.

3. To establish a corps in the Illyrian provinces,
which appears to me of the greatest importance as a
measure of police. Further, it is necessary that—

4. Your Majesty should declare to both the hostile
Powers that any infringement of territory will be
considered as a declaration of war. This declaration
without an available army is illusive, and a neutrality
without such a declaration is a nonentity. Lastly,

5. Your Majesty finds yourself in a position with
regard to France when nothing can be gained from this
Power, from the next war, beyond the improvement of
the present position ; and

II. In case of an active part being taken, Prince
Schwarzenberg must be ordered—

1. To make known to the French Emperor your
Majesty's decision to mobilise a *corps d'armée*, if

(*a*) Napoleon informs your Majesty that in case of
a conclusion to the war favourable to France, Austria
shall receive some real advantage, not merely compensation for the costs of war, but the improvement of her
position commercially and geographically ; if

(*b*) The French Emperor reveals views on Silesia,
the Illyrian provinces, and the Inn, including Salzburg.

2. In this case your Majesty would pledge yourself on
the re-establishment of the kingdom of Poland to add
to that kingdom a certain portion of Galicia as agreed
upon.

3. It must be expressly arranged that during the
course of the war there is to be no question of any
change in Galicia.

4. The army corps must be entirely under Austrian

generals, and only to act with France in general operations.

5. No marching of foreign troops will be allowed through your Majesty's states.

When your Majesty deigns to decide for one or other of these parts, then only can Prince Schwarzenberg usefully, and without risk of involving the highest interests, begin his journey.

Both courses require earnest thought in many respects. One of the most important considerations against the neutrality lies in the impossibility of avoiding complications in Galicia and Illyria—unavoidable complications, which Napoleon has foreseen long ago, as when he once said to Prince Schwarzenberg: 'If Austria is neutral, I should not revolutionise Galicia; but if that were done by my allies the Poles, I could not hinder it, and then we should certainly quarrel over it.' Neutrality would surely be the preferable part in case of a conclusion of the war unfavourable to France; but an active part will alone give us a chance of existence in case of a French victory.

Your Majesty's choice should therefore rest on the greater or less probability of the results of the future war. Calculating the probabilities beforehand, from former experience, everything points to a French victory. In respect to the costs and other burdens, I feel convinced that a strict neutrality offers as many difficulties as active co-operation.

If I nevertheless urge on your Majesty to come to a distinct and definite resolution, in urging this resolution I do not exclude an extremely cautious course of negotiation, constantly keeping in view that the initiative should be left to the Emperor Napoleon; I consider, on the contrary, caution so much the more needful as every unnecessary compromise is to be avoided, and in duty bound I must direct your Majesty's attention to the possibility that the French Emperor, convinced of your weakness, might under some specious pretext entirely withdraw from the negotiation.

This position, the most serious of all for us, seems, from the last news from Prince Schwarzenberg, to be only too probable. To bring this supposition to certainty must be the first care of your Majesty's ambassador, and in so doing he can only avoid a course most dangerous to himself and the state if he is thoroughly instructed as to the part decided on by your Majesty. I shall only then be in a position to make out the necessary instructions with the fullest details. In case the French Emperor should, however, act in opposition to the above hypothesis—which the next news from the ambassador must set forth—I will give to the same my most respectful attention.

METTERNICH.

I find the latter of the two alternatives the more suitable, with the addition that the greatest possible exertions must be made in carrying out the plan—to remove the burdens, as well in respect to active participation in the war as financially, as far as possible from my kingdom. With this design, I have accepted the above instructions for my ambassador, Prince Schwarzenberg.

FRANCIS.

Metternich to the Emperor Francis, Vienna, Jan. 15, 1812.

181. I have received from Prince Schwarzenberg an account, dated December 17, of the result of the audience granted him by the French Emperor.

For your Majesty's convenience I have drawn up a

sketch, giving the principal points in Prince Schwarzenberg's last despatches (No. 182), which contain :

I. Napoleon's political ideas with regard to Austria, and

II. His views on Austrian co-operation.

Ad I.—*Political Point of View.*

Prince Schwarzenberg's report explains that Napoleon, as usual, avoids expressing himself decidedly till we show more exactly the line on which we have decided. The most essential points which he touched on were,

(*a*) The guarantee or the exchange of Galicia at our discretion.

(*b*) Illyria as the object of compensation.

(*c*) His reference to the Turkish principalities and to a new frontier towards Germany as objects of acquisition.

I surely do not need again to submit to your Majesty my humble opinion upon the infeasibility of our ever being able to regard an acquisition assigned to the Porte as a compensation for the costs of war. If our political system should be favourable to the preservation of the Ottoman Empire, what we might attain by a burdensome war would not be looked upon by us as compensation for our efforts; the case is, however, different if meantime peace should be concluded between Russia and the Porte. Every concession which the latter Power might have been brought to make can only then turn to our advantage, and might afterwards be applied to make terms with the Porte if the new provinces should not lie conveniently for ourselves. The guarantee of the possession of Galicia appears to be at the present moment the best course to take, the rather as it would secure to this important province the continuance of internal peace at a time when this peace might be only too easily endangered. In the present aspect of things I assume Galicia neither as a whole nor in part to be suitable for compensation. And should the peace make desirable a frontier different from the present, supported by military advantages, many objects might be found to be taken as compensation from the Russian portion of Poland.

I regard the Illyrian provinces as the greatest and principal object of acquisition. It would be extremely desirable to assure ourselves of these, and still more so if the surrender of these lands, or at least of some parts of them, could be made at the very commencement of the campaign. How incalculably this would act upon the general feeling is so little to be mistaken that, in case your Majesty vouchsafed to approve of the present outlines of the instructions to be given to Prince Schwarzenberg, I would introduce this into it as one of the most essential points.

The question as to the frontier towards Bavaria might in any case be postponed to the time of the peace as well as that which concerns Silesia. I must, however, wish that an attempt should be made to maintain, if not the former frontier of the Inn, at least another differing from the present, and one which should secure better military and administrative advantages.

Ad II.—Austrian Co-operation.

To point out the peculiar character of the present war, I need only take the point of view set forth in my report submitted to your Majesty on November 28 last.

Your Majesty is carrying on neither a war of defence

against immediate attack, nor a war of conquest. Both these would require efforts which, in the present position of our finances, would be exorbitant. Participation in this war is a natural consequence of the position of affairs, and the internal and external circumstances of the monarchy : of the internal, because it is not possible to continue without a very great change in the states forming the greater half of your Majesty's kingdom, and this change is not possible without a war ; of the external, because among the consequences of the present war must be included the not improbable chance of annihilation by a foreign Power to which we shall abandon Austria, unless, by a vigorous interference in the affairs of Europe, we do our best to secure a better future. This war I can best describe as a war of self-preservation.

According to my humble judgment, the assistance which Austria can give must consist of a body of twenty-five to thirty thousand men, which should operate as the outer right wing of the French army, but quite independent of the other principal movements, which will be led by the French Emperor alone.

This corps should consist of the Hungarian and Galician regiments already existing in Galicia.

At the same time with this corps, which must be prepared as quietly as possible for war, all the German regiments not required for garrison service should be removed to Hungary, where they should remain till the time when they are required as a reserve corps of observation against Servia.

If your Majesty decides on these measures, it will be no less necessary in the impending negotiations to draw the attention of the French Emperor to certain points arising from our position. Among these I include—

1. The considerations proceeding from the still un-concluded Hungarian Landtag.

2. Those arising from the geographical position of Austria in connection with the destitute circumstances in which we find ourselves.

The necessary reservations in both these respects would be :

(a) The preservation of secrecy as far as possible for the present in everything showing a participation in the war.

(b) The right ourselves to arrange the day when we shall step forth and declare ourselves.

This last reservation is all the more necessary as the alliance between France and Prussia, if not yet con-cluded, is probable, and also it cannot yet be known whether peace may not be concluded on the Danube before the outbreak of the war ; and any of these cir-cumstances might necessitate different military arrange-ments. To contract these arrangements as much as possible is necessary from our internal position, and the question being mooted in Paris has the advantage of gaining us time, in which we may perhaps be able to discover the consequences which will follow the first operations of the French army.

The Emperor Napoleon wishes the command of the Austrian corps to be entrusted to Archduke Karl.

If the reasons against the appointment of his Impe-rial Highness seem to your Majesty insurmountable, the command should be given to Prince Schwarzenberg himself, and the notification of the appointment made in Paris.

The financial and military considerations of the necessary preparations will be self-evident, and are the natural consequences of the conclusions which your Majesty will deign to draw from the present report.*

Schwarzenberg's Interview with Napoleon, Dec. 17, 1811.

182. Prince Schwarzenberg's report of the audience which the Emperor Napoleon granted him on December 17 last shows two very distinct feelings. The Emperor while seeming to be unreserved, remained cold and calm. His expressions were premeditated and measured so long as it was merely the question of what we should ask in case of a war with Russia and the intentions of Austria. Prince Schwarzenberg even observed that in the first part of the conversation several marks of distrust escaped Napoleon because our ambassador had not brought his full powers, and that he did not know by whom the Austrian army would be commanded. But everything changed the moment it was a question of the Archduke Charles. The conversation became remarkably animated, and Napoleon's language became frank and even friendly. He was really at his ease for some minutes, and the ambassador ends by saying that it was not possible to say how strongly the French Emperor desires that his wishes in this respect may be fulfilled, and that he believed all the advantages from the sacrifices made by our august master were intimately connected with this choice.

Napoleon began by declaring:

1. That he asked nothing better than to enter into an arrangement with Austria; that an Austrian army

---

* The tenor of the Imperial resolution (seemingly verbal) consequent on this report is given at the conclusion of the treaty with Napoleon of March 14, 1812. The treaty is a treaty published in Martens, i. 427; Neumann, ii. 358; De Clercq, ii. 369.—ED.

of observation not only would be of no use to him, but that it could only inconvenience him.

2. That he asks of us an army of forty to fifty thousand men, in which there would be six thousand horse, the greater part in light cavalry, and sixty pieces of artillery. He would charge himself with the subsistence of this army from the moment when the operations should commence.

3. This *corps d'armée* should form the right wing of the army commanded by the Emperor Napoleon. It would form a separate body, under the orders of an Austrian general enjoying his confidence, who, however, would only act under the direct instructions of Napoleon.

As to the consequences of the war:

1. The Emperor of the French considers Wallachia and Moldavia as well as Servia as Austrian provinces, the Danube as ours, of which we must have the mouth, whether or not the Turks cede the said provinces to Russia.

2. Austria can, if she will, keep Galicia entirely, and Napoleon charges himself in that case to guarantee it. Austria can change this province for an equivalent, wholly or in part, in order to have a good military frontier.

3. Illyria must sooner or later go back to Austria; the port of Trieste is necessary to her; they can, therefore, serve for matters of exchange.

4. Napoleon only spoke very vaguely of our frontier on the German side; he made no objection against the arrangement, but seemed to wish to make it depend on those which might arise from the war.

5. The slightest fault committed by Prussia would decide the question of Silesia; and as, if the war is suc-

cessful, matters of compensation will not be wanting, Napoleon will very willingly dispose of Silesia in our favour if Prussia keeps to the line decided on, since any province would be acceptable to her, while Silesia is the only one which is suitable for Austria.

Prince Schwarzenberg observed that these different objects presented some very problematical aspects, and that only on the most positive explanations with the Duke of Bassano, to whom the ambassador had been sent by Napoleon, could they be cleared up.

They press the arrangement with Austria to know how they stand with us. Napoleon remarked that in business certain forms and facts were necessary to come to any result, and that a multiplication of words leads to nothing.

He makes war with repugnance, and only in the hope that a very long time of tranquillity will result from it; but since he cannot avoid it, he should make it vigorously. The Emperor on this occasion enumerated the forces at his disposal, and mentioned the middle of April as the time when the war would commence. He protested against the nomination of Marshal Bellegarde, if it were intended to give him the command of our *corps d'armée*.

ON THE ORGANISATION OF AN IMPERIAL COUNCIL OF THE EMPIRE IN AUSTRIA.

(Note 59, Vol. I.)

183. I now pass on to the closer explanation of the fundamental differences between the organisation of the existing Councils of State * and the consideration of the needs of our state.

I think the chief tendency of the different institutions cannot be better explained than by the following remarks :—

a. The organisation of Prince Kaunitz's council was nothing more than a ministry, with several heads instead of one premier.

This State Council clogged the very wheels of government itself. It had assigned to it a very important sphere of action, of which the advising of the monarch on prepared agenda formed only a small portion.

Besides, great jealousy with regard to places explained the tendency towards a premiership from the concentration of the Council itself. It could at the most consist of but eight members. One minister carried on everything. Prince Kaunitz, however, was too intelligent not to feel the drawback of a prime ministry (an organisation only calculated on the weakness of the monarch and the strength of one minister), and hoped

---

* This alludes to—1st the organisation of Kaunitz, 1760; 2nd, the Napoleonic Senate; and 3rd, the Russian Imperial Council of Alexander. —ED.

to neutralise this drawback by the co-operation of several members. It happened as was inevitable. Several could not have the strength of one. The Council of 1760 could not make up for the want of a prime minister ; it could not even support itself. Reckoned for a small number of experienced men, the work came to a standstill as they died, and soon there was only a state minister and a state councillor, without any common action.

b. The Council of State better organised, as I think, is in many points suited for a constitutional government.

c. The Russian Council is, on the contrary, suited for a new country, and in many respects it resembles a high court of justice ; in others, a court of exchequer. Of all the three, the least applicable is certainly that of Prince Kaunitz. Everything, and especially the experience of several years, speaks against it. The present total decline of this council is the result of its first faults of organisation.

This decline did not arise from want of men. I will venture to say that the more excellent, the stronger the council was, the less likely was it to endure in the future. Without deliberation, without oral debates, no council is possible. Instead of unity, a mere circulation of writings took place, the written notes showing differences of opinion without number. What a strong position have the later voters, who comment not only on the subject itself, but also on the preceding votes ; how timidly must the earlier voters go to work. How often would they (as is the case in all oral deliberations) not have modified their ideas if they had known the remarks of subsequent voters. Lastly, and these are the most important considerations, how little would questions be defined, how little would the monarch be placed in a position to obtain a thoroughly considered, correct, and well-argued opinion. Shall the monarch accept the judgment of one of the ministers or of the whole court, or that of the first, second, or third voter? The subject has circulated, and yet everything is in uncertainty. The monarch will be compelled to examine it all himself, which is impossible—or to lay it before one of the councillors, or some confidant. What frightful power thus falls into the hands of one man, who, unknown, without responsibility, may throw out the well-considered work of the whole council, simply by his single opinion! And if this does not happen, and the monarch gives only a partial confidence, it is but a separate, useless vote, which only increases the uncertainty. And if the monarch devotes his life to the work, and endeavours to overlook the whole range of affairs, will he not soon be convinced that time and human strength are quite inadequate? The public animadverts on one or other of the individuals, from whom it soon spreads to the whole council.

I make no mention of the State Council organised in the year 1807. It was the work of intriguing subalterns in the different ministries, who, under the pretence of this new organisation, wished to get the executive power into their own hands.

In December, 1809, your Majesty dissolved the Council of State, and announced the formation of a new one. That announcement gives the ground for the new work, the object of which, according to my judgment, must be:

1. The monarch to summon a council.

2. By increasing the number, to form a general deliberative Council of State, to take the place of single councillors working by themselves.

3. To give the central power more central feeling, and lastly,

4. To lighten the monarch's labours by obtaining greater calm and security.

To these ends the organisation of the French Senate, modified and limited to suit the locality and the present situation, seems to me to be the most suitable. Its principles must be essentially as follows:

1. Your Majesty will convoke a *Reichsrath*. I incline to this appellation because it includes the whole states, without distinction between German and Hungarian provinces.

2. The monarch to preside over the Reichsrath, which can be assembled only at his behest. In case of his Majesty not being able to preside, one of the Ministers of State must be delegated to that office. His nomination should be for one year.

3. The Reichsrath is only to deliberate on matters which are laid before it by the monarch.

4. The Reichsrath to consist—

a) Of Ministers of State.

b) Of Reichsräthe (members).

c) Of a director.

5. The minister and heads of offices are by virtue of their office, and as long as it lasts, members of the Reichsrath. Their votes count as those of minister and members (Reichsräthe). They cannot preside.

6. The Reichsrath to be divided into sections:

a) Legal and Judicatory.

b) Internal Affairs.

c) Finance.

d) Military Affairs.

7. The number of Ministers of State not fixed. They have a vote like each Reichsrath.

8. If the monarch nominates a minister for a section, he shall preside over that section.

9. The number of members not to exceed twenty.

10. Three members at least to form a section, of whom one presides.

11. His Majesty to appoint the members in each section every six months.

12. The *deliberanda* to go from his Majesty's closet to the Minister of State presiding for the time. He manages, through the director, according to the design of his Majesty, the appointments of presidents of the sections.

13. The president of the section shall lay the debated document before the presiding minister, who shall forward it to his Majesty.

14. The matters which are laid by his Imperial Majesty before the whole Reichsrath shall be sent to the minister presiding.

15. The president of a section shall nominate a member to state the matter in the section. If it should subsequently be laid before the whole Reichsrath, the same member to make the report.

16. A legal copyist from the *personnel* of the Reichsrath office to be appointed to each section.

17. In the assembled Reichsrath the director shall conduct the protocols.

These foundations, on which the complete edifice may be raised for the welfare of the state, I respectfully lay before your Majesty, trusting they may receive your Majesty's gracious approval.

If your Majesty deigns to accept this basis, the formal organisation for the conduct of business must first be worked out, which, as we have models already existing in France and Russia, as well as at home, will be but the work of a few days.

Such a Reichsrath will bring about the amalgamation of the different provinces of the empire. German and Hungarian councillors sit in the different sections. Purely Hungarian matters would naturally be given *ad referendum* by the president of the sections to Hungarian members, or to those members entrusted with the affairs of that kingdom.

By the formation of *maîtres de requêtes* and auditors, immense good may be done. Through them a number of the younger men prove themselves, and the Government gets to know them. Their inauguration must be considered after a time. In France they do not proceed from the *Conseil d'Etât*. The chief work must be arranged and set going before the finishing off can be thought of.

But however extended may be the Reichsrath, it yet cannot satisfy all needs. In France the Emperor has other councils; and if the same number and extent may not be necessary for us, at least a council of ministers is necessary.

Prince Kaunitz formed alongside his Council of State a conference for the management of foreign affairs.

A permanent conference for foreign affairs is, in my judgment, objectless and as little useful as the State Council of 1760. A cursory glance at the course of the business suffices to show the inadmissibility of a similar institution.

Foreign affairs are from their nature such as cannot be handled in the department itself. Foreign relations include the whole, and can only be conducted by one mind and one spirit, which must have the control of the whole, the open as well as the secret relations of the Powers, and keeps both foreign countries and the Fatherland constantly in view. The organisation of the conference, with its *circulandis* despatches, extracts, &c., cannot, and does not, still exist, because it was something formed out of nothing. Secret matters cannot be circulated, and the little light that newspapers can give—and such only were the extracts of despatches —on the true relations of the Powers is known from the nature of things. This organisation fell, like the Council of State, because the foundations of both made their existence quite impossible.

I should venture to propose that the present ministerial conference should be continued. Not only is its existence not unnecessary : it appears to me to be of essential use in connection with the Reichsrath, but we must bring it back to its proper meaning.

The heads of departments have on many occasions an urgent necessity to address your Majesty together, and together to make reports to your Majesty. Also, your Majesty may wish to explain some matter of a more secret kind to the whole ministry. Your Majesty yourself presides over such a conference ; and I believe that this conference, as it stands, may be brought into working order. Much less business would, however, come to it, for this conference has hitherto in many respects supplied the place of the Council of State ; but there will always be numerous matters which from their nature require to be debated in a council of ministers. The distribution (of business ?) to the conference or to the Reichsrath to rest with your Majesty. Besides the heads of departments—ministers or presidents—we have also State and Conference Ministers, who will all find their corresponding places in the new organisation of both councils. In the Reichsrath they will bear an honourable title, which in itself will be a prize, though with only the business of an ordinary Reichsrath in this category.

Which State Minister should be taken for the conference must depend entirely on your Majesty's wish, and must remain so. According to my opinion the minister should be *de facto* member of the Reichsrath, assessor (*beisitzer*) of the debates *in pleno*, but of the ministerial conference only by the express appointment of your Majesty.

I conclude the present report with a remark on the principal advantages of these institutions which I take the liberty of laying before your Majesty.

1. It is undeniable, as I have said before, that the monarch, the sole true central point of the state, the one point from which everything proceeds and to which everything returns, cannot give, without a duly organised council, fixity to Government, unity and consistency to the whole. The great and most requisite constituent parts of the art of Government lie, not only in the uprightness and the good, yea, the firm will of the monarch : they must be impressed on each and every part of the whole, down to the very lowest wheels of the machine. This miracle becomes possible only by the tranquil co-operation of a body one and indivisible. Finally, one spirit animates such a body : it is the one spirit which enters into it, in all its acts of administration, the present as well as those that are future ; without its existence the will of individuals governs, instead of that high consciousness of government which can only be the result of the moral, political, physical, and geographical relations of the whole. An imperial council, ministerial conferences like those proposed, may and must

serve as a school of Government, even to the heir of the throne; there the monarch learns to know his servants, the successor to the throne his duties, the statesman surveys the whole.

2. Your Majesty will establish something where nothing is, and will improve that which, notwithstanding the best intentions of a great Queen and a great statesman, did not and could not succeed, because the fundamental notions of the Constitution of 1760 were utterly false. The existence of a Council of State—of a true council of the sovereign—is useful not when it traverses the action of a department or impedes it by its interference, as was the case in the organisation of Prince Kaunitz. If the monarch deposits a part of his executive power in the hands of a minister, chief of a department, that minister must be free indeed. The security of the state with regard to him lies in his responsibility. How should this be possible if a committee, or what is worse, a single individual to whose talents the monarch has ventured to commit the management of a department in rare cases, can daily interfere with the management of the minister, suffer him only half to act where he ought to do it wholly? The Council of State must not interfere with the course of business; the principles for which the office exists the monarch must establish with an ultimate reference to himself, and must examine all measures proposed. The Council of State, according to its proper notion, cannot be an executive body. It advises the monarch, in whom all powers are united in his functions of making and guarding the laws. The power which is exercised by ministers is only delegated.

3. Two advantages, neither of them small, of a somewhat numerous Council of State are these: that in

its committees the best chiefs of departments are formed, and that it offers places to merit in later years.

4. Lastly, there lies in the existence of a well-organised council, filled with able men, ready to advise the monarch on every occasion with enlightened and impartial counsel, so high a degree of security for the whole body politic that this feeling will soon become general, and secure to the government strength and repose in equal measure.

1812.

ACADEMY OF THE FINE ARTS.

(Note 60, Vol. I.)

184. Metternich's opening Address as Curator, February 12, 1812.

184. Gentlemen! This day the Austrian Empire celebrates a day which excites in the patriot the most sacred feelings. The Academy of the Fine Arts joins in the general homage. What body more than that Academy owes to the monarch such renewed acts of beneficence?

On a day consecrated to commemorative expressions of gratitude, it is my duty to proclaim this beneficence to the assembled academical body. To invite the members of the Academy to a renewed activity, to direct the eyes of an illustrious assembly, and through it the eyes of the nation, to an institution whose sphere of action as deeply influences the noblest efforts of the human mind as the most important springs of industry and of the true wealth of cultivated nations.

A year ago, the confidence you reposed in me called me to the honourable duty of being the representative of your wishes for the advantage of art. With reciprocal confidence and united powers which you reposed in me, we proceeded to an important work. It was incumbent on us to enlarge the advantages of a subsisting, though too little known, institution, and to improve defects which the long experience of years had discovered.   We needed encouragement and support ; we afforded, therefore, to his Imperial Majesty a new opportunity of doing good.   Could our wishes remain unsatisfied ?

In order to give an exact statement to the academic body of that which has been done, I may be permitted to take you back to the earlier days of our Academy. In the history of the origin of this association, of its first germ, of the gradual extension of its original plan to the body as it now exists, there lies ample matter for well-grounded hope for the future.

The first traces of our national art lose themselves in the times of Maximilian I., Rudolf II., Ferdinand III. The first step to a real art-union was made by Leopold I. ; to him we owe the foundation in 1704 of an academy of painting and sculpture.   Joseph I. opened this school and placed it under the guidance of Count Lingendorf.

The government of the Emperor Charles VI. was still more favourable to the arts than that of his forefathers.   His epoch generated men of high artistic feeling.   The names of a Peter von Strudel, of a Fischer von Erlach—whose works are still the ornaments of the Imperial city—of a Kopetzky, of an Auerbach, of a Stamper, of a Flistenberger, belong to that time.   Eugene of Savoy, equally great as a soldier and administrator, appeared as a patron of art ; with him are associated the noblest of the nation : the works of masters were brought from foreign countries, galleries and noble buildings were erected.   Enthusiastic young artists received the most generous support to enable them to travel to the places of ancient classical art.

Vienna entered on a new period of culture, which, though retarded by unfavourable circumstances and

events, would yet not be retrogressive. The foundation was laid. Silently the spark glowed, the eyes of
rulers were at once directed to art. It was no longer
strange to the great men of the Empire. Where art is
encouraged, artists appear. In 1726 the Emperor Carl
enlarged the sphere of action of the Academy, Count
Gundaker von Althann became its most zealous patron,
Schouppen its director. Althann's active spirit infused
new life into the Academy ; he improved and enlarged its
action ; to the schools of painting and sculpture, a third,
the school of architecture, was added, and in less than
ten years there were found in all departments of art
men whose works are still esteemed. Daniel Gran,
Paul Troger, Unterberger, Janeck, Max Hämmel, the
elder Brand, Aigen Raphael, and Matthäus Donner, the
two Schuzer and Ledelmayer issued from those schools.

Count von Losse, the successor of Count Althann,
and Schouppen in the management of the Academy,
inherited the impulse given to it by their predecessors :
a few years reward their endeavours and those of some
active fellow-labourers.

We now draw near an epoch in many respects
never to be forgotten. Maria Theresa threw a halo of
glory over the Austrian throne. A man of lofty spirit
and active energy, a statesman of rare worth, Prince
Kaunitz, under whose protection a school devoted to
the art of working in metals had been instituted,
founded also in 1768 schools for design and engraving,
which were raised by the Empress to the rank of a
free Academy provided with its own statutes. The
supreme direction Prince Kaunitz undertook. Schumt-
zer, whose loss is still too fresh for us to estimate him
rightly, was made director of the new Academy.

Both these institutes flourished for several years side

by side. After the death of Count Losse the protectorate of both was entrusted to Prince Kaunitz. To this great connoisseur the union of all branches of art must be welcome : he knew how difficult it is for the one to advance without the other advancing at the same time. He wished to animate the whole with one spirit, and thus arose the Academy of the Fine Arts. The galleries were soon filled with genuine masterpieces. Rich stipends for the support both of students and of artists were founded. The number of travellers to Italy was increased ; the imperial treasures of art were opened up to artists.

Thus in less than half a century the arts in Austria had attained an elevation which placed our national institutions on a level with the first in Europe.

The Emperor Joseph II. mounted the throne. He, to whom our national industries owe so much, became convinced that one of the principal branches in the domain of art was still unfruitful. The Academy, hitherto a pure school of art, had not been brought into contact with the manufacturer : he therefore created a technical school. The taste of everyday life was to be guided by it and accustomed to true notions and fixed principles. Austria, according to the wish of Joseph, was not to remain behind any state distinguished by its industry in fabrics. His design was, by applying art generally, to make it therefore more generally useful. The Academy with all its branches was placed in connection with art manufacture. Each of these art manufactures should participate in its beneficial influence. It became the authority which had to decide on the privileges attached to guilds and companies. That the designs of the great monarch did not altogether fail to be attained, a daily experience shows. If we consider the stormy and desolating times which began with the last years of the Emperor Joseph, if we calculate the hostile influences of such disturbances upon the development of arts in a purely scientific and technical point of view, and call to mind that yet in this same period of wars, which lasted for twenty-one years, countless manufactures and fabrics rose and flourished, it is then seen how deeply based and considered had been the system of previous rulers, and how effective and productive was the protection of their successor.

We, gentlemen, are now called upon to satisfy great expectations. We are responsible to our predecessors for the use of the rich inheritance which they bequeath to us. Our contemporaries are entitled to expect from us the advancement and perfecting of the arts. Our honour demands that we should strive for the gratitude of our successors ; in this sense we examine the institutions as they have existed to this day. Sound as they appeared in their fundamental principles, they seem to us defective in their practical everyday application. One essential need was still unsatisfied, a want which became more perceptible with the enlargement of our experience.

Art in its higher stages is no longer satisfied with the common and vulgar. In the childhood of the arts the mere handicraftsman deludes himself with the notion that he is an artist. To an uncultivated people every display of colour is painting, every work of mere masonry is sculpture. The lofty spirit which makes an artist to be an artist; that feeling which communicates itself to the coarsest materials, to stone, to metal, to canvas, that life which issues from the works of the great masters of antiquity, stands far above the narrow limits of mere mechanical art. The feeling, the genius which the artist himself possessed, he only can communicate to the works of his art. Without this spirit which he has imparted, the colour remains colour, the marble under his chisel remains stone. If some artists, merely by felicitous though moderate talents, often only by mechanical facility, bring their works to such a point of perfection as renders them worthy of the attention of posterity, how great, how living must be the art in the man who communicates his own spirit to the works of a whole school inspired by him. A Phidias, a Praxiteles, a Raphael, a Rubens worked not according to mechanical art. What inspired them was of nobler origin. From the depths of their own inspired genius sprang forth the power which we see immortal in their works.

In addition to already existing institutions, these views seem to render a school educated to the theory of art desirable. It was reserved to the Emperor Francis to create this. The new statute establishes a professorship of the theory of art. The liberality of the monarch provides for the endowment of the chair. Scholars of distinguished ability will for the future be instructed in this new school in sciences which lie beyond the sphere of the common artist, without which, however, the truer and higher artist cannot exist. Teachers will hold up before the pupils of this Academy the great creations of antiquity, will initiate them into the mysteries by which, in the centuries of classical art, the path of perfection was shown to ingenuous talent, and irregular fancies curbed and restrained. Those preliminary studies which the artist in his later years could only rarely purchase, and then at the expense of much precious time lost for the exercise of his art, will be given to him in the new institution among the first elements of all future culture. By the untiring diligence of professors, under the guidance of the directors of the Academy, Vienna will one day possess a school which Italy and the Netherlands, under different climatical relations, instituted for the imitation of posterity.

In a state in which the true feeling of art is so vigorous as with us, in which many rich private individuals are ready to support the artist, another need is manifested. To the artist commencing his career the possibility of making himself known must be granted, and to the artist who has already made his position encouragement must be given by a well-directed competition, and the opportunity afforded for purchase. For many years France and England have given us the example of public exhibitions of works of art ; in galleries where living artists exhibit their works the progress of art from period to period is judged with the greatest certainty. In these the scholar aspires to the palm of the master, or the master fears to be surpassed by the scholar. The love of fame—a feeling which animates the minds of all—becomes the ruling spirit of those who compete. Mechanism disappears ; art comes in its place. His Majesty the Emperor has accordingly instituted exhibitions of the works of national artists. The first of these exhibitions is to take place in the year 1813, according to principles to be established by the Academy, and every three years they are to be repeated. All artists of the nation and every department of art claim the Academy as its honourable arena. Works though completed years ago will be admitted to the first exhibition ; for the following, only those which have been completed in the three preceding years.

We shall thus learn to know our present powers, the point from which we start, in order to be able the more correctly to estimate our progress.

Experience teaches what advantages art, both in France and England, has derived from well-directed and greatly-conceived institutions. Austria, with her artists, with her Mecænas, with the warm feeling of the nation for the good and the beautiful, should not be behind foreign nations. In order to reach the examples set by other nations, our concealed powers need only be brought to light; the unknown made known; the slumbering talent roused to life and activity. The nation will be astonished at its own treasures, of which it has hitherto been unconscious. The impulses of artistic life will not have been given in vain. A few decades will be sufficient to justify my hope.

These, gentlemen, are the views which the amended and enlarged institutions of our Academy seem to justify; but even as an association of art it must rise and spread.

Nothing is more cosmopolitan than science and art. The pure kinship of spirit, raised above every material condition, extends through centuries; distance does not interrupt its ties; no event of time weakens or dissolves its connection. Already the Academy numbers among its members the most illustrious of the nation. Happy the realm in which everything good and noble is furthered by the example of its ruler, and by that of his glorious house. I can only allude to the unobtrusive support which the sciences and arts daily receive in all parts of the kingdom, from the members of this illustrious house. True to this great example the nobles unite for the same great ends. More intimate still must be the bond which unites the Academy of the capital with similar institutions in the cities of the provinces.

The choice of the members of this Academy will not be confined to the limits of this empire. The names of the first in art, the names of the most distinguished connoisseurs and patrons of art, will be associated with an institution which in its extended sphere of action belongs in the first instance, indeed, to Austria, but then to art in its widest compass.

If we succeed in attaining the object which we have before us this day, then, gentlemen, we shall have earned the justest claims to the thanks of our country.

The study of art, the sense for all that is great and beautiful, the true national riches, inseparable from true national glory, will rise in like proportions ; our children's children will completely enjoy what their fathers have prepared for them. The Fatherland will present to them what we now have to seek under alien skies ; that soil from which those men proceeded whose names deserve to be glorified by their immortal monuments will evoke from its bosom works of art of immortal value worthy of them. From the genius of Athens and of Rome the voices of antiquity sounded through thousands of years to this very day. There glows in the works of their artists the lofty feeling which once animated them. Every one of those works speaks with a louder and more significant voice than all the cold and lifeless ruins of past greatness.

The new statutes, which we owe to the favour of our monarch, I now present to the Academy. Join your voice with mine, gentlemen, in the sincerest expression of thanks. Join your voice with my voice in the salutation, Long live the Emperor !

AT THE TIME OF THE ALLIANCE.

(1813—1814.)

1813.

METTERNICH'S CONFERENCE WITH NAPOLEON IN DRESDEN.

(Note 67, Vol. I.)

185. Metternich to the Emperor Francis (Despatch), Dresden, June 28, 1813, 9 o'clock in the evening.
186. Abstract of a Conversation with the Emperor Napoleon.

185. I arrived here yesterday at two o'clock in the afternoon, having made the journey in twenty-four hours. The Emperor had gone to Königsbrück, but returned at ten o'clock. I spoke with the Duke of Bassano, and handed him my memoranda, to which he made no reply, and at eleven o'clock I received a summons to go to the Emperor. He received me directly I was announced, and our conversation lasted from a quarter before twelve to half-past eight without intermission. It consisted of the most wonderful mixture of heterogeneous subjects, of mutual friendliness and outbreaks of anger (No. 186). The result is that I cannot decide on the length of my stay here. I received a direct command to remain here at least till to-morrow, and I must await the official answer to my memoranda, which the Emperor promised to give me to-morrow, as he assured me to-day he had not yet read these notes, which is, however, very improbable.

I shall not, therefore, return in any case before Monday next, or in the course of Tuesday, and I implore your Majesty, respectfully, not to leave Gitschin before that time. I have ascertained here with certainty that a very large quantity of corn will be smuggled into this country from Bohemia. I believe the *prefect* ought to have his attention called to this circumstance, and that very severe measures will be necessary.

Abstract of a Conversation with the Emperor Napoleon.

(Supplement to No. 185.)

186. Having arrived at the Marcolini Gardens I was announced immediately, and his Majesty received me alone in his private cabinet.

He came towards me, and asked me with a very serious air for news of the Emperor. After a little time I began the conversation by saying that I presented myself before him in consequence of his invitation, and, according to my conviction, at the most important time for the future relations between the empires, and for the whole of Europe. ' It depends on your Majesty,' said I to him, ' to give peace to the world, to establish your government on the surest foundation —that of universal gratitude. If your Majesty loses this opportunity, what limit can there be to revolutions ? '

The Emperor replied that he was ready to make peace, but that sooner than make one that was dishonourable he would perish ' I have written to the Emperor,' he continued. ' My honour before all things, and then peace.'

I replied that dishonourable propositions could

never enter into the calculations of the Emperor
Francis. ' Very well, what do you understand by peace ? '
the Emperor interrupted me with ; ' what are your conditions ? Do you wish to rob me ? Do you wish for
Italy, Brabant, Lorraine ? I will not give up one inch
of ground. I make peace on the basis of *status quo ante
bellum*.

' I will, however, give a part of the duchy of Warsaw
to Russia ; I will not give anything to you, because you
have not beaten me ; I will give nothing to Prussia, because she has betrayed me. If you wish for Western
Galicia, if Prussia wishes for a part of her ancient possessions, that might be arranged, but with compensations. You will then be obliged to indemnify my allies.
Illyria has cost me three hundred thousand to conquer ;
if you wish to have it, you must sacrifice an equal
number of men.'

I replied to this first attack that I was not called on
here to discuss the conditions of the future peace, but
simply to insist on the most speedy assembly of the
negotiators under the mediation of Austria, or to
announce the refusal of the Emperor to negotiate under
this mediation. If the negotiators assemble, and no
opposition is made to a discussion on the basis of the
pacification, Austria will fulfil the part of mediator with
the most entire impartiality.

METTERNICH'S INSTRUCTIONS FOR THE CONFERENCE AT PRAGUE.

(Note 68, Vol. I.)

187. Metternich to the Emperor Francis (Report), Brandeis, July 12, 1813.

188. Emperor Francis to Metternich (Imperial Resolution), Brandeis, July 12, 1813.

187. At this time, when I am beginning the great business of negotiation, I consider it an indispensable duty respectfully to lay before your Highness the following concise points of view, which, with your approval, will at the same time serve me as instructions.

Your Majesty stands on the highest point which in the condition of peace and under existing circumstances can be reached. But this highest point itself leads necessarily to the moment of decision.

Our former course has reached its end ; we go onwards to meet a most decisive crisis, which it is not in our power to avoid.

Your Majesty can only save yourself and the monarchy, if your Highness acts with the greatest decision, and if I can rely with the most perfect confidence on the greatest firmness and perseverance being shown in the course prescribed for me, when once decided on. Without this decision my steps from day to day will be hesitating and incoherent, and even dangerous to the last degree. With the purest and most earnest desire for the good of the state, I should under such conditions only be the means of its possible ruin.

Without any exaggeration, either in abstract principles, or in their application to everyday life, I cannot help thinking two principal conditions to be necessary to the very existence of a great State.

Material force: for without that the body sinks to nothing, however extensive it may be.

Political consideration: this is the result of material force, and, far more still, of the monarch's personal influence and the direction of his cabinet.

How much influence these two considerations have had on my administration is shown by the situation in which we stand at present. In the year 1809, when all the resources of the monarchy lay shattered at the feet of your Majesty, and the whole Ministry looked on the ruin of the state in peace or war as inevitable, your Majesty alone kept up his courage. Your Highness thrust on me the heavy weight of the government. Favoured by fortunate circumstances, full of confidence in the strong sense and certain support of your Majesty, I did what duty and principle required of me. We have in this manner in less than four years again reached the first position in Europe. But we can no longer follow the same course, hitherto crowned with success ; it fitted the passing weakness of the monarchy. In the knowledge of this weakness lay the possibility of following this course, in order to become once more strong. In an abstract sense—reckoning the monarchy alone—we are far removed from being so strong as we were ; but the weight in the scale is the part, the preponderating part, which Austria plays, and this consideration, the only right one, I see is too little thought of by us. This consideration must now have the most direct influence on all your Majesty's decisions ; it is the only possible basis for our policy in the present decisive moment. Your Majesty has come forward as mediator for peace, because—

1. Your Highness wished to admit every possible chance for peace.

2. Because the forces of the monarchy unfortunately are not sufficiently strengthened at present, if the theatre of war were transferred beyond the frontiers of the empire.

Our strongest endeavours have been exercised to lead to a negotiation. This negotiation will exhaust the first of the above-mentioned motives. On the higher point of the development of the national forces, we can come to no other conclusion but that which we reached on the 10th of August. Hitherto, we have gained some advantage by our own addition of strength which the opposite party have obtained from the prolongation of the armistice ; later delay would bring loss to us, and certainly advantage to France.

Your Majesty has laid down conditions as a foundation for co-operation with the Allies, which show the moderation of the views of the Austrian cabinet. These views are such that they might be declared by the Allies to be acceptable.

Out of this state of affairs arise, therefore, three chances :

1. Of peace on the preliminaries already accepted.

2. Of Austria's co-operation in favour of the Allies, in case France refuses the preliminaries.

3. To take up a fresh position free from all ties, in case France should accept the preliminaries, while the Allies reject them.

In the first case, the question decides itself. The

discussion, therefore, can only be about the course to be decided on in the other two cases, and about these I must be armed with the undeviating commands of your Majesty before I begin the negotiation.

Your Majesty has declared the preliminaries of peace as the minimum, because it has at least the impress of peace, and because an agreement to it on the part of France affords the only possible evidence that Napoleon's designs are not entirely directed to the dispersion of the present coalition, the disarming of the Powers, and their partial destruction. In that case your Majesty could, as little as Prussia, escape such destruction. Russia would immediately withdraw from the game, and would be compelled to take the only part which could afford her any security, that of allying herself with France, and joining with her in our destruction.

This truth is too evident for me not to consider the following principle as completely established :—

That your Majesty, in the case of France not accepting the preliminaries of peace, should remain true to your word, and seek for preservation by the closest union with the Allies.

The Illyrian question stands as one of the possible modifications of the four preliminaries of peace. Illyria belongs to your Majesty. The Powers might certainly lay claim to Illyria as a *conditio sine quâ non;* but, no one can compel your Majesty to go into a war against your Highness's judgment, for a sacrifice which concerns the monarchy alone.

Whether this modification should be considered in the last moment of the negotiation or not, appears to me must be decided by the then existing circumstances, but that it must never overstep the limit of eventually securing the restoration of Illyria by the maritime peace appears to me completely established.

The possibility that your Majesty should unite with the Allies and France in a dishonourable peace, I do not think worthy of consideration. But what part should we take, in case the Allies should not accept our preliminaries? This question can and must be decided precisely at the moment, when it comes under discussion.

But it can only be to the advantage of the Allies, in case of their chances having been estimated lower on the 10th August than at present; or, and in apparently the worst case, they can only lead Austria into an armed neutrality. How much this would degrade us in the eyes of everyone, is so easily estimated, that it should not be accepted entirely on my own authority, wherefore, I take the liberty of entering upon a further discussion of these circumstances.

I confine myself in the present humble despatch to this short summary of my opinions. On the question, Can I rely on the firmness of your Majesty, in case of Napoleon not accepting Austria's preliminaries of Peace; is your Majesty unalterably determined, in this case, to entrust the right cause to the arms of Austria, and the whole of united Europe? lies the whole of my instructions, and according to my view, the foundation stone of our future policy. I must allow no shadow to pass over my soul, otherwise all my steps in Prague would, without the most precise definition of the will of your Majesty, bear the impress of ambiguity. We should lead on the general animosity to a possible decline of the monarchy, instead of to the chances of peace or an advantageous war; and I should, with the best intentions for the good of the State, certainly become the unhappy instrument for the destruction of all political consideration, of all moral tone, and of the loosening of all the inner and outer bonds of the administration of the State.

Emperor Francis to Metternich, July 18, 1813.

July 18, 1813.

188. I have to thank you chiefly for the present glorious political situation of my kingdom. I depend on you in my endeavours to maintain it. Peace, lasting peace, is certainly that which is most longed for by every sensible man, still more by me, as the miseries entailed by war fall so heavily on faithful dependencies and beautiful countries to which I am attached with heart and soul. We must strive to attain this end ; we have hitherto been in treaty for this ; we must now go further. We must not be deceived by momentary advantages or by increase of territory. What I conceive to be the basis of a lasting peace (although that this is so has been strongly questioned) is to make it such that it may be possible to be attained. To avoid as much as possible everything which can be derogatory to the honour of the Emperor Napoleon has been already so much considered that he can hardly have one sensible reason for not accepting. Henceforth, in the negotiation now about to begin, you must hold fast to what I have already declared as the minimum, showing the Powers that they and you can obtain more by using their energies in negotiations than by coming to an open rupture. Besides, you should carry on the transaction in the best possible mode to bring it into the right track, to remove all bitterness, and lead the affair to the wished-for end. Should you find that France makes the bringing about of a general peace contingent on the restoration of Illyria, I permit you, after you have exhausted all other means, to give in to this, in order to show a proof of my wish to promote the general good. You must firmly insist on that which I have decided on as the minimum, although I might wish that the point about the Hanse Towns could be arranged, for I only look on it as important in so far as it was an indispensable condition for ensuring Russia's continuance in her present conduct. You will also in this matter do all that is possible. Moreover, you can rely on my firmness in carrying out this principle, and you will receive amongst the notes for your use many reports having reference to Galicia, Illyria, and the ceded part of Austria. Should it come to pass that France accepts my minimum, the other Powers not being willing to agree to it, I shall expect that you will be good enough immediately to give me information on the subject.

FRANCIS.

NAPOLEON'S ABDICATION AND COUNT VON ARTOIS'S ARRIVAL IN PARIS.

(Note 76, Vol. I.)

189. Metternich to the Emperor Francis (Despatch), Paris, April 11, 1814 (2 A.M.),* with the Imperial Resolution.
190. Metternich to the Emperor Francis (Despatch), Paris, April 11, 1814.
191. Emperor Francis to Metternich, Troyes, April 12, 1814.

189. With regard to the affairs of the French Emperor, I find things stated in the following way :—

Your Majesty knows the new proposal which the Russian Emperor has made to Napoleon.† This proposal was introduced by the appearance of three marshals, who announced the abdication of the Emperor Napoleon, under certain conditions. In the answer, which your Majesty, as before mentioned, is acquainted with, Napoleon declared himself ready to sign his abdication. He himself delivered this document to Marshals Ney and Macdonald and Herr von Caulaincourt, with the request that they would make out a treaty according to his instructions.

On this treaty these plenipotentiaries, with Count Nesselrode, have worked for four days. But the Russian Emperor wished that I should be included in its arrange-

* The reader will see from the date of the document that its hasty compilation is explained.

† The fixed determination that Napoleon as well as Marie Louise should be dethroned, and that only the Bourbons would be acceptable to France and Europe,—ED.

ment, as one of the articles concerned a separate establishment for the Empress and the King of Rome.

This evening I have had a sitting of three hours
with the French plenipotentiaries and Count Nesselrode,
with the addition of Lord Castlereagh, in which we
settled everything in regard to the treaty. I considered
the duchies of Parma, Piacenza, and Guastala afforded
the most appropriate provision for the Empress, to
which all parties agreed. The signatures are therefore
complete ; to-morrow the final ratification will take place,
and the Provisional Government having agreed to the
whole, this important document can be published in the
course of two or three days. The Emperor Napoleon
will therefore immediately be sent to the island of Elba.
To-morrow, with Prince Schwarzenberg and the French
marshals, we shall determine on the best way of carrying out Napoleon's immediate removal. This will depend on the answer we expect from Augereau's army.
The marshals have no doubt that Augereau, Soult, and
Suchet will return immediately. So the war with one
stroke will come to an end.

Napoleon has still twelve or fifteen thousand men at
Fontainebleau. Marshal Macdonald declares he has
not two connected ideas. Amongst the many reasons
which call for the speedy removal of Napoleon, the
maintenance of this army is not one of the least.

The marshals have declared that Napoleon should
die if he does not abdicate ; and in the opposite case
they would immediately swear themselves under the
banner of Louis XVIII. All these things have decided
me not to wait for your Majesty's arrival to ratify the
treaty.

You have acted quite rightly in this matter, and I

thank you heartily as a father for all that you have
done for my daughter on this occasion.

FRANCIS.

Metternich to the Emperor Francis, Paris, April 11, 1814.

190. Your Majesty has probably been already informed by Count Bombelles that the Count d'Artois
intends coming here. He will probably arrive the day
after to-morrow. I beg your Highness to hasten your
coming here as much as possible. I have secured the
hotel of the Princess Borghese for your Majesty. It
lies close to that of the Russian Emperor.

This town appears most perfectly tranquil. When
I arrived yesterday there were thousands on the Boule-
vards. The voice of the people is entirely for the
Bourbons. That of the army is less so, so long as the
regiments remain together; but they will very soon be
disbanded.

Your Majesty is expected by this people with great
impatience. I have made all arrangements with Talleyrand for your having a suitable reception.

I have found the Russian Emperor in a very sensible mood. He is far less vacillating than I should
have imagined, and Prince Schwarzenberg is also pleased
with him. Indeed he can hardly contain his joy over
the whole course of events, which have overcome all
difficulties.

I dined to-day at Talleyrand's house with Marshals
Ney, Macdonald, Marmont, Lefebre, General Dessolle,
and many others, who were all unanimous in their excited feelings against Napoleon. It is difficult to form
an idea of this feeling without having actually seen it.
The Government carries on its direct course, and never

finds any opposition in its fulfilment. On all other points the most perfect tranquillity prevails.

I would venture to advise your Majesty to make use of the post in coming here. Your Highness could easily in coming here, with relays, make the journey from Troyes to Provence in one day, and on the following reach here from Provence. In this case it would be well if your Majesty could arrange to arrive here in the day-time. At the post stations between Provence and Paris your Majesty will easily find forty post-horses, and even more, by sending an order twenty-four hours in advance.

It seems probable from some vague information that Soult has been again beaten by the Duke of Wellington.

The Constitution has appeared, and is similar to the English, but with some sensible modifications. The Senate sits in the Upper House, the Legislative Corps in the Lower. The old nobility are reinstated, the new are confirmed. The endeavour has been carried out as far as possible to retain the old form in the present amalgamation. It is above all a very constitutional monarchy.

The Emperor Francis to Metternich, Troyes, April 12, 1814.

191. Dear Prince Metternich,—To your information received on April 11, I must reply that I can find neither horses nor forage here; to-day I travel with my own to Ponte on the Seine; to-morrow I proceed to Paris as best I can. I thank you for everything you have arranged for me. The principal thing is to get Napoleon out of France, and, please God, as far off as possible, therefore you have done quite rightly to conclude the treaty without waiting for my arrival, for only by this can we bring the war to an end. The island of Elba does not please me, for it is a loss to Tuscany; they give to others what belongs to my family, which cannot be allowed in future, and Napoleon remains too near to France and Europe. At any rate it must be arranged that Elba, if this matter cannot be prevented, shall come to Tuscany after Napoleon's death, that I shall be guardian of Parma, &c., for the child, and that in case of the death of my daughter and the child, these states shall not be reserved for the Napoleon family. In conclusion, the father thanks you heartily for everything you have done for his daughter.

FRANCIS.

AT THE TIME OF THE BEGINNING OF THE PEACE ERA.

1815.

THE VIENNA CONGRESS.

(Note 80, Vol. I.)

192. Memoir by Frederick von Gentz, February 12, 1815.
193. Metternich to Hardenberg, Vienna, December 10, 1814.
194. Talleyrand to Metternich, Vienna, December 12, 1814.

192. Those who at the time of the assembling of the Congress at Vienna had thoroughly understood the nature and objects of this Congress, could hardly have been mistaken about its course, whatever their opinion about its results might be. The grand phrases of ' reconstruction of social order,' ' regeneration of the political system of Europe,' ' a lasting peace founded on a just division of strength,' &c., &c., were uttered to tranquillise the people, and to give an air of dignity and grandeur to this solemn assembly; but the real purpose of the Congress was to divide amongst the conquerors the spoils taken from the vanquished. The comprehension of this truth enables us to foresee that the discussions of this Congress would be difficult, painful, and often stormy. But to understand how far they have been so, and why the hopes of so many enlightened men, but more or less ignorant of cabinet secrets, have been so cruelly disappointed, one must know the designs which the principal Powers had in presenting themselves on this great battle-field, and the development which particular circumstances and personal relations have given to these designs. The following observations will serve to characterise them.

Designs of the Powers at the Opening of the Congress.

The Emperor of Russia has come to Vienna, in the first place to be admired (which is always the principal thing in his thoughts), and next to direct personally the important arrangements which should fix the boundaries and future position of the many states who claim their share of the immense spoil which is placed at the disposal of the Allies, by their success against the common enemy. The three principal objects of the Emperor Alexander were : 1st, to take possession for ever of the whole, or almost the whole, of the Duchy of Warsaw, with the exception of some small portions, which he would give to the two neighbouring powers; 2nd, to prevent Austria from profiting too much by the advantages of her new position ; 3rd, to enrich Prussia as much as possible, not only to compensate her for her ancient Polish provinces, which he had carried away from her by surprise, and which he retained because it pleased him to do so, but also to make her a useful and powerful ally, the only one on whom he could rely in the future. Such were the *real* objects he had in view ; the *ostensible* object was to mingle in all the affairs of Europe, and to pass as the arbiter of their destinies.

On arriving at Vienna the Emperor was already more or less embroiled with Austria, England, and France. His displeasure with Austria was chiefly on account of the many and deep grievances which he had, or pretended to have, against Prince Metternich. The first and true origin of these grievances dated from

the opposition of that minister to the Emperor's proposal to become himself the commander-in-chief of the
allied armies. His resentment, which was restrained
during the first period of the war, and even hidden
under an appearance of great friendliness, broke out
for the first time in the month of December, 1813, on
the occasion of the Allies entering Switzerland, a plan
which all good generals had approved, but which the
Emperor opposed, because, in one of his philanthropic
moods, he had given his word to some Vaudois apostles
of liberty that the neutrality of Switzerland should be
respected. Since that moment there has been no return
of harmony. Angry and bitter discussions took place
almost every day during the last part of the campaign,
and by the time the Allies reached Paris they preserved,
with difficulty, the outward appearance of a friendliness
which had no longer any foundation. The Emperor
accustomed himself to look on M. de Metternich only as
a permanent obstacle to his designs, as a man occupied
without intermission in opposing and thwarting him;
at last, as a sworn enemy. The calmness and serenity
which M. de Metternich always opposed to these prejudices, instead of softening the Emperor, appeared only to
embitter him the more; private feelings, above all a strong
jealousy of M. de Metternich's success, both in politics
and society, increased this irritation. At last it reached
the point of an implacable hatred, and during his stay
in Vienna, his daily explosions of rage and frenzy
afforded an inexhaustible fund of curiosity and amuse-
ment to frivolous minds at the court, whilst sensible
men deplored them as a great calamity. This hatred is
the key to most of the events of the Congress ; if it has
done infinite harm to the affairs, and essentially spoilt
the most important interests of Europe, we have at least

the poor consolation that it has not turned to the personal advantage of the Emperor. His perpetual tirades against Prince Metternich, the details into which he entered with twenty women of society, to indoctrinate them with the crimes of this minister and designs for overthrowing him, as badly conceived as foolishly carried out, and only succeeding in adding to his credit —all this has given the Emperor Alexander an irreparable blow in public opinion; and it is perhaps one of the most useful effects of this Congress, and one of the greatest benefits it has given to Europe, to have cooled the general admiration with which some of this sovereign's brilliant qualities had inspired almost all his contemporaries. The true worth of his character is now seen, and if men have ceased to admire, they have also entirely ceased to fear him.

His relations with England (a Power which he had always cordially detested, and which he only cultivated either from interest or fear) have been sensibly disturbed since his visit to London. Lord Castlereagh was particularly disagreeable to him; he called him cold and pedantic, and there were moments in Vienna when he would have treated him as he did M. de Metternich, if extreme fear of openly compromising himself with the British Government (the only one before whom he trembled) had not forced him to dissimulate. Neither was the Emperor inclined to friendly relations with France. He had not pardoned the King for having adopted a system of government contrary to the advice which he had wished to give him; he was furious against Prince Talleyrand, who, at the time of the Allies entering Paris, had appeared to recognise no law but the will of the Russian Emperor, and who, four weeks afterwards, had found the means of rendering himself

independent. In the first months of his stay in Vienna
there were some violent scenes between the Emperor and
M. de Talleyrand; subsequently Talleyrand understood
how to impress the Emperor by his cleverness, his re-
partees, and his *savoir-faire*; but the secret aversion
remained the same. The King of Bavaria, although his
brother-in-law, was odious to him on account of his
close relations with Austria, and because he believed
Marshal de Wrede to be one of the blind instruments of
Prince Metternich. The King of Denmark was equally
insupportable to him, because he had had the courage
to reproach him for his wrongs and evil conduct. The
King of Prussia, therefore, was the Russian Emperor's
only friend, a prince whose personal attachment was
secured by his gratitude, his weakness, his infatuation,
and by his distrust of everyone else, whose cabinet, foreseeing the general opposition to its schemes for self-
aggrandisement, had allied itself with Russia, and made
the first principle of her policy a blind submission to
the will of that Power.

Prussia only brought to the Congress an immoderate desire for extending her possessions at the expense
of all the world, and without regard to any principle of
justice or even of decency. This passion for conquest
had its origin neither in the character of the King nor of
his Prime Minister; for the King, although below medio-
crity in intellect and judgment, is yet at bottom a good
sort of man, and Chancellor Hardenberg one of the best
that ever existed. But the system of this court does
not depend after all either on the King or Prince Hardenberg. This system, founded and pursued for the
last century, has found fresh support in the general
enthusiasm of the nation, in the energy of the army,
and in the irresistible power which a certain number of

distinguished military men exercise at present on the cabinet. Since the moment of Prussia's resurrection, the principal object of this party has been the total acquisition of Saxony. Being neither able nor willing to compete with Russia, they transferred all their designs to Germany; the acquisition of Saxony, however enormous it was, was for them but the beginning of a grand series of political operations, by which they hoped sooner or later to unite to Russia the largest part of the north of Germany, to efface the influence of Austria, and to put themselves at the head of the whole German Confederation. Reckoning on the help of Russia in the execution of this vast scheme, they wished at least to carry away from the Congress the foundation stone of their new edifice ; and if Austria has not been able entirely to thwart them, she still deserves some merit, in having at least prevented a considerable part of their schemes. England appeared at Vienna with all the brilliancy which she owes to her immense successes, the prominent part which she had played in the coalition, to her influence without limits, to a condition of strength and solid prosperity which no other Power has attained in these days, and lastly to the respect and fear which she inspires and which govern her relations with all the other governments. In profiting by these advantages, England could have given the law to all Europe ; by making common cause with Austria, whose interests were also hers, she might have prevented the aggrandisement of Russia, made Prussia fall back within her own boundaries, re-established a true equilibrium in Germany, and guaranteed for a long time the repose of Europe. England renounced this noble privilege, for reasons which I prefer to explain on another occasion, and which touch on the most delicate ground in this history. It is true, Lord Castlereagh for some time resisted the ambitious schemes of Russia, but he ended by abandoning this opposition. Guided by the purest intentions, but with some radically false views, he first supported Prussia's designs on Saxony to their utmost extent, returned later to a course more in conformity with just principles, and more favourable to Austria, but, stopping half way, he finally only saved a part of Saxony by a thoroughly bad arrangement. He observed in all the other questions (with the exception of those directly concerning England, such as the establishment of the House of Orange, the slave treaty, &c.) a neutrality often astonishing. But, though capable of being the arbiter for Europe, he gave her only weak and partial support. This was, without doubt, the principal cause of the unsatisfactory issue of the Congress.

The part of the French Ministers at this Congress was decidedly the most simple and agreeable of all. Everything relating to France having been regulated by the Treaty of Paris, they had nothing to demand for themselves, and could confine themselves to watching the conduct of others. Defending the feeble against the strong restrains each Power within its proper limits, and to working in good faith for the re-establishment of political equilibrium. To do them justice, their general course has been in accordance with these principles, for they have made no proposal, started no scheme tending directly or indirectly to the least change in the stipulations of the Treaty of Paris, to the slightest extension of their frontiers, or to any pretension whatever, incompatible with the rights of their neighbours or general tranquillity. In spite of all the lies which are current in society, of all the schemes, measures, and intrigues which inveterate hatred against

France has falsely and even absurdly attributed to her
ministers, a faithful history cannot refuse them this
honourable testimony ; and I, who have been a close
observer of everything, and am better able to write this
portion of history than anyone else, I am the first to
give them this testimony.   But if M. Talleyrand and his
colleagues have never worked *against* the general good,
it is also true that some special obstacles have prevented
their co-operating in it, in any efficacious manner.   In
the first place, the secret article of the Treaty of Paris
which authorised the formerly allied Powers to arrange
the division of the countries conquered by France,
' according to arrangements agreed on between themselves,' was a terrible barrier to all their measures, and
if the Powers who, like Austria, only demanded order
and justice, or, like England, were willing to give up the
power which this article allowed them, Russia and
Prussia, who were solely guided by ambition and desire
of acquisition, would never have suffered it.   This, and
the often exaggerated fear of the other Powers, of appearing to conspire with France, will explain to you in
a great measure the nullity of the French plenipotentiaries in all the negotiations, and above all during the
beginning of the Congress.   Another cause contributed
very much to this.   To hold a firm and imposing attitude against cabinets such as the Russian and Prussian, who considered their wills as almost irresistible,
France must be prepared and perfectly decided for war.
She pretended to be so, but was not in reality ; and,
when once the secret of her policy was suspected, her
arguments could no longer encourage her friends, or
her menaces terrify her enemies.   The present French
Government longs only for peace ; believing it indispensable for reorganising the Government, the finances,

the commerce, and all the resources of France, it looks on peace as the only means of solid security, whilst a fresh war would bring alarming chances of danger and revolution.

The energetic demonstrations by which the French Ministers are sometimes carried away, contrast too much with what we know of the true intentions of their cabinet to produce a great effect; and if M. de Talleyrand is to be reproached with a mistake, and still more his coadjutor Duke d'Albert, it is perhaps that of having in their communications and private conversations, above all at the beginning of the Congress, held a language somewhat too haughty against people who did not want for means of knowing up to what points they would support them at Paris. However, I do not wish to imply by this observation, that if Austria and England had preferred war to hurtful concessions, France would not have allied herself to these Powers to take part in it. I believe the contrary; but what I wish to remark is, that France was not decided enough to give an impulse to the Powers who, for causes which you will find explained later, only wished to fight with the pen and in conferences, and would prefer in secret the most detestable arrangements to a fresh explosion, which they feared above all.

Austria found herself, between these four Powers, in the most embarrassing position. She could not look on the Emperor Alexander, in spite of all his protestations of friendship for the Emperor, but as a declared enemy, and Prussia, always carried away by her own rapacity and ambition, as the inseparable ally of this enemy. She was deterred from too great a friendship with France, not by any reason of direct repugnance or distrust, for she was perfectly convinced of her loyal and friendly disposition, but by what is called respect of mankind, that is to say, by the fear of lowering herself in public opinion, by leaguing herself openly with a Power which had formerly been the common enemy of Europe, and which still preserved its bad reputation in the minds of the multitude, led away by the hypocritical declarations of the Russian and Prussian party.

Another consideration also stopped Austria. Perfectly agreed with France in her views on the affairs of Poland and Germany, she was not so in regard to those of Italy. France had a natural interest in regaining her old influence in Italy, by the re-establishment of the deposed branches of the Bourbon family at Parma, and principally at Naples, whilst Austria wished first to consolidate her own power ; then, to preserve Parma, which a recent and formal convention had secured to the Empress Marie Louise ; also to support the King of Naples, whose cause she had embraced from the wisest and most powerful motives. The cabinet of Vienna had therefore to fear that, by allying herself too closely with France, whose support was essentially useful in her contests with Prussia and Russia, she might have to sacrifice to this Power a part of her great interests in Italy. This is why, during the three months of the Congress, Austria has always remained somewhat separated from France, and it is only since the beginning of this year that a real intimacy has been established between the ministers of these two Powers. There remained then only England as any support to Austria ; but England wished for peace, peace before everything, peace—I am sorry to say it—at any price and almost on any conditions. Thus Austria was absolutely in the position of having to rely on herself alone, against Russia and Prussia united ; she had but one ally, who would follow her at the first call, Bavaria ; if war broke out, she could rely on the help of France ; but this help would be tardy and constrained, and would turn the opinion of all the rest of Germany still more against her. As to England, decided not to quarrel with anyone, she would not even give a subsidy to Austria. By reflecting on this *ensemble,* you will understand the course of the negotiations, of which, in this preparatory paper, I am about to give you a very short but exact abstract.

The Affairs of Poland.

On arriving at Vienna, the Emperor of Russia declared, through Count Nesselrode, at the first conference (which, as well as all the others of the first month, was attended only by the ministers of Austria, Russia, Prussia, and England), that he demanded as a just indemnity for his sacrifices the possession of the Duchy of Warsaw, and at the same time the power of regulating its position and future constitution according to his convenience. This declaration was regarded as a first attempt, and received with indifference. Persuaded that the only means of treating with the Emperor Alexander was by confidential conversations, Prince Metternich, although quite aware of all the inconveniences of this mode of negotiation, determined to try it. He had four or five private conferences with the Emperor ; he found him so obstinate that nothing could move him ; his exasperation and violence even increased from one interview to another ; and at last the interview of October 24 was so stormy, that the Prince declared to his friends that after the scene which had just taken place he neither would nor could see the Emperor again in private. He has kept his word ; with the exception of one explanation, which the honour of the Prince rendered inevitable, he has never again set foot inside the Emperor's door. They are still seen at the court, and at large assemblies given by a third party; but since October 24, the Emperor will not go to any ball, to any *fête* at Prince Metternich's house; the remonstrances of his sisters, of the Archduke Palatine, his brother-in-law, of several of his friends, of all the women whose acquaintance he cultivates at Vienna—nothing can conquer this repugnance; and whilst affecting to treat Madame and Mademoiselle Metternich with marked consideration, he always maintains that the Prince has offended him too mortally for them ever again to have any personal communication. I have no need to add that the accusation was absolutely false; that the Emperor, carried away by his passion, was alone to blame in these interviews, and that M. de Metternich has conducted himself up to the present moment with all the wisdom and politeness which are characteristic of him, and with all the propriety inherent to his person and manners.

This first great instrument, and certainly the most skilful of all, put *hors de combat*, Lord Castlereagh entered the field. He addressed to the Russian Emperor three private memorandums, in which he showed with much vigour, and sometimes with little tact, the injustice of his conduct and his pretensions, and the dangers with which his projects would threaten Europe. He spoke to him in these memoranda, sometimes in his own name, but more often in the name of his Government. The Emperor replied to each of these papers by bad arguments, sometimes in an evasive manner, sometimes with disdain; but always with extreme bitterness. This private correspondence was not only useless, but absolutely hurtful to the success of the negotiation. Lord Castlereagh was wrong in undertaking it; we were wrong in consenting to it. Arguments were wasted that should have been reserved for a formal negotiation which alone can be of any use, and which should never have been renounced, for the very reason that the Emperor opposed it with all his might.

It is true that a presentiment of the failure of all these measures had excited Austria and England to put in train a veritable negotiation; but the method of conducting it was not happily chosen. Prussia having, at least in appearance, a great interest in reclaiming her part of the duchy of Warsaw, it was thought possible to associate her in the measures that the two other Powers intended to take for moving the Emperor of Russia, and it was decided to make him understand that the affairs of Saxony would be more easy if he conducted himself well in those of Poland. You will see from the following article what were the terrible effects of this resolution on the great quarrel about Saxony. Its perfect uselessness for the end directly in view was soon recognised. Prussia, after having affected for some weeks to associate herself in the course of Austria and England with respect to Russia, and to second their combined plans, declared all at once, towards the middle of November, that having reflected on all the consequences of this plan, sounded the intentions of the Emperor Alexander, and seen the impossibility of effecting any change in his projects, she could no longer continue this course, and had no better counsel to give to her friends than that of giving in to Russia with a good grace. From this moment the whole edifice crumbled away. A rupture was pronounced between Austria and Prussia. A reciprocal animosity took the place of those intimate relations which had united them since 1813, but which the last events of the war had already greatly shaken and changed. England wavering for some time between these two Powers, Austria found herself, in this painful interval, isolated on the field of battle. There was no longer any question about the affairs of Poland ; they were tacitly regarded as lost.

Meanwhile the most lively debates took place about the territorial arrangements of Germany, and above all on the unfortunate affair in Saxony. Austria, seeing the pretensions of Prussia increase and strengthen, and the quarrel growing more bitter day by day, made at the end of the year 1814 some indirect attempts to conciliate Russia. Abandoned by Prussia in her plans for thwarting Russia, she hoped to be able to make use of Russia, up to a certain point, in moderating the projects of Prussia. Russia pretended to agree, but she exacted first the arrangement of the affairs of Poland in the sense of her previous demands with some modifications. Austria, persuading herself that she could not save both Saxony and Poland, decided to allow the latter to fall.

Meanwhile, on December 29, the famous conferences began between the ministers of Austria, Russia, Prussia and England, to which at last M. de Talleyrand was admitted on January 8. Since December 30 the Count Razoumowsky, appointed for these conferences because the Emperor believed Count Nesselrode too much attached to Austria, communicated the proposals of Russia relative to Poland. The Emperor declared that he demanded the whole of Warsaw, with the exception of the ancient palatinates of Gnesen and Posen, and some old districts of Western Prussia, the whole amounting to 850,000 souls, which he would give up to Prussia, and a small territory on the right bank of the Vistula, opposite to Cracow, in which are situated the salt mines of

Wieliczka, which he would give to Austria, as well as the circle of Tarnopol with 400,000 souls, ceded by that Power according to the Treaty of Vienna. Cracow and Thorn should be declared free and independent cities. This scheme was adopted without any discussion. Austria had taken her part. Prince Talleyrand, finding it impossible to contend alone against Russia, declared that all the wishes of France had been for the independence of Poland; but this question being abandoned by the Powers most directly interested, could not be supported by France alone. Lord Castlereagh contented himself with sending a memorandum on January 12, in which, while submitting to the projects of the Emperor of Russia, he confined himself to expressing some empty regrets, announcing some sinister presentiments, and giving some philanthropic advice to the three Powers. In reply to this note, Count Razoumowsky returned on January 19 the most remarkable document which has appeared at this Congress. The most striking part of this document is the clear and positive manner in which the Poles are informed that all hope of the re-establishment of their independence is lost. It is astonishing that the Sovereign who for two years has not ceased to flatter them with this hope, should be the very one who informs them now of the ' impossibility of restoring that ancient political system of Europe of which the independence of Poland formed a part.'

The constitutional government with which they have been deluded so long is only vaguely mentioned in this document; it is believed that the Emperor feels the difficulty so much, that he no longer dreams of bringing it about, and he believes he will satisfy his admirers by offering them some phantom of the so-called nationality which will shut their mouth as to the new arrangement. It is certain that he has gained sufficiently in carrying the territorial question, and that so marked an advantage will soon make him forget all his constitutional dreams.

Such has been the end of the Polish affair, by which the Empire of Russia has gained one of the most fertile countries of Europe, and three millions and a half of new subjects, after subtracting the 850,000, which she gives to Prussia, and the 400,000 which she gives to Austria, in the province of Tarnopol. When I say the end, I speak only of the Congress and of actual negotiations, for the ulterior consequences of this event are incalculable. No one can conceive how Austrian Galicia, although Russia has offered to be her guarantee, can remain for two years in her present state ; and how, after the enormous progress of Russia which this last acquisition has brought to its height by the menacing position which it gives her with her neighbours, and with the domineering and ambitious spirit which she has constantly manifested in these transactions, the equilibrium and tranquillity of Europe will be exposed to perpetual dangers and the most frightful revolutions.

However, no treaty has been signed or drawn up at present on this 'new distribution of forces,' to use the ominous terms of the Russian note. Austria does not wish definitely to subscribe to this division of the Duchy of Warsaw, till those of Germany shall be terminated, and the Emperor Alexander, less out of complaisance for Austria, than by an affectation of delicacy for Prussia, has announced the same intention.

Territorial Affairs of Germany.

There are in Germany, besides a great number of secondary interests, and independently of the question of a future constitution uniting all parties in Germany, two territorial questions of the first importance to decide : one, on the means of reconstituting the Prussian monarchy on its old dimensions ; the other on the indemnities of Bavaria for the provinces which she should cede to Austria. The first of these questions has most occupied the ministers of the Congress, which embraces all the other political subjects, and for several months it has stopped and absorbed all the others.

The same motives which determined Austria and England not to approach, during the continuance of war, the knotty question of Poland with Russia, compelled them to keep silence about the pretensions which, since the end of the year 1813, Prussia had openly made to Saxony. It appears, even, that, as to the latter, they were not content with simple temporisation, but that they had several times given Prussia strong hopes. However that may be, this Power, protected and warmly encouraged in this project by the Russian Emperor, arrived at the Congress with a fixed intention of taking possession of the whole of Saxony, as equivalent for its ancient Polish provinces, lightly and imprudently (perhaps even craftily) ceded to Russia by the treaty of Kalisch. Austria, in the unfavourable relations in which she found herself with the Russian Emperor, could not resist this project of Prussia's, except with the open and determined assistance of England ; for the opposition of France, although strongly marked from the beginning, could not suffice to support Austria in a contest which might terminate in war. There were several reasons for believing that the English Government would make common cause with Austria in this important affair, to which the equilibrium of Germany, and the future relations of these two Powers, were

directly bound. This expectation was disappointed.
Lord Castlereagh, drawn on by the great interest which
he attached at first sight to the affair about Poland
(completely abandoned afterwards)—by some false ideas
of the necessity of strengthening Prussia, and many other
reasons, which there is not time to unfold—joined the
project of Prussia, and employed his means of influence
and persuasion to engage the Cabinet of Vienna to consent to the execution of this project. You know from
several of my despatches the powerful objections of
Austria against this measure, objections which were
never replied to, except in representing the horror and
the dangers of an open rupture with Prussia and Russia.
These representations alone would not have made
Austria accede ; but the entreaties of England, joined to
the deceptive hope that Prussia would second her measures against the aggrandisement of Russia, produced a
momentary effect, which other circumstances soon rendered irretrievable. It was promised to Prussia, in a
confidential note of October 22, as the condition of her
assistance in the negotiations, that war should be entered upon with Russia ; that if no other means could
be substituted for this, to satisfy the just pretensions of
Prussia, the Emperor would even consent to the incorporation of Saxony with the Prussian monarchy. This
step, which has given M. de Metternich more grief in
three months than he has had in all his life, was accompanied by the verbal consent of Austria and England to
the provisional occupation of Saxony ; and, to complete
the misfortune, it was interpreted immediately by Prussia (in spite of all the conditions and restrictions which
had been attached to it) as an absolute and definite
consent.

Prussia having fulfilled none of the conditions which

Austria had attached to her eventual consent to the acquisition of Saxony, the Cabinet of Vienna would have had, without any doubt, the right of rejecting any ulterior negotiation on Prussia's favourite design. But once the provisionary occupation of Saxony granted to this Power, there could be no hope of their being dislodged from this country by simple representations; and, on the other hand, it was always hoped that she would employ at least some of her influence with the Emperor of Russia to persuade him to concession in Poland. Thus, although bitterness was already in every heart, the outward appearance of friendliness was preserved, and, instead of retracting altogether, Prussia was allowed to understand that there would be no objection to a *part* of Saxony being given up to her. At this time the dispatches from London announcing the angry feeling that the news of the Prussian projects, supported by the English Ambassador, had produced, and the formidable attacks on Parliament from the Opposition relative to this question, warned Lord Castlereagh that he had gone too far, and although he did not entirely change his system, these despatches and the anger that he felt towards the Prussian Ministers on account of the equivocal part they had played in the affair of Poland, determined him to modify his course, and to abandon, once for all, the idea of consenting to the total incorporation of Saxony with the Prussian monarchy.

It was under these circumstances that Prince Metternich addressed his memorandum of December 10 (No. 193). This document shows both the resolution already taken at this epoch to regard the question of Poland as lost, and the repugnance of Austria to give up opposition to that of Saxony. To understand thoroughly the sense of this note, you must know that in the programme which is annexed to it Prussia is offered, besides all that she has gained in Westphalia and on the Rhine, nearly 430,000 souls of the population of Saxony, in giving up to her Basse-Lusace, more than half Haute-Lusace, and the province of Wittenberg on both sides of the Elbe. The terms of the note were extremely moderate and conciliatory, and, if one can find a fault in this document, it is that of too great a compliance with a court whom Austria cannot, without perfect blindness, consider as her friend and ally.

The surprise was, therefore, so much the greater when it was known that the Prussian cabinet looked on the note of December 10 as an insult, and as an evident proof of hostile intentions on the part of Austria. This cabinet was so familiarised with the idea of absorbing Saxony entirely, that the proposal to content herself with 430,000 subjects in that country, and to re-establish the King of Saxony, who it believed deposed for ever, could only alarm and embitter her. All the Prussians and all their partisans cried murder. The text of the memorandum was only known to a few persons; only the bare proposals were divulged, accompanied by the most perfidious commentaries. The Emperor of Russia joined in the chorus with the Prussians. On the other side the friends of Austria, the French, the Bavarians, and, one may add, all the honest and sensible men in Germany, took fire against the outrageous pretensions of Prussia. The storm which rose was such that for a fortnight, and up to the end of the year 1814, those who were behind the scenes regarded war as inevitable. Energetic preparations were made in all parts. Troops were concentrated everywhere; nothing was spoken of but the speedy dissolution of the Congress. The Emperor Alexander denounced M. de Metternich to his sovereign and amongst all classes in Vienna as the disturber of public peace in Europe. Prussia would not even answer the note of December 10, finding the proposals which it contained beneath her dignity. This deluge of injustice and extravagance was at last put an end to by the calm and intrepid bearing shown by the Emperor Francis and Prince Metternich, by the firmness of Austria and Bavaria, by the wise reflections and cutting sarcasms of M. de Talleyrand, who brought all thinkers and mockers to his side, and by the peaceful exhortations of Lord Castlereagh ; and last, by the perceptible fall of the authors of this chicanery in the opinion of the world. It is to this time of agitation that the letter of December 19 of M. de Talleyrand to Prince Metternich relates, which is found amongst the annexes of this report (No. 194), a document extremely remarkable from more than one point of view, written with as much fire as force and nobleness, and containing grand truths and the most striking insight. It will interest you so much the more that it is the only formal and official document which the plenipotentiaries of France have sent during the whole duration of the Congress. Everything that the gazettes have written about other pretended French memoranda belongs to fiction.

The conferences, which began on December 29, and of which I have spoken before, opened in the midst of the outbreak of all these passions. But several days afterwards the storm abated. The Emperor of Russia had made some serious reflections. He looked forward to the moment when England, in spite of all her moderation, irritated and excited by the obstinacy of Prussia and Russia, would openly take action against these Powers. Already a project was talked of for future agreement between Austria, France, England, Bavaria, and Hanover, and this rumour, which was not without foundation, caused the Emperor Alexander to tremble, and made him lower his tone prodigiously in a few days. He promised even to do his best to persuade Prussia to content herself with the half of Saxony.

Chancellor Hardenberg, sincerely devoted to peace, and an enemy of all exaggerated projects, profited by this opportunity to gain ground against the party who, under the standard of Baron de Stein (the real disturber of the public peace in Germany and Europe), laboured without intermission to draw the King into a fresh war. The conferences took up a fixed position; each Power, consulting together in good faith, discovered that it did not wish for war; peace was again the order of the day.

In the project for reconstitution sent by Prussia to the Conference on January 19, she still demanded the whole of Saxony; she avowed at the same time that with the countries which she claimed on the Rhine she would have 680,000 more subjects than at the epoch of her greatest splendour. But this scheme did not alarm anyone; as it was certain that Prussia could be brought down very much in her demands. Austria and England laboured for a fortnight at another project. This period, without being comparable to that of the last fortnight of the month of December, was still extremely agitated, and sometimes very stormy. The impatience of the Prussians was extreme. Their movements and their military measures, which they did not discontinue, still caused offence to the cabinets and great uneasiness to the public. On the other side, Austria and England were no less agreed about the definite proposals to be made. Lord Castlereagh only aiming at peace and at what he called (often very gratuitously) a just division of forces, little sensible to the powerful objections of the Cabinet of Vienna, to the disproportionate aggrandisement of Prussia, and completely indifferent to the fate of the King of Saxony, adopted grounds which Austria, and with her France and Bavaria, could not admit.

There were, besides, enormous difficulties on the subject of the important place Torgau, to the cession of which Austria was most strongly opposed, whilst Lord Castlereagh treated it as a bagatelle. The military chiefs in Austria, judging quite differently, embittered and excited besides by the conduct of Russia and Prussia, began to demand war, and it required all the skill of M. de Metternich to prevent the Emperor himself from being drawn into their opinions. At last, after the most painful discussions, of which those alone who were actors or witnesses can form an idea, the counter-project was sent in on January 29. Prussia was offered 800,000 subjects in Saxony and 1,400,000 on the Rhine. Her population was thus increased to above 10,000,000 souls.

Although this most moderate counter-project was supported by England and France, Prussia made fresh objections and fresh demands. She admitted tacitly the principle of the division of Saxony, although she had never agreed to it in all its forms, but she found her share below her expectations. She insisted, amongst other things, on the acquisition of the town of Leipsic ; the other Powers had decided not to cede this point. This difference would not have been settled at the time it was—it would perhaps have required a month or more of negotiations—if a particular and unforeseen circumstance had not brought it suddenly to a conclusion. This circumstance was the recall of Lord Castlereagh to

London. This minister, not wishing to lose the results of his hard labour, and to leave Vienna without having arranged the Saxony affair, made some last attempts to accomplish his aim. He showed extraordinary activity and perseverance ; he worked day and night, now with the King of Prussia and the Emperor of Russia, now with Prince Metternich and Prince Hardenberg, and he succeeded at last, on February 6, in coming to a definite understanding with the latter minister about the arrangement which terminated this great question. According to this arrangement, Saxony will be divided into two parts nearly equal, of which the one remaining to the King of Saxony is the most populous, that which falls to the lot of Prussia the largest in area. The King of Saxony keeps about 1,200,000 subjects, with Dresden, Leipsic, Bautzen, and all the frontier along Bohemia. To console Prussia for Leipsic, which she has fought for with such ardour, the Emperor of Russia will give her Thorn with its environs, which in consequence will not be a free city like Cracow.

You will observe in all these arrangements there is no longer question of the King of Saxony, who would appear indispensable for the legitimate cession of so large a portion of his States. But the conduct maintained towards this unfortunate Sovereign is a blot on the history of the Congress.

It might have been predicted that Prussia and Russia, in consequence of their system of spoliation, would persist in treating the King of Saxony as a dethroned prince and a prisoner, and his kingdom as a conquered country. But that the English Government, adopting nearly the same manner of seeing and acting, only recognised in the discussions about Saxony a simple difference between Austria and Prussia, and declared the consent of the King superfluous to sanction the result of a negotiation to which he remained an absolute stranger,—this was a circumstance that would have been more difficult to predict, but which nevertheless occurred. Austria and France have for a long time supported the opposite principle, the only true and just one, and have never formally abandoned it ; they have, however, ended by not insisting on it. It is therefore understood now that the King of Saxony is bound by the common decision of the great Powers, that he will be brought out of his state of captivity to be informed of the position which has been prepared for him, and to propose to him to enter into possession of the States which remain, and in case he should not wish to agree to this arrangement, there will be a provisionary government of the part of Saxony which belongs to him, reserving the ulterior disposition of it to his family. According to all the ideas which we have gathered up to the present time, we might believe that he will refuse everything, but those who know him best are secretly of opinion that he will accept ; his best friends even advise him to take this line, and to await some event which the present state of things may lead to only too soon, to regain all his possessions or lose the rest.

My intention was only to give you a faithful history of the Congress. I abstain from any reflections which the *dénouement* of the affair might suggest, with the exception of presenting you with my general ideas on the relative situation in which the Congress of Vienna is about to leave the principal Powers of Europe. The only observation which I cannot help making is that the division of Saxony, entailing necessarily the ruin and despair of that country, will produce a painful sensation in Europe, and will be, as a political transaction, perhaps more badly thought of than the terrible partition of Poland was in its time.

The second object of territorial arrangement in Germany is that which relates to Bavaria.

Without being as important as the one I have just been considering, it is still not without difficulty or complication. Bavaria ought to give up to Austria (according to the treaty of Ried, concluded at the time when this Power acceded to the coalition) all that she had gained in the wars of 1805 and 1809, obtaining for this satisfactory indemnities.

One part of this engagement is fulfilled. Bavaria has restored Tyrol and the Vorarlberg, and has received, as an equivalent, the former Grand Duchy of Wurzburg, and the greater part of that of Frankfort. She is still in possession of two provinces of Upper Austria and of the Principality of Salzburg. The provinces of Upper Austria are fertile and productive, the revenue of which, under Bavarian administration, more severe, but much better organised than the Austrian, yields nearly 3,000,000 florins.

She demands now as indemnity for these countries 670,000 subjects to be taken from the possessions of the King of Würtemberg, the Grand Duke of Baden, the Grand Duke and the Elector of Hesse, these princes to be indemnified by other arrangements on the banks of the Rhine. This difficulty would be still to overcome. But there is another, much more serious, arising from the promise that Austria has made, to procure for her the Town of Mayence in exchange for Salzburg, independently of any other indemnity. Prussia and all the rest of Germany, specially excited against Bavaria, unanimously opposed this arrangement. At first Prussia wished to keep Mayence (occupied by a mixed garrison of Austrians and Prussians) for herself, and demanded it with much arrogance. They have, however, withdrawn this pretension, and they are now satisfied that Mayence should be declared to belong to the German federation, as formerly did the fortresses of the empire (Philippsbourg, Brisach, &c.). But, on the one hand, this federation is still only a vague project, and no one knows when, and in what condition it will be realised ; and, on the other, what is more serious, Bavaria, notwithstanding her present intimate union with Austria, persists in not giving up Salzburg (a place which the Austrian Kingdom can no longer do without) unless Mayence is assured to her.

The formal debates on this thorny question will commence as soon as the affair of Saxony is definitely terminated. There will be great storms yet.

The discussions on the Federal Constitution of Germany were broached at the beginning of the Congress. The Plenipotentiaries of Austria, Prussia, Bavaria, Hanover, and Würtemberg, formed the private Committee who dealt with it. But the numerous claims of the other Princes of Germany, and above all, the great tension which the affair of Saxony has established between Austria and Prussia, have interrupted this work, and since the 16th November it has been entirely suspended. It is proposed to resume it forthwith.

Affairs of Italy.

After the union of Genoa to Piedmont, the fate of Upper Italy is decided, except one single point, which regards the possession of the Duchies of Parma and Placentia. The right of the Empress Marie Louise to the possession of these two countries is clear and incontestable; they revert to her by virtue of the famous treaty of the 11th April 1814, which the allied Powers signed with Napoleon, and which has been since sanctioned by the Royal Government of France. On the other hand, the Queen of Tuscany and her son, deprived by the despotism of Napoleon of the Grand Duchy of Tuscany, which had been given to their family in compensation for Parma and Placentia, have doubtless some indemnity to claim. Spain defends her rights with much zeal, often even with a haughtiness which little agrees with her extreme feebleness. To France, the second in this affair, the re-establishment of one more branch of the Bourbons in Italy is a subject of great interest. They had at first cast their eyes on a part of the Legations, of which they might dispose without scruple; the predecessor of the present Pope having formally ceded them by the Treaty of Tolentino. But the difficulties which were foreseen on the part of the Pope, and the solemn protestation of the Queen of Tuscany,—a very devout Princess, who will not touch territory belonging to the Church;—probably also, the secret influence of France, who likes to see this branch of the Bourbons better at Parma than at Ravenna, seem to have made them abandon that project. The Empress is now offered a pecuniary revenue, double or triple that which Parma and Placentia yield her; she has even been offered the Ionian Islands; but this is evidently only a pretence, for they know quite well that England, in possession of these Islands, and guarding them under pretence of preserving them as an indemnity for the King of Sicily, will never yield.

Up to the present time the affair of Parma has not been regularly in train, the discussions with Russia and Prussia having absorbed all the time of the Ministers.

Her turn will soon come. Opinions, even at the Court of Vienna, are divided on this affair. Some, and I am of the number, maintain that it will be inconvenient to deprive the Emperor's daughter of that possession, and dangerous for the future to give it to a Princess who will be under the immediate protection of the Bourbons. Others maintain that with the exception of Placentia,— a military station of the first importance for the defence of our Italian provinces, — Austria might let these provinces go, and that a considerable appanage would be more convenient to the Empress, and especially to the future condition of her son, who, after having seemed destined to govern the half of Europe, would be happier as a rich private individual, than to be reduced to the slender inheritance of a small State of 280,000 souls. Nevertheless, everyone is agreed that we cannot do without Placentia.

The boundaries of the Pope's territory are still subject to many uncertainties. For, on the one hand, they dispute about a part of the Legations, Austria considering the possession of Ferrara as indispensable for the safety of her frontiers, and having offered to the Queen of Tuscany only a part of the same Legations ; on the side of Naples, the Pope is for ever deprived of that which is called the Marches, a country which contains a population of 400,000 souls, and one of the first places of Italy, Ancona, the key of the Adriatic. This occupation of the Marches is directly connected with a subject, on which I must enter more fully.

Among the questions which relate to Italy, the most problematical, the most difficult in general, and the most critical for Austria in particular, is without contradiction the question of Naples. This question will bring in a short time great disputes and great collisions between the Powers; and if we are not delivered by some unforeseen accident, I fear that this alone will render the last part of the Congress still more painful and more stormy than even the first part has been.

Austria signed on April 10, 1814, a treaty of friendship and alliance with the King of Naples, by which she solemnly promised him help against all his enemies. The relations established by this treaty have guided Austria up to the present time in all her proceedings with the Government; and the Emperor himself has declared and confirmed on all occasions that he would never abandon the King of Naples. All the allies of Austria, at the time she formed these engagements, knew of and approved them; the ministers of England even made corrections in the Act of the treaty, and, in signing on the same basis an indefinite armistice with the King of Naples, declared that peculiar circumstances alone prevented them from signing the peace in due form. The French Government itself, by comprehending in the Treaty of Paris 'the allies of Austria,' without excepting the King of Naples, or without ever making mention of him in any of the negotiations of that time, appeared tacitly to recognise him.

By a secret article of the Treaty of January 11, 1814, an article specially approved by the English ministers, there was stipulated in favour of the King of Naples an increase of territory amounting to four hundred thousand souls in population, to be taken from the possessions of the Pope. In virtue of this stipulation, the King of Naples, after having evacuated and restored to the Pope all the rest of his States, continued to occupy the Marches. Nevertheless, shortly before the Congress, the Pope had opened a negotiation with this sovereign with a view to the restitution of the

Marches; and the King, advised by Austria to arrange
the best possible terms with the Pope, was on the point
of yielding, reserving only to himself the military occupation of Ancona up to the end of the Congress, when
all at once the Pope, directed by the Bourbon party,
declared to him that he could not recognise him as a
King before being informed of the intention of the other
Powers.

The Congress had hardly assembled, when the plenipotentiaries of France and Spain expressed themselves
very forcibly on the necessity of restoring the throne of
Naples to the legitimate sovereign of that country. The
question of knowing whether the plenipotentiaries of
King Joachim would be admitted to the Congress or
not was rather eluded than decided; means were found
of escaping from this question, by admitting without
distinction all the full powers presented at the Congress,
and not joining the commission which was to judge of
the legality of these full powers. The question of Naples was never directly approached; when anyone
touched upon it by chance in the Conferences, M. de
Metternich contented himself with declaring that Austria
having concluded a treaty with King Joachim, he could
not discuss that question. Lord Castlereagh, every
time it was presented to him, seemed to be walking on
hot coals; he would not declare for or against, fearing
to commit himself in either case; and he departed from
Vienna without ever giving a decided opinion on the
subject.

Now that the great questions of Poland and Saxony
are decided, we can foresee that the Ministers of France
and Spain will attack the subject of Naples with much
vigour. Their instructions are very positive on this
point; the King of France, in principle and family in-

terest, holds strongly to the re-establishment of the branch of the Bourbons in Sicily. Austria, on the other hand, although on the best terms with France, thinks she has decisive reasons for opposing the project. Her general interest impels her always to weaken as much as possible the influence of the House of Bourbon in Italy; she is, besides, bound to King Joachim by solemn engagements which it will not be easy to break; and seeing the state of fermentation which is reigning in all parts of Italy, an enemy such as Murat, who will certainly defend himself to the last extremity, would be much more dangerous for Austria than for any other power. The French plenipotentiaries are convinced themselves that they cannot demand from Austria that she should open up Italy to a foreign army; they maintain that they can attain their end by a maritime expedition; but the great object they wish to attain at the Congress is that the King of Sicily should be formally recognised King of Naples by all the Powers, and that Austria should join in that declaration. Such is the new difficulty which we expect; if Austria finds a way of finishing the Congress without coming to a decision on this point, the affair of Naples may sleep for some time, and later on take a different turn. This question will become very much clearer in a few weeks.

General Observations.

The sketch I have traced will show you that there are not more than three principal affairs to be treated of at the Congress: that of the Bavarian indemnities, with which the territorial questions of Germany will be concluded; that of the Germanic constitution, to which a number of others are united; lastly, that of Naples. Thus, this Congress, which has only been, as I had for some time foreseen, a source of embarrassment and trouble to everybody, and particularly to Austria, and the results of which will do little towards the foundation of a lasting peace in Europe, approaches its conclusion. Without being able to calculate exactly what time it will still require to finish its career, I think it will end with the month of March; and it is not likely to last much longer.

The foreign Sovereigns will leave us, apparently, at the end of the present month; the Emperor of Russia and the King of Prussia, having finished their affairs, may even depart sooner if they wish; but they seem so settled at Vienna, and so delighted with their visit, that they will most probably stay to the end. The departure of the Empress of Russia was fixed yesterday for the 20th of this month.

The departure of Lord Castlereagh for London is an epoch in the history of the Congress. He has been the most active and the most influential minister of all; and if, by right of the excellent qualities which he possesses, Lord Castlereagh had arrived at Vienna with a system more suited to secure the permanent interests of Europe; if he had more profoundly studied the affairs of the Continent; if he had used more energy in maintaining some one of his theses; lastly, if peculiar circumstances had not made him a little too cold towards Austria, and a little too warm towards Prussia and France—he would have been able to do much more good. But having regard to the manner in which things have passed here, it is impossible to any one who has followed their progress not to be convinced that England, take it altogether, although having held the first place at the Congress, has nevertheless played a part mediocre enough as to its results. The Duke of

Wellington has been up to the present time quite passive; he did not put himself forward till after the departure of Lord Castlereagh, and I have more than one reason for believing that he has held to the instructions of his predecessor, and not mixed himself with affairs more than was absolutely necessary.

Metternich to Hardenberg.   Vienna, 10th December, 1814.

(Supplement to No. 192.)

193. . . . . The first, as the most important, of the questions reserved for the negotiations of Vienna, has without doubt been that of fixing the fate of the Duchy of Warsaw. The question contains in reality every facility necessary to regulate the general affairs of Europe, in a political point of view; and of territorial distribution, either that the former Polish Provinces had, wholly or in part, been united in a political independent body, placed between the three northern courts, or that the division of the territory of the Duchy of Warsaw between these same courts had furnished the means of completing the extensions of territory foreseen by the treaties of alliance of 1813.

From the time that the fate of the Duchy of Warsaw has ceased to form a subject of discussion, and that, by its destination to serve for the aggrandisement of the Russian Empire, the question was reduced to the valuation of certain points of frontier, the Emperor determined to yield for the general good that which was only connected with the private interests of his kingdom, for he does not hesitate to subordinate to his desire of preserving peace, and friendly relations with Russia, the pretensions which he had formed besides of the possession of Cracow with a suitable radius.

He must nevertheless desire that this city, as well as that of Thorn, should be restored to Austria and Prussia, to be incorporated with their States. The independent existence of these two cities would equally menace the tranquillity of the three neighbouring Powers; placed beyond all direct influence, they would soon serve as centres for conspiracies and disturbances.

The lines of the Wartha and the Nidda offering the best natural frontier, and the only one which is still based on a military plan, the Emperor must attach much importance to a plan which undertakes to obtain them. The course of the Nidda alone is, however, of such great importance for Austria, that his Majesty wishes to make this object a condition *sine qua non* of his arrangement with Russia; in exchange, all increase of territory which your Highness may obtain for Prussia in the Duchy will be regarded by the Emperor as a veritable amelioration of the general arrangements.

His Majesty places these questions in the hands of your Highness, and he believes that the final settlement of the radius of Cracow and of Thorn, as well as the future boundaries of Austria, Prussia, and Russia in the Duchy of Warsaw, must be at once entrusted to staff officers of the respective armies.

Besides, his Majesty will not refuse, if the Emperor Alexander insists upon it, to accept a clause, which would be placed among the definite arrangements with Russia, to the effect that the city of Cracow should be no longer fortified.

The Emperor having found nothing in the verbal note of your Highness which relates to the constitutional question of Poland, or to the union of the ancient Polish Russian provinces to the new acquisitions of

Russia, His Imperial Majesty has told me to call the attention of the Prussian cabinet to an object so essential.

The demands which we have the right to make on this subject from Russia result from the engagements which the Emperor Alexander has made spontaneously, and of his own accord, to us, to compensate in some measure for his pretensions to these territorial acquisitions. It appears impossible not to make mention of this condition in the progress of our ulterior negotiations, and to join the Emperor's promises on this subject to the guarantees which we have the right to claim for our former Polish possessions.

There remain to settle with Russia many subjects of negotiation not less important, among which may be mentioned the stipulations in favour of the freedom of the navigation of the Vistula, &c.

The Emperor has commanded me to submit these matters in direct conference with the Russian minister, and to follow the same course with his Majesty the Emperor Alexander, on those subjects which your Highness wished to bring to the knowledge of his Imperial Majesty.

The second question is that of the incorporation of the kingdom of Saxony with Prussia.

The details into which we have entered in the different discussions which have taken place, as much verbally as by writing, between our two cabinets, and the trouble we have bestowed on the examination of this question, have shown too clearly the interest which the Emperor takes in the reconstitution of Prussia, on the scale determined by these treaties, for us to be able to dispense with making it again the object of our studies.

The territorial arrangements desired by the King are nevertheless in opposition to the wishes of the other Powers. It is important, therefore, that your august master should not remain in doubt as to the motives which guide the determinations of the Emperor in this important negotiation.

The reconstitution of the Prussian monarchy has appeared so necessary to the Emperor, that it has been established by him as one of the first bases of the triple alliance. We repeat it, Austria entertains no jealousy against Prussia; on the contrary, she regards that Power as one of the most useful weights in the balance of the forces of Europe. Of all the Powers, it is she whose position has most conformity with our own. Placed equally between the great Empires of the East and West, Prussia and Austria complete their systems of respective defence; united, the two kingdoms form an impregnable barrier against the enterprises of any ambitious prince who might perhaps one day occupy the throne of France or that of Russia. Both German Powers, they find simple and natural relations in their reciprocal influence in the Germanic Federation, an influence generally desired, because it offers an assured pledge of peace. Everything should unite our two Courts; but it is necessary to render that union possible. The Congress must not end in the miserable spectacle of a quarrel between the Powers most directly called upon to cement the peace of Europe.

Germany must constitute herself a political body; the frontiers between the great intermediary Powers should not remain undecided; the union between Austria and Prussia must, in a word, be perfect, for this great work to be consummated.

It is as an impediment to that union, as an insur-

mountable obstacle to the arrangement of the Germanic
Federal agreement, that we condemn the entire incorporation of Saxony with Prussia, and not only from the
point of view of the enlargement of this last Power.
The incorporation of Saxony contains an obstacle to
our union, because the principles of the Emperor, the
closest family ties, all our neighbouring connections
are opposed to it. It contains also an obstacle not less
difficult to surmount in the arrangement of the affairs
of Germany, because the principal German Powers have
declared they do not wish to join a Federal agreement
on a basis so menacing for their own safety as that of
the incorporation of one of the principal German States,
carried out by one of the Powers called on to protect
the common country. France having also decided
in a most peremptory manner against the entire conquest of Saxony, the union of Austria and Prussia,
for the support of this conquest, would only serve to
place the protectorate of Germany in the hands of the
French Government ; and what excuse can the Emperor
find in his own eyes, to explain his compliance in a
question so repugnant to his principles, when it is
directly connected—as indeed would be the case—on
the one hand, with a compliance of our two Courts, not
less complete, with the projects of the aggrandisement
of Russia ; on the other, with the loss of the beneficent
influence which the two Powers are called upon to
exercise over Germany ?

The Emperor is thoroughly convinced that in refusing to agree, in the present situation of affairs, to the
incorporation of Saxony, he is acting as a real and
watchful friend, and not as the rival of Prussia.

But it is important to find the complement of the
additions of territory reserved to Prussia by these

treaties. A sketch made according to the scale of valuation established by your Highness proves that these additions are not impossible to attain. We believe we have furnished the proof by the enclosed table, to which I beg you to attach no greater value than that which I have given to it. The distribution of territories in Germany is connected with so many considerations, that we hesitate to approach alone the details of this question, however ready we may be to enter on this important discussion with the Cabinet of his Prussian Majesty, by consulting the views of the German princes the most directly interested in the fate of the countries provisionally administered. I must make one remark on the above-mentioned table. It proves that the dimensions of Prussia can be increased in two ways: on the one hand, by concessions on the part of Russia more suitable to the plans proposed by Prussia for delimitation in Poland; on the other, by acquisitions in Saxony compatible with the continuation of her political existence.

For the rest, the Emperor has no difficulty in again declaring that he is too anxious that the possibility of arrangements in Germany should not stop at the single question of the possession of Mayence, for him not to be ready to enter into the discussion on the proper means to reconcile it, as much with the interests of the divers parties who make pretensions to that place, as with those of the whole German country.

This negotiation being, however, inseparable from arrangements concerning the distribution of territories, and the establishment of strong federal places, we must reserve it to the discussions relative to these subjects.

It depends now upon Prussia to advance the termination of the great transactions which it remains for us to conclude. This end will be seen whenever his Prussian Majesty, yielding to the wish that Austria should share with the other Powers, will take the middle course necessary to reconcile views so opposed as are those which now stop the negotiations. No Power is more the friend of Prussia than Austria, none more truly recognises the rights which the King, his people, and his army have acquired to the gratitude of Europe, by the most noble constancy in misfortune, and by the most sustained efforts in favour of the general cause ; it is even in consequence of this conviction, and participating in these sentiments, that the Emperor expresses himself with the most entire frankness to the King, and that he cannot conceal from him his profound conviction that, in his opinion, the true interest of the Prussian Monarchy is much more dependent on a perfect agreement among the Powers of the centre of Europe, and on the sole possibility which still remains of establishing a system of peace by the completion of the German Federal agreement, than by the incorporation of the Kingdom of Saxony, which would not be consolidated either by the submission of its King or by the recognition of the great Powers. His Imperial Majesty is ready, and has expressly commanded me to propose to your Highness to employ without reserve his good offices, as much for the benefit of his Majesty the King of Saxony, as for those Powers which have declared in favour of his cause, so as to arrive, with the least possible delay, at an arrangement which includes, in favour of Prussia, such concessions as are necessary to complete her share, and which, invested with all these sanctions, would eminently serve to bring the negotiations of Vienna to the speedy termination so much desired by the whole of Europe.

We await, with the utmost anxiety, the determinations which your Highness may be pleased to send me on these important questions.

Talleyrand to Metternich. *Vienna*, 12*th December*, 1814.

(Supplement to No. 192.)

194. My Prince, I am anxious to fulfil the intentions of his Imperial and Royal Apostolic Majesty, expressed in the letter which your Highness has done me the honour to write to me, and I have brought to the cognisance of his Most Christian Majesty the confidential note (No. 193) which you addressed on the 10th of this month to the Chancellor of State, Prince Hardenberg, and which you officially communicated to me.

It is sufficient reply to the satisfaction which the declared determinations in that note gave the King, to compare them with the orders which his Majesty has given to his ambassadors at the Congress.

France had there no object of ambition or personal interest. Replaced in her ancient boundaries, she does not wish to extend them; like the sea which never overflows its banks except when tempests stir it up, her armies, full of glory, no longer aspire to new conquests. Delivered from that oppression of which she had been much less the instrument than the victim, happy at having recovered her legitimate princes, and with them the repose which she was afraid she had lost for ever, she had no claims to make, no pretensions to bring forward. She had raised none; she will raise none. But it remains for her to desire that the work of restoration should be accomplished for the whole of Europe as well as for her, that everywhere and for ever the spirit of revolution should cease, that all legitimate

rights should be considered sacred, and that all ambition, or unjust enterprise, should find condemnation
and a perpetual obstacle in an explicit recognition and
formal guarantee of these same principles, of which the
Revolution has only been one long and terrible oblivion.
The desire of France must be that of every European
State which does not blind itself. Till such an order
of things is established, none can be a single moment
certain of its future.

Never was a more noble aim offered to the governments of Europe ; never was a result so necessary, and
never could there have been so much hope of obtaining
it, as at a period when the whole of Christendom was
for the first time called upon to form a Congress. Perhaps it would already have been completely obtained if,
as the King had hoped, the Congress had, when first
assembled, laid down the principles, determined its
object, and marked out the only road which could lead
to it. Doubtless we should not have then seen the
Powers making a pretext to destroy what it could only
have been meant to preserve. Truly, when the treaty
of May 30 proposed that the ultimate result of the
operations of the Congress should be a real and durable
equilibrium, it did not mean to sacrifice to the establishment of that equilibrium the rights which it should
guarantee. It did not mean to confound, in one and
the same mass, all territories and all people, to divide
them again according to certain proportions ; it wished
that every legitimate dynasty should be either preserved
or re-established, that every legitimate right should be
respected, and that the vacant territories, that is to say,
without a sovereign, should be distributed conformably
to principles of political equilibrium, or, which is the
same thing, to principles conservative of the rights of

every one, and the repose of all. It would be, besides,
a very great error to consider, as the sole elements of
equilibrium, those quantities which political arithme-
ticians enumerate. 'Athens,' says Montesquieu, 'had
in her breast the same strength, when she ruled with
so much glory, and when she served with so much
shame. She had twenty thousand citizens when she
defended the Greeks against the Persians, when she disputed the empire at Lacedemonia, and when she attacked
Sicily ; she had twenty thousand when Demetrius of
Phalera numbered them, as one counts slaves in a
market.' The equilibrium would not be then but an
empty word if one made an abstraction, not of that
ephemeral and deceitful strength which the passions
produce, but of the true moral strength which consists
in virtue. Now, in the relations of people to people,
the first virtue is justice.

Penetrated with these principles, the King has prescribed as an invariable rule to his Ambassadors to seek
before all that which is just, not to swerve from it in
any case or for any consideration ; not to subscribe or
acquiesce in anything which would be contradictory to
it, and, in the course of legitimate combinations, to attach
themselves in preference to those which can the most
efficaciously contribute to the establishment, and the
maintenance, of a true equilibrium.

In all the questions which must be considered at the
Congress, the King would have considered as the first,
the greatest, the most eminently European, beyond all
comparison, that of Poland, if it had been possible for
him to hope, as much as he would desire, that a people
so worthy of the interest of all the others by its antiquity, valour, the services which it formerly rendered to
Europe, and by its misfortune, could be restored to its

ancient and complete independence. The division which erased it from the number of the nations was the prelude, partly the cause, and perhaps, up to a certain point, the excuse for the revolutions to which Europe has been a prey.   But when the force of circumstances, prevailing over even the noblest and most generous dispositions of the Sovereigns to whom the former Polish provinces are subject, had reduced the question of Poland to a simple affair of division and boundaries, which the three interested Powers discussed among themselves, and to which their former treaties had rendered France a stranger, there only remained to the latter, after having offered, which she has done, to support the most equitable pretensions, the desire that you should be satisfied, and she is so, if you are.   The question of Poland could then hardly have, not only for France, but for Europe and herself even, that pre-eminence which it would have had in the above-mentioned supposition, and the question of Saxony has become the most important and the first of all, because there is no other at this moment where the two principles of legitimacy and equilibrium would be compromised at once and to such an extent as they are by the disposition which it is intended to make of this Kingdom.

To recognise this disposition as legitimate, it would be necessary to admit—that Kings can be judged, that they can be so by those who covet and can deprive them of their possessions ; that they can be condemned without being heard, without being able to defend themselves ; that in their condemnation are necessarily involved their families and relations ; that confiscation, banished from the codes of enlightened nations, should be, in the nineteenth century, consecrated by the general agreement of Europe, the confiscation of a

Kingdom being doubtless less odious than that of a simple cottage; that these people should have no distinct rights with those of their Sovereigns, and can be assimilated like the cattle on a farm; that Sovereignty is lost and acquired by the single fact of conquest; that the nations of Europe are not united among themselves by any other moral ties than those which unite them to the islanders of the Australian Ocean, that they only live together by the pure law of Nature, and that what is called the public law of Europe does not exist; that, although civil societies in all the world are entirely or in part governed by customs, which are to them laws, the customs which are established among the nations of Europe, and which they have universally, constantly, and reciprocally observed for three centuries, are not a law for them; in one word, that everything is legitimate to the strongest. But Europe, to whom these doctrines have caused so many evils, to whom they have cost so many tears and so much blood, has only bought the right of detesting and cursing them. They inspire equal horror at Vienna, St. Petersburg, London, Paris, Madrid, and Lisbon.

The disposition which they wished to make of the Kingdom of Saxony, pernicious as an example, will be still more so by its influence on the general equilibrium of Europe, an equilibrium which consists in a reciprocal agreement between the forces of aggression and resistance in the different political bodies; and these it will injure in two ways, both very serious.

1st. By creating a very strong aggressive force against Bohemia, and thus threatening the safety of the whole of Austria. For the special force of resistance of Bohemia must be proportionally increased, and this can only be at the expense of the general force of resistance of the Austrian Monarchy. Now, the safety of Austria is of too great importance to Europe, not to excite the particular solicitude of the King.

2nd. By creating in the midst of the Germanic body, and for one of its members, an aggressive force out of proportion to the others, putting the latter in danger, and forcing them to seek support from without and thus render void the strength of resistance which, in the system of à general equilibrium in Europe, the whole body must offer, and which it can only have by the intimate union of its members.

France can say with truth, like Austria, that she entertains no feeling of jealousy or animosity against Prussia, and it is precisely because she is really interested in her, that she does not wish to see her obtain apparent advantages, which, acquired by injustice and dangerous for Europe, must become sooner or later fatal to herself. Let Prussia acquire all she can legitimately; and not only will France not oppose her, but she will be the first to applaud her. Let it be no question of what the King of Prussia will cede of Saxony to the King of Saxony; that would be a confusion of all ideas of justice and reason. But if it is a question of what the King of Saxony will cede of Saxony to the King of Prussia, and if it is to restore more completely to Prussia an existence such as she had in 1805, then cessions on the part of the King of Saxony are necessary, and the King of France will be the first to induce that Prince to make such as are in the interest of Austria and the interest of Germany, which on this occasion means the general interest of Europe. Your Highness seems to me to have indicated the right measure in the tables which were enclosed in your note.

His most Christian Majesty invariably decided not to

sanction, even by his silence, the execution of projects formed against the King and the Kingdom of Saxony, but, wishing to believe that these projects are the fruit of some error or illusion, which a more attentive examination will cause to disappear; full of confidence in the personal uprightness and the sentiments of his Majesty the King of Prussia, who has also known misfortune; knowing all the influence of his Majesty the Emperor of All the Russias, and all which he has a right to expect from the noble qualities which distinguish him; persuaded, in short, that he should never despair of a just cause, has not despaired of that of Saxony. He will be still further from despair on learning that his Majesty the Emperor of Austria, by a determination worthy of him, has boldly taken up the defence, and declared that he will never abandon it.

OTTENFELS' MISSION TO BASLE.

(Note 84, Vol. I.)

195. Metternich to Ottenfels, Instruction.
196. Metternich to Fouché, April 9, 1815.

195. M. d'Ottenfels will go to Basle under the name of Henry Werner. He will alight at the inn of the 'Three Kings.'

If there should arrive there a person who says he has been sent by the Duke of Otranto, and identifies himself by means of a copy of the enclosed (No. 196), M. d'Ottenfels will express himself to that person in the following terms :—

'He will tell him he has been sent to Basle by the Austrian Cabinet to have an interview with a person of confidence, sent by the Duke of Otranto, in virtue of an invitation which had been directly addressed to him at Paris. He will add :—

'1st. That he is informed that the Duke of Otranto had learned by that direct communication the object of the mission of M. d'Ottenfels. That he knows that the Duke of Otranto has been told of the firm resolution of the Powers not to treat with Napoleon Bonaparte, because they find no chance of safety in any transaction with him.

'2nd. That, nevertheless, they do not wish to interfere in questions entirely national. That they do not wish to lay down the law to France, but they are forced to give up all idea of seeing Napoleon Bonaparte retained at the head of his Government. That the Duke of Otranto having been invited to make choice of the person who may replace Napoleon Bonaparte, M. d'Ottenfels is ready to transmit immediately the ideas of that Minister. These ideas can only reasonably refer to the following questions :—

'(*a*) Louis XVIII. ; (*b*) the Duke of Orleans ; (*c*) the Regency.

' As for Louis XVIII., if France wishes it, the Powers will undertake to bring about his return in virtue of a new compact. They desire to serve the national interests by removing the *émigrés*, as well as the impediments put forward by those who surround the King to prevent the establishment of a new order of things.

' If France wishes for the Duke of Orleans, the Powers will act as intermediaries to persuade the King and his line to desist from their pretensions.

' If, lastly, she wishes for the Regency, they will not withstand her ; but Austria, for one, is far from desiring it :—

' (*a*) Because a long minority of the sovereign offers infinite chances of disorder, &c.

'(*b*) Because Austria is not anxious to exercise a direct influence in France, of which she would soon be accused by that nation and by the other Powers of Europe.

' M. d'Ottenfels will not make his overtures until he has heard what the messenger from the Duke of Otranto may have to say to him. He will in any case give him nothing in writing, and will call himself specially my confidential agent.

' He will be ready to return to Vienna immediately with the overtures which may be given to him by the person furnished with the communications of the Duke of Otranto.'

Metternich to Fouché.   April 9, 1815.

(Supplement to No. 195.)

196. The Powers will not have Napoleon Bonaparte. They will make war against him to the last, but do not wish to fight with France. They desire to know what France wishes, and what you wish. They do not pretend to intermeddle in national questions, or with the desires of the nation concerning the government; but they will in no case tolerate Bonaparte on the throne of France. Send a person who possesses your exclusive confidence to the place which the bearer will indicate to you. He will find there a person to whom to speak.

JOURNEY TO PARIS.

Metternich to his daughter Mary.
Heidelberg, June 22, 1815.

197. The details are now arriving as fast as possible, and all prove that a battle more disputed, and consequently more bloody, has perhaps never been fought. Bonaparte himself led all the attacks. The English repulsed the attack on points which the French assailed with forces often quadrupled, for Bonaparte had massed all at one point. At last the arrival of Blucher at the rear of the enemy decided the successful issue of the affair, and no one has any idea of the confusion. Napoleon's hat and cloak were taken. It was hoped that we should end by taking himself. Hostilities have commenced on our side. In a short time more than five hundred thousand men, who have not drawn a

trigger, will pay a visit to Napoleon, who must be very
ill at ease.

Metternich to his daughter Mary.
Heidelberg, June 24, 1815.

198. Pfeill arrived here yesterday.   He assisted
at the battle of the 18th.   He pursued the French with
Blucher, and came near a carriage, from which issued
loud cries.   He approached, and some one said to him :
' Spare a poor wounded man who has been slain ! '   He
found that some Prussian soldiers had rifled the wounded
man.   Pfeill asked him his name.   The wounded man
replied that he was General Piré.

It appears that General Lefebvre-Desnoettes is also
taken by the English.

Old Blucher, who is always at the head of the sharp-
shooters, was there as usual on the 16th.   He had just
led a column to the attack, when his horse was struck
by a projectile ; the horse started off, and carried him
straight into the ranks of a body of the enemy's cavalry
who were preparing to charge the Prussians ; there the
horse fell, and the whole charge passed over his body.
Blucher pretended to be dead, and the French returned
over his body ; he arose, shook himself, and remounted
his horse, without having received anything but two
bruises.   It was a chance, indeed !

. . . I also send you the literal copy of a letter from
Blucher to Knesebeck, a letter worthy of a man who,
mourning for his wife, said, ' Yes, the toad was beautiful, like the deuce, and she had the feeling of a thousand
devils.'

Copy of the Letter.

The most splendid battle has been fought, the most
glorious victory won.   The details are now being car-

ried out. I think the fall of Bonaparte is almost complete.

La Belle Alliance! 19th, early morning. I cannot write more, for I tremble in every limb, the exertion has been too great.

BLUCHER.

19th, 2 A.M.

Metternich to Talleyrand. Mannheim, June 24, 1815.

199. Here, my dear Prince, is an address to the French which I have composed, and to which the Prince of Schwarzenberg has put his name. I flatter myself that you will find it correct in principle and in words, and above all in conformity with our measures.

M. de Vincent, and failing him, M. Pozzo, has received orders to protest against the nomination of Royal Commissioners to our armies. The thing would militate entirely against the King. I refer you under this head to what I have commanded Vincent, and I send you, for your private perusal, the enclosed copy of a letter which I have written to Lord Wellington, in reply to one in which he wished me to point out the advantage which would result from requisitions made in the King's name. I can see in it only inconvenience and useless complications with the allied Generals, and also grave difficulties with the interior of the country. Remain faithful to your idea, make the King go to France; in the south, in the north, in the west—where you will—provided he is there, surrounded by French, far from foreign bayonets and foreign assistance.

It is sufficient to trace Bonaparte's system to be convinced that the great weapon he wishes to use is that of emigration. The King ceases to be an *émigré* the day he enters France, and is in the midst of his own people. It is necessary that the King should govern, and that the Royal armies should operate at a distance from the allied armies; as soon as the King has formed a centre in the interior, we shall send there all who desert to our armies.

Vincent's wound makes me very uneasy. I am waiting to hear whether I must send you a substitute, for in every respect it is most essential that you should have near you some one who will act as intermediary.

Here, all goes well. Now that the Russian armies are in line—and that is a good and useful step—operations are being pushed forward with great vigour. The great Austrian army crossed the Rhine towards Basle on the 25th; the army of Firmont will be at Geneva on the 26th. Another army crossed Mont Cenis the same day, and a third will disembark immediately in the south.

Yesterday, in the centre, the advance-guard passed the frontier. The news which reaches us from the interior proves that the agitation is increasing very much. Fouché's report is sufficient to prove that fact. I hope to see you again soon, my dear Prince, in some way or another.

Text of the Address to the French.

Frenchmen!

Twenty years of trouble and misfortune have crushed Europe. The insatiable thirst for power and conquest of one single man had depopulated and ruined France, had devastated the most remote countries, and the whole world was astonished to see in an enlightened century the disasters of the middle ages.

The whole of Europe arose ; one cry of indignation was sufficient to rally all the nations.   The Allied Powers in 1814 might have exercised on France the just vengeance so long provoked by her ; but the great monarchs, united in one single and salutary object— the re-establishment of peace in Europe—will not confound the author of so much evil with the people of whom he made use to crush the world.

The allied Sovereigns declared, under the walls of Paris, that they would never make peace or truce with Napoleon Bonaparte.   The capital itself arose against the oppressor of Europe ; France, by a spontaneous movement, rallied round the principles which will restore and guarantee to herself liberty and peace.   The allied armies entered Paris as friends.   So many years of misfortune, so much spoliation of the country, the death of so many millions of brave men, fallen on the battle-field, or victims to the scourges inseparable from war, were all forgotten.   Bonaparte solemnly abdicated a power which had brought nothing but evil on the world.   Europe from that time had no enemy to fight.

Napoleon Bonaparte has re-appeared in France ; he finds the whole of Europe under arms against him.

Frenchmen ! it is for you to decide for peace or war.   Europe wishes to be at peace with France, but she will make war against the usurper of the French throne.   France, by admitting Napoleon Bonaparte, has overturned the first foundation on which rested her relations with the other Powers.

Europe does not wish to encroach on the rights of a great nation ; but she will not allow France, under a chief recently proscribed by herself, to threaten again the repose of her neighbours.

Europe wishes to enjoy the first benefits of peace.

She wishes to disarm, and this she cannot do as long as Napoleon Bonaparte is on the throne of France.

Europe, in short, wishes for peace, and because she wishes it she will never come to an agreement with one whom she regards as a perpetual obstacle to peace.

Already in the plains of Brabant Heaven has confounded his criminal enterprise. The allied armies have passed the frontiers of France. They will protect peaceable citizens; they will fight against the soldiers of Bonaparte; they will treat as friends the provinces which have declared against him, and they will recognise as enemies only those who maintain his cause.

From head-quarters at Heidelberg, June 23, 1815. The General-in-Chief of the Austrian Imperial and Allied Armies on the Upper Rhine,

THE MARSHAL DE SCHWARZENBERG.

Metternich to his daughter Mary. Saarburg, July 2, 1815.

200. We have been here for some hours, after a very distressing march. The main road from Saverne to Paris passes by Phalsbourg, and as that paltry little town still holds out, it was necessary to make a road across the mountains to avoid the place. Our baggage was sent on this morning at two o'clock; we left at six, and I made a little excursion to see a place near at hand. We were regaled with two bullets, which passed over our heads, and after saluting the shooters we went on our way. This affair was not hot, but the day was infernally so. When one is on horseback from seven to eight hours in a burning sun, on a perfectly white road, and in the midst of five-and-twenty thousand men, and six thousand wagons, cannon, &c., one has a taste beforehand of the pleasures of one of the outer courts of Lucifer. Every moment men and horses fell dying or dead—the first of apoplexy, and the second from that grand spirit which makes the horse drag on till he dies.

Except for the fatigue of our march, it was necessary to know that we were making war to suspect the fact.   Every one received us well, and begged us to make haste and finish whatever we intend.   Our presence in France is a benefit which may be compared to an amputation.   We shall do much good and some harm by the way, at the same time.

The people are annoyed that Napoleon should have reappeared, and caused the loss of sixty thousand men, and then fled.   They maintain (and they are not far wrong) that he had calculated everything while he remained at the island of Elba.   The King is generally liked.   All the hatred is concentrated on the Duke de Berri and M. de Blacas.   They also detest the *émigrés*, of whom one dare not pronounce the name.

The French Commissioners who came to seek us at Haguenau have departed as they came; they are convinced that there is nothing to be done but to submit, and all they want is to save themselves.   I did not see them, but Laforest and Sebastiani have written and said the most beautiful things in the world; they have declared their attachment to all, and consequently also to me.   The latter has also entreated me to lodge nowhere in Paris but at his house.

Metternich to his daughter Mary, Saarburg, 3 July, 1815.

201. We have news from Paris of the 28th, 29th, and 30th.   The English advance-guard was at Versailles on the 29th and you will see by the news which I send to Vienna that the cause of Louis XVIII. seems triumphant at Paris.

Bonaparte has asked from the Provisional Government permission to retire to America; and, not wishing to expose his person, he has begged for a safe-conduct and passports to England, which have been refused him. As the danger to Paris was increasing, the Provisional Government made him depart without more ado. Before entering his carriage, he proposed to the Government to name him Generalissimo; he added that he had a certain plan to prevent the English and Prussians from pushing on to Paris, and he pledged his word, as Emperor and soldier, to return to solitude after having fulfilled that task. They declined the offer of his services, and he departed with Bertrand and Savary, who has sold his estates and follows him. It is much to be desired that he should be sent across the sea.

Metternich to his daughter Mary, Paris, July 13, 1815.

202. I can imagine the joy you would feel at the good tidings which have successfully reached you, and certainly with a rapidity which the boldest wishes could hardly expect.

I am settled at last, and that not so badly. I am with a M. Lemarre, banker, Rue-Neuve-des-Capucines; I have taken this apartment because the house faces the Emperor's, who is living with Berthier.

It is curious to observe Paris just now. The people do not know in the least what they want. Everyone cries ' Vive le Roi !' without any person, with few exceptions, knowing what good the King can do by reigning over people who do not wish for order. I would not be in his place for anything in the world, and he will need much skill to be able to maintain it. If we seize Bonaparte, the aspect changes in many respects, for from that moment, the seditious will have lost their rallying points.

He is still at Rochefort, and that place, including the port, is so completely blockaded that we have every hope of being able to capture him.

Our affairs here will occupy six weeks at least, reckoning up to the 1st September; then the Emperor wishes to make the following circuit. From here to Marseilles, Toulon, Nice, Turin, Milan; remaining some time at Milan, and then some time at Venice; then to go to Rome and Naples; return by Florence to Milan, and then to Vienna. The journey from here to Milan will take nearly three weeks. I should like you to come straight to the latter city—that is to say, as near as I can guess, you should come towards the end of October. The greater part of the winter will be spent in Italy, and we shall not return to Vienna till about the spring.

See what man proposes and what God disposes!

Schwarzenberg arrived here to-day. He is staying with Queen Hortense. As for me, I have changed my abode, for I was very uncomfortable. I am now living in the Faubourg Saint-Honoré, where your mother met the Princess Elisa. This house belongs now to the former Minister of Marine, Decrès. He is delighted to have me, because I do not impose upon him, and I am glad to be comfortable. I have the whole of the first floor and the view on to the Champs-Elyseés, which are transformed into an English camp.

The King went yesterday for the first time to the Opera. I arrived there late. The King was received as every sovereign is who is seated on the throne of France. If I were placed there to-morrow I should create the same excitement. The cries and the airs of

' Vive Henri Quatre !' ' La charmante Gabrielle !' all
have had their course. The play was ' Iphigénie ' and
the ' Dansomanie ; ' the last was wonderfully well done.
The Gosselin danced like an angel. M. Anatole and An-
tonia, Delille, Gardel, Manille, &c., &c., as usual. I
was in my box as if I had been eight years younger.

I dined yesterday with Blücher, who has his head-
quarters at St.-Cloud. He inhabits that beautiful
château as General of Hussars. He and his aides-de-
camp smoke where we have seen the court in full dress.
I dined in the room where I have conversed for hours
and hours with Napoleon. The army tailors are established where they had the theatre, and the musicians
of a regiment of Chasseurs fish with a line for the gold
fish in the lake, under the windows of the château. In
crossing the grand gallery the old Marshal said to
me : ' That man must have been a regular fool, to have
all this and go running after Moscow !'

On seeing from the balcony this immense city, still
brilliant with all its towers and spires in the setting sun,
I said to myself : ' This city and this sun will still
greet one another when there are no longer any tra-
ditions of Napoleon and Blücher, and least of all of myself.' These are the immutable laws of nature—this
specific weight of the masses will always be the same,
while we, poor creatures, who think ourselves so important, live only to make a little show by our perpetual
motion, by our dabbling in the mud or in the shifting
sand ! Let us at least carry away the remembrance of
having done some good—and in this respect I would
not exchange with Napoleon.

*Metternich to the Empress Marie Louise, Paris,
July, 1815.*

203. Madame,—I promised before my departure
from Vienna to inform your Imperial Majesty what
was decided concerning the fate of Napoleon.

You will see by the enclosed article, an extract
from the *Moniteur* that he has surrendered to the
English vessel, the 'Bellerophon,' after having vainly
tried to escape the surveillance of the cruisers which
had been placed before Rochefort.

According to an arrangement made between the
Powers he will be sent as a prisoner to Fort George,
in the North of Scotland, and placed under the surveillance of Austrian, Russian, French, and Prussian
commissioners. He will be well treated there, and will
have as much liberty as is compatible with the certainty
that he cannot escape.

The persons most directly involved in the con-
spiracy of last March are mentioned in the same
Moniteur of the 18th. They have left France, or are
on their way to leave it. M. de la Bédoyère will be
arrested unless he makes his escape. Ney is in Switzerland.

Madame Mère and Cardinal Fesch left yesterday
for Tuscany. We do not know exactly where Joseph
is. Lucien is in England under a false name, Jérôme
in Switzerland, Louis at Rome. Queen Hortense has
set out for Switzerland, whither General de Flahault
and his mother will follow her. Murat seems to be
still at Toulon; this, however, is not certain.

Metternich to his daughter Mary, Paris, July 26, 1815.

204. They gave us yesterday a new *ballet de circonstance*; I send you the programme. The dances at the end were charming. The scene represents the garden of the Tuileries. The whole of the château is seen, for it is supposed to be taken from under the great avenues almost in the middle of the garden. Albert, but especially Gosselin, who is perfect, danced marvellously. There were loud cries of 'Vive le Roi!' If the devil had appeared suddenly he would have been equally well received. Provided that a Frenchman can shout, he is content. During the last days of Bonaparte, a crowd was always assembled under the windows of his residence. This crowd was composed only of the dregs of the people; for it was proved that out of every ten admirers there was never more than one who wore a hat. They paid a sou to these tramps and blackguards, and called that patriotic meeting *la criée*. 'Are you going to *la criée?*' 'Have you received your *criée?*' was said among these people just as we might say, 'Have you been to the theatre?' 'Have you got on well?' When a man well known happened to pass, *la criée* stopped him, and proposed that they should try to make the Emperor appear. If he consented, the performance cost twelve sous. Then *la criée* commenced by 'Vive le père la Violette! Vive le bonhomme! Vive le Caporal! Vive l'Empereur!' and this only ended when *le père la Violette* was made to appear to his good children.

Metternich to his daughter Mary, Paris, August 9, 1815.

205. . . . . Our last news from England gives some details as to the manner in which Napoleon has received his sentence of exile. He asserts that he will not go, for he would die there in three months, after being accustomed to ride twenty leagues a day on horseback, and that he could not stand the heat of the climate. He said all this at first; and then he begged to be allowed to stay in England on his word of honour. But, in the meantime, the ' Northumberland,' which is to transport him, will have arrived at Torbay, and the affair will be over. Stürmer begs for the place of Austrian Commissioner at St. Helena. He reckons on marrying here, taking his wife with him, and returning at the end of two or three years. I think he is sensible. He is young; it is a splendid voyage. He will see the Cape of Good Hope, and the Island of St. Helena; it is said that country is the most beautiful in the world; and he will be made much of on his return. He will be sunburnt a little; but that is nothing, for he is not very white now. I am going to see if the Emperor will consent to his project. He will not find many competitors.

Metternich to the Empress Marie Louise, Paris, August 13, 1815.

206. Madame,—Napoleon is on board the ' Northumberland,' and *en route* for St. Helena. We have no news of his departure from Torbay, except by telegraph, but we know that it was in open sea that he left one vessel for another. He was made to set out on the ' Bellerophon,' because there was such a crowd of curious people surrounding that vessel, that they were not perfectly sure that some unlucky event might not happen. . . .

Metternich to his Mother, Venice, December 6, 1815.

207. . . . I left Paris on November 26, and arrived at Geneva on the 28th. I spent the 29th and 30th there. I continued my route by the Valais and the Simplon on the 1st, and arrived here on the morning of the 4th. I avoided Turin, so as not to encounter the court, and have fallen among Republics. We have done so much good in Switzerland, and particularly at Geneva and at Valais, that the Austrian name is in every heart. I was received at Geneva in the same way as the Emperor would have been, and as the Father of the country would be. The Diet of the Valais was assembled at Sion, and there I fell into a terrible trap. In order not to stop at Sion, I dined at Martigny; the unfortunate innkeeper gave us, Floret and myself, twenty-nine dishes. I arrive at Sion. I find the deputation from the Diet at the entrance to the town; they drag me to the Guildhall, and press me to a supper composed of one dozen guests and seventy-nine dishes, making altogether a hundred and eight dishes offered to me in the space of four hours! Do not therefore be astonished if I tell you that during my eight days' journey I have eaten only five times.

The Simplon, which everyone dreads at this season, because sometimes one is buried there under thirty feet of snow, has been perfectly well behaved to me. . . .

I have been charmed with the great lake and its beautiful islands, the southern plants, the splendid sun, all the peasants sitting at their cottage doors, as they can scarcely do with us in the month of May, and this after three hours' journey which transports you from the climate of Lapland to the beautiful Italian sky.

I passed through Milan in the night. I saw nothing there but the hotel at which I stopped. I arrived here early in the morning. As I had nothing more to see except what water could not spoil, I allowed the heavens to rain. I embarked at Mestre. I crossed the Grand Canal in a gust of wind which you would hardly have arranged for me, and I descended here at the Gritti Palace, near the Place St. Mark, where the Emperor is staying. I found him in perfect health, and as pleased with his stay here as the Venetians are with him.

The suite of the court are very weary of it, because there is nothing to do, and Venice resembles one vast ruin. The Empress is at Modena.

Will you accept a box which I bought for you on taking leave of the Palais-Royal at Paris? It seemed to me so pretty that I could not refuse myself the pleasure of sending it to you. I kiss your hand, and also my father's.

END OF THE SECOND VOLUME.

S. & H.

LONDON : PRINTED BY
SPOTTISWOODE AND CO., NEW-STREET SQUARE
AND PARLIAMENT STREET